BUT WHAT DO YOU ACTUALLY DO?

Kissinger's Year: 1973
The French Revolution
Age of Napoleon
Friend or Foe
Seven Ages of Paris
Telling Lives (editor)
How Far from Austerlitz? Napoleon 1805–1815
The Lonely Leader: Monty 1944–45 (with David Montgomery)
A Bundle from Britain
Harold Macmillan: Volume II, 1957–1986
Harold Macmillan: Volume I, 1894–1956
The French Army and Politics, 1870–1970
Napoleon, Master of Europe, 1805–1807
A Savage War of Peace: Algeria 1954–62
Small Earthquake in Chile
The Terrible Year: The Paris Commune 1871
Death of a Generation
To Lose a Battle: France 1940
The Fall of Paris: The Siege and the Commune, 1870–71
The Price of Glory: Verdun 1916
Canada and the Canadians
The Land Is Bright
Back into Power

BUT WHAT DO YOU ACTUALLY DO?

A Literary Vagabondage

ALISTAIR HORNE

Weidenfeld & Nicolson

LONDON

First published in Great Britain in 2011
by Weidenfeld & Nicolson

1 3 5 7 9 10 8 6 4 2

A CIP catalogue record for this book
is available from the British Library.

ISBN: 978 0 297 84895 0

Typeset by Input Data Services Ltd,
Bridgwater, Somerset

Printed and bound by CPI Group (UK) Ltd, Croydon CR0 4YY

The Orion Publishing Group's policy is to use papers that
are natural, renewable and recyclable and made
from wood grown in sustainable forests. The logging
and manufacturing processes are expected to conform to
environmental regulations of the country of origin.

Weidenfeld & Nicolson
Orion Publishing Group Ltd
Orion House
5 Upper Saint Martin's Lane
London, WC2H 9EA

An Hachette UK Company

www.orionbooks.co.uk

For Sheelin
Whose smile keeps the writer writing

and

For Gaynor and Paul
Who have helped keep the show on the road for at least ten books

CONTENTS

PREFACE

'I know you write books, but what do you actually do?' The unexpressed rider was that writing is something people do in the evening or at odd moments over a wet weekend. It was a standard conversation-opener from bright young things back in the 1960s that I would come to dread. So here I am going to try to respond. Literary vagabondage? Is that such a derogatory notion? I have shamelessly flitted, sometimes like an errant butterfly, drunk on nectar, from history to biography and back again: from Germany to America, to Canada, to France, to Latin America and the Middle East. I have drained the cup wherever I found it, and moved on. I don't apologise.

But I have a problem. From artificially inflated celebs to camp fashion pundits revealing all about flings with princelings, these days everybody seems to be writing their memoirs. My wife warns me that, if I tell all, she will divorce me; but, if I don't, no one will buy the book. It is a narrow parapet for an author to creep along, and I suffer from vertigo. So this is simply an account of a writer's life, with less about loves than dislikes, and prejudices. To their considerable relief, my family is largely absent. I am old-fashioned enough to think that, just as secret intelligence should remain secret, so no one's most private life should be opened up as territory for Ramblers Unlimited.

Chronologically, this is to some extent a sequel to an earlier book, first published by Macmillan in 1993 and entitled *A Bundle from Britain* (Macmillan, 1992) which recorded my life up to the age of eighteen, focusing on the wartime experience of us children who were known as Bundles from Britain, sent to America to escape from Hitler.

1

WELCOME HOME!

Aspiring to fly a Spitfire, August 1943, Moncton, New Brunswick.

''Allo, 'allo, 'allo! Now just what do you think you're doing? Name, number and unit? Let's have a look at your papers, now.'

The RAF police sergeant's voice was full of suspicion: had he caught a real-live Nazi spy? The scene was the Liverpool docks tube station, some time in the autumn of 1943. A bedraggled, recently seasick bunch of airmen, AC2s (Aircraftman Second Class), the lowest form of animal life, had just disembarked in the middle of an air raid from the SS *Mauretania*, having been onloaded at Halifax, Nova Scotia. As we waited interminably for a train, I spotted on the platform one of those elegant pieces of cast-iron workmanship of pre-war England, a chocolate-vending machine. It was the first happily familiar reminder of home, and – aged seventeen and a half – I could have killed for a bar of chocolate. I put in a couple of large round pennies and tugged the drawer. Nothing happened. I thought it must have become jammed, so I tugged a little harder, then bent down to find out what was wrong. It was sealed up – as it doubtless had been since the early days of the war. At this point the heavy hand of authority descended. After scrutinising my papers, suspicion replaced by disbelief, the sergeant's next question was 'Where have you been all these years?'

I mumbled out the word 'evacuee', too abashed to add the qualification 'returning home to fight'. The sergeant now showed barely disguised contempt. He grunted, 'War-dodger, eh?' and moved on. Sometimes the image of that sealed-up chocolate machine and the RAF MP comes back to me over the years, whenever I have encountered an example of the upraised nanny hand of British bureaucracy, saying '*No*, it can't be done!'

So this was England! Hardly the most auspicious home-coming after just over three years. But then nor had my departure in July 1940 been auspicious. Shortly after France had fallen and the Blitz was about to begin, without any warning – let alone consultation – my father summoned me out of school, to London, and told me that I was off to the USA 'for the duration' as one of thousands of 'Bundles from Britain'. There was no discussion. My mother having died in a car accident when I was five, I was a spoilt and petulant only child and for no very clear reason my father felt my fourteen-year-old frame worth preserving from the ravages of Hitler for some unspecified future career. With that extraordinary mystical sense of belief in a special relationship with God, my father assumed – in common with millions of other 1940 Britons and against odds quite impossibly overwhelming at the time – that Britain would defeat Hitler in the space of a few months, and that the 'for the duration' meant until some time around Christmas. Then the prodigal son could return safely home. But the war went on grimly, in fact from bad to worse, through 1940, 1941, 1942 and into 1943, without any prospect of my returning home. It was hellish at first. I yearned for my home, for my dog, for my trains, for my father – possibly in that order, as he was a shy, distant man who spent most of his life alone in London. America was a strange country; its inhabitants ate peanut butter and squash that had the texture of a string vest and drank a revolting drink called sarsaparilla, played baseball and spoke a language that was not always intelligible. Some didn't even seem to appreciate, or want to know, that it was only the mighty Royal Navy that stood between them and Hitler. Be an ambassador for England, they exhorted; I'm not sure how far I succeeded in those early days.

But I was lucky, very lucky. In fact America almost certainly saved my life, in more ways than the one. A mass of tangled complexes, I found myself thrown into an extended, noisy, extrovert, dedicatedly eccentric and wonderfully warm-hearted family – the Cutlers and Breeses. I was sent to an excellent school in New York State, Millbrook, where I encountered a brilliant history teacher, Henry Callard, whose precepts were to remain with me all my life. I made some excellent friends, many of whom remained my friends for as long as life itself – not least my old room-mate, who was later to find great fame, William F. Buckley Jr. I came to love this sometimes crazy but always great-hearted country that still warms me every time I hear American spoken, and I enjoyed myself in those three years of exile – though not unashamedly. There was always the spectre of burning London, of humiliating military reverses such as Crete and Singapore, of personal losses (husband of my one and only first cousin, Cecil, was killed commanding his brigade at Gazala in the Western Desert), of anxiety about my father when his letters (always numbered) failed to arrive. The war, grinding on and on, seemed interminable, despite the bright moment – especially for us Bundles – when America entered it in December 1941.

I remained English, indeed supremely English. I knew that when I graduated from Millbrook in the summer of 1943 I would head for home and join up. There were enticing options; I could have accepted a scholarship to Harvard and joined one or other of the officer training programmes, as several of my Millbrook classmates did. Then I would have become American, and some of my fellow Bundles did just that. But these weren't real options. There was a debt to repay; the call from England was clarion clear. At Millbrook we had been superbly brainwashed. The headmaster, Ed Pulling, the 'Boss', who had served in the Royal Navy, ensured that we had a steady flow of British fighting men come to lecture to us at school. Most were airmen from the RAF, come to the States to have terrible facial burns repaired, or to train. From 1940, the year of the Battle of Britain, I knew that it had to be the RAF for me. I had to fly a Spitfire.

So, on a hot summer's day, I presented myself to the British Consulate in New York. I had some anguishing doubts. I could lie that I had never had asthma, as long as I didn't wheeze, but would I pass the eye-test? On a good day I could make 20/70 or a little better; 20/60 was the accepted minimum for aircrew. So all that summer I had practised ocular exercises, and chewed raw carrots till I became slightly orange in colour. But that day at the Consulate the good Lord was (at least temporarily) on my side. The doctor examining me gave off the rich aroma of a man who had had rather too good a lunch, and seemed slightly unsteady on his feet. Halfway through the examination, nature called and he left the room. I could hardly believe my luck. Before he returned I had memorised that elusive third line from the bottom of the eye-chart, and I qualified with a spanking '20/50, correctable to 20/20'. I lied convincingly about the asthma (the strange thing was, for the next four arduous years in the services I never once suffered from it, but back it came with a vengeance when the time came for 'demob'). The Consul gave me the long-coveted golden pass to the RAF, a pat on the back and a one-way train ticket to Moncton, New Brunswick, and a whole one-dollar note 'for expenses'. I was over the moon. I was in. It did not occur to me for a single second that other, more stringent tests might lie ahead. At the time, it seemed the happiest moment of my life, but the wheel of fortune was to spin with brutal swiftness.

Not without pangs, I left the country and people that had been so good to me over the past three years for the Great Adventure. There was no time for tears, nothing but excitement. As the train rattled across the border into Canada, there on the railway tracks of Moncton in the late summer sunshine, waiting for transport, were dozens of those legendary gods, flight lieutenants, squadron leaders and wing commanders, mostly in their early twenties, plastered with DFCs and DSOs, wearing that enviable gold 'VR' (Volunteer Reserve) on their lapels and chattering away like magpies – all on their way for a quiet spell as instructors, away from ops. I gazed at them in awe and envy. We new recruits, a strangely heterogeneous crew, found ourselves squadded into a unit with the exaggeratedly romantic title of the Western Hemisphere Squadron. Most of us were conspicuously young, including several Bundles from Canada or the US like myself. (One was Ian Cole, whom I had known before and who would accompany me the furthest in our military careers.) There was an American rapist on the run from New York State, and a playboy from California, all of twenty-six, with a receding hairline and Clark Gable moustache. There was a self-contained group of seven or eight Newfoundlanders, the sons of isolated, poverty-gripped cod-fishermen and lumberjacks in what was still Britain's oldest Crown Colony. They were glum people. To them the air force offered tremendous prospects of social and economic betterment, but they were backward and ill-educated, and I often wondered how many of them got their wings. Unkindly, we nicknamed them the 'Neanderthalers'.

The largest group, and the most impressive, however, consisted of about a dozen blacks from the Caribbean, mostly Jamaican. Looking back on them, shivering in the Canadian winter, I remain filled with respect and admiration. They had absolutely no reason to volunteer for the mother country, so many miles away; she hardly treated them well on their home islands in those days and was to show them scant welcome in post-war Britain. I often wonder how they made out, how many became aircrew – or survived the war – and what happened to them afterwards. One of them, Arthur Wint – highly educated, with that wonderfully melodious West Indian lilt – made his name as an Olympic gold medallist of the 400 metres in both 1948 and 1952, and later became Jamaican high commissioner in London. His athlete's frame, 6 foot 6 inches tall, gave me encouragement, for if they could cram Wint, A., into a Spitfire cockpit, then there would certainly be room for my meagre 6 foot 2½.

Little did we know, alas, that the magical Spitfire or even the equally glamorous Mosquito light-bomber was not what we, any of us, were going to be trained for, at that point in the war. By 1943 it was bombers, bombers, bombers. Oh, the pride when we got fitted up in our uniforms of air-force blue; with what swank we marched around Moncton's dreary parade ground, to the strains of the Royal Air Force March. In the slang of the time, it was all absolutely wizard. We felt we were on the way somewhere, somewhere important. Was there ever a happier time, despite all the regimentation? Perhaps we were a bit like those starry-eyed German schoolboys of 1914, so evocatively described in Remarque's *All Quiet on the Western Front.* Looking back on our squadron from a vantage-point of six decades I often wonder at the adhesive that bonded us together. It was not something to be bragged about, nor false heroics, but we had luck; we had a cause.

After our initial training at Moncton, we were on our way westwards, to Flying Training Schools on the prairies, with exotic-sounding names like Moose Jaw and Medicine Hat. But that was the moment when the weather changed. The sun went in, and it would not come out again for a long time. Unexpectedly, in November 1943, we were subjected to another medical, this time an impressively professional Royal Canadian Air Force check-up. There was no fudging this eye-test. The Canadian medical officer was icy and unsparing: 'You're barely 20/70 at best. I can't think how you got this far' – as if I had somehow been wasting the valuable time of the combined RCAF and RAF. The MO stamped my form 'UNFIT FOR AIRCREW', appending, as a final insult, the handwritten observation 'No evidence of malingering', and called out, 'Next!' Cole went in and came out white. He, too, had been ploughed, for bad eyesight. There were several others of us.

It was the worst moment of my life. I exaggerate, of course, but I some-times wonder if this was how poor disgraced Dreyfus felt when he had his sword broken in front of him on the parade-ground of the Ecole Militaire. I remember the pain of it, every detail, even now. Why is it that the defeats of one's youth seem so inconsolably graver than those of later life? Perhaps because, then, there seemed to be no alternatives. And, indeed, what alternative could there be; what was the point of soldiering on in groundcrew, servicing the planes of the aces, denied the opportunity to play any active part in the war? It seemed like the end of the world. I felt rejected, disgraced.

So that was how, a forlorn little group of failures, we found ourselves on the inimical tube platform in Liverpool, bound for a groundcrew Manning Depot at an awful dump called West Kirby on a bleak hill in the Wirral. There, while the Russian Army heaved itself heroically westwards back across the Dnieper, while the Eighth Army pushed on up through Italy and while the rest of Britain readied itself for D-Day the following June, we waited – for what? Nobody quite knew what to do with us. We were unemployed and apparently unemployable. While some unknown bureaucrat decided our fate, they set us to work on the vital war service of fumigating officers' blankets. Many years later some lines of Rupert Brooke's –

> the cool kindliness of sheets, that soon
> Smooth away trouble; and the rough male kiss
> Of blankets

– reminded me of this procedure. I can still remember the smell, of rather ancient plum pudding. What a waste of all that bursting teenage energy! What a loss for the war effort! We were the dregs, the failures combined with the men of no ambition, the motley groundcrew returning on posting from Canada, the cooks, the clerks, the sweepers, the general-trades, the types whose sole and not unadmirable wish was simply to survive the war.

Our own little group, survivors of the glorious Western Hemisphere Squadron, were reduced to a dispirited handful, including Cole and myself. Even the American rapist talked about getting back to the US, to face the rape charges and try to join the US Army. Urged on by a fiery, elderly squadron leader, Brian Nixon, Cole and I had another go at aircrew – this time as flight engineer, an infinitely less glamorous role than pilot of a celestial Spitfire (we imagined a kind of airborne mechanic prowling about the innards of a great lumbering bomber with an oil can between his teeth). But at least it would mean being in action. Nevertheless, we flunked that one too, as our eyes let us down once again: why on earth, we grumbled, couldn't a flight engineer carry out his duties in specs?

Amid all this, there was a passing moment of joy, one bright spot. I was given leave to go up to London, to rediscover the father I had not seen for three and a half years. I was prepared to find him changed, but I was shocked. Now sixty-eight, he had visibly aged and seemed so much smaller. His whole world had got smaller, too, shrunk within itself and poorer. Our family home was long gone, sold up. Too old for war work and a lonely widower, he was living in a tiny two-bedroom house, eating out every night at his club, the Oriental, a half-mile walk there and back in the blackout, where he would hobnob with his old pukka-sahib friends from Indian Raj days. Occasionally his rations would be supplemented by a food parcel from Wales, from a new lady-friend, determinedly in pursuit, the formidable head of a girls' finishing school that had been evacuated from London. His seemed a sad and empty life. I was struck by what I now realised must have been the drabness of his existence during those years that I had been away. Never once had he complained in any of his letters, and now I suddenly felt dreadful for having deserted him – though the decision that I should cross the Atlantic had of course been his.

What should I call him? Here was an immediate problem. When I had left, in 1940, he was 'Daddy' and had remained so in our letters. But that seemed the language of a child, and now I was a grown-up airman, 2nd class. I tried 'Father', but that sounded too formal, and slightly ecclesiastic. For the short time there remained to us, it was never quite resolved, illustrative of how great a chasm had been opened by our years apart. We talked about America, and the beloved friends he had sent me to. It all seemed a million miles away. Nevertheless, there was all at once an implicit and unspoken warmth between us. He affected great pleasure in the simple presents I had brought him from Moncton, including a rather tatty Canadian trapper's beaver-fur hat, complete with earflaps, which he wore to show his chums in the Oriental Club. How they must have ribbed him! I was older; I could appreciate his droll, dry sense of humour and could understand the quaintly old-fashioned formality that wasn't in any way coldness, but which made it difficult for him to put an arm round me. He was so touchingly pleased to have me back, proud of me, gawky in my AC2's uniform. We talked about the future. He wanted me to go to Cambridge, then into the City, become a chartered accountant ('That's where the money will be') or an electronics engineer ('That's where the future will be, but I don't think you've got the maths, poor old boy'), or maybe a diplomat ('Hard exams, but I think your mother would have liked that – all those foreign countries'). More imperatively, we talked about my immediate future. He was plainly relieved that I had failed aircrew, and soon the subject of a 'nice quiet Guards regiment'* came up. He and his brother, my uncle Newt, who had all sorts of cronies in posh places, would try to arrange for me to get a transfer. He seemed to know most of the regimental lieutenant-colonels by their first names, or at least knew somebody who did. Well, if that was the only way to get into the war, I was beginning to think, to get away from fumigating blankets in my beloved RAF, then why not?

It was glum, returning to West Kirby, back to the blankets, after that first leave at home with my father. Looking back on it now, from the very different standpoint of the cynical and worldly-wise twenty-first century I am faintly amazed at our mad ardour to get into battle and more than a little relieved that things turned out as they did. For by the end of 1943 the RAF no longer wanted those glamorous Spit pilots, the Douglas Baders and the 'Cocky' Dundases of 1940. So the great Lancasters, plodding gamely over Germany night after night, losing an average of one in ten planes each time, would have been our fate. If I had managed not to be shot down, there was a fair chance that I would have survived the war with a guilt complex about what we had done to those German cities and their inhabitants. One statistic, little appreciated, continues to trouble me to this very day – namely, that the 57,000 British lives lost with RAF Bomber Command almost exactly equals the number of officers killed in the holocaust of the First World War. Those officers were called the 'Lost Generation', whose absence gravely diminished post-1918 Britain; were the dead of Bomber Command, a technical elite, the Lost Generation of post-1945 Britain?

---

* It should perhaps be added that, at this juncture in the war, the Guards had been suffering heavier losses even than the RAF. So much for that 'nice quiet Guards regiment'.

COVENTRY? LONDON EAST END CHURCHES
THE BAEDEKER RAIDS?
NEVER FORGET!

Uncle Newt was as good as his word. With the enthusiastic connivance of the bellicose Squadron Leader Brian Nixon, invisible wires began to be pulled. One day AC2 Cole and I were summoned to Birdcage Walk in London for an interview with the Regimental Lieutenant-Colonel of the Coldstream Guards, M. F. Trew. We looked as smart as we possibly could, but in our somewhat bluer-than-blue RCAF uniforms, among all those rigidly drilled, short-back-and-sides, stamping and saluting Guardsmen, with their peaked caps crammed down over their eyes, we must have cut the most incongruous of figures. From the stares one might have concluded that no aircraftman 2nd class had ever dared cross the thresh-old of Wellington Barracks. The Regimental Sergeant-Major, with fierce handle-bar moustaches, who ushered us one by one into the godlike presence, looked incredulous. There was, after all – though we were too green to realise it – something quite insufferable about presenting ourselves thus, clearly as second choice, to a body that so proudly lived upon its ancient motto of *Nulli Secundus* (second to none).

Colonel Trew was warm and encouraging but – godlike (one was soon to learn that the highest deity in the military hierarchy was not the Chief of the Imperial General Staff but the regimental lieutenant-colonels of each regiment of the Brigade of Guards). He didn't think such a transfer had ever been done before, but he couldn't see any reason why it should not – if that was what I really wanted? Nervously, just turned eighteen, and wondering apprehensively what lay behind all the shouting and stamping, and the terrible tales we had already heard of the horrors of the Guards Depot Caterham, I assured him that, yes, it was what I wanted. With the technical and mechanical training we had already received in the air force, he thought we would be well suited for the new and as yet unblooded (it was waiting for D-Day) Guards Armoured Division.

Interviewed separately, we left proudly with two slips of paper. Mine said, 'I am prepared to accept this man for potential officer training,' and so on; Cole's mysteriously contained the enhancement 'without hesi-tation'. We were now ranked equally as 'Guardsman Recruit' and had two new regimental numbers which, as had been the case in the RAF, were consecutive, because we had signed up at the same minute of the same day. But what had he said in the interview, I asked a little covetously, that I hadn't? 'Oh,' said Ian, 'I told him I liked cricket.' Oily bastard! Never mind, we were in. In the post there followed a little placard, emblazoned with the State Colours of the Coldstream, to proclaim to family and parents that (as of 26 February 1944) I was 'serving King and Country as a soldier (No. 2666732) in the Coldstream Guards'. God willing, in twelve months' time we would be battle-ready second lieutenants in command of a handful of tanks, with their guns pointing at the Hun.

The Birdcage Walk procedure gave me the opportunity to sneak a couple of days' leave with my father. He was delighted by this development, though I suspect that, out of the same protective motives that had caused him to despatch me to America, he might have been still happier had I been found a non-combatant role digging potatoes. We got on famously. As a treat he took me round to the Connaught Grill, where we saw the American Ambassador, John G. Winant, dining quietly in a corner. My father introduced me: 'My boy, just back from America – did him so much good.' Seated at our own table I watched with greedy expectation as the head waiter, surrounded by the august panelling that remains unchanged to the present day, with great ceremony whipped off silver domes to reveal reconstituted American dried egg, scrambled on toast. I felt a warm happiness that evening. After the bitter disappointment of the RAF, I had found a new friend. Whatever grim passages may lie ahead, one day the war would be over, and, with my father, I could look forward to a bright new world.

Cole and I returned to West Kirby, in a state of limbo, to await summons to the Guards Depot at Caterham. Blanket-fumigating no longer seemed quite so intolerable. Then, one grey December day, there came an urgent summons for me to report to the Squadron Leader. I blanched. Had I committed some misdemeanour? Had Colonel Trew changed his mind? Nixon treated me with more than usual friendliness, asked me to sit down and offered me a cigarette. A signal had just come through from the Air Ministry: my father had been knocked down by a car and was in St George's Hospital, Hyde Park Corner. Nixon didn't know the details, but from his face he clearly thought it sounded bad. Was history repeating itself? He was kindness itself, sending me back to London on immediate compassionate leave.

Uncle Newt took me to the hospital and filled me in. It seemed that my father had been dining at the Oriental Club, celebrating my return with some friends. He was walking back from Hanover Square in the funereal dark of the blackout. Very probably he had had one too many. A car knocked him over. They took him to St. George's. His skull was fractured and he had not recovered consciousness. The surgeon, a natty figure wearing a pink bow tie, could not offer any encouraging prognosis. I went and sat with him, in the accident ward, every day. His poor old head was swathed in bandages, and he seemed peacefully asleep. I longed for him to open his eyes, smile and say something. Once he seemed about to wake up, muttering unintelligibly about 'ginger wine'. But he never came to, never spoke again. With what seemed like great determination, he lingered on unconscious for another six weeks, getting visibly frailer, and died on 4 February 1944. He never lived to see me in that 'nice quiet Guards regiment'.

That Christmas, in austere, battered London, while my father lay in hospital, was the cruellest and loneliest I can remember. Uncle Newt and Aunt Ursie did their best, but they had never had children of their own. We were not close and I felt no warmth. The ardent lady from the finishing school in Wales disappeared overnight, and so did the food parcels. From distant America the letters (there was no telephone connection) were wonderfully consoling. I missed them all terribly, but the thread never broke. Regularly the incredibly generous food parcels arrived from New York, the rich home-made plum cakes, to be scoffed by greedy Guards recruits at Caterham and Pirbright. My friendship with Bill Buckley, now a comrade in arms at a US Army boot-camp, remained, tenuous though it was thanks to the vagaries of wartime communication. He wrote encouragingly: 'you would annoy me more than I can say if you should go and get yourself killed one of these days'. But, with the cheery self-assurance of eighteen-year-olds which alone makes war possible, none of us really thought that *we* could possibly be killed, let alone maimed.

I was living during those weeks in the bleakness of my father's empty house. From there I made frequent expeditions to Charing Cross Road to buy second-hand books about Mongolia and Central Asia and dream of exotic travels in the future. I started writing a first book, about those three years in America, and contemplated a novel to alleviate the emptiness I felt. Apart from my uncle and aunt, I knew not a soul in London. Then, after my father had at last died, the war intervened, providing a blessed distraction in the shape of the summons to Caterham. It was tough, tougher than either Guardsman Cole or I had ever anticipated. Arriving (there was no other option) in those bright-blue Canadian uniforms before trading them in for khaki battledress and stiff-peaked cap, we inevitably became marked men. The remaining traces of transatlantic accents hardly helped. 'So you've come back to 'elp us win the war, 'ave you now – like Errol Flynn, eh?' was the standard NCO's friendly quip that followed the invariable parade-ground reproaches of 'dirty rifle', 'idle' (that is, just plain bloody exhausted) or 'dirty flesh' (a couple of whiskers that missed the matitudinal razor). Though, at eighteen, we felt older hands than the others – some, hot out of school, were entitled to extra milk, much to the derision of the Trained Soldier* – in fact our RAF training availed us naught, or worse than. It was a bit like hoping that a passing acquaintance with classical Greek at prep school might help you with demotic Greek. There were many times when, in nostalgia for the RAF, I felt like ex-AC Ross, alias T. E. Lawrence, as he complained on transferring to the army: 'the difference between Army and Air is that between earth and air, no less.'

The two of us, Cole and I, were, however, experienced enough – just – to recognise that all the shouting, the terrible 'chasing' (changing, in three minutes flat, from one 'kit' to another, six times a day), the folding of blankets daily so tight that a sixpence would bounce off, the seemingly pointless 'bulling up', painting the hearths white and the fuel black for Company Commander's inspection, was all part of survival-of-the-fittest, breaking down the unfit, and – though this was sometimes hard to perceive – it was basically good humoured. We lost a few: one passed out during the MO's introductory lecture, accompanied by gory slides on VD; another dropped out following the statutory harangue by the second-in-command, a much decorated veteran of two wars, on the theme that Guardsmen-die-but-don't-surrender; a third went berserk when having a TAB (triple typhoid) injection, chased around the room by the Sergeant Orderly, syringe in hand ('Only nancy-boys are frightened of pricks,' observed Gas-Sergeant Crabb, the Company wit); a fourth was found

---

* A rank unique to the Brigade of Guards: an old sweat who was in fact the barrack-room nanny, or mother-hen, whose job was alternately to bully and cosset young recruits.

crouching under his bed after a rifle had crashed on to the ground during an air raid.

Before we even saw a tank, we learned how to crawl under barbed wire with live ammunition fired above our rumps; how to strip a Bren gun, that hardy perennial of the 1939–45 war; how to prepare for battle under a mustard-gas attack. Several nights in a row a touch of reality was added to all the training when the Luftwaffe carried out desultory raids on the camp. Our platoon officer was a forty-year-old, Lieutenant Barnard, with an MC from the Great War, which shows just how close the two world wars were, and what that generation had endured. Surprisingly gentle for the depot was our sergeant, Bill Young, a delightful, human figure who had fought through the retreat from Dunkirk. Infinitely more terrifying was the Company Sergeant-Major, Ronnie Nott. Striding across the parade ground, the inseparable pacing-stick tucked under his armpit, he had an extraordinary capacity to froth at will white spittle at the corners of his mouth in simulated – or was it real? – rage over sloppy drill. And faced by drill, day after day, one often wondered what was the point of it all for us future tankies. Then, at the end of each week of hell, came the special treat of marching to the music of the regimental fife-and-drums. Somehow the stirring strains of 'Milanollo' (the Coldstream official march) would make the slouchiest of us stand taller and march like proper Guardsmen. 'Oh, the brave music of a distant drum . . .' Later one began to understand the magic whereby, after the worst battles in Tunisia or Italy, a battered Guards battalion would be drawn out of the line and resuscitated by marching to regimental music.

Though it seemed endless, even the hell of thirteen weeks of Caterham came to an end and in April we were shipped to Pirbright Pre-OCTU (Officer Cadet Training Unit), at the other end of Surrey, for our first acquaintance with tanks, courtesy of the Guards Armoured Training Wing. Meanwhile, the Red Army was pushing on unstoppably towards the Polish frontier; and southern England was filling up with Allied tanks in preparation for D-Day. Proudly we exchanged our uncomfortable stiff-peaked caps for black tank berets. But there was little let-up or change in the tempo of training, the shouting and the stamping – all the internals that afforded the Brigade its admirable elitist mystique. The French use a word, *engrenage*, to describe being caught up in the system; it sounds like the meshing and gnashing of gears, and indeed that is what it was. It was all a great machine, with the sole ultimate purpose of testing our spirits to destruction, with the object of sorting leaders from non-leaders. More of us dropped out along the wayside, with the dread initials RTU (Returned to Unit) appended to one's name. A kind of pecking order swiftly established itself. Cole (Colonel Trew had clearly spotted some hidden talent there) became a recruit leader, near to the top of the pyramid; I was considerably lower down, clearly more suited by temperament to the individualism of that notional Spitfire than to parade-ground discipline. My battledress (surely the least battle-like kit any Second World War army was equipped with?) seemed always to bulge in the wrong places. Looking at the old group photos, Cole invariably looked soldierly and reliable, almost Prussian, his stiff cap brimming with self-confidence. How childlike we all looked, tiny boys compared to the hefty sergeants and trained soldiers – some of us still on extra milk and dependent on Mars Bars handed out weekly by motherly Church Army ladies. Many of these men are dead now, though few were killed in battle; some became generals; one became a television millionaire, another a QC.

Pirbright brought the added interest of introduction to that imposing instrument of war, the tank. Two hundred of them, American Shermans, British Cromwells, roared, whined and wheezed away like modern dinosaurs in the tank park. They looked vast and persuasively impregnable – until, studying weapon-recognition in the classroom, one noted details of the opposing enemy armour. Even to the eye of the novice, they looked so much more businesslike than ours. Where we had the bulky Sherman, thrown together at speed by General Motors (and nicknamed by those who fought in it the Ronson – 'one flick and it lights'), and the fast but diminutive Cromwell, with its puny 6-pounder peashooter, the Germans had tanks with altogether more sinister silhouettes – none of which, as of spring 1944, the unblooded Guards Armoured had yet encountered. There was the Panther with its slinky low profile and thick sloping armour and the Tiger with its huge and lethal 88mm ('Looks like a bloody great telegraph pole sticking out in front,' one old sweat from Tunisia recalled). Better even than driving a bucking, roaring tank, learning to fly cross-country on a motorbike was quite the best fun the army could offer to date. Apart from that, indoctrination in the technical secrets of the tank was interesting. We were taught how to operate that wilful instrument, the No. 19 wireless set. But why, I always wondered, the Morse code? Nobody I ever knew who actually fought in tanks ever had time to tap out an emergency call, known as a 'Mae West'. We learned how to strip down and clean in record time the breech block of the thoroughly inadequate chief armament, the 6-pounder peashooter.

In the wartime Brigade of Guards the NCOs ruled through their trenchant, macho humour. In the barrack room the Troop Sergeant, the redoubtable Sergeant Brown, a Geordie former coalminer, reigned with devastating wit and a capacity for mimicry. He made a careful study of the foibles of each member of the squad, and it was his recommendation that decided whether candidates for Sandhurst would make it or not. We eighteen-year-olds were justly terrified of him and his acid tongue. On a thirty-six-hour pass, one cadet – later to become a duke – went alone to see a film in Oxford and partially lost his virtue to two beefy Land Girls who molested him from either side during *Mrs Miniver*. He was much distressed. 'But why didn't you protest, fight back?' we asked him. 'Because I kept thinking of Sergeant Brown, and all that stuff about "conduct unbecoming".' So he suffered in silence. If we sensed that, fundamentally, S'arnt Brown was on our side, it was not the same with the PT instructors. Admittedly, they had a horrible job – to make us weeds fit to kill the enemy – but they did revel in it. Dedicated perverts they seemed to be: it was hard to guess what form of activity would attract them in civvy life. As we were made to climb rope netting with full kit and rifle, grinding with hobnailed boots the fingers of those below us, to swing over chasms on a rope, to crawl under barbed wire with thunderflashes thrown at us to lend reality, we hated them with a passion.

It was on one such assault course that my progress on the way to fighting the Hun next became derailed. I gashed my right shin and it promptly went septic. Within days it had swollen up and was painful to walk on. A Guardsman hobbling on the parade ground was hardly inconspicuous. Sarn't Brown had me despatched to the Pirbright sickbay. There an eldely MO, a Lieutenant Smith with a distinctive aroma of whisky, put me to bed for a couple of days and treated the injury with a variety of Wellingtonian preparations such as silver nitrate. I returned to duty, but once again the leg swelled up, worse than before. The septic sore became a deep ulcer. I was back in Lieutenant Smith's care, this time for a week or more. He made discouraging noises: 'If it doesn't heal, we may have to have it off.' More immediately threatening, the rest of my squad – Cole and the others – moved on, and I was left behind, not once but several times 'back-squadded'. From my sickbed I could hear the rumble of the Guards Armoured tanks pulling out from the tank park in preparation for Normandy. Once again I was missing the war; it went on being fought without me. That was painful – even more painful than the leg.

Yet, like so many things in life, it had compensations. A former inmate of the sick-lines, some surprisingly erudite Guardsman, had left behind Aldous Huxley's novel *Point Counter Point* and Compton Mackenzie's *Winds of Love*. I read them avidly and was immediately seduced. Was there really, somewhere out there, a world 'that has such people in it' – such as Huxley's Lord Tantamount, Spandrell and Illidge, Rampion and the dreadful hypocritical prototype of the champagne socialist, Walter Bidlake? I longed to know it, and in that frustrating sickbed dreamed of Huxley's world. Suddenly I knew what I wanted to do in life; it had to be, to write. Over the next months on leave I would buy and read every Huxley novel I could lay my hands on. But perhaps I was even more immediately drawn to Mackenzie's eastern Mediterranean of adventure, spies and high romance.

But what hope of all this, of writing like Huxley, participating in adventures like Mackenzie's, while incarcerated in the sickbay at Pirbright? Survival was still the key. D-Day took place. In the run-up to it, all leave was cancelled. Instead, as a sop, we cadets were sent to Medmenham to practise river crossings on the Thames. (Little could I have known that I would come to spend some of the happiest years of my life at nearby Turville.) The Guards Armoured Division broke out of Normandy, and after a fantastic, exciting chase liberated Brussels. It was now the autumn of 1944. I was back on duty, but I had lost weeks (and my friends) and the leg was still not properly mended. The ulcer healed, but left a nasty, weeping kind of sore. Sandhurst would not accept me until it was cured. Eventually, in despair, I sought out a civilian doctor, who sent me to Guy's Hospital in London. There an amazing, bright-blue ointment based on gentian violet did the trick. Hitler, however, nearly brought an end to all the misery. London was under attack from the V-1 and V-2 bombs. One day in Guy's I was just getting out of bed when there was a brilliant flash outside; something prompted me to duck behind a partition, and a second later the whole window flew past me. A V-2 rocket had landed just outside.

I finally got to Sandhurst, but with something akin to despair. The war was coming to an end in Europe. The newspapers showed photographs of Belsen, as British troops liberated the first of Hitler's concentration camps. We studied them in stunned silence; if ever justification was needed for 'fighting the good war' there it was. Ian Cole was commissioned, but even he saw no action. We celebrated Victory in Europe Day, on leave together, but somehow feeling we didn't really belong to the victory, among all the heroes. Compared with Caterham and Pirbright, Sandhurst was wildly civilised; we were almost officers and gentlemen – 'I call you sir, and you call me sir. Do you see, sir!' the RSM informed us. There the greatest enemy of promise that lurked, like the last long serpent on the Snakes and Ladders board, took the shape of the black-denimed civilian engineers from Rolls-Royce, protecting their beloved engines and waiting to pounce if any wayward cadet dared fail to test a Sherman radial for hydrostatic leak. The war carried on in the Far East. The hatred I had nurtured for the Germans was replaced by anger at the cruelty of the Japanese, with their bayonet practice on living civilians and prisoners of war. But, traditionally, the Brigade never went east of Suez, so its regiments would be left behind to police Germany and the Middle East. I went to see the C. O. of our squadron. Could I not transfer to the Airborne? Or what about the Yorkshire Hussars, supposedly bound for Burma? A Coldstreamer himself, he was unsympathetic. 'Go back and finish your training, and shut up' was the message. So I did. I got my commission, after two years of training, but for what? That same week the first atom bomb was dropped on Japan. It was all over.

SO, IN ACTUAL FACT, 4/W DID NOTHING !!! — WASTE OF CHAPTER !!

2

ENSIGN OF THE GUARD, UNWANTED

Guards Armoured Training Wing, 1944. Sergeant Brown is on the front row, fourth from right; AH, back row, far left.

A profession which makes bad men worse.

Laurence Sterne, *A Sentimental Journey through France and Italy*

A few years ago I ran into a pal who had graduated from Sandhurst with me that month of August 1945. We had been good friends, but had not seen each other since; he lived in northern Scotland. We met at a convivial Christmas party. Conspiratorially he drew me into a quiet corner: 'Alistair, tell me, do you sometimes very secretly wish the war hadn't ended just then?' I started: 'Frankly, I've been thinking about it ever since!'

Of course I had my private regrets, but they were selfish ones. There was all that time wasted on training, learning how to kill efficiently, all that firing up, over two long years. But there was a huge element of self-gratification. Aged eighteen, we all wanted to experience the Great Adventure, to prove ourselves, to come out the other end, knowing that one could take being under fire and not get it wrong. Then, looking back as a military historian, how much would it have helped to have heard the crack of an 88 in battle? the shriek of a Nebelwerfer? to have had the experience of commanding four tanks in action? One will never know. But anyone in the British armed forces still lucky enough to be alive in that August of 1945, with any vestige of humility, got down on his knees and thanked his God.

And there were other consolations: there were the girls. I had received a disheartening rebuff in Moncton, New Brunswick, when my seventeen-year-old's advances were repelled by a Canadian girl called Irma with the words 'Oh no! I'm keeping it for an officer'. Eventually I succeeded in losing 'it' to a businesslike Piccadilly tart in the blackout. That put me off 'love' for a while. Then there appeared a sweet girl who lived close to Sandhurst. I borrowed Cole's ancient and highly unreliable MG to take her out for the weekend, and we ended up in the Maida Vale flat of a girlfriend. There we wrestled all night with the problems of a hymen which seemed to be constructed like the gateway to the Tower of London. Faced with our youthful ineptitude, the hymen won; she declared that it was all 'rather horrid'. Indeed so it was. More dead than alive I rattled back to Sandhurst. As I turned in though the main entrance my foot failed to connect with the dodgy brake, and I torpedoed the venerable gate. Cole's MG was extensively damaged, and I had to buy it off him – for the vast sum of £125. An expensive early lesson in 'love'.

But there were better things in store. I met an immensely pretty blonde actress, understudy to one of the stars of the day. Junie was only nineteen, but had been around, had the pertest of behinds and was engagingly uncomplicated. So too was her divorcee mother, who profoundly shocked George, a fellow Coldstream ensign, by grabbing his belt in a vigorous attempt to lead him upstairs at Junie's coming-out party. His shock, principally, was that anyone so old should still have desires. Junie's mother was, I recall, a robust thirty-seven.

Arrival back at the Guards Armoured Training Battalion in Pirbright, as an ensign with one glittering star on the shoulder, inevitably a let-down. The war was over. One was swiftly made to feel not entirely wanted. With the Guards Armoured being disbanded, there was a sudden surfeit of young officers and not enough employment. The reception was polite but frigid. The Commanding Officer, Lieutenant-Colonel Ririd Myd-delton, was a fearsome figure with a prominent jaw, made fearsome (so I learned from his son Hugh many years later) by disappointment at having been recalled from commanding a tank battalion in Normandy without the customary DSO. The company commanders were veterans, majors of twenty-four, tired before their age, waiting either to be demobbed or to get on with peacetime soldiering. But perhaps the most difficult to come to terms with were the freshly blooded subalterns, who had just seen a shot or two fired in anger. Although barely more than six months to a year older than us ensigns, they perceived themselves to be a different generation – and, indeed, for the rest of time, that relationship has endured. There were, of course, the exceptions. Most notable was Andrew Cavendish, future Duke of Devonshire, a company commander with an MC about which he was characteristically modest, wonderfully laid-back, friendly and accessible. I have enduring memories of Andrew, supposedly conducting some boring exercise, fast asleep beneath a gorse bush. But how some of our contemporaries did fawn on the future master of Chatsworth!

Much of the life at Pirbright was disagreeably snobbish, even by the standards of 1945. We were issued a pamphlet, 'Instructions to Young Officers Joining a Battalion', written – it was alleged – by Nancy Mitford. It contained such gems as 'Speak about "Plain Clothes" – Not "Civvies".' 'Pardon', 'perfume', and 'up-to-town' were equally proscribed. 'Don't spring to attention like a "Frenchman" when you come into the ante-rooms and find yourself confronted by the Colonel ...' It also featured this chestnut: 'Never openly discuss any possible lapse of virtue on the part of your mutual female friends.' (In fact, in the mess very little else was ever discussed! One lucky fellow ensign collected a £50 wager from a party of us for copulating with his girlfriend under a table in the 400 nightclub, while the band played on.) 'Remember,' this invaluable document continued, 'they may be discussing you too.' Finally it enjoined: 'The only female you may walk arm in arm with in public (other than down the aisle) is your aged mother.'

We newly commissioned ensigns were, some of us more than others (I was one of the former), a bolshie lot. I found one kindred spirit in a fellow ensign, Mark Norman, who had also wanted to join the RAF, where his father had died a hero's death in one of the first airborne operations. The war over, we both now wanted to get out of the army as quickly as we could, and meanwhile have as much fun as possible. We set about flouting rules and regulations, and raising hell, as regularly as we could. It was a wan dawn that greeted England the morning after VJ-Day. Britain was cold, hungry and bankrupt. The Training Battalion was awash with spare young officers with nothing to do – especially those, like us, who had had their toys, their tanks, taken away from them. Now we were to be retrained as infantry platoon commanders, our smart black berets swapped for dim khaki ones. And, except for the oldest and longest serving, there was no hint of demob. Boredom was unrelenting.

Consequently, whenever we ensigns could, we would set off for London, forty minutes by car – stopping by the obliging Mr Jarrett of Jarrett Motors in Datchet for a fill of black-market petrol on the way. In London we would splurge our allowances drinking or, with luck, go dancing for free. Amazingly, so soon after the end of the war, there were already

ambitious hostesses throwing parties for their daughters, sending out
invitations by the score to anonymous officers at Pirbright, often at
elegant premises near Hyde Park Corner, No. 23 Knightsbridge. Then we
would hurtle back to camp at 6 a.m. for first parade. One morning
I arrived back with so little voice after a night of carousing that the
Company Sergeant-Major amused himself by making me quick-march
my platoon off in the direction of the Brookwood Canal. 'Then, sir, if you
please, "*about turn*" just before they reach it. Try not lose them now.' At
the crunch moment, I could utter no more than a falsetto squeak. In the
best tradition of Brigade discipline the platoon marched on, to the very
brink of disaster, until a stentorian roar from the CSM halted them.

Ten days' commissioning leave came along. Uncle Newt and Aunt Ursie
kindly offered space, but conversation with them was limited to who was
who in Brigade circles (of which I had no idea), the iniquities of the
new Labour government of Clement Attlee, and my own stressed bank
account. So I took myself off alone to a modest hotel, and started to
write a first novel. Though optimistically thinking myself a Huxley or a
Compton Mackenzie, the results were depressingly autobiographical –
growing up, and the war. That was all I really knew anything about.
After a few laboriously handwritten pages, I fell in love instead. I began
collecting notes, filed away under 'Literary material', which were to grow
into box after unused box, for the novels that would never be completed.

At one of those parties at No. 23 Knightsbridge somebody introduced
me to a cluster of three girls sitting out on the staircase. I invited the
prettiest to dance; she was very blonde, beautiful and almost as tall as me,
but seemed a bit older. Her name was Jo, for Joanna. As we danced I felt
something rough on her left ring-finger. 'Are you married? engaged?'
I asked. 'No,' she said, as she placed her cheek against mine. 'I'm a widow.
My husband was killed with the Irish Guards, in Normandy last August.'

What could one say? What was there to be said? I felt very insignificant.
She was very sweet, smiling and friendly. We danced most of the evening
together. She let me have her address. We met for dinner the following
week, and went on to the 400. Gradually I realised I had fallen head over
heels in love. For once there would be no bed at the end of a (preferably
brief) pursuit. This was no Junie – who now disappeared briskly out of
my life. Where was the beast desire? Could there be a different category

of desire? But where could it all possibly lead? I wasn't yet quite twenty; she was twenty-three, with a two-and-a-half-year-old baby girl, sharing a tiny Chelsea flat with her parents and working as a Red Cross volunteer. For the next weeks, months, we spent every possible moment with each other. Those short hours were the happiest I could remember. But what could I possibly offer her? Certainly not security. I could make her laugh, drive away the bouts of despair that would suddenly well up. Her eyes would twinkle with gaiety, then suddenly turn sad, and I knew she was thinking about her husband. He was never far away. How much was my Brigade uniform a kind of touchstone for her, I sometimes wondered? On the other side, how much did I regard her as a kind of earth-mother surrogate? Ours was to be, sadly, a Winter's Tale; none of the joys of spring, the gentle warmth of an English summer; and, essentially, it was a wartime affair – with all the stresses, and desperation – and Jo had been through it all before, only a few months earlier. To try to cheer her out of her bleaker moments I would play over and over the title song of Noël Coward's 1945 musical *Sigh No More*, wistful words that reflected the feelings of so many women who had lost husbands or lovers in the brutal war that had just ended:

> Sigh no more, sigh no more,
> Grey clouds of sorrow fill the sky no more.
> Cry no more, die no more, those little deaths at parting.
> New life and new love are starting,
> Sing again, sing again,
> The winter's over and it's spring again.
> . . .
> Sweet and beguiling lady sigh no more, sigh no more,
> Sweet and beguiling lady sigh no more.

It was all the war, the war. We were totally – painfully – chaste; no bed, just clasping on the dance floor or frozen good-night hugs in Jo's unheated Baby Austin. We were strangely happy, for all that denial – or just possibly because of it.

Indirectly, I suppose, the rushing up and down to London to see Jo was to lead to a fundamental change in my whole future. One night I was offered a lift up to London from Pirbright by a Coldstream captain,

Richard Fortescue. His car was so ancient that the accelerator was somehow located between the clutch and the brake. On the way back, in the small hours, the car started weaving down the road. 'Christ, I fell asleep!' he exclaimed. 'You take over.' I did. All went well until we reached the camp, when the rows of grey huts had a soporific effect on me too. I suddenly saw the white mass of the Officers' Mess looming up at me and jammed my foot on the brake. But of course it was the accelerator. (I seem not to have been lucky with cars in those days.) Fortescue's vile old crock bounded up the steps, straight through the double front doors of the mess building, which were brought down on its roof with a thunderous crash, accompanied by two bangs and a whinnying sound like a dying horse as both front (black-market) tyres exploded. It must have been about 6 a.m. Out of the ghastly wreckage appeared the formidable figure of the Commanding Officer, Lieutenant-Colonel Myddelton wrapped in a kimono. At the best of times, he had a jaw like an angry crocodile; on this occasion it would have crunched a Drill-Pig's pacing stick in one snap.

The immediate result of this catastrophe was several extra pickets, confinement to barracks (and no Jo) and a further financial haemorrhage to pay for the mess doors and Fortescue's tyres, not to mention ruinous games of poker in the mess with grandees like Andrew Devonshire. More significantly, it also meant that I was top of the Colonel's blacklist for an early posting away from the regiment. Daily propositions of such delights as Army Hygiene Courses (how to instruct Guardsmen about the clap) came my way – then, at last, a slot at the School of Intelligence. 'I really think this may be just up your alley, Horne – if you're capable of any intelligence' said the Colonel with the deprecating sniff reserved in the Brigade for such arcane, long-haired subjects – coupled, unmistakably, with relief at this opportunity to rid himself of a tiresome, supernumerary young officer.

I packed up, unaware that I was not to return to Pirbright, sword drill or regimental training – or even the Regiment – ever again, and took myself off to the Army School of Intelligence. It was located in a requisitioned Surrey prep school at Frensham Ponds called Pierrepont House. As I drove through a discreet gateway, I noticed an odd-looking dead elm, made apparently of papier-mâché, and with a pair of eyes peeping out of it – or could I have imagined it? Inside the school, seated under a large-scale Intelligence Corps badge (defined by rude, and envious, outsiders as a 'pansy resting on its laurels'), I was greeted by the Colonel, a man with a small moustache and protuberant eyes, somehow mirrored by the similarly aggressive genitals of the bull-terrier that sat between his feet. His welcome was not overwhelmingly friendly. He clearly shared the generally held view that all Guardsmen were, by definition, dim, so what was I doing at Pierrepont House? Dismissively he asked if I had noticed anything unusual as I entered the school. 'Yes, sir. There was a phoney dead elm by the drive, with a man inside. Come to think of it, it's gone now!' With a surprised grunt, the Colonel made a note, and I was in.

The course of several weeks that followed proved hardly designed for the creation of future 007s. It was largely focused on the role of a battalion IO, or intelligence officer. We did exercises based on the 1940 retreat from France. A major from General Slim's Fourteenth ('Forgotten') Army, with the stress of Burma still writ large across his furrowed brow, took us into the Surrey woods and had us hunt for plastic mule droppings. From their pattern, he assured us, a skilled Naga tracker could tell which way the mule – and *ipso facto* the Japanese – were heading.

At the end of the course we had a passing-out exam, an exercise in which we were all IOs operating in the heat of battle. To add reality, a major who also bore the unmistakable look of a man only recently re-covered from shell-shock brought a motorbike into the corridor of Pierre-pont House and revved it up at full throttle, screaming 'Stukas!' We all passed the exam. The colonel with his pop eyes and priapic dog inter-viewed me and asked if I'd like 'an I-job'. I said yes, and was transferred to the I-Corps depot currently sheltered in the grounds of Wentworth Woodhouse, the biggest private house in England, just outside Rotherham in Yorkshire, to await posting abroad. I left Frensham feeling that I had not learned a great deal about the mysteries of contemporary intelligence work, and a bit like the hero of Compton Mackenzie's famous spoof, *Water on the Brain*, the naive but well-meaning Major Blenkinsop.

In truth, what I had mainly on my brain wasn't papier-mâché elms but Jo. I continued to spend every possible free moment with her. She would drive down to Frensham on these wintry evenings, still dressed in her

Red Cross uniform, in her ancient Baby Austin. We would eat in a pub, then sit for ages in the draught-riven little car, just chatting. Or I would rush up to London, and we would dance the night away in the Orchid Room. (There was a curious arrangement under London's wartime licensing laws whereby nightclubs were not allowed to sell drinks on the premises, so small boys would fly around to all-night liquor stores collecting bottles of gin – on which you then wrote your name and it would be there waiting for you on the next visit to the club.) For a fiver you could dance all night, to the seductive strains of Edmundo Ros or the groovier Harry Roy. Nevertheless, £5 was half my weekly allowance (highly generous, in those days), on top of my ensign's pay of eleven shillings a day. Soon I was again in financial difficulties. Newt, my uncle and trustee, was scorchingly vituperative. I was on a Hogarthian road to ruin; if I went on being overdrawn he would cancel my account at Coutts, he would report me to the Regimental Lieutenant-Colonel. (I still have the letters, masterpieces worthy of Lord Chesterfield.) Never mind: *omnia vincit amor*.

I declared my love for Jo. I expected nothing. Anyway, *à quoi bon*? I was only just twenty, a second-lieutenant with no very clear future, except a posting abroad. She parried, and wrote me a long letter of explanation. After Mick's death, she had 'almost gone mad', had had suicidal moments. Briefly, crazily, she became engaged to his brother. Then, when I met her, she had a semi-understanding with a fellow officer in her husband's battalion. Mick's ghost was everywhere, not to be exorcised. She just wasn't ready to think about love. Her parents were wonderfully sweet and surprisingly receptive to me. I spent Christmas 1945 with them in their Chelsea flat. It was an austere, bleak time in England, but for me, after the two previous, lonely Christmases, the most cheerful since I had left my American family. In fact, Jo and her parents and her baby daughter Jenifer became a kind of surrogate family. Here was suddenly a world full of sunshine and hope. Then gradually – or perhaps it was more sudden than that – I found my love being reciprocated. We were as one. We got engaged, officially. We bought a ring; it was announced in *The Times*.

Reactions were curious. Jo's parents were warmly supportive; I had some charming telegrams of congratulation and encouragement from America; my one and only first cousin, Eve, whose husband had been killed in the desert four years previously, and who would never marry again but would drink herself to an early death from cirrhosis, was manifestly disapproving. So too was Uncle Newt, ever the pessimist and clearly (rightly, too) concerned about the financial realities of the whole proposition. To my future in-laws he wrote, 'it seems to me the height of folly so young a man wishing to marry anyone, don't you agree?' He was surprised by the contrary response this elicited. But the mother of my friend Ian Cole (a thoroughly disagreeable old bat) wrote me an unsparingly direct note: 'we felt sure it must be a joke – however as we can see it's true we both wish you good luck and happiness. We hope we can rely on you to do nothing to encourage Ian to follow your example ...' Much more to the point, and rather wise for someone of our tender years, a letter from my closest (platonic) girlfriend, Margaret Ewart, sister of a brother officer and whose loved one had also been killed in the last year of the war, gave it to me straight, citing C. S. Lewis on love as opposed to 'being in love':

> putting 'being in love' to one side (for just one minute), you must consider Jo as the one woman to be your life-long companion – the best word I can think of. Is she the woman you want to share your joys, troubles and sadnesses, and to be the mother of your children? I'm not saying she would not be ideal but I do think these things should be considered not through love's ecstatic glasses but through the lens of cold reality ...
>
> When you are 45 and still a man in the prime of life – Jo is going to be a middle-aged woman. Do you love her truly enough to give up many many things which a man with a wife several years younger than himself is able to enjoy? ...
>
> Is Jo giving – or going to give rather – you her best or is it only second best ... you deserve the best ...

I winced, smiled and binned the letters (at least, I thought I did; they were to turn up in an old envelope nearly sixty years later). Love instructed otherwise. It was a strange sensation of total commitment – particularly strange at twenty. So what did we really have in common? Was it just the bond of the war, that elusive grail I had been questing after in those tedious months since joining up in 1943? In the long term – had there been a long term – the verdict of history would most probably have been unfavourable. It was, after all, fundamentally the war and its cruelty which had brought us two rather disparate people together – just as eventually it would drive us apart. Intellectually, we shared little; Jo's education had ceased in her teens. But then, especially in those days of what was still a wartime atmosphere, that one little word, Love, was enough. And there was trust, absolute. And still we were chaste.

My posting to Intelligence Corps Depot, Wentworth Woodhouse, came through. The alternatives were clearly Germany or Palestine. If the former, it would offer frequent leave; in which case Jo and I would almost certainly have got married. But my orders were to 'proceed' (why do all military orders always say 'proceed' instead of, simply, 'go'?) to Palestine, to join a unit of General Staff Intelligence with the appetising acronym of GSI(X). The expectation was that it would mean a three to six-month absence before I returned for demob – and a wedding. I had a week's embarkation leave. Jo came with me up to Rotherham and we stayed in the Crown Hotel for £1 1s 6d a night in two single rooms.

Rotherham at the war's end was the grimiest, gloomiest town I ever remember. The Crown was equally depressed, and depressing, freezing cold graced with frayed carpets and tiny gas fires you had to feed with shilling pieces. One elderly and grumpy maid hobbled about with tea trays, complaining of being 'gone in the legs'. In a small single bed in that comfortless place, we embraced each other for the first time, with half-chilled fumblings of inexperience. It was not a success, but it was a token, a tryst; and, of course, it was semi-respectable as we were officially engaged. Having gone through all the agony of losing her husband, the pain of renewed separation for Jo was, I recognised, very tough. She was stoically philosophical. Yet, for me, Palestine was an exciting though not particularly dangerous posting (or so it appeared at the time). It sounded full of Compton Mackenzie-like promise. Undeniably, it was pro-fessionally challenging, compensation for all the effort and boredom of the previous two years. And, anyway, we assured ourselves, it would only be for three months or so. Then Life with a capital 'L' could begin.

3

CAIRO: THE GREAT GAME

Cairo, 1946. AH (top) and Capt. J. Linklater MBE (below) in GSI-14.
Note the wall map of Balkans.

In that package of letters that turned up nearly sixty years on, I found a
green rail ticket: 'HM forces on leave', Brighton to Newhaven, one-way,
Third Class. After all these years still it gives me a pang – so much was
bound up in it. Jo left me there, at military-controlled Newhaven. From
the port I boarded the troop transport for Dieppe in February 1945. Thence,
on the intricate MEDLOC (Mediterranean Lines of Communication)
route ferrying personnel by the thousands to and from the Middle East,
we crept across ruined France by train, making a wide sweep around
Paris. All the signs of war still abounded – bridges down, embankments
blasted, flat cars loaded with smashed German tanks on their way to the
smelters to fuel France's recovery. At last we reached the transit camp at
Hyères, where we waited several days for a boat. It was the first time I had
seen the Mediterranean; the spring sunshine had a wonderfully liberating
effect on all of us. Somewhere George Millar wrote of that first sight of
the Med, 'opening like a flower at the touch of the sun of peace'. Some
bold fellow officers of the Brigade managed to take off to Cannes, where
they lost weeks of pay on the tables. I sat and suffered a typical soldier's
yearning that Jo should have been there, wrote to her, sent her some scent,
and tried to keep a writer's diary. After embarking at Toulon, we stopped
off at Malta, where the beer had a nasty brackish taste. At Port Said, it
was train and bus to Cairo – or rather to another vast transit camp at
Heliopolis, on the fringe of the desert, the sort of place where only the
British Army could put down a camp. We arrived at night. I awoke in the
morning under a dazzling sun, feeling I was on the edge of a vast beach.

Surely the sea must be just over there? In my total naivety I walked for a few hundred yards before taking on board that it was some 90 miles away.

My orders were to 'proceed' to Jerusalem, to join GSI(X). This sounded enticingly mysterious and exciting. In fact, all the (X) stood for was '10', or 'Topo,' which handled topographical intelligence. I was to join a four-man mapping expedition in what was then called Transjordan. It was not exactly the highest level of intelligence work that I had been hoping for. Jerusalem was still, roughly, a city at peace. I stayed a couple of nights in the YMCA, a massive stone-built edifice with its landmark tower, just across the road from the equally massive King David Hotel, which housed (apart from paying guests) the most important organs of the British High Commission, including intelligence services. It was all reassuringly solid, and British, with a presence that seemed as solid and permanent as that grey Judaean masonry. There I met my new boss, Captain Stan Hilton of Lancashire and the Intelligence Corps, and the rest of our team. He explained that our task was to recce and map every route in Transjordan to check whether it could be passable to a Russian T-34 tank. As there were at least two countries, Turkey and Syria, to traverse before the T-34s could reach Transjordan it seemed like a footling and faintly recondite mission, and I imagine the results were swiftly forgotten in London. But it had its moments. We were based on Mafraq, a tiny desert cantonment on the oil pipeline to Iraq, only thirty years previously a station on the Hejaz railway targeted by Lawrence of Arabia. To allay boredom, every morning at dawn before the day's recce I took some target practice with the deadly 1917 German Luger Jo's father had 'liberated' in the First World War and had given me at our farewell in London. Protected behind a stone wall, a small Arab boy would toss up empty 'M and V' cans for me to pot in mid-air. I like to think that I am not fibbing, but I am sure I became expert enough to get two if not three in the air at once.

Every day we would take off on our recces, endlessly note-taking, photographing, sketching. There could hardly have been a single track, culvert or bridge in the whole kingdom that remained unvisited. I came to love the Jordanian desert, in all its novelty, the wonderful purity of its air, the deceptive beauty of its floating mirages, even the bitter cold at night, around a fragrant campfire of aromatic scrub. In Transjordan at least it was seldom monotonous – the terrain sometimes pink, then ochre, grey and even (close to Mafraq) black from the volcanic lava which in, biblical times, had destroyed Sodom. In the fertile hills round the Roman site of Jerash, the land of Gilead, sloping down to the River Jordan, and the Valley of the Yarmouk on the border with Syria, there were tranquil groves of olives and gnarled oaks inhabited only by goatherds. There was one constantly reassuring landmark, a ruined Turkish fort from the era of T. E. Lawrence, Qasr Kerane, which you could see from over 40 miles away, shimmering in a mirage, confirmation on our return through the unmapped desert that we weren't hopelessly lost.

It was all very pastoral, but there were also hazards. Azraq was a fascinating oasis on the fringe of Saudi Arabia, peopled by blond Circassians in their vivid native costumes, left behind by some migration or other. Once an important base for Lawrence a bare three decades earlier, in summer Azraq was marked on the map as desert scrub; in winter, when the rains came, as a vast lake. It was dry, so we decided to cross it in the jeep. Then it began to rain. Little rivulets began to form between the tussocks of reeds. We couldn't see over the tussocks, and we had no radio communications. We got to the other side perhaps half an hour before the rivulets formed an uncrossable lake.

More dramatic was a disastrous attempt to reach the legendary city of Petra – the difficult way, via the biblical Wadi Arnon in the Mountains of Moab, and transported in an unwieldy Humber, taking with us for the jaunt both 'Mate' the driver and his eighteen-year-old co-driver. Halfway down what looked like the Grand Canyon, the track suddenly disappeared. With a drop below of thousands of feet the Humber bellied down, immovably. Again, no communications. We looked at each other and – as the most junior officer – the lot clearly fell to me to walk and get help. We had passed a small town called Madaba on the way, about 15 miles back.

I clambered out of the canyon, on to a track that had once been a Roman road. In the failing light I walked, and walked, and walked. As night fell I could see the twinkling lights of Bedouin encampments in the far distance. I fired the Luger several times, to attract attention, but the Bedouin were too far away to hear. It became bitterly cold, and still I walked. Finally I stumbled into Madaba, in a state of dilapidation, feeling a bit like Scott of the Antarctic. It must have been about midnight. I was led to the home of the Mayor, a charming, friendly Christian Arab, who warmed me up with sweet tea and potent arak, and put me to bed for the night. To my great embarrassment, he spotted me placing the Luger securely under my pillow (standing orders for a young subaltern) and gently removed it, with the remonstration: 'Here you are among friends. You won't need that!' I felt deeply ashamed – as indeed I was many times, in years to come, when remembering the friendliness, almost amounting to affection, of the Jordanians and their deep trust in the British, as we disingenuously persuaded them that we would never let them down, above all that we would never quit Palestine.

The next day the splendid Arab Legion, complete with red-and-white chequered keffiyeh and mounted on camels, came and hauled the Humber out of the canyon. For my exploit of the previous night, I was permitted the great honour of riding out on a camel. It was a castrating experience; even the Humber would have been more comfortable.

The Wadi Arnon excursion more or less marked the end of our sojourn in Transjordan. By way of R&R we made a detour via Beirut on our way back to Cairo. Still nominally under British Army occupation, and before its grisly civil war in the 1970s and 1980s destroyed it, Beirut was a city of easygoing, tensionless, idyllic Mediterranean delights. I shall always remember the sheer magic of crossing the Bekaa Valley (now a haven of the Hezbollah) and descending on Beirut from Aleh in the mountains behind, as the sun sank into the sea through nacreous clouds that kept changing colour. In the few days we were there I bought a box of oil colours and tried with excessive ambition to paint the sea front from the St George's Hotel. I was regularly distracted by a Eurasian woman, with the sexiest walk I have ever seen, gyrating past me. When I asked the barman in the hotel about her, he replied, 'That's Tinky-Tonk, from Indochine. But', he added, glancing dismissively at my humble subaltern's two stars, 'much too expensive for you, sir!' I was stung with embarrassment; I had convinced myself that my query had been prompted by nothing more than curiosity. It was Jo I wanted and longed for. Nevertheless, after those weeks in the desert and as the heat of the Levant rose, that certain prickliness in the loins was not to be denied. But how long before the finality of demob would come along?

The reply came, in the most brutal fashion, on our return from Beirut.

The Chief of the Imperial General Staff, the illustrious Field Marshal Montgomery, 'Monty' himself, was visiting the Gaza strip. All available GHQ officers were summoned to be addressed by the great soldier in what I recall was an enclosed real-tennis court. There was an element of farce because, when the little Field Marshal rose to speak, a flock of pigeons took off and fluttered cooing round the court. Irritated, like a latter-day King Canute, Monty ordered his chief of staff to 'get those bloody birds out of here!' The general passed the order down to a colonel, who passed it on to a major, and thence all the way down until some wretched subaltern was sent aloft with a butterfly net. The pigeons insouciantly continued their racket. Above it Monty began his speech, with grim news: as a result of 'imperial requirement', notably in India but also in Palestine, demob was going to have be deferred for six to nine months. It was a shocking blow. I hardly knew how to communicate it to Jo. She was understandably upset, but sweet and reassuring.

Back in Cairo I was set to work, in GSI(X), writing up the results of our recce. It was a dreary process. Captain Hilton was not exactly my ideal of a Compton Mackenzie spy-master; and, additionally, as part of the Attlee government's economies in defence brought out with Monty, we junior staff officers were pulled out of the fleshpots of Cairo and lodged in a soulless mess at Maadi, nearly an hour up the Nile. There was something infinitely uninspiring about the rows of knobbly knees below those ill-fitting KD (Khaki-drill) shorts, as the 3-tonners which had been converted into buses wheezed and ground slowly out of Maadi at dawn and back again with the dusk. Yet, to a young subaltern translated from the deprivations of 1940s Britain, Cairo was exciting and mysterious. There were its myriad smells, horse sweat and camel dung, spices, old leather, drains and humanity, but above all the scent of jasmine after dark. There were the noise, the braying of invisible donkeys, the violent rows in the street that never seemed to end in blows, the cooing of doves at eventide (a celebration of having survived the day's heat, as the disappearing sun turned their wings to pink), the howls across the city after a sudden storm inundated the shacks of the Cairo poor, squatting on rooftops. There were the gully-gully men, the incredibly persistent street vendors and conmen who would try to sell you a pyramid, the pimps promising the exhibitions – woman and donkey, for example – that would never materialise, or 'my sister, waiting for you at home, all pink-and-white-inside, just like Queen Victoria'. As persistent as the terrible flies of Egypt, they never gave up, but their inventiveness and their sense of humour were beguiling. There were the tarts with kohl-rimmed eyes, languidly promenading in the heat, and the mysterious female spies plying between the Continental and Shepheard's Hotels. At Shepheard's the immortal Joe Scialom, the Italian-Russian barman at the famous (men-only) Long Bar, was the best-informed man in Cairo and the most discreet – wooed by every intelligence service – a figure straight out of *Casablanca*.

As one got gradually into the swing of Cairo social life, there were fun parties out at the Pyramids or on feluccas on the Nile; there was tennis and golf, or languid buffet lunches by the pool at the secluded Gezira Sporting Club. Gezira was select in that any British officer could join; other ranks and so-called 'Wogs' (except the hand-picked princely few) could not. Cairo seemed incredibly cheap; even on a subaltern's lowly pay of fourteen shillings a day (I had been promoted), plus a modest increment for 'discomfort' and 'foreign service', one could enjoy a marvellous life. With its various interlocking communities of Greeks, Copts, White Russians, Jews and Lebanese, Cairene social life was wonderfully diverse – and inviting to a GHQ officer. It was a popular joke that, when the students rioted (as they did regularly) in anti-British protest, they would go and sack a few Greek grocers' shops; in consequence, the Greeks supported the British 'occupation', out of fear of what might follow. Jews, such as the affluent Mizrahi clan, though torn by events in Palestine, would do the same; so perforce did the other minorities. Thus in all of their manifold salons representatives of the British Empire were by no means unacceptable. As one observed even humble privates clip-clopping round the city in horse-drawn cabs or gharries, in retrospect one should have wondered whether this was not the last fling of Empire. If it was, it was certainly not a fling to be missed – and a great palliative to the drudgery of GSI(X).

As of 1946, the elephantine GHQ Middle East Land Forces was by far the biggest command left to the British Army. Its numbers were variously estimated at 10,000 to 100,000; as one watched the ants in their KD shorts swarm in and out of Cairo's Garden City compound, which had been almost entirely taken over by GHQ since wartime, the higher figure was all too believable. Out of Grey Pillars, a block of requisitioned flats in its centre, GSI ran an empire within an empire. Embracing all forms of military intelligence (only the highly secret, more political organs of MI6 and MI5, under their transparent acronyms respectively of ISLD and SIME, stood apart), its remit ran far beyond the geographical Middle East to the borders of Austria in the north and to Kenya in the south, and from the frontiers of India to Tunisia. At the head of this powerful organism were two remarkable and totally distinctive figures. The BGS(I)* was a peppery Highlander, Geoffrey Macnab, his short fuse probably exacerbated by the humiliation for so proud a Scot of having been taken prisoner in Italy. From Cairo he subsequently became a legendary military attaché in Paris, refusing stoutly to compromise with the French language and leaving an indelible imprint when his staff car was bashed by a huge *camion* on the Faubourg Saint-Honoré one day. Fuming with rage, he got out and, wielding the car's starting handle (an essential piece of equipment in days when batteries and self-starters were not as dependable as today), smashed in the *camion*'s headlamps. Then, sticking a furious Scottish face into the cab, he roared at the startled driver, 'Eh maintenant, vous fucker, nous sommes égal!'

In Cairo Geoffrey Macnab was regarded with both respect and affection. Immediately under him, the real brains of GSI was Lieutenant-Colonel Claude Dewhurst, a truly brilliant intelligence officer. Always wearing an unconventional silk foulard, Claude was unashamedly gay. Without harassing, he was especially thoughtful to the juniors on his staff, and shared a flat on Zamalek Island with two dedicatedly heterosexual young captains, Doric Bossom (a fellow Coldstreamer and son of a prominent Tory MP, Alfred Bossom) and John Linklater. Claude delighted in eighteenth-century usages; people were either 'most agreeable' or 'entirely preposterous', and he expected a high standard of literacy from his juniors. A flamboyant man, he ran an immense 8-litre Mercedes tourer (nicknamed 'Merky Bey') which had been liberated from some SS grandee. It did about 8 miles to the gallon and could cruise smoothly at 125 mph (a considerable achievement in those days), and Claude would

---

* Brigadier General Staff (Intelligence).

boast proudly that it took two Egyptian mechanics to lift out the car-
burettor. In its rear dicky-seat a kind of giant paperclip held you by the
knees to prevent your being thrown out if the car hit a hump in the desert
road. Its starting-up roar proclaimed to all Zamalek that the G-1(I)* was
on his way to the office. (Fortunately there were no terrorists lurking in
those days.) But Claude's brown eyes missed nothing. Rank was irrelevant
to him and, however outrageous, he was always fun to be with.

One happy day Claude summoned me up from GSI(X). 'I've been
watching you. I think you're wasting your time in Topo – I want you come
up here to GSI(14) and take over as IO Balkans.' I was stunned and
delighted. In this job, for the first time I was writing – even if only reports
on Soviet-bloc troop movements in the Balkans. I shared a spacious office
with John Linklater, no less than Claude an unusual personality. In his
mid-twenties, half British and half Czech, he had been decorated for
carrying out covert ops with SOE in Czechoslovakia during the war. A
manic personality, he was brilliant but highly flawed. Sent on a special
mission down to Eritrea he came back with a thirty-five-page report
which, Brigadier Macnab declared, suggested that the author was either
'a genius, or mad – or possibly both'. John was obsessed by Freud and
Jung, and by every kind of sexual activity, if not deviation, and had a
ravishingly pretty nineteen-year-old White Russian girlfriend called
Irene. The mix of Slav temperaments was explosive, their relationship
constantly on/off; when it was on Claude would complain that, in their
sexual rampages, they had wrecked their flat, the fridge torn off its hinges.
One day I was horrified to find that he had brought Irene into our
supposedly off-limits office to translate some secret Soviet documents.
Such was security in Cairo in those happy-go-lucky days. But John was a
truly good friend to me, and he taught me a lot about the craft of
intelligence work. Years later he made me godfather to his eldest daughter.

Behind my desk in Grey Pillars was a vast map of the Balkans and
Greece, which covered the whole wall. It seemed bizarre that it all lay
nearly 1,000 miles from Cairo. That map in turn was covered with little
flags, in various colours and shapes, which John Linklater (G-3 Greece)

---

* General Staff Officer, Grade 1 (Intelligence), a Lieutenant-Colonel in rank. G-2 was Grade 2,
and so on.

and I, as IO Balkans, moved daily. A massive preponderance were coloured red, representing divisions under Stalin's control, Soviet or satellite. My responsibility stretched from Trieste and the borders of Austria to the Black Sea and from the shores of the Adriatic down to the Greek frontier – where John took over. One of the major concerns of contemporary British foreign policy was which way the Yugoslav leader Marshal Tito would jump. He was then solidly in the pocket of Stalin, and had at his behest a battle-hardened army far bigger than the British, aggressively orientated and much of it poised on the borders of Greece. Communist guerrillas, supplied and supported by Tito and Stalin jointly, were in control of large tracts of northern Greece. It was a thoroughly dangerous situation, and an imposing responsibility for a green subaltern to keep an eye on it all.

Among the other engaging personalities I had to deal with in the course of duty was a full colonel, with a complexion of old port (from which it was doubtless derived), called Godfrey Hobbs, who ran a neighbouring office with the title of Allied Liaison Services (ALS), yet another deceptive abbreviation. Through Colonel Hobbs's ALS was funnelled all the intelligence of the numerous Allied services quartered in Cairo. Well before midday Godfrey would suggest, 'Let's have a look at the top-secret files,' and a bottle of gin would come out from inside his safe. Through him and his cohorts I came to recognise that, perhaps second only to the Vatican and Mossad, the Poles were supreme in the field of intelligence. Their tortured history dictated that they had to be. Many a time did I seek out one or other of Godfrey Hobbs's Polish operatives for the most up-to-the-minute intelligence. Their deep hatred of the Soviets helped ensure that their knowledge of what was going on in the Balkans was infinitely superior to ours.

Altogether, it was huge fun. For the first time since I had joined up, I had to use my brain. Meanwhile, under pretext of the exigencies of intelligence work, Claude – bless him – had engineered my escape from the dread Maadi Officers' Mess. On chic Zamalek Island I found and rented a suffragi's, or servant's, apartment atop a private house. It consisted of one small room, bed, kitchenette and shower, though for most of the year I lived out on the roof under the stars. To look after me I found a marvellous jet-black Nubian called Osman, who would stand in his blue ankle-length galabiyeh silent and motionless as a Thebes statue while I ate what he cooked. It was a good life, all on a subaltern's pay. Psychologically it might have been better not to have been alone, but at the time there were no other options. I missed Jo terribly, and there were moments of acute loneliness when the *afreets* – the Arab equivalent of what Winston Churchill called the 'Black Dog' – struck. But I was fortunate in being so preoccupied with a fascinating job.

There were no private telephones in Cairo; it was anyway virtually impossible to get a line, to ring England. Did Jo and I speak once? There was no chance of getting home leave, or for her to come out to Cairo. So our life-line was those flimsy, circumscribed blue air-letter forms, so unsatisfactory. I could write little about what I was doing; her letters tended to dwell on a life committed to bringing up a tiny child: 'Went to zoo, came back and J. hd a lovely glass of orange juice,' or 'Went riding in the Park.' Occasionally there was a note of desolation. We wrote to each other virtually every day, letters filled with love and hope: the optimism of youth.

Then came a pause in her letters. But on 29 June 1946 a thick one arrived. I tore it open in eager expectation, trying to imagine what she had written. What I found was this:

My beloved darling

There is something I must tell you. I have been meaning to for some time, but now things have come to a head, so here goes. As you know I have been riding a lot in Rotten Row with R [her riding-master]. Well unfortunately R fell in love with me, and I admit darling that I was rather taken by him. I told him that I was engaged, and I knew he was married but didn't get on frightfully well with his wife. I went out with him once or twice, and we had some very good times together. Then suddenly the most terrible thing happened ...

While Jo was away with Mick's family in Ireland, a letter had arrived, marked 'Urgent'. Her mother opened it, was horrified by what she read and insisted that Jo write to me at once and tell all. It was from R's wife, now a desperate woman whose husband had run from her when she was ugly and unattractive in the latter stages of pregnancy. She beseeched Jo to leave him alone: 'Please give me this one chance – keep out of his life utterly and completely for six months.' Jo went to see Mrs R and promised she would not see R again.

> ... I felt awful leaving him like that. I dread to think how this letter will hurt you, darling. It has been a great weight off my mind and I feel so much better now. I can't tell you how it happened – it was just one of those things. ...
>
> From having read all this, darling, do you feel inclined to break off our engagement and hate me? I know I deserve to be treated like that, but I hope you won't. I suppose I have been a bloody fool. I do love you – will you ever forgive me for what I have done? (Apart from everything else I adored riding.)
>
> ... Darling, I will wait for you for ever. I will wait anxiously for your letter. Say what you like – I deserve every bit of it. I have told you everything ...

I reeled, I shook. I remember wandering through the streets of Cairo, bemused, aimless, with all the pain of the cuckolded lover through the ages. I read and reread the letter, again and again. How could it have happened with us? And it was little more than three months since we had parted. How could she have? Her immediate reactions shocked me. First, she had been angry that her mother had found out; then, she felt distress at having to give up R – and the riding (no concern at all about the anguish Mrs R had suffered); and thirdly, and only thirdly, or so it seemed, she was concerned about me, concerned that I would break off our engagement. I raged for a day or two. Then anger gave way to a kind of comprehension. It was not her fault; it was the fault of the beastly war and its aftermath, for killing Mick and separating us. I tried to think of what she must have suffered when he went off to Normandy, and now to have to face a comparable separation all over again. Hadn't I been asking just too much of her? Perhaps I was growing up. Anyway, in those few brief but intense months we had invested too much emotional capital between us to let it all be squandered. And, selfishly, she was my rock. I just could not imagine returning to an England without her, indeed I could not imagine any life without her.

I tried to telephone, but it was – as always – impossible to get a line. Once again I tried to get home leave: impossible, too. So I telegraphed, reassurance and enduring love. The same came back, with grateful sweetness. The riding-master and his distraught wife were relegated to history.

Yet something, imperceptible at the time, had cracked. The summer heat was now gripping Cairo, and with it came the inevitable stirring of the loins. I had resisted so far, but abnegation of the flesh had never been, and never would be, a particular forte of mine, while on every side availability beckoned. There was a tacitly adopted policy of don't ask questions now; like Lois in *Kiss Me Kate*, I could say 'I'm always true to you, darlin', in my way.' I permitted none of those brushes on the stairs in Cairo to affect me. After all, Cairo was not serious life. As with adventures at the Carnival, nothing really counted. The emblem of Jo remained paramount. Yet, and yet, something had cracked – on both sides.

So I forgave. Her letters, those blue letters, flowed in more loving than ever. Our relationship resumed its course. Of course I knew how much harder it was for her than for me; any woman will tell you, it always is. She had a child to care for, a boring job and very little money. I had my job, getting more exciting all the time, and Cairo, which I had come to love in all its moods. Months passed by. Then there was a financial problem. With only her Red Cross job, Will's pension and a tiny allowance, Jo was finding it hard to manage. I wrote to Uncle Newt, begging for help. Back came a furious response. It was all most improper. Had Jo become my mistress? Supposing I didn't get married at all – altogether most likely? I reacted angrily. After all, it seemed only proper that I should help. Had it not been for the exigencies of Monty I would be home, we would be married and I would (somehow) be supporting her. Newt climbed down, and a cheque was sent to tide Jo over.

I went back to grappling with Tito's order-of-battle in the Balkans. In Grey Pillars my ability to master my wide-ranging responsibilities was tested one day by a sudden visit from the DMI (Director Military Intelligence) himself, one of the most remarkable (and indeed alarming) personalities thrown up by the British Army post-1945: Major-General Gerald Templer. Preceded by the Brig, he exploded into to our office and, without any preliminary niceties, thrust his swaggerstick* like a matador's

---

* An accoutrement of rank that officers carried in those days.

sword into the heart of Albania, barking, 'Now tell me what are the Communist dispositions in Rumania?' I swallowed, gasped and, catching Linklater's eye, managed to give a two-minute dissertation (always at attention) on the state of Tito's forces on the Greek border. A grunt of approval and the caravanserai of red tabs moved on.

· That September of 1946, my capability was tested even more dra-matically. It was the month the Nile rose, as indeed it had done ever since the pharaohs. It was the worst time of humidity, heat, pollution and *cafard*. Lawrence Durrell writes evocatively of that 'palpitant moist heat, dense from the rising damps of the river and aching with the stink of rotten fruit, jasmine and sweating black bodies'. Men beat their wives and abandoned their mistresses. Camels went mad and killed their drivers (I actually once saw this happen, down in Luxor). Anybody with any sense fled the city.

So it was in GSI-14. Of our little set-up, John was away on leave, Major Guy Wilmot-Sitwell, the G-2, was (I think) sick, and Claude was off goodness knows where in Merky Bey. I found myself alone with the Brigadier, and no one in between. But nothing was happening. Then, suddenly, there was the BGS(I), his knobbly Scottish knees vibrating with the sudden call to action, waving a top-secret signal at me. 'Where the fucking hell's Linklater? Where's Sitwell? Only you? Christ!' The signal was from the general in command of the British Military Mission in Bucharest. It ran roughly as follows: 'Most reliable source warns Soviets may be planning surprise attack from Bulgaria southwards on Istanbul night of 16/17 September.'

Christ indeed! The 16th/17th was less than a week away. I looked at the wall map. Certainly a lot more red flags had accumulated inside Bulgaria over the last week or two, facing that very narrow strip of Greek Thrace between Istanbul, Salonika and the sea – where the Greek Communist guerrillas were substantially in charge anyway. And what had we got in the area? A couple of under-strength brigades? A flotilla of ships somewhere in the Aegean? The Americans? It was barely six months since Winston Churchill's 'Iron Curtain' speech in Fulton, Missouri had alerted the United States to the danger in Eastern Europe, and there were no US forces anywhere in the area. For months past we had been noting growling noises from Moscow about control of the Dardanelles (a time-honoured

Russian obsession) and other menaces to the eastern Turkish provinces of Kars and Artvin. And now? 'Horne, I've got to do an appreciation for the Chief of Staff, by this afternoon. For God's sake come up with an answer. One page only, typed. Is it "Yes" or is it "No"?'

What could the youth presuming to be IO Balkans do except toss a coin and pray? My recollection is that I rang up one of Godfrey Hobbs's Polish colonels and guardedly enquired about Russian intentions in Bulgaria. He put out feelers with his Bulgarian contacts and came back with a clear *no* answer. ('Tell General X in Bucharest to get rid of his mistress' was his opinion of our 'most reliable source'). It was pure sabre-rattling by Stalin, just large-scale troop manoeuvres, the Pole assured me. I presented my one page to the Brig; he rephrased it for the chief of staff to the Commander-in-Chief. And we waited. The deadly night of 16/17 September passed uneventfully. We, those in the know – and there could have been barely half a dozen in the whole vast command – breathed again. But these constant Soviet pinpricks and alarums continued to pester us, perhaps to test the mettle of the West. Our team returned from wherever they had been. Claude was congratulatory: 'Poor fellow, what a most disagreeable experience! But you did well – just imagine if you'd tossed and come up tails!' I had won my spurs.

Then, quite soon after the September crisis there followed a major reorganisation in GSI-14. John was summoned to Haifa, to be the IO of 6th Airborne Division, the unit in the hottest seat in Palestine, where the situation was worsening daily. I was truly sad to see him go. One day, I was called to Claude's office. I was going to be translated, to work in a mysterious office called SIME – Security Intelligence Middle East – under the equally mysterious Lieutenant-Colonel Maurice Oldfield. Brushing aside my bleats that I was very happy and really didn't want to leave him and GSI-14, Claude took me across the road to a separate small building, a once chic villa just inside the GHQ Garden City compound. With its own guard and liberal coils of barbed wire, it was, in effect, now housing the Middle East branch of MI5, the Security Service. Like its sister organisation MI6 (or ISLD), SIME was linked to Claude's GSI set-up, but was totally independent. The heavily protected SIME villa was like a tabernacle within the temple of GHQ; and within SIME, where none dared tread or even ask what went on, was a small holy of holies, manned by strange signals personnel and topped by a tangle of aerials. That was in fact the very heart of British intelligence, where all the intercept work of SIGINT (signals intelligence) went on – of which none of us normal mortals had an inkling until three decades later, when the story of Ultra and Enigma came to be revealed.

That day Claude introduced me to one of the most remarkable men I was ever to meet, one who would have an enduring influence on my life and who would himself ultimately become a legendary and controversial head of MI6. As of 1946, Maurice Oldfield was not quite thirty – he was young when he made the rank of Lieutenant-Colonel, even for those days. He was the éminence grise to a curious figure called Brigadier Douglas Roberts, the head of SIME. It was in fact a kind of Hindenburg–Ludendorff relationship, although here the Hindenburg input was often hard to discern. Born in Odessa, Roberts was one of the rare Russian-speakers in the Middle East and had been involved with the White Russians since the First World War. Supposedly he had even met Lenin. Was this his one raison d'être? He was, and continued to be for many years, an imposing figurehead. Oldfield, as number two, did the work, and the thinking.

Maurice, physically, reminded me a little of Charles Laughton playing Captain Bligh. My initial impression was of an enormous round head, a pasty face which had not drunk deeply of the Egyptian sun, with thick Billy-Bunter tortoiseshell glasses. Behind them the eyes were penetrating, but warm and friendly. His KD uniform was nondescript, calling out for the *dhobi* and looking more suitable to an Intelligence Corps sergeant – which, indeed, Maurice had been not so many years previously. His cloth badges of rank seemed deliberately faded and obscure, if not purloined. Everything about the man (in contrast to the ever dapper Claude) was low-key, designed – except that it was not designed – for anonymity. It was often said subsequently, but hotly denied, that John le Carré had taken 'MO' (as he signed himself) for his model of the unsmiling George Smiley in novels such as *Tinker, Tailor, Soldier, Spy*, while Alec Guinness had also drawn on him heavily in portraying this faceless hero. Only, unlike Smiley's face, Maurice's was seldom unsmiling. (Poor man, he suffered from appalling psoriasis, perhaps aggravated by stress, and it plagued him all his life, getting steadily worse with age.)

For a senior officer holding down one of the most important I-jobs Britain could offer, Oldfield's background was unusual. The eldest of eleven children, he was born a north-country farm boy (his parents were struggling tenant farmers), his whole existence flavoured and influenced by his birthplace of Over Haddon near Bakewell in Derbyshire. Over Haddon, in the Peak District, was always close to his heart, and whenever he gained promotion he would send off a cheque to buy a new cow. A religious man, he would sit down and play the church organ whenever one was available. He attended the local grammar school, whence he graduated with dazzling distinction, before going on to Manchester University. There – with further distinction – he studied history under two stars, A. J. P. Taylor and Sir Lewis Namier, and was set for an academic career in medieval history (notably on the role of the clergy); only for the war to intervene.

As he would frequently observe to us neophytes, history was closely akin to the Great Game of intelligence. And so it would prove for me. Indeed, the best thing about working for Maurice Oldfield was that it was like having a series of the highest-quality tutorials. It was not coincidence but a compliment to him that the great majority of his young men in SIME, having been demobilized and obtained university degrees, went and joined him in MI6. I was to be one of the few exceptions.

Shortly after joining up in 1941, he transferred to the much derided Intelligence Corps and was despatched to the Middle East, with the unglamorous job of checking passports on the Suez Canal. From there he was sent to Syria (taken by the British from the Vichy French) and promoted sergeant in the Field Security. In 1943 he was picked for a commission, and shortly afterwards was spotted by Brigadier Douglas Roberts – then head of DSO (Defence Security Office, an MI5 offshoot) Syria. Thenceforward, his advance to the rank of lieutenant-colonel was both meteoric and, in those far-off days of privilege when smart regiments tended to fill all the senior posts, highly unorthodox. With Maurice in tow as his deputy, Roberts gravitated to become head of SIME in Cairo. During the war SIME had been an immensely powerful and successful body, independent of MI5 in London and running many skilful (and largely unsung) operations of it own. Under an inspired officer, Brigadier

Dudley Clarke,* it had specialised in the arts of deception, of turning round German agents whom the Abwehr poured into the promising territory of Egypt. This in turn became a speciality (indeed a lifelong interest) of Maurice. An integral part of this work took place at the Maadi Interrogation Camp, just up the Nile from Cairo, where methods of psychological pressure were used with great success – but which undoubtedly would not be acceptable under modern human-rights legislation.

That day of my first interview, after questioning me closely about my work in GSI-14, Maurice (I was immediately instructed to address him by his first name) explained that an important new section was being opened in SIME to concentrate on combating all forms of Soviet subversive penetration in the Middle East. SIME was currently low on manpower and brainpower; through demob many of the wartime stars had departed. In a vast GHQ thousands strong, SIME was in a bit of a vacuum. Almost apologetically he continued, 'By their very nature intelligence bodies suffer from a disease of time-lag, like cars starting up after the lights have changed. In counter-intelligence, we're still fighting the last war. Even though the war's well behind us and the Germans defeated, it's taken us a long time to get the machinery round to pointing at the next big threat – Soviet Communism.' Meanwhile our biggest jobs here were the preserving of security in the Middle East, especially and increasingly in Palestine. He added: 'I want you to start up the new section. Claude says you've got experience of this particular problem as IO Balkans.'

He went on to say that – although, because of the post-war vacuum, I would in substance be doing a major's job – there would be no immediate promotion, not even to captain, as the command was tough on the intelligence establishment ('the funnies' they called it). An organisational chart of MI5 in 1946 shows, under SIME, in the middle of a large empty space, 'Russian Inspired Activities: Satellite Powers: Lt A. A. Horne'.† It was an ambitious role to be filled by a twenty-one-year-old subaltern. But

* An extraordinary operator, once photographed by wartime Spanish intelligence disguised in drag.
† Unearthed by Professor Christopher Andrew in the course of writing his official history of MI5, *The Defence of the Realm* (2009).

soon more senior people would come out from London. Like a university tutor, he sent me off with two books to read and discuss over the weekend: one was Arthur Koestler's grim *Darkness at Noon*, the second the Royal Canadian Mounted Police official report on the recent Soviet spy case in Canada prompted by the defection of Igor Gouzenko, a cipher clerk at the Russian Embassy in Ottawa. 'These', he said, 'will give you an idea of what we're up against.'

They also gave me a first insight into Maurice's passionate abhorrence of Soviet intelligence (soon reorganised as the KGB) and the inhumanity it represented. His dedication to the war on Soviet Communism, the Cold War as it later became, reinforced by my reading of those two books and of the material that passed across my desk, was infectious and profoundly influential. In my teens, the valour of the Red Army in the fight against Hitler had made me staunchly pro-Soviet. Now I became lastingly disabused.

4

A USEFUL APPRENTICESHIP

The 'Green' Security Card. Note the wide-ranging authority,
in the 'execution of his duty'.

The great advantage of being a writer is that you can spy on people.

Graham Greene

I was in clover. At SIME I was doing real intelligence work, what I had longed for after that first confrontation with the phoney elm at Frensham, and I was still short of my twenty-first birthday. It was the most fabulous job imaginable. In those first weeks I worked in closest contact with Maurice, received sparkling tutorials and studied his style. He did not believe in the narrow need-to-know principle where officers worked in small cells and were not encouraged (or even permitted) to see what was going on elsewhere. For Maurice the history don (who, as a good historian, always had one eye on the portents of the future), those he trusted had to see the whole picture. Of course it was no doubt suitably edited; but he applied the same principle throughout his career, not least in his dealings with journalists, among whom he became renowned for his candour – with sad consequences towards the end of his career. His own office in Cairo was somewhat indicative of the man and his style. It had three doors; one led into the main office; the other two, at opposite ends of his office, housed waiting rooms in one of which Teddy Kollek of the Jewish Agency in Jerusalem (his good friend) often would be found, and in the second Kollek's Arab counterpart. Somehow they never collided.

As far as Palestine and the war against Jewish Terrorism was concerned, it was a minority view that MO took – as exemplified by that second door to his office. It was certainly not shared by either the pro-Arab Foreign Secretary, Ernest Bevin, or by the vast majority of British soldiery in the Middle East. Intellectually as well as emotionally, Maurice strongly believed in the Jewish right to a state in Palestine. All through his career he fostered the closest contacts with the Jewish intelligence community, as represented in 1946 by Teddy Kollek, which was later to evolve into the redoubtable Mossad. Most of the time these contacts were highly beneficial to Britain. The Palestinian Jews helped with their links to the huge oppressed diaspora still living in the Soviet Union; because of terrorism in Palestine, 1946–7 was almost certainly the worst patch in Anglo-Jewish relations – though it has been alleged that MO helped the Jewish cause by indicating safe routes out of the USSR. While he particularly admired, and studied, the sophisticated deception techniques of the 1946 paramilitary Haganah, his nightmare was Soviet penetration, or turning, of the Jewish community. For their own cynical purposes, the Soviets were backing a policy of getting the 'British imperialists' out of Palestine, where, uniquely in post-1945 history, it found itself at one with the US, as President Truman allowed policy to be driven by the Jewish lobby. Maurice despaired when he felt Bevin's policy was playing into Soviet hands. But equally, with hard-eyed pragmatism, he always retained a hope that he would be able to make use of a friendly Jewish intelligence establishment, with its renowned skills and contacts among the millions of Jews inside the USSR, in order to penetrate the monolithic Soviet apparatus.

Ever since the Irgun's brutal bombing of the King David Hotel in July 1946 (which had not only killed ninety-one people but had inflicted a shattering blow on British intelligence records), things had been hotting up in Palestine. Officers were now ordered to carry side-arms and to walk in twos. Progressively the 100,000-man British force there found itself under siege. Passions rising against us among the Jews were exacerbated by the policy of refusing the 'Illegal Immigrant' ships permission to discharge their pathetic cargoes, survivors of Hitler's Holocaust, instead redeporting them to camps in Cyprus. It shocked many of us, too. From the point of view of intelligence-collecting, the consequence was to create a void: virtually to a man, and woman, the Jews turned against us. There were no informers, those essential handmaidens of good intelligence work. Nevertheless, or perhaps because of this, and at odds with Maurice's natural inclinations, by far the biggest section in SIME was the one dealing with 'Jewish terrorism'. Second came the section focused on the Arab irredentist movement and then – a long way behind – mine dealing with Soviet incursions.

Always a man in a hurry, Maurice had an off-puttingly brisk manner on the telephone: 'Oldfield, Oldfield. Yes. Yes ...' But this belied great courtesy, and a genuine, supportive interest in the lives of all those working for him. He was perhaps especially popular with the girls working in SIME. All of them carefully hand-picked, well-brought-up 'nice' girls, many were highly attractive, and – locked away behind the barbed wire in our tabernacle – they made us the envy of others in GHQ. Several of them married officers within the compound. At their head was a dragon (though she too must have been under thirty) called Pat Robinson, Head of Registry, who knew (and kept) almost as many secrets as there were in Maurice's own vast cranium. Liked by women, and with numerous platonic girlfriends, Maurice never married, though he claimed he came close to it at least once. I often suspected he was a closet homosexual, which indeed was to cause his tragic downfall many years later. But it was never an issue in SIME; certainly he was never overtly gay like Claude. As I often wondered in later years, how was it that the two most brilliant intelligence operators under whom I worked were both homosexual? Was it perhaps that they had more acutely developed sensitivities than the rest of us? If so, the era of 'positive vetting' that followed Burgess and Maclean may well have caused a loss of talent to the secret services comparable to Louis XIV's ill-conceived expulsion of the Huguenots from France.

As even the Soviet agent Kim Philby admitted in his mischievous autobiography, Oldfield was a 'formidable' figure. Working under him, we were a heterogeneous and perhaps rather raw lot – few of us older than twenty-five, drawn from all three services, and with very diverse backgrounds. Joining my section was a brilliant young flight lieutenant, Alexis Forter, a Russian-speaker, son of an émigré officer of the Imperial Russian Guard and imbued with a passionate hatred for the regime which had murdered so many people of his parents' world. He had a brilliant mind and incisive wit. After SIME Alexis took a double first at Oxford in Farsi and Arabic. On his return to the Oldfield clan, his first posting sent him to Iraq where he received a decoration for destroying the secret files during the Revolution of 1958. He died after becoming head of the MI6 office in Paris.

Then there was Michael Wrigley, an old Harrovian Rifle Brigade subaltern who joined the Arab section. Over six foot tall, usually clad in huge fawn-coloured brothel-creepers with a gait that put one in mind of a camel, even at twenty-one Michael was a wonderfully eccentric figure who came increasingly to resemble Charles de Gaulle. With an eminently kind heart well concealed beneath an extensive lexicon of swear words in every language, he developed (and enjoyed) the exterior of a hearty Yorkshire squire from the Turf Club – perfect cover for his subsequent spell as our man in Bangkok for twelve years. Like Alexis, Michael became a lifelong friend of mine. A close protégé of MO's was the nineteen-year-old Tony Castle (he later changed his name to Cavendish), a grammar school boy. His father managed a hotel in the Swiss Engadine, and as a result Tony had the great asset of speaking flawless German, with a Swiss accent. Another Arabist was Miles Ponsonby, who was to end his career as ambassador to Outer Mongolia (then a most important MI6 listening post).

A mysterious figure, who kept himself to himself and whom few of us knew was a Major Sugden, in the Signal Corps, who disappeared daily into the inner sanctum, sprouting with aerials. No one knew exactly what he did, he was uncommunicative and anti-social; only years later was it revealed that his outfit had been the Middle East end of the great Bletchley Enigma or 'SIGINT' secret. It was his equipment that tracked the wretched Jewish 'Illegal Immigrant' ships all the way from Eastern Europe to be seized by the navy on the shores of the Promised Land.

One of the old guard left over from wartime was a flamboyant and controversial figure named Jimmy Brodie, a twenty-five-year-old captain in the Gurkhas, who had been wounded in the desert. Born in Basra of a Scottish doctor and Turkish mother, Jimmy in his Gurkha beret closely resembled a young Saddam Hussein, at least in looks. He spoke perfect Arabic, was an expert in interrogation and perhaps even more of an adept in the wheeling and dealing of the souk. This was something he could never resist, which earned for him the nickname of 'The Thief of Baghdad'. Jimmy was to play a vital role in my departure from SIME and return to England.

Among outsiders, SIME had close relations with the Special Branch of the Egyptian Police, as represented by the elegant, tarboosh-wearing Riadh Bey and his pockmarked deputy, Youzbashi (Captain) Youssef, who rivalled The Thief in his knowledge of the souk. We would supply them with information on hashish-traffickers, and they would brief us on Communist activities. Then there was Walter Emery, the distinguished

Egyptologist, a former senior officer in SIME, who could open doors everywhere; and, another Egyptologist, the representative for American Central Intelligence in Cairo, John Hoag. John was a good friend, and exchanges between him and SIME were of the closest – except when, as US and British policies on Palestine began to diverge, an increasing number of documents would be marked 'TOP SECRET & GUARD' (that is, on no account to be shown to the Americans). And, of course, there were the outstations, spanning the region from Khartoum to Istanbul – most notably the weighty set-up in Jerusalem of DSO (Defence Security Office) Palestine.

To help me carry out my duties, I was issued with a most imposing document, a Green Card with a photograph of me in civvies which bore the inscription, in both English and Arabic: 'The bearer of this card is engaged in Security Duties. He is authorised to be in any dress at any time in the execution of his duty. All persons subject to Military Law are enjoined to give him every assistance in their power and all others are requested to give him all facilities in carrying out his duty ...' This did not, of course, automatically give me access to the belly-dancers at Madame Bardia's Opera House, but in those happy days the Green Card did carry considerable weight in Egypt.

So what did I actually do? Over the course of more than half-a-century, many of the details have become blurred, erased deliberately or otherwise; some remain under wraps. As a result of his wartime background in the field of double-agents, Maurice was able to pass over to me to track such legendary names out of the world of old-time espionage as Alex Rado, former head of the Soviet-controlled LUCY ring in wartime Switzerland, and Leopold Trepper, the genius behind the Rote Kapelle (Red Orchestra), Moscow's most successful network in Occupied Europe, who later went to live in Israel. Another wartime legacy (though it had no Soviet connections) which I had to deal with was trying to track down the traitorous Greeks who had betrayed to the Gestapo (for money) a network of brave SOE operatives called (after the naval commander at their head) the Cumberlege Mission. I never learned whether the culprits were found. If not, it certainly would not have been for want of effort.

Nevertheless, apart from the occasional 007 work of contacting, briefing and debriefing agents, and travel to exciting outposts such as

Jerusalem, much was fairly unromantic deskwork. In Compton Mackenzie's *Water on the Brain*, 'N' warns Blenkinsop that 'our work doesn't
consist entirely of meeting mysterious Polish countesses in old castles. Of
course, we have our little dramas, but the greater part of the work is
routine stuff. Card-indexing, filing, making out lists, putting agents'
reports into proper English . . .' That was true. The last item might take
the form of secret reports from ISLD; these would be assessed, rather like
a *Guide Michelin* entry, according a rating of 'reliable' and 'well-placed'.
Each had a tear-off slip on which the recipient would grade the report
from 'very good' to 'useless'. In the latter category would come a torrent
of reports from our operative in the Lebanon, a man with one eye and
clearly limited sight in the other, given to referring to 'my Aleppo source'.
Once I had cause to query the accuracy of a report and received back the
riposte 'As my Aleppo source can neither read nor write, this is difficult
to check.' Henceforth anything that smacked of the *One Thousand and
One Nights* was labelled 'an Aleppo'.

As Compton Mackenzie shows, the comic, the absurd and the occasional disaster are seldom far removed from intelligence work. There was
the occasion when SIME was brought in to check on a major loss of top-
secret material which its sister firm ISLD had despatched to its office in
Jerusalem. The trouble was that ISLD, fearing that its cover name was
widely blown – which indeed it was, with every *suffragi* working in GHQ
knowing what it stood for – decided, abruptly, to change it to the equally
transparent CRPO(ME), for Combined Research and Planning Office.
Immediately it was nicknamed 'Creepo'. Over a week or two, instead of
sacks and bags of vital documents pouring into Jerusalem, there was total
silence. Put on the case, the sleuths of SIME discovered that the missing
material, much of it to do with Jewish terrorism, was piling up inside a
small office – the Command Regimental Pay Office (ME) – manned by a
locally employed (that is, Jewish) sergeant. There he sat, totally baffled by
this sudden surge of top-secret documents which had nothing to do with
pay. Red faces all round.

Then there was the famous, or infamous, Kim Philby, currently MI6's
man in Istanbul. I would often meet his old, distinguished father, St John
Philby – who had 'gone tropo' – dressed as a Saudi Bedoun, fiddling with
his prayer beads, on the terrace of the Continental. With equal regularity

a thick file on his wayward son would pass across my desk. Almost exclusively the contents dealt with the dedicatedly heterosexual Kim's ill-chosen liaisons with Hungarian dancers, who were suspected of being Axis spies (we were still hunting Nazis, even though the war had ended months previously). Much later Maurice would claim that he had suspected Philby's Soviet affiliations even then, but the frivolous thought often crossed my mind in subsequent decades that he had escaped investigation because, after spy scandals involving Guy Burgess, John Vassall and Anthony Blunt the hunt was on for homosexuals; when that fat file on Philby surfaced, did the reassuring cry go up, 'Nothing queer about old Kim! He must be all right'?

We also had to face the sorry debacle of the Nazi prisoners of war. It was learned that a number of quite senior Wehrmacht POWs, who had escaped during the war, had set themselves up prosperously under cover in Cairo and were busy fomenting anti-British activities among nationalist elements in the Egyptian Army (such as were subsequently to bring forth Gamal Abdel Nasser, who overthrew the monarchy only a few years later). SIME decided to mount an operation to round them all up. With great courage and skill, young Tony Castle, posing – with his immaculate Engadine Schweizerdeutsch – as a friendly Swiss-German, managed to penetrate their circle. Heavily armed Field Security personnel in plain clothes swooped; the Nazi escapees were piled into trucks and driven off to a camp in the desert. Unfortunately, they were too clever for the young guards. By simple guile, they overpowered them, relieved them of their weapons and their clothing, then left them in their underpants to walk home in the desert, and drove off with their captured vehicles. More red faces.

So what did we really achieve? Perhaps I was too junior a cog, operating for too short a time, to pass sensible judgement. What can the flea tell you about the hunting successes of the dog on whom he resides? In terms of penetrating the various Jewish terrorist organisations, of course we failed. With the Americans ranged against us, and with a local population that was almost 100 per cent against us, it was a sea in which no fish could swim. There were virtually no defectors, no potential double-agents. But, in the longer term, as far as the Cold War against the KGB was concerned, I like to think that some of the early steps taken under the brilliant aegis of MO did eventually bear fruit. At least we learned what we were up against, long before the Americans did. But, in terms of purely personal advantage, for me – for what was to become my future career as a historian – the sheer joy, the inspiration, the mental discipline and training of work under MO were to prove of incalculable value. After all, what is really the difference between the work of the analytical intelligence officer, the journalist, the foreign correspondent and the historian? Very little.

But these were thoughts for the future. At the time, when my attention strayed from my work, my thoughts were never far from Jo. In England the winter of 1946–7, the coldest in living memory, crunched down. Coal ran out; frozen trains were unable to transport it. There were endless power cuts. The food ration diminished still further. I agonised for Jo, with this added misery, and sent parcels when I could, while I basked in the Lucullan comforts of Cairo.

Maurice departed. His demob number was long overdue. He was what was known as 'sweating on demob'. The Brig joined him. Shortly thereafter they reappeared as a team running R-5 in MI6, the section which embraced the Soviet desk. Maurice became known as 'the Brig's Brains'. As before, it was often hard to decipher just what were the Brig's contributions to the world of intelligence. Whenever I met him in years to come the conversation ran along the lines of 'What clubs do you belong to? What kind of car are you running these days, Horne?' With some misgivings, Maurice gave up for ever any thought of an academic career. We, his accolytes in SIME, went into deep mourning. He would remain a lifelong friend (as, indeed, did my first 'I' boss, Claude Dewhurst) and an important influence; but working in SIME would never be the same again. Maurice and the Brig were replaced by a triumvirate of ex-army 'I' officers: Derek Hamblen, David Stewart and James Robertson.

At their head was a fairly unimpressive figure called Alec Kellar. With a lisp, protruding teeth and a small grey moustache, Kellar looked like a nervous water rat; he was a through-and-through civilian bureaucrat and as such marked the beginning of the new, peacetime era. His second name was caution, and his favourite expression 'We musn't exercise ourselves.' Out from England to head my section, by now vastly expanded, came a much decorated Battle of Britain squadron leader, Peter de Wesselow. One felt he was perhaps more adept at shooting down Heinkels than nailing spies. Michael Wrigley and I were made captains – long overdue, we thought, given our responsibilities. Gone were the glory days of MO's regime.

But, perhaps worst of all, because of Bevin's undertaking to 'evacuate' Cairo, GHQ MEF (Middle East Forces) was moved, lock, stock and barrel, out into a dreary, dusty cantonment on the Suez Canal at Fayed. It was a major logistical operation. For the second time since the dark days of 1942 when Rommel had threatened Cairo, the air around Garden City was filled with the smoke and the smell of burning paper. As anyone knows who has attempted it, paper is extraordinarily difficult to burn in large quantities. Young staff officers, including me, scurried about the streets, retrieving partially burned top-secret documents from the gardens of pashas. I regretfully packed up the apartment on my Zamalek rooftop. The silent, faithful Osman wept what seemed like genuine tears at my departure; doubtless a future Egyptian master would not be as easy-going as I had been.

At Fayed, which was eventually to become Britain's main surviving base in the Middle East until Nasser cleared us out once and for all after the Suez Crisis of 1956, nothing was ready. It was a drear patch of desert on the Bitter Lake, full of scorpions and sandflies, and sand-blasted by the hot Khamsin wind off the Sahara. We staff officers, spoiled by the lotus-eating of Cairo, now found ourselves sleeping in tents, tended by dispirited German POWs instead of Osmans. SIME's offices were lodged in temporary huts in a separate compound where once again, wired off from the rest of GHQ, our girls became the source of the greatest envy, given the shortage of women on the Canal. It was wildly insecure as German POWs, nomadic fellahin and even the odd camel wandered in and out. Secret documents had a habit of disappearing and turning up in strange places. It all seemed symbolic of the decline of Empire, not least the empire of GHQ MEF which had once stretched from Kenya to Thrace. Everybody wanted us out, including our American allies, and the Attlee government had neither the resources nor the will to remain. The situation in Palestine was worsening by the day; the terrorists were winning and we were losing, despite endless military reinforcements. And, according to the rationale of imperial purpose, Palestine was there to protect the Suez Canal, while the Canal was there to assure the route to India. But the Jewel in the Crown was being flogged off (Britain abandoned the Raj in 1947), so why all the residual back-up? With the situation deteriorating in Palestine, there were signs of increasing unrest in Egypt. At SIME, as more and more effort was diverted to Palestine so, inevitably, it lessened the focus on what Maurice and the Brig had rightly identified as the number-one threat – Soviet penetration. The role of my section seemed to become less and less important. That was a serious misjudgement. But at least, I would always feel, we had established an important bridgehead in what was to become the Cold War.

There was much disaffection, particularly among veterans like Jimmy Brodie. Most of us just longed for our demob number to come up. But, yet again, because of the demands imposed on Britain's overstretched forces, my demob was postponed. There was, all too understandably, a note of mounting coolness, distance and almost despair in Jo's letters. From them I could glean little idea of her everyday life; in return there was very little I could write about mine. Our letters became less frequent, though still loving, in both directions. The distance was killing us, but still we clung on, sustained by a kind of resigned optimism that things would work out when I returned at last. Yet, in the rare moments when I had time to think about the future rationally, I wondered what I was going to do, once demobbed? How was I going to support a wife and somebody else's child? I had an inchoate yearning to empty my mind of military things and to write, but what? How should I start, and what could I earn?

To counter the rising malaise and tedium at Fayed, those of us in SIME who had the excuse to do so would make trips back to the fleshpots of Cairo (in civilian clothes, naturally) for R&R. On one such occasion, after a dinner out at the pyramids, I managed to write off my second MG in a near-fatal collision with a city bus. I still cannot remember exactly what happened, but woke up with concussion in hospital after kind and friendly Cairenes had brought me in, more dead than alive. Photographs of the wreckage made my blood run cold, but out of it came a blessing: The insurance company would not pay up the price of a new car, so I settled instead for a second-hand Citroën (an Onze Légère, with one of the first front-wheel drives on the market, and only just pre-war). It proved to be a fabulously sturdy and reliable car. But how could I get it back to

England? I was at long last due for demob. So was Jimmy Brodie. We decided to drive the Citroën home, together. It would, I thought, take a week or two (it would turn into more than a month) and it would give both Jo and me time to think about the unclear future.

And so we set off. I wrote in the diary I started keeping for what we enthusiastically called 'Operation Press-off': 'After months and weeks of preparation of the most gigantic order, and all the setbacks and trials of Job one could imagine, we finally left Fayid, on the Suez Canal, for Ismailia – our starting line, at 9 pm on 1 August ... we slept (only for a few hours) at the Timsah leave camp ...' Montgomery could not have prepared for Alamein with greater attention to detail. Stacked in a dozen miscellaneous boxes and holdalls inside the Citroën, right down on its torsion bars, were cases of Naafi gin (at knockdown prices), 6,000 cigarettes, soap, sponges, pouches full of uncut Alexandrine stones (surprise, surprise, they turned out to be fakes), and of gold rings (to me they looked to be straight out of a Christmas cracker, but JB knew a market). There were Jerrycans of petrol strapped on the back and, slung from the headlamps, two amazing canvas chaggles, essential to the Indian Army which, holding several gallons of water, miraculously sweated and thus kept cool both for the radiator and for human consumption. As we left the Gurkha quarters (where JB had been lodged), the friendly Sikh doctor urged on us one most important piece of equipment, a small attaché case containing sufficient condoms for a battalion going on home leave, pills, syringes and every antidote for every known form of VD. 'You never know ... You meet very many funny women. Must take care your good health, my good friends.' There were tears in his eyes.

The only commodity we lacked almost totally was any form of currency. But Jimmy had no worries; he knew the market for everything, from Cairo to Paris. I soon learned, when he disappeared off into the souk on 'business', that it was better not (if not actually pointless) to ask questions. I just prayed, every night, he wouldn't go too far. In return, I was in charge of seeing that the car kept running and that we didn't get lost. Oh yes, and most important of all, JB had managed to produce a Movement Order, addressed to all intelligence formations along the way, notifying them that the above officers were travelling 'on duty' from Fayed to London, via – and I had a lurking suspicion that JB had had these destinations typed in *ex post facto* – Jerusalem, Damascus, Beirut, Ankara, Istanbul, Salonika, Athens, Naples, Rome, Berne, Paris. All addressees were enjoined to give us all possible assistance. In those happy far-off days the web of the British intelligence community, with its assistant military attachés, Visa Offices, British Military Missions, MI6 residents, Field Security outposts and so on, truly did reach from Cairo to London, and far beyond. We would be in good hands. Our bumper stickers, reading 'Cairo–London' in English and Arabic, showed the confidence we felt – though, as far as we knew, as of 1947 no one had undertaken the journey, certainly not across the heart of mysterious, closed Turkey.

But on the first morning we hit a snag. On the Canal, at the entry to Sinai, at 6 a.m. a sleepy Egyptian official told us that the papers were out of order and the car could not be exported. A lot of shouting and wheed-ling by JR, three hours wasted, finally bakshish of our first hundred Philip Morris produced the vital rubber-stamp, that hallmark of Egyptian bureaucracy. Then, after a bumpy trip across Sinai, we reached Jerusalem, the last of several trips for both of us, where we stayed in the legendary YMCA building. Across the road stood the King David, with its shattered wing still covered with tarpaulins. There was an atmosphere of tension, anger and gloom pervading this beautiful sunny city. How suddenly it had changed. Only the previous week the Irgun, in its most brutal operation to date, had kidnapped two young British Field Security sergeants, garrotted them and then strung up their booby-trapped bodies. Road blocks were everywhere. It was a repellent crime.

The Old City was out of bounds. Three senior officers of the DSO joined us for dinner at the 'Y'. They literally dived into that solid building. They knew they were marked men. One of their much loved colleagues had been murdered the previous year, and having been driven out of the King David they were, I noted in my diary, 'living like rats – bolting from one hole to another – with the fatalistic conviction that their number would be up sooner or later. They have all our sympathy. I personally would be a nervous wreck within a month.'

All were still visibly shaken by the fate of the two young Field Security sergeants, Martin and Paice, who had been working under the SIME umbrella. Inexperienced, one still in his teens, they should never have been exposed to the work they were given. It is hard, so long after the event, to evoke the horror which the beastliness of the murders aroused in Palestine – especially among those of our people responsible for those two boys – and the anger. The media have hardened us to terrorist horror today, but nobody in 1947 had experienced anything like it. Jewish shops in Britain were sacked; in Tel Aviv soldiers of 6th Airborne ran amok, indiscriminately killing five Jews, and wounding fifteen others. A deep rage had been unleashed. Perhaps more than any other single act of terrorism it was what decided the Attlee government to get out of Palestine the following year. We drove down to visit my regiment, the Coldstream, whose 3rd Battalion was stationed at Natanya, just 500 yards from the grove where the bodies had been found, and had been engaged in the fruitless search for the sergeants. Strictest discipline was in force; no one was allowed out of camp, to avert anything like the outrage in Tel Aviv. The atmosphere was grim. There were old friends from Pirbright days – Mark Norman, Rupert Strutt and George Edwards – but none of the cajolery of those days, no jolly talk about duck-shooting in the Jordan marshes. The schooboys of only eighteen months ago had become bitter, tough and very angry veterans.

We drove on up to Haifa, to see my old GSI-14 mate John Linklater – now 6th Airborne's intelligence officer. Living in a requisitioned convent atop Mount Carmel, he had grown a moustache and seemed more febrile than ever. True to his admirable spirit of eccentricity, he had also become passionately pro-Jewish, even Zionist. We got into his jeep and drove – or rather bounced – down the hair-raisingly steep steps that divided Upper Haifa from Lower Haifa. Hundreds of small Arab children came from nowhere, shouting and cheering the crazy British. Then, suddenly, we were in a silent and sullen Jewish quarter where people moved away from us, 'I just wanted you to see', said John, 'how close the two communities live to each other. Any thought of "partition", which they're now talking about, is just ridiculous. The moment we leave, those silly Arabs will be pushed into the desert. You'll see.' And, of course, within the year, the British did leave, and later so did the terrorised Arabs.

The next day, Tuesday 5 August, we got officially demobbed, in Jerusalem, but why? It remains a mystery. In my SIME work I had no direct connection with Palestine, with Jew or Arab. But JB, deeply involved with the Arab community, did. We were kitted out with the most ethnic demob suits of baggy trousers and fedoras. I wish I had kept them; instead we handed them to some friendly Turk on the way home. We were still permitted to wear uniform, while JB's bogus Movement Order remained valid.

We were bidding farewell to our friends Jimmy and Marjorie Sales in the DSO office after lunch, just starting the car, when an almighty explosion close by shook Jerusalem. As one much accustomed to such things, Sales said calmly, 'You've had it now. The siren will go in two minutes, and you won't be able to move!' So it did. We went upstairs, and listened in to the police net over a communications receiver. I took my hat off to the remarkably efficient, quiet way the police carried out the whole operation. Apparently Jewish terrorists had planted a bomb in the Labour Office, which had blown up when three British constables tried to remove it. The body parts of one policeman were found out in the street and on a neighbouring roof, the remains of two others were buried under the wreckage and a fourth was severely injured, as was an Arab constable. All this came over the air with matter-of-fact grimness. After a couple of hours, the all-clear went and we got under way at once, passing close to the area where the bomb had gone off. We drove in a fury with the terrorists. I wrote, 'My legs were trembling so much with uncontrollable rage I could hardly drive.'

We reached Haifa that afternoon, and left for Damascus the next day, via Tiberias and the bleak, empty Golan Heights that were to become such fierce battlefields decades later. We stopped at the summit and gazed back over shining Galilee, over the whole expanse of northern Palestine laid out beneath us. The Jewish settlements below were so close you felt that an Arab throwing a stone off the heights could almost hit a settler. But it was all so beautiful, so beguilingly tranquil. 'Goodbye bloody, horrible, beautiful Palestine', I muttered to myself. 'Goodbye you cursed and damned country.' I hoped I would never see the place again. How little did I know!

At the Syrian frontier what could have been an awkward moment, given all the contraband concealed around the car, was transformed instantly as Brodie produced one of his miraculous letters, this time from the Syrian Consul in Cairo. Once inside Syria, from being soldiers we became tourists. We visited the cities of Homs and Hama, and were beginning to succumb to the tranquillity of it all when the valiant Citroën's dynamo started acting up. We limped into Damascus, where Brodie, true to form, discovered a garage run by a former SIME agent, who patched up the dynamo. That evening we had drinks in a Russian bar with the Assistant Military Attaché. From his pocket the Attaché produced some highly sensitive notes about Soviet espionage activities in Syria; then he left his jacket, complete with notes, behind in the bar. We returned, to be greeted by the Russian bar owner, holding up the mislaid jacket with a smile. We were not impressed. On to Aleppo and the magnificent, looming Crusader fortress, Krak des Chevaliers.

On 12 August, we crossed into Turkey and the really exciting part of the trip began. As of 1947, Turkey was terra incognita, whose mysterious interior had been visited by few over the last decade. Nobody one knew had driven across it; there were few cars, and fewer filling stations. The roads were an unknown quantity. We had a long, winding climb of some 60 miles, on a robust (and completely empty) road built by German military engineers. Passing through wild mountain scenery, we reached the Cilician Gates, a great gorge cut into mountains 12,000 feet high, with room only for river and road to pass at the bottom. We encountered occasional fierce-looking Anatolian peasants, all of whom were deeply curious about the Citroën: they gave the impression of never having seen a car before.

After the Taurus it was uninteresting, prairie land. In the distance one could see a massive snow-capped mountain rising out of the plain with a salt lake at its base, the classical Mount Argaeus. Just behind it lay Kayseri, St Paul's Caesarea, capital of Cappadocia, and almost the dead centre of Anatolia. That evening, with some difficulty, we found one hotel. The manager was on the street to greet us practically before we arrived, with 'Bonjour, messieurs!' in perfect French. It was encouraging to meet the first person in Turkey who spoke a language we understood, but we soon found that that was all he knew. I was more or less incapacitated by a hornet sting on the palm of my hand received that morning, which was extremely painful. So Brodie set about finding petrol. There no sign of a filling station – we had to get the Mayor's permission. With great goodwill, this friendly official drained 4 gallons from what appeared to be the only fire engine in this town of largely wooden houses.

Over many of the next 200 dusty miles the road either ceased to exist or had been deliberately blocked, perhaps due to fears of Russian invasion. Finally we reached Ataturk's artificial and charmless capital, Ankara, and were glad to push on towards Istanbul. We broke the trip at Göynük, one of the loveliest places I had ever seen. Cresting a very high ridge, all of a sudden right below there was this wonderful little village, shaped rather like a bowl, with beautiful old houses of plaster and half-timber that could have belonged to unspoilt Tudor England – except for a large white mosque at the bottom. On Friday 15 August, ten days after leaving Jerusalem, we arrived at the heights overlooking Üsküdar, Florence Nightingale's Scutari, to see the famous skyline and the thousand spires of Istanbul. Below there were myriad small boats and ferries, bustling, scuttling and hooting their way across the Bosphorus. It was wildly exciting: after two years in the heat and dust of the Middle East one felt perhaps what an Ancient Greek army had felt as they cried 'Thalassa! Thalassa!' when they at last saw the Black Sea after a 1,000-mile march. There, across the water, was Europe. We had got out of the murderous Middle East, through the Great Unknown of Anatolia; we were halfway home. We felt quite proud of ourselves. Our next stop was Athens where we were planning to put the Citroën on a ferry to Italy – Yugoslavia being out of the question (I recalled my great map in GSI-14, with its abundance of red flags).

We contacted Arthur Whittall, scion of an illustrious Anglo-Turk family, located in the Visa Section (otherwise MI6) of the Embassy. He was adamant: we could not attempt the journey, whether by road or by rail. Greek Communist partisans or bandits would ensure that we were never seen again. For intelligence officers, it was out of the question. So there we stuck. In the event, the only alternative was to catch a 2,000-ton Italian cargo ship, the *Lido*, leaving Istanbul for Naples on the 22nd or 23rd, and taking at least seven days. This was depressing news; we would be losing at least another ten days. In theory, there could hardly have been a better place to be stuck than Istanbul in 1947 – had it not been for my eagerness to be reunited with Jo. Turkey was opening up after all its years of isolation during the war, and was keen to meet its new friends, the British. The old German *feldgrau* uniforms were slowly being replaced with a mish-mash of Western kit, the Luger sidearms of the police with the British Army's useless Smith & Wessons. Brodie sold off our hoard of gin and whisky, and his deals made us rich – temporarily. We lived it up.

While Brodie was on his financial expeditions (sightseeing and tourism were never his thing), I prowled around the Galata and up the exquisite, still-unspoilt valley with the enchanting name of the Sweet Waters of Asia, goggled at the mosques of Hagia Sophia and Suleiman the Magnificent and at the splendours of Topkapi. I went out to the ravishing Princes' Isle in the Bosphorus, Prinkipo, and enjoyed the endless movement of the little vessels darting back and forth. I fell in love with Istanbul, and with the hardy, courageous and dependable, Turks. I longed to return.

We spent several evenings with Arthur Whittall. If Cairo was the intelligence hub of the Middle East, Istanbul was its close rival. Spies, defectors and deserters from the Eastern bloc flowed in and out from the Balkans across Turkey's rugged eastern frontier or on boats that plied the Black Sea. It was a vital Western listening post. For that reason MI6 had a heavyweight office in Istanbul. But, alas, at its head currently was the accomplished traitor Kim Philby, who later boasted in his own memoirs of the coups he pulled off while in Istanbul (which were relevant to my work in SIME). Barely two years previously (in August 1945), perhaps the most important KGB defector since the war, Konstantin Volkov, working under cover as Soviet Vice-Consul in Istanbul, had approached the British for asylum for himself and his wife. He claimed to know the names of three Soviet agents working in Britain – presumably Burgess, Maclean and Philby. This vital intelligence came to Philby's desk in London via C himself. Philby, closer to panic than at any other moment in his odious life, played for time, 'to dig into the background', as he put it. Meanwhile the KGB was alerted. My old boss in SIME, Brigadier Douglas-Roberts, incredibly the only Russian-speaking intelligence officer in either the ME or London able to interrogate Volkov, was on home leave. He was ordered forthwith to fly to Istanbul: 'But, don't you read my contract? I don't fly!' was his response. So the Brig went by slow boat to Turkey; by the time he had arrived, three weeks had elapsed, and, thanks to Philby, Volkov and wife had been spirited back to Russia. They were never heard of again.

We never met Philby while in Istanbul – I think he was away on leave. Brodie – years later – told me that he thought Whittall had even then harboured suspicions about his boss. Many lives and much damage might have been saved if he had managed to expose him then.

On 23 August we at last embarked from Istanbul aboard the ancient SS *Lido* and apprehensively watched as the Citroën was winched aboard in a big net. The cog on the hoisting crane seemed to have a tooth missing, so every yard or two the car would make a sickening jump, its mudguard buckling and unbuckling. Finally it sat, in solitary splendour, above the forward hatch. The *Lido* was a tiny tramp steamer designed for ambling round the fringes of the Mediterranean. Among our fellow passengers (there were only a handful of cabins) were an Italian priest, an elderly American professor and his wife and a pretty Italian girl. The girl was deposited on board by a weeping mother who, with menacing looks at Brodie and me, placed her under the personal care of the Italian captain. He assumed his *in loco parentis* responsibilities with Latin dedication; shortly after sailing she moved into his cabin and was hardly seen for the rest of the voyage.

And what a voyage it turned out to be! At every port along the route, as we sauntered southwards, the holds were filled with dried beans and peas, or emptied of them. The air was thick with dust and the poor gun-metal Citroën, proudly seated up on the bow, became the colour of desert camouflage for the remainder of the voyage. The crew were as genial as only unpressured Italians can be, singing Neapolitan songs all day. But I was in a hurry. Each day took us closer to where we had started off from, in Egypt, and further away from England. I had no mail from Jo, obviously; once again there was no telephone communication, and I could only send a desultory card from each island.

Finally, after the best part of two weeks, we hit Naples. We had seriously lost time, and at once set forth in the dusty Onze Légère on the last leg of our Odyssey. It wasn't long before we discovered that one piece of baggage had gone missing: the benison of the Sikh doctor at Fayed, the attaché case stuffed with condoms and anti-venereal medicaments. I giggled at the thought of how surprised the Neapolitan thief would be, what admiration he must have had for Anglo-Saxon virility! But Brodie went ape. I had never seen a man in such a transport of perfect rage, kicking and lashing out at every unfortunate Italian who came within reach. I told him he was being ridiculous – to have worked his way through the missing case would have required a lifetime of dedication by a Casanova and a Don Giovanni combined.

We then treated ourselves to a night out at the grandest hotel in Sorrento. We paid the bill in cigarettes, the accepted currency then in Italy. With solemn dignity the manager counted them, then locked them away in his safe. From there we rushed northwards, following the route of Monty's Eighth Army only a few years previously. We drove past Monte Cassino and its monastery, still shattered as if hit by an atom bomb. We stopped a couple of nights in Rome, then Florence, which neither of us had ever glimpsed before. We then had to make a detour to Venice, where Brodie had some notional liaison task to perform. There we stayed at the Danieli, then a British officers' hotel; no cigarettes accepted, but only 3s 6d a night. Sitting out on St Marks Square, I listened to the ageless musicians at Florian's strike up 'I Love You for Sentimental Reasons' and was overcome with a longing to be home, to be with Jo – to face whatever uncertain future lay ahead. I chided myself for letting the trip run on.

We romped at top speed through Switzerland, gorgeous in September sunshine – clean, neat and orderly, as if nothing had happened to it during the war, as indeed it hadn't. Then finally, Paris. It felt good to drive the travel-stained, indestructible Onze Légère, down the Champs-Elysées. Ever after I would have a residual tendresse for French cars, those pioneers of *traction avant*. How I looked forward to taking Jo through Hyde Park in it! But here came one last hitch. We learned through the Commercial Department at the British Embassy that we would not be allowed to import it into England. With Egyptian registration it would be quite unacceptable to the socialist bureaucracy of the times, although Britain was crying out for workable cars. The sensible French, on the other hand, were anxious to acquire an Onze Légère, of such recent vintage. It took, however, several days to go through the bureaucratic hoops in the wing of the Louvre which then housed the Ministère des Finances. More time wasted. Never mind: through the disposal of the remains of 'Brodie's Booty', that remarkable Aladdin's Cave, and a comfortable profit on the car, we had money to whoop it up in Paris. Suddenly we seemed to have a lot of new friends.

With a few hours on my hands, I thought I would look up the great fashion designer Elsa Schiaparelli, inventor of 'shocking pink'. She had been my father's (and my uncle's) girlfriend in pre-war days and fairy godmother to me. To this day I still do not know why their relationship had gone cold. But a lot of water had passed under the bridge, not least the war. All insouciant, I telephoned her at her sumptuous house on the Rue de Beni. Recalling all the hospitality she had received from my father I was confident that, thrilled to see me grown into a dashing captain of the Coldstream Guards, she would kill every black-market fatted calf in Paris, and assail me (in place of Meccano kits) with voluptuous models. Alas, all I got was a cup of tea and a first introduction to the true meaning of Parisian froideur.

Brodie and I crept back into a rainy England, aboard a Channel ferry similar to the one that had taken me away from Jo nearly two years before. It was the end of a kind of life: the end of Operation Press-off, the end of SIME, the end of the Middle East, the end of the army. It was also to prove the end of Jo.

5

COME TO JESUS!

Cambridge Ice Hockey Team, 1948–49 (AH, back row, third from right; Jud Gale on my
left; the goalie, George Lindsey, seated, second from right).

When Brodie and I got to London there was a short note from Jo waiting for me. She was in Dublin – and she wanted to break off our engagement. I booked a flight to Dublin; she tried to put me off coming.

Dublin was rainy and cold – in every sense. We met as strangers. Jo wanted out. Someone else had entered her life; in fact, he was the former MO (doctor) of Mick's battalion. Of course I understood. Perhaps, after all this time, I wasn't even sure what I felt. It had been just too long; the gap had become too great. Life had to move on. I could only wish that this brave and beautiful girl would find happiness again. But, for me, a bleak chasm yawned. England seemed as lonely a place then as it had four years earlier when I landed at Liverpool off the *Mauretania*.

On the plane back from Dublin, I began to take stock of my life, a life without Jo. I decided I would try to go to university, to read English and if possible Russian. But the combination wasn't possible; so I chose English, on the absurd assumption that after four years stultification away from books it would prove the easiest option. Then I would write. Through a cousin, I had one contact (because that was how things were done in those days) in the university world. He was the Senior Tutor at Trinity College, Cambridge – George Kitson Clark, *ex officio* one of the most important men in Cambridge. Tremulously, I wondered what I had to offer. A 'College Entrance pass' from Millbrook School, New York, and a four-year-old offer of a scholarship to Harvard? In effect, all I really had to show was my uniform, or so I thought. I stayed up late polishing my Coldstream buttons, and presented myself thus.

Kitson Clark was a plumply self-satisfied figure, a specialist in Victorian history. He had a room straddling the gate, overlooking Trinity Great Court, and as I glanced through the window at that breathtaking masterpiece of Renaissance architecture, my heart jumped: that was where I wanted to spend the next three years. But Kitson Clark was not to be impressed. I had to make up my mind: Eng Lit or Russian – one or the other, not both. I opted for English. He asked me when I wanted to come up. 'Would three weeks' time be convenient?' I replied. He seemed taken aback: 'I'm afraid we're taking men in now for five years hence.' Then, looking disdainfully at the shiny pairs of buttons I had slaved so hard at, he added, 'Since you were in the Brigade of Guards, may I suggest you try Magdalene on snob value?' So that was the end of my dream of studying at Trinity; henceforth I would only tiptoe across its Great Court as a guest. However, some years later, thirty-six to be precise, I was invited to deliver the Lees Knowles Lectures at Trinity and could hardly wait to relate this anecedote. The students loved it, the Master less so. The awful Kitson Clark had long gone, but revenge was sweet.

Fairly desperate for any academic home back in 1947, I took Kitson Clark's advice and shuffled round to see his opposite number at Magdalene. But even elitist Magdalene could not be enticed by military snobbery. Thoroughly despondent, and having no lead on any other college, I was making my way back to the station when a voice hailed me in the street. It was someone I had last seen in the Middle East, a former flight lieutenant working in intelligence. 'Hey, what brings you here?' he shouted. I told him, and then asked, 'But what are you doing?' 'I'm a Fellow at Jesus. Come to Jesus!' The invocation sounded like the summons of a Jehovah's Witness, but who was I to hesitate? So I 'came to Jesus'. Michaelmas term had already started, so it would make sense if I waited and came up in January. Matriculation was perfunctory; all I had to do was get hold of my US College Entrance papers, of 1943, and send them in asap. It was all wonderfully informal.

I now had a couple of months to spare, to sort myself out, get some proper civvies and chase away the mental cobwebs of four years by doing some basic reading on English literature. Meanwhile, my wartime crush from Bundle days, Judy Cutler, was getting married in New York. I got a seat on a plane, an unconverted wartime transport with stretchers down the side, that was flying back American shipcrews. It was noisy and incredibly uncomfortable, and put down at dreaded Gander, a backwoods airbase in Newfoundland. But it took me home to my wonderful family in America. The rejoicing, the partying, the friends rediscovered – the sheer fun of that couple of weeks was prodigious. I was welcomed with unbelievable warmth and generosity. Most of the Cutler–Breese clan had come home safely from the war; some had had extraordinary adventures. Judy's brother Jack had walked home across Eastern Europe dressed as a German slave-worker after his bomber had been shot down in the Balkans. All were celebrating, in a state of post-war euphoria – all, that is, except women like Judy's sister Pat, whose husband Bob had gone down with his destroyer, the USS *Duncan*, off Guadalcanal shortly after Pearl Harbor. However, America was in party mood; Churchill may have recently made his cautionary 'Iron Curtain' speech, but Europe and trouble seemed to belong to another planet. America had won the war, a horribly hard war, the boys had come home; it was time to get going again and have a good time. Judy was marrying a delightful ex-Burma flyer from St Louis, called Jackson J. Shinkle. (Mischievously 'Aunt Rossy' Cutler queried in a loud voice, 'I do wonder how she could have met one of those Germans from the Midwest. But they seem quite nice!') Like an Arab wedding, the celebrations seemed to go on for a week. I got swept up in all of them, capitalising for all I was worth on being the 'Limey Captain – guards the King, you know!'

I went up to my old school, Millbrook, to see the 'Boss', my headmaster Edward Pulling, and to retrieve my papers to send to Cambridge. Only one of our tiny class of thirteen had been damaged by the war: Whit Landon had lost a leg in the Battle of the Bulge. I rediscovered my room-mate, Bill Buckley, who had come out of the US Army. His war service had paralleled mine. Commissioned in the army, he had not left the US, but had stood duty on the FDR funeral cortège, then served briefly in the CIA in Mexico. He was now already a year or two into Yale and making a name for himself on the college newspaper, while teaching Spanish at the same time to make up for the shortage of teachers. Time seemed to have made no dent in our friendship. As we always would for the next six decades, we started off just where we had left off. Bill whirled me up to the family home at Sharon, near Millbrook, and introduced me to the barbarities of the Harvard–Yale football game. And, God, how we all drank! It all seemed to be *de rigueur*. After the few short weeks I had spent back in battered, austere Britain, I was staggered by the sheer affluence, the boisterous insouciance, of the post-war USA. To most Americans, there seemed to be not a cloud in the sky.

But the ending of the wartime partnership seemed to have divided us, British and Americans. There was Palestine. How could you Brits behave so harshly to those wretched survivors of Holocaust, Ally! It was good-humoured but difficult to parry, difficult amid the party mood to talk about the King David, the two sergeants, about our commitment to the Arabs, about the facts of 'Illegal Immigration'. There was a cloud between Britain and America which had not been there four years previously. How simple our war had seemed then, in 1943. I now felt a constant, unspoken rebuke about Palestine and the Jewish claim.

There was worse to come. Up in Boston, I was having a drink with some Harvard Cutlers at a bar called the Merry-Go-Round in Copley Plaza. Foolishly, though I still had a few other smart clothes, I was in uniform – perhaps improperly, possibly showing off. The bar itself rotated slowly round the tables. Each time it passed our table, I noticed a man shooting looks of ever increasing ferocity in my direction. Finally he leaped off the Merry-Go-Round, grabbed me by the lapels and accused me of being a 'murderous British officer, as bad as the Nazis, what you're doing to our people in Palestine!' It was profoundly embarrassing. The last thing I wanted was any kind of scene. Then suddenly the situation was saved by a tiny Irish Bostonian woman placing herself between me and my Jewish assailant and attacking him vigorously with her umbrella: 'Now just you leave that British officer alone!' Times change! I doubt I would have been rescued in similar circumstances by an Irish Bostonian from the 1970s onwards.

Nevertheless, it was wonderful to be back among the family and friends, the generous-hearted people to whom I had become so deeply attached in the Bundle years. There were moments even when I wondered – not for the first or the last time – whether my true home wasn't really on that side of the ocean. Should I not be taking up that scholarship at Harvard, go to the American instead of the British Cambridge? But no, I was British, perhaps too fundamentally British. Those four years on His Majesty's Service had somehow affirmed it. I sailed back, steerage, on the *Queen Mary* with a great big lump in my throat, a lump that returns almost every time I set foot in the US.

Sad as it was to leave them all again, the Cutlers and Breeses and Buckleys, life has a way of providing consolation. At the rails of the *Queen Mary* as we hooted our way out of the Hudson River, I made the acquaintance of a ravishing young Viennese girl with exquisite skin. Not yet twenty, Gloria had married a GI in Vienna – anything to escape the awful *Götterdämmerung* of 1945. She had followed him back to California, but it hadn't worked; now she was on her way home, one more failed GI bride. Generously he had given her a first-class one-way ticket. We became friends, more than friends – a part-cure for each other. I spent the rest of the voyage scurrying from the steerage to the more elevated departments of that great ship. On arrival in Europe, I accompanied her on her way home as far as Paris, which was then in the depths of the most bitter freeze without much central heating. As a good Austrian Gloria had two passions, the opera and animals. It was a glum, cold and hostile city. We froze to death in *Lohengrin* at Garnier's exquisite opera house, and I half longed to be aboard that *Lieber Schwan*. Gloria, a passionate animal lover, upbraided a man with a pony-cart for maltreating his horse. A crowd gathered and there were ugly growls of 'Sale boche!' The hatred aroused by the Occupation had hardly abated, and I feared for Gloria's beautiful golden locks. I hastened her up an alley and away. She returned to Vienna; we corresponded for a while, and then silence. I often wonder what happened to Gloria. Did she stay in Vienna, or return to try her luck again in California? But, for me our encounter was only a diversion: Jo was always there, somewhere at the back of the picture.

I sent my precious Millbrook papers up to Cambridge, and waited for the summons. December passed, and still no response. Anxiety! Then one day the papers came back to me, clipped to a peevish note from the Senior Tutor of Christ's College, Cambridge, complaining that he had never heard of me, and who the hell was I anyway? Suddenly the penny dropped: amid all the carousing in America I had got confused and sent the papers to the wrong college. Hastily I redirected all to my friend at Jesus. I hoped he would never learn what had happened.

Cambridge in January 1948 seemed a strange place, a world apart from Cairo. What I recollect most of that winter were the bells, bullying, cajoling and comforting, all in the freezing mist exhaled by the Cam. And the cold and the hunger. In our antique rooms we were permitted one electric fire of 650 watts (I hadn't known they made them that small). So, working in my rooms, I would pull on a thick woollen dressing gown inherited from my father and place the wretched fire perilously inside it. With rationing stiffer then than it had been even at the height of the U-boat threat – thanks to the incompetence of the vegetarian Chancellor of the Exchequer Sir Stafford Cripps and the Labour government – food in College was inadequate and generally revolting.

So were eating habits. To get to the back benches along the long tables in hall it was customary to clamber over, plonking one's muddy shoes on the table between the plates of fellow undergraduates – not exactly the manners encountered in the Brigade of Guards. (Fortunately the advent of women students in 1979 refusing to reveal all as they climbed over to the back benches reformed these Tudor customs. The College carpenter simply cut access routes through the massive tables.) To stave off starvation I joined the Pitt Club, a cheerful establishment given largely to blood sports. Just up Jesus Lane, the Pitt enabled one, *in extremis*, to put down two lunches a day. To a chocoholic like myself, almost as grievous as the food situation was the prolongation of sweet rationing, by those kill-joy socialists affecting concern about the state of our molars. It was all a terrible shock to the system after the Capuan delights of Egypt.

Strange too, to schoolboys coming up and to us veterans alike, was the laissez-faire, sink-or-swim attitude of university life. There were no schoolteachers, no sergeant-majors or colonels, to tell you what to do and when to do it. You attended what lectures you wanted, without being checked in or out; you chose what sport you wanted to play – they didn't recruit you; you joined what clubs you wanted, they didn't come after you. You could, I reckoned, if reclusive by nature, easily spend three years at Cambridge without anyone (except, just possibly, your tutor) knowing you were there. The large majority of undergraduates in my day were, I suppose, returning veterans like me, who had been two, three, maybe five years away in the forces. We were, undoubtedly, a strange lot, betrayed by the worn British Warm greatcoats and the dyed (generally maroon or viridian) service dress trousers, each with hangups we had brought home with us. Between ourselves and the apple-cheeked eighteen-year-olds come up straight from school there was a generation gap not dissimilar to that between ourselves and our blooded seniors who had savoured action in the Second World War. Things were evidently not very different at contemporary Harvard and Yale: 'How do you handle freshmen back from Omaha Beach?' Bill Buckley once asked rhetorically.

At Cambridge, for instance, was it not a little bizarre for a friend of mine, a twenty-five-year-old decorated lieutenant-colonel, to have to go to the former flight lieutenant Senior Tutor to ask permission for an exeat to go and sleep with his wife in London? A strange lot: on some, the war had left its imprint more indelibly than on others. There was Robin Howard, a huge heroic figure of a man, grandson of Prime Minister Baldwin, both of whose legs had been removed above the knee by a landmine at the age of nineteen. Stumping around Cambridge with a single stave of Little John proportions, Robin never acknowledged defeat, and afterwards put all his energy and money into companies fostering modern dance, something that his disability would forever put out of his own reach. Another was Mike Barnes, a diminutive Scot who – having survived the war with a Military Cross – had his leg blown off in a foolish training exercise. Bicycling round Cambridge, Mike kept all his pencils and slide-rules in the empty prosthesis. At one Burns Night binge, he found himself about to be sick in the middle of his speech, turned round, unscrewed the leg, discreetly threw up in it and continued.

In our urge to become normalised, to make up for lost time, many of us overplayed the notional role of the student. My friend David Montgomery, escaping the rigid discipline of his father, the Field Marshal, risked his neck night after night to scale the most perilous pinnacles to place a jerry atop King's Chapel. A harmless but by today's sophisticated standards absurdly childish activity was the stealing of bobbies' helmets. Another friend of mine had an obsessive's collection. Once, short of the requisite number of trophies he had set himself for the term, he was struggling to climb in over his college wall when an obliging bobby helped with a leg up. Ungratefully, he grabbed his benefactor's helmet as he disappeared over the other side of the wall. Conscience-stricken, he threw a party at the end of term for the Cambridge constabulary, and handed back all his trophies.

Such infantile trophy-hunting nearly proved my undoing at Guy Fawkes Night in my second year. Traditionally a wild scene, in 1948 all hell broke loose, with a vast force of police patrolling in the Market Square. Always greedy for the bigger prize, I fixed my eye on a chief inspector's hat, enticingly decorated with scrambled egg like a senior naval commander's. I tracked my prey round the square, then – as I lifted my hand to grab his cap – I was in turn seized in a savage half-nelson from behind. My assailant turned out to be the Chief Constable himself, in plain clothes, who had divined my malign intent and had in turn been stalking me. I spent the night in police cells, thoroughly bored with myself by morning having recited every line of poetry I knew. Boredom, if nothing else, would have led me on to the straight and narrow thenceforth. But it had been a menacing scene that night: the party had got out of hand, serious damage had been done (some idiot had let off a stick of dynamite all too close to the priceless King's College Chapel windows) and the police were in vindictive mood. In court I was summarily fined the draconian sum of £7 10s. Possibly it saved me from being sent down, as it was regarded by my tutor, Vivian Fisher, as excessively punitive. What's more, in the long run, quite by chance it materially helped on the next stage of my career.

Especially for those of us who had been around, the rules governing women inside men's colleges and vice versa seemed positively antediluvian. The old Anglo-Saxon notion prevailed that nice young people can only make love in the dark, so college gates closed at 10 p.m. But you could do pretty well anything you wanted before then. On one occasion, 'after hours', I found myself being pursued down a corridor at Newnham by a female don making a noise like a rhinoceros in full charge. I spotted a stretch of concrete glistening in the moonlight through a first floor window and I jumped down on to it to make my getaway. Alas, the concrete had been laid the previous day. I sank into it up to the knees, just managed to struggle out, but leaving behind a pair of shoes and socks (worth, in those days, 2½ valuable clothing coupons). Then, with my corduroys setting hard, I had to bicycle back to Jesus to face an arduous climb in rigid trousers over the wall of the Master's Lodge. Jesus was renowned for having the toughest perimeter to climb over of the whole University. The College porter, a lean and leathery ex-Marine called Captain Austin, took personal delight in oiling every week the revolving spikes that were guaranteed to disembowel any incautious nocturnal climber. Captain Austin also displayed a pronounced interest in the personal lives of his charges. I once received a letter of alarm from a girl, expressing fear that something had gone awry with her calendric calculations, but happily she was able to add a PS on the back of the envelope: 'Thank God, it's all right!' Captain Austin was on to that in a flash, enquiring solicitously each day for the rest of my time at Jesus 'Everything *all right*, Captain Horne?'

Eng Lit was no sinecure; I had had no idea how ill read I was. Almost total neglect of Latin at Millbrook, USA, left me floundering with classical allusions in *Paradise Lost* and as for Dryden's *Absalom and Achitophel* ... Frankly I found Dryden a pretentious bore. Pope was prissy and waspish, but I was awestruck by the skill of his couplets; Dean Swift stunned me by the force of his invective, which sometimes seemed almost demented. I wish I could have heard Johnson teasing Boswell and inveighing against my frightful countrymen, the Scots. I hooted with pleasure at Byron's irreverent stanzas in *Don Juan* and *Childe Harold*, and – my current mood – nodded assent to his fierce views on womanhood. I was thrilled to discover unknown (to me) medieval England through *Piers Plowman* and the Paston Papers.

In my day, Cambridge had to offer perhaps the most brilliant galaxy of Eng Lit lecturer talent of all time. There was the impassioned 'Dadie' Rylands and F. R. Leavis, F. L. Lucas and – in my own college – A. P. Rossiter (who always conjured up for me the image of Mephistopheles) and the Master himself, E. M. W. Tillyard, still the universally recognised authority on Shakespeare's world picture. How many of us really took advantage of this treasure trove? I certainly did not, and every time I go back to Cambridge these days I wish with the hankering of frustrated old age that I could just have it all over again. My one personal opening, of which I think I did take advantage, came in the shape of a brilliant and delightful supervisor, Graham Storey. Graham truly burned with what Walter Pater would have called that 'hard, gem-like flame', and did his best to make me understand what was really Hamlet's problem. When it came to poor silly Othello, of course, how I empathised with his agonies of jealousy. As a teacher, Graham was of the Maurice Oldfield genre; he became a lifelong friend and spent the next fifty years editing the letters of Charles Dickens.

For us returning old sweats, the healthy pursuit of pleasure was not easy. In those hard-fought days before the pill, of the handful of comely female undergraduates almost all were cast-iron virgins. Those who were demonstrably not were hugely in demand, possibly overworked. In Eng Lit lectures I spotted a girl with a magnificent bosom and dark, cascading hair à la Rossetti. I tracked Ellie down and brought her to bed feeling immensely pleased with myself. However, at what the French would call *le moment critique*, she leaped up and proclaimed, 'You're the thirty-third this term!' – a remark guaranteed to result in instant detumescence. (The term was, I reflected, barely halfway through.) But how dare one condemn those few girls who behaved like men. In the words of Browning:

> Girls must have boys.
> Why, let girls say so then,
> Nor call the boys and men, who say the same,
> Brute this and beast the other as they do!'

Many years later I re-encountered Ellie. The luxurious brown hair had turned to white plaits neatly coiled up, a governessy creature coaching my daughter in Eng Lit. I speculated at what point she had stopped the comptometer.

In the more morally elevated pursuit of 'nice young women', finding a surrogate for Jo, I was even more unsuccessful, inflicting hurts along the way. At parties I found myself tongue-tied, totally inhibited. A sophisticated and suave ex-Coldstreamer tried to take me in hand. In chatting girls up, he explained, 'You can't just stand there saying "yes" and "no" – it has to be "yes, and ... " or "no, but ... "' Under his guidance I met a sweet-faced debutante whom I managed to persuade to come up to the Trinity May Ball, a major event at £10 a head. For months when I should have been struggling with Potts on Criticism, I dedicated myself to organising a hundred ancillary drinks-parties and other entertainments to delight my partner pre- and post-Ball. On the big day itself she rang to say she had a cold and could she just come up for the Ball? When she arrived, she was so frosty it was I who felt I had the cold, if not pneumonia. As soon as the Ball was over, remarkably recovered, she spryly announced that she had to flee to Ascot. Years later I met her again too, unrecognisably obese, marinated in gin and deserted by her husband. W. S. Maugham would have made a good short story out of it.

A large part of the problem of gratifying the ever-pressing beast side of the beastly male lay in the nature of Cambridge University, the dreadful regulations laid down by Captain Austin and his ilk. Thus one eagerly perused at the start of the year a thick booklet entitled *Extra-Curricular Activities*, scanning for those activities which required regular and constant absence from the monastic courts of our chosen fount of education. First my eyes lit on gliding, a palliative I thought to those thwarted dreams of flying a Spitfire. But half-a-dozen winter excursions to Marshall's Airfield, frost-bitten at the controls, or – worse – waiting one's turn to be winched aloft on the open tarmac with the wind blowing straight off the frozen fens from Siberia, cured me of all Icarian urges. Then there was the Cambridge Ice Hockey Club. Now there I found a winner. With no ice-rink in Cambridge, every weekend – with the blessing of the University proctors – we would bus up to London for practice. We certainly needed all the practice we could get; we weren't very good. Half the team were Canadians or Americans, the rest – like myself – had been Bundles sent off to school in North America. Our captain was a soft-spoken son of a bishop, Chris Tubbs, who later became a cleric himself, and did his best to curb our expletives on the ice and even win a game or two. We had a sensational goalie, a humorous Canuck scientist called George Lindsey, who in later life made a name for himself developing electronic anti-submarine defences. It was said that Oxford had a lousy goalie but a good team, Cambridge a lousy team but a good goalie. But then the other university had all those Rhodes Scholars to choose from. The epigram was not strictly true though: we also had Jud Gale, a classic all-American athlete from Harvard, who played left defence (in fact, *was* our defence) opposite me, in defence. Jud carried so much weight and kinetic energy that when we succeeded in double-checking an enemy forward I would find my spindly frame hurtling over the boards and off the ice altogether.

We were a jolly, homogeneous group who became, and remained, great friends. But the best aspect of the CUIHC came in the winter vac, when we were invited to play around Switzerland, all expenses paid. At a time when British travellers were allowed only a derisory £25 per annum to take abroad, this was a real bonus and the generous Swiss gave us a marvellous time. I don't think we won many matches, but the excitement of the game, plus the impressive (but synthetic) physique all the armour lent us, assured us of an unprecedented success with the girls – followed by disappointment as the removal of shoulder-pads and codpiece revealed the puny creature within.

Jud, my American co-defenceman, was particularly successful, as well as being a perfect gentleman in his discretion. Towards the end of our tour we both collapsed, I with flu, he with sheer exhaustion, and were left behind at Wengen. As we licked our wounds in the sun, a postman struggled up the street with a heavy parcel for Jud. Inside was a vast, heart-shaped box of chocolates from the hotelière at one of our stops, with a card: 'Darling Jud, You have left me with many memories. Ruth (PS I do hope that's all!)'. Blushing, he admitted his liaison, and revealed there had also been 'an incident'. One night their love-making had been disturbed by the cries next door of a woman in obvious distress. Ever the clean-living all-American boy, Jud rushed to the scene, broke down the door to be confronted with a naked young girl and a man equally naked – save for a pair of ski boots, with which he appeared to be doing a *zapateado* on his partner. To the rescuing knight's consternation and dismay, the two united to throw him out. The next day the Spanish Consul in Geneva filed a complaint with the proctors that the Cambridge Ice Hockey Team had compromised him on his honeymoon. In consequence, the snooty Blues Committee in Cambridge refused, for several years, the awarding of a blue for our strenuous sport.

Meanwhile, outside the cloisters of Cambridge the world ground on. Austerity grew harsher and harsher as Attlee's egalitarian wizards wasted Britain's ever-shrinking assets on hare-brained Laputan projects such as the infamous East African Groundnut Scheme. In America the tough-eyed President Truman would do nothing to help the USA's former ally. In India Muslims and Hindus were hacking each other to pieces by the hundred thousand as Mountbatten's premature and ill-conceived partition plan went into operation.

In Palestine, where the Union Jack had been run down in favour of the United Nation flag, those of us who had served there watched in rage and gloom as the incompetent Arabs lost every battle to preserve their Palestinian homelands. The Jews fought back with astounding zeal and chilling efficiency. Begin and his ruthless Irgun teams gave a new spin to the name of terrorism by massacring a whole village of defenceless Arabs at Deir Yassin, throwing over a hundred men, women and children down a well. After Deir Yassin, Arabs stampeded in mass panic out of their homes, leaving the victorious Israelis to occupy empty areas that had once been allocated to the Arabs on the UN's map of partition and to which they would never be allowed to return. At the Cambridge Union I spoke up, in disgust, a couple of times about our commitments to the Arabs of Palestine, to a thoroughly apathetic audience. Then gradually contempt for the venality of the Arab armies, their sheer inability to present a united front, began to replace my sympathy for the displaced Palestinians. I wished a pox on both their houses and turned my eyes from the Middle East.

With my old friend from SIME, Michael Wrigley – whose job it had been to keep an eye on Arab irredentism – I found a sympathetic ear. I spent one happy and restful Easter hol with him, his enchanting mother Audrey and highly eccentric father 'Old Joel' – the only Master of Fox-hounds who blew a referee's whistle on the hunting field, instead of the horn he had never been able to manage, amid the rolling Wolds of East Yorkshire. Mike was reading history at Worcester, Oxford, but was rather more interested in cricket and was largely marking time till he could rejoin Maurice Oldfield in his newly acquired world of MI6, 'the Firm'. As holiday work, I was supposed to be reading up on the Metaphysical poets for Graham Storey, who said I might also cast an eye on Bertrand Russell for the philosophical background. I did more; curious to know more about what made me, this disastrous animal, tick, I slogged manfully through *A History of Western Philosophy* from start to tedious finish. Next I picked up Huxley's *Perennial Philosophy*, then moved on to Jung and Freud. I didn't get around to Donne and Marvell. Graham wasn't pleased, but how easy it was to get distracted by books – wasn't that perhaps the purpose of all university education?

The next holiday, the long summer vac of 1948, I became even more distracted. I was invited up to stay a month with Uncle Newt and Aunt Ursie in their small Cotswold house at Tadmarton. Manifestly relieved at the collapse of my engagement to Jo, they were sweetness itself and we established a new entente. It was a blissful month; I worked happily and peacefully away in their barn – this time supposedly on Shakespeare's 'problem plays', set me for holiday reading by Graham. But something enticed me to read *Richard II*, and from there I read, and revelled in, every single one of the history plays. Suddenly everything I had been learning about the Aristotelian principles of high tragedy began to make sense. What could possibly be more dramatic than the rise of a great king, and then his fall through some fatal error or some fatal flaw within? I read and reread the famous speech of Ulysses in *Troilus and Cressida*:

> Take but degree away, untune that string,
> And, hark! what discord follows.

Therein surely lay the whole sweep of English history, as Shakespeare saw it, indeed of world history. The vital interplay of character with historic destiny, that was worth writing about. I began to wish I had been reading history – and that, maybe one day, I could *write* history. That summer's vacation reading left a permanent mark on me. I did nothing about it at the time, but the seeds were there – overlaying Maurice's analytic education in SIME – to germinate more than a decade later.

Then there were the even more exciting distractions of real holidays. Suddenly Bill Buckley and a gaggle of sisters burst in upon the tranquillity of the Cotswolds. I accompanied them to nearby Stratford, then to Cambridge and revealed to them the art of climbing in and out of colleges. They were all sharing a house on the Left Bank, in the Square Montsouris – Douanier Rousseau's old haunt – why didn't I come and join them? Elder sister Priscilla was working with AP and knew her way around. I was only too happy to accept. As their guide they had a wonderfully eccentric White Russian, a former colonel of the Imperial Guard named Valerian Bibikoff. Married to a (very grand) niece of Tolstoy, Bibi had fallen on hard times. Before the war he had worked as a guide to Paris for the Buckley clan. During the war, passionately anti-Communist (his brother had been executed by Stalin for working with the Germans), Bibi emerged on some kind of French blacklist. His punishment? He was banned for several years from having a telephone, surely the kiss of death for anyone struggling in the tourist trade – a Mikado-like but also very French punishment. A man of boundless courtesy and Russian good humour, Bibi taught me two things: one, to drink the strongest vodka at mid-morning at White Russian *épiceries* on the Left Bank; two, to venerate the glories of Chartres Cathedral and twelfth-century Gothic (to Bibi, there was none other). We set off for Chartres almost every day. It was reputed that, with one group of Americans burning to see Rheims, resentfully Bibi set off from Paris in an easterly direction only to perform a great wheel, like General von Kluck in 1914, to end up, once more, at the glorious portals of Chartres. In visits to the Jeu de Paume, I also fell deeply in love with the Impressionists' view of the world. After a wonderful week of gaiety and laughter I had developed an incipient passion for Paris, and for France.

France took hold of me once more while I was at Cambridge. Wrigley, not one of nature's linguists, had been told to learn a smattering of French to assist him in his passage to rejoin Maurice in MI6. So we set off across France, heading for Agen in the south-west to stay as paying guests with a local family. We arrived at a moment of tension. There was no running water in the house, only a vaguely nasty odour of bad eggs emanating from the taps, and the family – unwashed for several weeks – added their own particular flavour. Worse still, the paterfamilias, an octogenarian Pétain-lookalike always addressed as 'Monsieur le Président' (though what he had once presided over – perhaps the local boule team – never became clear), was in deep disfavour. It transpired that, on a recent shopping visit to Agen, he had been greeted too effusively by an unknown dog. Investigation by a suspicious Madame revealed that the unknown dog's mistress was also M. le Président's – a carefully kept secret, apparently, over some twenty years.

Such was the local accent (you could cut it with a knife) that neither Wrigley nor I learned much serviceable French. We headed off towards the fleshpots of the Riviera, and then home. How we survived, frequenting equine restaurants, on our £25 allowances I cannot think. But France then was amazingly cheap, extremely friendly, with empty roads and only a sprinkling of tourists. Truly, as Germans used to proclaim before 1914, one could be *heureux comme un dieu en France*. I have never since ceased to be enchanted by *la France profonde* where over every range of hills there always lies a valley, a pocket paradise, as yet undiscovered. I restarted painting (something I hadn't done since Cairo), ineptly.

In the summer of 1949 came the day of reckoning at Cambridge – Part I of the English Tripos. I was hoping, vaguely, to be allowed to return for a third year, to do philosophy and psychology and have time to read more good books. I even contributed a special paper on my hero, Aldous Huxley. But, as we awaited exam results, it was also a time of serious partying, during which I managed to commit my final, fatal misdemeanour – of amazing undergrad silliness. In my rooms on the top floor at No. 2 Chapel Court I threw a party for members of the Boat Club. It grew rather wild. It was also the time of year when hapless undergraduates tended to top themselves under stress of exams. The room below was tenanted by one Antony Armstrong-Jones, the cox of the Jesus and later of the Cambridge boat, younger than most us, who tended (then) to take himself rather seriously. Some bright spark suggested it might be diverting for me to be dangled out of my window on the primitive fire escape, with heels drumming on the future Lord Snowdon's window. In extreme agitation Tony rushed to alert the Senior Tutor, Vivian Fisher: 'Horne's hanged himself!' The splendid Vivian may have been torn between emotions of alarm and private relief at being rid of a troublesome student. But, publicly, he was not amused and I endured a very *mauvais quart d'heure* in his chambers.

Then, for all his and Graham Storey's generous insistence that I should get a first-class degree, when the results came in I didn't do very well – a miserable 2.2 in fact, a lower second. Of course I had my excuses: I had arrived in time to complete only five short terms out of six; my American education, sterling though it had been, had not really prepared me for Eng Lit. Then I had let myself get too readily distracted, by ice hockey, by extraneous reading – of the history plays, for instance – but worse by my own inner confusions of identity, which often made concentration difficult. I had spent many hours working, too many hours in nugatory questing after love, but had ended up with neither a good degree nor the right girl. Perhaps one militated against the other. Looking back on those two years when I had had at my disposal the greatest galaxy of talent in Eng Lit, I fear that I offended against the old principle of never wasting an hour or a man.

As it was, the combination of my Guy Fawkes Night imprisonment, the hanging episode and finally the lowly 2.2 meant that even the gentle and long-suffering Vivian couldn't see his way to granting me a third year. Forlornly, tail between my legs, I trooped off to the University Employments Board to see what they had to offer. Still doubting my ability to make a profession out of writing, I proposed myself for the Diplomatic Corps. 'Out of the question', snorted the much decorated old Colonel heading the board 'with a 2.2!' Then, looking down coyly, he added, 'But there is of course a back door to the Foreign Office.' 'Thank you, sir,' I think I replied, 'but as I came out of that door to go to Cambridge, I don't really want to go back through it again!' Somewhat crestfallen, the old spy-recruiter finally came up with 'Well, how about Events Secretary at the English Speaking Union? Unpaid of course.' Meanwhile, in London Uncle Newt was urging respectability at last on me, a nice 9–5 job with a stockbroking firm. I still wanted to write. I reflected on my future all through the summer of 1949.

It was, I suppose, some mild consolation that most of my fellow veterans had done no better than 2.2 either. Most pretended it didn't matter – indeed to some it didn't. Nevertheless four of us (one of them Philip Goodhart, later a Conservative MP, who became a lifelong friend) clubbed together to rent a Cam riverboat for a farewell party, the *Countess of Bury* ('Her lines like a floating jerry' was a line I composed for the invitation). It duly floated slowly up and down the Cam most of the night, with a skilful jazz group aboard. To economise, instead of glasses – which it seemed was tempting providence for the disorderly to chuck overboard – we had paper cups. Unfortunately the punch brewed by Phil (again, I suspect, an economy) was powerful enough to melt the glue retaining the bottom of the cups. After a few hours sailing there were wails all up and down the *Countess* as disintegrating cups shed their contents on to prettily dressed laps. It didn't seem a very promising start to our entry into the real world.

6

HACKING FORWARD

1952, the Yugoslav Dancers.

Journalism is the last resource of the educated poor who could not be artists and would not be teachers.

Henry Adams

How the human mind rejoices in seeking out excuses for its own defeats! But it would be less than truthful to pretend that persisting misery over Jo was not one of my preoccupations in the Tripos Hall of 1949. When I first went up to Cambridge, there were few lonesome nights when I did not think about her, wonder how she was, was she happy? Might she ever think of me? Would I ever see her again? A laugh, a swirl of the skirt, a wisp of someone else's blonde hair, an ancient Baby Austin, would set me yearning, remembering. Sometimes, the longing was replaced by flashes of anger; in her repudiation she had not been very kind. But the flashes passed, the sadness remained. As the months rolled by and distractions at Cambridge moved in, so the pain gradually lessened. Occasionally moments of good sense even reminded me of what a fundamentally hopeless relationship it had really been.

Then, one summery day in London I went into Peter Jones, a hundred yards from where Jo had once lived in that Chelsea flat with her parents. There she was, slowly descending the famous circular staircase, cool and blondely radiant in the sunshine, dressed in the semi-chic clothes of post-war Britain, looking slimmer than I remembered and utterly ravishing. Of course I had never seen her in summery clothing. My heart pounded. We said hello. I sent her a note. She agreed to meet for lunch. It was painful, the conversation forced. We talked commonplaces. The war was over. She was waiting for her man, the doctor, to get a divorce. Twice she got up to telephone, to say, I knew, 'It's all all right, darling, nothing to worry about. He's not being difficult.' We parted with a formal kiss. It was the last time we ever met.

I cogitated throughout that summer of 1949 on what to do. Cambridge had been altogether too short. In five terms, I had hardly got moving.

I still wanted to learn; there were still books, many, that I wanted to read. And that novel I wanted to write. But had I courage and conviction enough to bury myself away and work on it? In the event I decided to do just that. I rented rooms off a young couple with a small boy in Montague Road, a quiet bywater on the other side of the Cam from Jesus. They were kind people and spoiled me with fried breakfasts and little suppers. I took out of the University library books on psychology and philosophy that would have been my set works had I achieved that third year, and attended an occasional lecture. It only made me troublesomely introspective. I fear I learned little about either man or myself at the end of it all, let alone how to cope any better with the paralysing bouts of depression, the Black Dog that has plagued me for much of my life. Freud's *Psychopathology of Everyday Life* was entertaining as a work of art, and I found delight and echoes of my own questing in Huxley's *The Perennial Philosophy*. Huxley seemed approximately to be in search of what I was after – or perhaps what we all, the confused post-war generation, were after. But much of the rest struck me as phoney pomposity. It would be excessive to write off a whole profession, but in subsequent years I can recall meeting no more than one or two shrinks who weren't in the game on account of their own problems.

With greater joy I read up on the Impressionists and all the uncomplicated joys of the Belle Epoque that they conveyed. I longed for France and the colours of the Mediterranean. In the afternoons, I painted. At least, as Winston Churchill so charmingly discovered, when wrestling with the yellow ochre one simply cannot think of anything else, certainly not of oneself. And I started, once again, fearfully and hesitatingly, with many procrastinations, to write the novel. Revealingly, I called it 'Sigh No More'. It was painfully (but, I hoped, uncomplainingly) autobiographical. After struggling away for some 300 laboriously handwritten pages, I found that I couldn't bring it to any effectual conclusion. It took its place, with other incomplete novels over the years, in the *tiroir des réfusés*. And, by the summer of 1950, I still had no job. It had been a somewhat lonesome year, as I was of course no longer able to enjoy the company of a noisy, jolly college, and many of my friends had departed from Cambridge, already earning daily pennies, embarked at last on real life.

Then, out in that real world, something happened to wake us all up a bit. North Korea invaded the South. Momentarily it looked as if the Third World War might be upon us. I was called up for service as a reserve officer by the Coldstream. Depressingly, my Sam Browne belt no longer seemed to fit in quite the way it had just three years previously; nor did I have the same lust for action that had grabbed me back in 1943. After a few spiritless exercises on hilltops and convivial meetings with old chums, we were stood down, and I think all of us were quite glad that the Korean War managed without us. Then came a much more enticing invitation, from my old boss in GSI-14 in Cairo days, Claude Dewhurst. Now military attaché in Belgrade, a key intelligence posting, he suggested I come out to stay there and then take off round the country. It was a time when big things were happening in Yugoslavia. And, said Claude, in coded terms, I could help him out with a thing or two. One would be to pick up large sums of black-market dinars in Trieste on the way out, at seventeen times the ludicrous official rate, both to finance my own holiday and to pass on to young Yugoslavs whom Claude was helping escape.

I leaped at the invitation. I started reading everything about Yugoslavia that I could get my hands on, above all Rebecca West's classic *Black Lamb and Grey Falcon* and Fitzroy Maclean's recently published *Eastern Approaches*. With its superb blend of adventure, war, political writing and description of people and places Maclean's was, I think, one of the finest books written in the twentieth century. How I wished I could have been just ten years older, to have joined Fitzroy and his Partisans.

In great excitement I boarded the Orient Express, complete with paint-box, easel and canvases (at Claude's suggestion). In Trieste I found Claude's black-market financier. Within minutes I became a millionaire, but alas the grubby dinars he handed me were in small denominations, enough to fill a small suitcase. I spent the night secreting them around my luggage, in my shoes, under the tray of my paintbox. From Trieste the Orient Express dwindled to one coach, with Balkan peasants and their chickens clinging to the roof. It ambled up to the Istrian frontier, and villainous-looking guards with red stars and sub-machine guns came on board the train. So these were the hostile forces represented by all those little red flags I had been moving around the great map in Cairo just four years before! They looked most unfriendly as they set to searching luggage presumably looking for black-market currency. I admit that my heart thumped when one of them opened my paintbox and squeezed a tube. Was this going to be the end of the line, up against a stony wall in Istria? After a few nerve-racking moments, he and his comrades disembarked and the train with its peasants and livestock moved on.

At Belgrade station Claude, now wearing the red tabs of a full colonel, greeted me in his Austin Atlantic coupé, a hideous car and a notable come-down from Cairo's Merky Bey. 'Funny, they don't like German cars here!' he said. As we arrived at his quarters, his housekeeper – a surly Serb – was putting down the telephone. 'She's just been calling UDBA [Tito's secret police]. They'll be wanting to know who was the tall man I've just picked up at the station. It's all a great joke: she knows I'm a spy, and I know she's a spy. You'll find everybody here is a spy, of some sort.' He shook with laughter as he ran through the anomalies of life in Tito's beleaguered fiefdom. The Marshal had broken with Stalin less than two years previously, and there had been much mystification as to what it really meant; was it genuine? Was Tito's Yugoslavia, once the most virulently anti-West and militarily threatening of the Soviet-bloc countries, going to become an ally in the Cold War? It was Claude's function to find an answer. Meanwhile there was fear and suspicion everywhere. It was a typically Balkan situation. Several high-ranking dissidents had escaped across the border into Bulgaria, or had been shot trying to do so. In this shakily stuck-together nation, Serb mistrusted Croat, old Partisans hated and brutalised the survivors of General Mihailović's rival Chetniks; the Catholics of Slovenia and Dalmatia, oppressed by the Communists, loathed the regime, and so did the Bosnian Muslims. Only Tito, much helped by Stalin's clumsy menaces against this eminently proud and brave country, kept it all together. But no one went to bed at night without the fear that dawn might bring Stalin's massed T-34s rolling across the borders of neighbouring Hungary, Rumania or Bulgaria into the suburbs of Belgrade.

Staying in Claude's residence, in the mornings I would be awoken by the trains down by the Sava River below. They whistled at a peculiar, eerily high pitch which somehow gave voice to the tension all round one. Across the river in Zemun lay the skeleton of a vast unfinished building, the new Presidium, supposedly already sinking into the ground – like hundreds of other buildings round Belgrade, unfinished either because of the inefficiency of Titoist planning or because of shortage of vital materials that would once have flowed in from the Soviet bloc. The small British Embassy, excited by the new world it found itself in, had its own particular problems. It was still trying to decide whether it lived in a hostile camp or among potential friends. The answer was probably both. In practical terms it meant that its unmarried officers were discouraged from having intimate relations with any local, who would almost certainly be in the pay of the UDBA. This no-fratting policy resulted in a great deal of sexual frustration. At the helm, the Ambassador was an engagingly laid-back and popular figure, Sir Charles Peake. He had a somewhat disquieting eccentricity of addressing remarks to a visitor indirectly through the medium of his dog, a kind of West Highland terrier: 'Bonzo, do you think Mr Horne would like another drink? No? He's got to leave, has he? Well, goodbye – it was so nice of you to drop in.'

One of the senior members of Sir Charles's staff, a bachelor whom I shall call Bertram, suffered horribly from eczema of the hands, which HE found uncongenial. One day Bertram was called in by HE, who (doubtless hiding his embarrassment by channelling his remarks via Bonzo) told him that he was to go on home leave to London and 'get a woman there – sex'll cure those hands'. Obediently, Bertram trotted off to London where his brother provided him with an ex-girlfriend, an obliging young actress called Meg. After several weeks Bertram noted that his hands were miraculously cured, and having enjoyed the cure greatly he decided to smuggle Meg back into Yugoslavia. Back in Belgrade, he lost his nerve and jibbed at introducing her to HE (thus dodging the pain of a possible Bonzo interrogation). So Meg remained on the black market in Belgrade, passed from one frustrated young diplomat to another. (When I met Bertram some years later, he had become an ambassador; as we shook hands, I noted they were bad again.)

Only one man at the Embassy, John Priestman, a brilliant young secretary (and former fellow Coldstreamer), sought to solve his personal problems differently. He bedded down, secretly, with his Serbian cook, who was fantastic in the kitchen but a rather plain woman. In the course of his posting she had one if not two children by him. All went swimmingly, until he requested permission to marry her. This was too much for the complaisant but snobbish FO, and a potentially brilliant young diplomat had to seek employment elsewhere. Belgrade was not an easy place for a young unmarried British diplomat to serve in – nor, for that matter, for anyone.

Quite different to all the rest in Peake's star-studded Embassy was Lawrence Durrell, who became a good friend. Larry was serving nominally as public affairs officer, but we both (correctly) suspected each other of being involved in the Great Game. It was several years before he wrote his great classic, *The Alexandria Quartet*, which made him properly famous; but he was then married – uneasily – to the woman fictionalised as either 'Melissa' or 'Justine', I forget which, and was a relatively unknown, 'difficult' poet. He had stubby, unartistic fingers and chubby proletarian features, unmemorable in a crowd, but restless, reflective eyes that missed little. One day when we where swimming and lunching together off a raft in the Danube, he mused, 'Have you noticed anything odd about people in this Embassy?'

'Such as?'

'They've all got guilty consciences. They're all engaged in a dirty game.'

Possibly I was too callow at the time to grasp the drift of what he was saying, but I did afterwards – and Larry was dead right. During those critical days as the 1940s became the 1950s, the West as a whole had a collective guilty conscience about Tito – call it double standards. We were treating him as a knight in shining armour, almost a saint, who, by his single-handed, super-courageous stance was going to show the embattled West the way to defeat Stalin. Of course, his breach with the Soviets was undoubtedly the most exciting international event of the post-war era to date. And yet in many ways Tito was just as nasty as Stalin. His Yugoslavia was a dedicated Communist state; his wartime competitor Mihailović had been shot along with many of his Chetnik supporters. He had locked up the Catholic archbishop, Stepinac, and many Catholics in Croatia and Slovenia had also been imprisoned for their beliefs. The prisons were overflowing. It was a thoroughgoing police state, riddled with the UDBA. And yet Tito, having liberated Yugoslavia from the Nazis through his leadership of the Partisans, now stood out as the one bright star in an otherwise dark and menacing firmament in the Cold War.

Undeniably Tito was achieving some positive things. Most notably he was keeping this explosive bundle of nationalities together, united by the external threat of Stalin. He was repairing miraculously, and now without outside help, the war-shattered economy. On the cultural scene he was striving meaningfully to establish rightful pride in the national heritage. Nowhere did he succeed better than in the encouragement of national dance and music. Based on the Serbian Kolo, Yugoslavia had an incredibly rich mine of folkloric dance. Night after night Claude and I would go to watch and hear whatever was available of the curiously off-key, whirling accordion music, the friule (shepherd's flute) or the tamburasko (a kind of mandolin from Croatia, played at enormous speed) – sometimes doleful, singing of cruel battles or unhappy love, or full of gaiety and fire.

On several days Claude took me out 'manoeuvre-hunting'. It was one of the most vital parts of his mission. Which way was the bulk of Tito's huge army pointing? Eastwards or westwards? Trieste – which is now Italian and was then an independent city-state under the UN – had been briefly occupied by Yugoslav forces in 1945 and was still threatened by Belgrade, whose army was immense on paper. Again and again we returned empty-handed. Then, one afternoon, south-east of Belgrade and close to the Bulgarian frontier, we suddenly ran into a vast cloud of dust. The whole plain was alive with tanks, trucks, horses and carts, as far as the eye could see. It was the grand summer manoeuvre Claude had been trying to track. 'Quick,' he said, 'get a pencil and note down the first three figures of all the armour – then we can check back at the office which divisions are committed.' Alas, between us, two trained British intelligence officers, we had neither pencil nor paper. 'Never mind,' said the ever resourceful Claude, 'get out and trace the numbers in the dust on the side of the car – don't let them see you.' I tried, but by the time we got back to Belgrade, fresh dust had settled, rendering my hieroglyphics quite illegible. Water on the brain! But Claude had enough information to prove that the manoeuvres were facing east, that is against the threat of an attack by Stalin, no longer against Trieste or Greece – which was what Western governments needed to know. The point was made; the op had succeeded.

I left Claude's cheery hospitality and took off down to the coast, to Dubrovnik, armed with my paints and my illicit dinars for the next 'little job' Claude wanted done, and quite glad to escape from the hothouse intriguing of Belgrade. The plane, a wartime Dakota, bounced on to a grass field where pretty girls in Dalmatian national dress (a yellow tassel on the bosom signifying they were nubile but unmarried) shooed goats off the runway. Immediately there was an overpowering fragrance of the

Med, and of Dubrovnik. I set up my easel, my cover, and started to paint. Strange thing, I painted rather well. But, then, who could not find inspiration in Dubrovnik, then a glorious, unspoilt city in which I was virtually the only tourist. In the evening if you laid your cheek against its cobalt-mauve-gold walls, back came the warmth of the day's sun, plus a thousand years of history when those fearless Ragusans had faced down both mighty Venice and the dread Turk. I completed more than half-a-dozen canvases, and cheekily sent two to the Royal Academy the following spring (they accepted one, but didn't hang it).

I was never again to paint so well as I did that summer in Dalmatia. But it left me with an abiding passion; and, as a cover it was, I suppose, moderately effective. The Yugoslavs were so incurably suspicious of everybody. Spying seemed to be the main national pastime. Men would follow me to where I set up my easel, then furtively disappear. It was worse in Dubrovnik's Excelsior Hotel. Using the simplest MI5 techniques of detection – placing hairs on suitcase catches and so on – I could tell that my luggage was being searched, rather crudely, virtually every day. Fed up, I bought a mousetrap and hid it under a handkerchief. To my shame the next day the nice buxom lady who cleaned my room appeared with her fingers bandaged and a look of reproach on her face. We had a tearful confrontation: it was part of her job, she explained; ashamed, by way of compensation I gave her a sleeveless bright-yellow pullover. To my horror she wore the incriminatingly English garment, barely containing her ample bosom, solidly for the next week around the hotel.

I made contact with the family of dissidents Claude wanted to help flee from Tito's paradise. They were very Catholic, very Italianate Dalmatians; the son, Milos, was a brilliant twenty-three-year-old electronics technician. They had all suffered greatly in the post-war persecutions. My role was simple: to hand over some of the funds I had acquired in Trieste; and to recce a boat-launching spot on the neighbouring island of Lokrum, then help arrange their reception across the Adriatic in Italy. But the coast was heavily patrolled, and the penalty for failure – for them – a stiff gaol sentence (only a short while previously they would have been shot). But the lust for freedom among the descendants of ancient, proud Ragusa was overwhelming. For me, an eccentric-looking tourist, an artist to boot, the task was not too excessive. Had I been caught, I suppose I would have savoured the inside of a Titoist gaol too.

On returning to the UK I learned that Milos had made it, rowing with six others (including a middle-aged architect, who left behind a wife and children). For three nights and two days they had rowed across the treacherous Adriatic in Milos's 10-foot dinghy, until they landed in Bari, 120 miles away, before moving on to Canada. The family gave me an ancient flintlock pistol, an heirloom which had seen service in the wars against the Turk. I treasure it to this day. I often wonder how Milos got on in Canada.

Saint Tito! Sveti Broz! How the magi from all over the world flocked in to worship at his temple, lay offerings at his feet in those days. At one end of the scale, from England, came the extreme left-wing Independent MP for Gateshead, Konni Zilliacus, affecting to be the Marshal's new best friend and freeloading dedicatedly all summer long at Tito's sumptuous Villa Scheherazade on the cliffs outside Dubrovnik. At the other end of the spectrum came Fitzroy Maclean – my new hero, and then a recently elected Tory MP – with his rumbustious wife Veronica. Though Churchill was still out of power (just), and Fitzroy had been out of favour with Tito during the ugly years when Stalinism had reigned, it was clear that as the dashing figure who had helped the Marshal to victory during the war – he was now back on the inner track, reopening his old closeness of Partisan days. He was a spirited and friendly companion, and introduced me to many interesting and influential Yugoslavs. He was particularly drawn to the Serbs and Montenegrins, and I was amused when he extolled the Montenegrins to me as 'incredibly brave, headstrong – and treacherous, just like us Highlanders!' Years later I discovered him using roughly identical words about the Georgians. He excused himself: 'Oh, well, aren't all mountain people a bit similar!' Little escaped Veronica's beady and humorous eye. 'Do you know you're known throughout Dubrovnik as the "painter-spy?"' she told me. A wonderful foil to Fitz, she was placed under my charge when he had to fly back to England for a crucial vote in the House of Commons. It was an onerous task to be appointed a trusted Sir Galahad to such an attractive woman, but we survived and remained close friends for the rest of her life.

My glorious weeks in Dubrovnik at an end, I got a lift back to Belgrade with Claude's secretary. The roads were totally empty of any civilian traffic, but inside Bosnia it soon became clear that we were being tailed. I got the number of the car, and my companion confirmed that it was an UDBA block number. Just at that moment, we hit a large pig with a resounding thwack. The pig trotted off, but the car came to a halt. Two young men got out of the UDBA car and politely got us up and running again. 'We'll be behind you as far as the border,' said one helpfully, 'and then someone else will pick you up and be with you all the way to Belgrade.' He saluted and they got back into his car. Never did I imagine that secret policemen could be quite so useful!

From Belgrade I sped back home. Yugoslavia had been a fantastic experience. I felt I had learned a lot. Now I had to get down to finding a job, a serious job. I took myself off to 135 Fleet Street, to the *Daily Telegraph*, humbly (with my 2.2 in Eng Lit) asking to be taken on as a journalist. The assistant editor, responsible for hirings and firings, a man called Stowell with a toothbrush moustache and a watery smile who seemed the incarnation of Mr Salter in Evelyn Waugh's *Scoop*, was not unfriendly. Yes, the *Telegraph* could find me a job in the newsroom, but first I would have to do a year on a provincial paper. My heart sank; visions of becoming one of those intrepid foreign correspondents I had met in Belgrade, let alone a Fitzroy Maclean, receded briskly. Which paper? Well, how about the *Cambridge Daily News*? You should have some useful contacts there. My spirits rose, marginally. I put 'Sigh No More' away in a drawer and did not take it out again for fifty years. Then I packed up to go back once more to Cambridge.

Working my apprenticeship on the *Cambridge Daily News* gave me – I came to reckon in later years – one of the happiest, most relaxed and pain-free years of my working life. Those self-inflicted blues of the previous four years had at last begun to dissipate. I was back in dear, familiar Cambridge, lodging with a motherly widow, Mrs Peel-Yates, in a house at the gates of Girton. The *CDN*, then located next to the University Arms Hotel and (conveniently) opposite the police station, was an engagingly harmonious place to work in. Its editor, Henry (yes) Higgins, with his pipe and comfortable shapelessness, was central casting for a British provincial editor of the 1950s, and the *CDN* was a tight ship seemingly loosely run. Treading a careful path between Town and Gown, it endeavoured – in the very best sense – to be all things to all sections of the community. It did not believe in sensational scoops, and it prided itself on its political neutrality, as I was to discover in my one and only run-in with Mr Higgins. My first couple of weeks I worked at a small table, at the side of W. C. Fincham, the sub-editor, an ectomorphic figure who seemed to live in his bicycle clips, and whose clacking dentures didn't quite fit. The silence would be broken regularly by exclamations of 'Bilge!' and a terrifying chatter of teeth as he struck through somebody's copy with a thick blue pencil. 'I'll ruin this woman!' he cried as a lady correspondent submitted a five-page report on Empire Day. Yet, a true weeping heart, he would be kindness itself when the offending contributor appeared in the office. One morning, seated at my little table, I noted a regular drip coming down from the ceiling. Each time a drop hit the table there would be a fizz and a small puff of smoke. A greenish crater in the wood was growing steadily larger. I reported the phenomenon to Mr Fincham. 'Oh, God, it's those bloody photographers again,' he said and rushed upstairs. Before the acid rain could start up again, I was translated to another department.

Writing up local weddings, I came to recognise that the Cambridgeshire bride invariably wore 'organdie and tulle', but many years passed before I discovered exactly what these materials were. In the evenings, I took a course in shorthand, thinking it essential to the qualified journalist; like the Morse code imposed by the army, I never used it. (In fact some employers such as the *New York Times* would not employ those with shorthand as foreign correspondents, on the grounds that they would be inhibited from seeing the wood for the trees.)

Possibly my main contribution to the *CDN* lay in my police record, handed down from undergraduate days. The Chief Constable, Bebbington, had often expressed his regrets (no doubt they were crocodile tears) at having had to arrest a Jesus man, and his team across the road (headed by the very Chief Inspector whose enticing headgear I had tried to grab in that night of excessive ambition) treated me with indulgent good humour, almost amounting to affection. The feeling lingered that I had been treated with undue harshness; there was almost a sense that the Cambridge Constabulary owed me a favour or two. The main problem facing Bebbington's team seemed to be incest, curiously prevalent in the Fenlands – perhaps on account of those deep ditches not easily surmountable by fugitive daughters. So every day I would pop across the road to hobnob with the friendly Cambridge rozzers or meet one or two over a pint in the pub next door, and come away with advance knowledge of all the hot cases about to come up in court.

The joy of being a reporter on a provincial paper in those days was that you became, inevitably, jack-of-all-trades. 'Fitter Fell into Repair Pit', 'Man on Probation Took Cycle', 'New Master of Trinity' were some of the earth-shaking topics I covered. Only once, I think, did I offend the paper's strict canons of political neutrality. It was during the general election campaign of 1951. Hamilton Kerr, the sitting Tory MP, was standing for re-election. I was not canvassing for him, but one day I encountered his Liberal opponent, a Miss Josephy, driving down the centre of the road with both flippers out (in those days cars had plastic, illuminated indicator-signals that flicked out on either side). It was too good to miss. I rushed back to the office and drafted a humorous piece about the Liberals' confusion between pointing left or right. Mr Higgins came down on me like a ton of compositors' lead slugs: had I forgotten the fastidious political neutrality of the *CDN*?

I was book-reviewer and art, cinema and theatre critic; I covered flower shows, royal visits and stately-home openings; I even ran – by default – the Women's Page. I found reporting humdrum events like school pageants curiously moving, in the surety of bonds between little children, their beaming teachers and proud parents. It was all charmingly innocent, and devoid of stress or much challenge. In a strange way, this world seemed to bring one to the cutting edge of life. But was this real life? I began to yearn for the bigger, more demanding world. I also wanted to go back to Yugoslavia.

The radiant warmth of the stones of Dubrovnik, the shrill hooting of the trains in Belgrade, the pungent aroma of slivovitz, the whirling melodies of the dancing, the exciting mystery of it all, had never left me. That winter I read every book on Yugoslavia, the Eastern bloc and Sovietology that I could lay my hands on. Partly, it was where I had left off in SIME. Maurice Oldfield, now high up in MI6, whom I often saw, regularly invited me to rejoin the Firm; as regularly, I declined. I wanted to combat Communism 'my way' – through journalism and books. But we never lost touch.

I asked to take my summer holiday from the *CDN* in Dubrovnik. Apart from the bus subsiding into a ditch and overturning on the way from the airport, it was as delightful as it had been the year before. It was also more relaxed; I was not spied on at every turn. I had no trouble in rediscovering old friends from the previous year; with Enka, a spirited former Partisan from Croatia, I travelled up and down the glorious Dalmatian coast. When I returned, Mr Higgins generously allowed me to write some articles on Yugoslavia (under the byline of 'Anthony Heron' – why the imposed pseudonym I never quite understood), and – perhaps rashly – gave me my head. The result was five of the longest articles the *CDN* would probably ever print on a foreign country. But these feature pieces at least presented me with a useful springboard to my next employer, the London *Daily Telegraph and Morning Post*, who had promised to take me after twelve months' apprenticeship in Cambridge.

In the autumn of 1951 I started work for the *Daily Telegraph and Morning Post*. Before the two papers amalgamated, my mother had written travel and fashion articles for both of them a generation earlier. In those days, the *Telegraph* resided in a stately stone and marble building at 135 Fleet Street, almost abutting its racy competitor, Beaverbrook's *Daily Express*, a building that glistened like anthracite. After the cosy mateyness of the *Cambridge Daily News* it was rather like going from a small prep school to a large, impersonal public school. As one entered the foyer there was a busy, respectful hush which became more accentuated as one rose in the lift. At the top of the building, on the Fifth Floor, a veritable Mount Olympus, resided the hallowed proprietor, Viscount Camrose, and his son (the effective chairman of the newspaper) Michael Berry, known as 'Mr Michael' – a shy, unobtrusive man with a powerful wife, the Lady Pamela, daughter of the legendary F. E. Smith, who also relished having a share in the running of the newspaper.

Throughout the Camrose empire, the 'Fifth Floor' was always referred to in sanctified quotes, as well as in an impersonal, passive tense. No names were ever mentioned, but if a piece drew comment it would be said to have been 'well received on the Fifth Floor', or the reverse. Worst was the sinister utterance: 'There was an inquest on the Fifth Floor.' As from Mount Sinai, from the Fifth Floor there issued a page, printed in blue, of accepted and unacceptable usage. Woe betide any reporter who used the terms 'big business' or 'tycoon'. These were decidely 'not liked on the Fifth Floor'.

On the fourth and third floors, as I recall, resided the business staff, who maintained the paper's solvency in some mysterious way, and the venerable editor-in-chief, Colin Coote DSO, a veteran of the Great War and a one-time Liberal MP who had all the gravitas of the headmaster of a posh (an adjective also not liked on the Fifth Floor) public school. Around him, and beneath him, were cells inhabited by the various leader-writers, among them old Cambridge chums Colin Welch and later Perry Worsthorne, and, not least, the mercurial deputy editor Malcolm Muggeridge. Malcolm's rasping voice could be heard echoing through the corridors (and it must have been clearly audible to Coote) proclaiming regularly that the paper was 'neither run nor edited'. It would not be long before he left the *DT* to infuse life into the moribund *Punch*.

A pixie-like figure, with the blazing blue eyes of a true fanatic, Malcolm made the deepest impression on me of any of the 'prefects' on the paper. In his earliest professional life, he had done time in Lenin's Moscow, coming to it all as an ardent Fabian and an enthusiastic would-be fellow-traveller. But having to report on the mass starvation of the kulaks opened those blue eyes wide. Then, in the war, MI6 had sent him to North Africa and then to post-Liberation France. He simmered with an anger at having been deceived by Communism, and had become the most vehement of Cold War warriors. It was with the same kind of personalised passion that – abandoning his many 'profane loves' (according to Graham Greene, who may have been jealous, 'his underpants conceal a stiletto') – he, like John Donne, subsequently embraced God, to become the most ardent of Catholic converts. As old members of the same fraternity – that is, the secret services – metaphorically turning back our lapels, we recognised each other, the old lag and the younger one. He became a valuable ally during the short time I served in No. 135.

The second floor was tenanted by a dignitary who was to become another key figure in my *Telegraph* career – S. R. Pawley, the foreign editor, also a wartime intelligence officer. Somewhere in a back room hid the staff of 'Peterborough', the nearest the Fifth Floor would allow to a gossip column, headed by the irascible, bibulous and extremely snobbish Hugo Wortham. Under him was Bill Deedes, already an MP but not a particularly noteworthy journalist in those days, though he was to become one of Britain's greatest, getting better and better as he moved from his eighties into his nineties. Also on 'Peterborough', struggling to find items that were witty but not libellous, news but not meretricious, was another old friend, Phil Goodhart, who also soon became a Tory MP.

But the real hub of the mighty machine was located on the first floor, stretching across the whole of the front behind the great clock on Fleet Street: the newsroom. Although I worked only six grisly months in this hell of dense tobacco smoke, clattering typewriters and crumpled copy and carbons (who under forty can even remember what carbon paper was?), I feel I can still recall intimately its layout, and its rigidly established pecking-order. At one end, ruled the Trinity of the news editor – a hard-bitten Glaswegian called Archie Maclaren – and his two deputies, Hill and Sandrock, facing the herd of reporters. Behind them came the longer-serving newsmen, including the heroic John Armstrong. Just two years older than me, John had lost an eye and both hands to a grenade in Burma. He had had a primitive artificial hand fitted which allowed him, miraculously, to peck away at a typewriter. Even more miraculous was his ability to shake a match out of its box with his two stumps, and somehow light a pipe – which he was never without, and which contributed its own special haze to the impenetrable pall of the newsroom. For many years, John managed to arrive at No. 135 immaculately turned out with a monocle in his waistcoat pocket and (as his obituary in April 2000 had it) 'a determination to beg no privileges'.

Finally, behind John, at the very furthest point from the news editor and his two myrmidons, there skulked three of us newcomers – all public school boys, all ex-wartime officers, all Oxbridge, all with names beginning with H. There was John Herbert – son of the famous A. P., and one of the most agreeably indolent men I have ever known, who left the paper after a few undistinguished years to pursue a brilliant (and highly profitable) career at Christie's in charge of PR. There was the immensely genial and even more unambitious Michael Hogg, later becoming the eighth baronet and spending over thirty years on the paper, much of it in long liquid lunches at El Vino's wine-bar. And then there was me. All three us would endeavour to hide behind John Armstrong's smokescreen, pretending to peruse the bound copies of the paper at the back of the room, flinching from the summons of 'Ogg, 'Erbert or 'Orne from Maclaren, knowing that it would be to send one of us off on some trivial mission such as covering a 'four-pump fire'. Compared with the cuttings book I maintained on the *Cambridge Daily News*, those originating from six months in the *DT* newsroom look meagre. 'Choir Held Up by Fog', 'Where do Snails Go in Winter?' and a court case concerning trespass and damage by errant ducks. Positively spicy was a scoop that Madame Tussaud's were having to melt down one of Attlee's Cabinet ministers to make way for Churchill's new, taller and broader team. Were it not for the bonhomie of a lunchtime, or a day, ending in the nearby Cheshire Cheese or in the Punch Tavern down at the bottom of the street, or in El Vino's at the top when one was feeling rich or posh, the boredom would have been inexpressable. No wonder so much promising talent fell to melancholy or cirrhosis.

Then there were the hours. The normal, or rather optimum, day ran from a civilised 10 a.m. to 6 p.m. but there was also the anti-social 3 p.m. to 10 p.m. and the grisly 'graveyard shift' from 5 p.m. to 1 a.m. On the last the almost empty newsroom was ruled by a new figure, the night news editor, a courteous but unsmiling figure in a stiff white collar with, appropriately enough, the look of an undertaker about him. One regular hack on the graveyard shift always kept a trilby on his head – unless Lord Camrose telephoned, when he would automatically doff it to take the call. But the names of 'Ogg, 'Erbert and 'Orne seemed to come up with inequitable regularity on the night roster. And all this for about £13 a week.

The only recognisable key to escape from the slough of the newsroom was to get one's name in print, on an op-ed feature. Between them Maurice Oldfield and Malcolm Muggeridge provided a first opening. In my studies of Sovietology, coupled with a close reading of the press, it occurred to me that a new trend was now afoot in the Eastern bloc that could have the greatest significance. In the early days of Bolshevism many of the Comintern leaders, men like Trotsky, Kamenev and Zinoviev, had been Jews, members of an oppressed minority and victims of pogroms under the tsars. All had been purged by Stalin, save Lazar Kaganovich, a hardline Stalin loyalist who managed to survive. Over Palestine in 1946–8 the Soviets had come out with a strongly pro-Zionist line, for once supporting US policy, opportunistically – in order to get Britain out of the Middle East. But since the ending of the Mandate things had changed radically. In 1951, Rudolf Slánský (alias Zaltsman), the all-powerful Communist Party Secretary of Czechoslovakia, was arrested on ominous charges of having been in 'the service of American imperialism' and Zionism. At the same time, the Czech premier, Antonin Zápotocký, savagely attacked 'Jewish capitalists'. Slánský was executed after a show trial the following November, conducted in an atmosphere of old-style anti-Semitism. In Hungary and Poland there were parallel purges, while in Rumania even the all-powerful Ana Pauker seemed to have fallen from grace. More significant, in the long run, was the block that was now placed on Soviet Jews obtaining exit passes to leave for Israel – something which was not to be ended until the Nixon–Kissinger deal of 'grain for emigrants' in the 1970s.

This new trend, if indeed it was a trend, struck me in 1951 as having powerful implications in the incipient Cold War. I ran my thesis past Maurice; he endorsed it enthusiastically, and provided me with some extra material. Malcolm was delighted and ran it, under the provocative heading 'Soviets Copy Nazi Anti-Jewish Repressions' on the centre op-ed page, with that ardently sought-after byline. As per *Telegraph* principles they cut it to a stark 1,200 words. Nevertheless, an important statement had been made; my foot was in the door. Some encouraging correspondence flowed in.

Meanwhile, in my life outside the *Telegraph* there were exciting developments. I had managed to infect a literary agent, Osyth Leeston, with my enthusiasm for the Yugoslav dancers. She introduced me to a theatrical producer, Peter Daubeny. Peter was very much in the public eye at the time, having brought over the marvellous Spanish flamenco dancer Antonio. He was an engaging figure, who had lost an arm when landing with the Coldstream Guards at Salerno and would flap the empty sleeve with enthusiasm for a new project that caught his imagination. Like most stage figures he was vividly indiscreet about his encounters, describing for example how Somerset Maugham had recently made a pass down at the Villa Mauresque, then – on rejection – petulantly wouldn't offer him a farewell 'g-g-glass of ch-ch-champagne'. Inseparable from Peter was his impresario and hatchet-man, Leon Hepner, a vast Georgian with the jowl and lugubrious eyes of a bloodhound. Peter flew to Belgrade, saw the 'Kolo' team of dancers and their inspired director, Olga Skovran, and came back as keen as I was. It would be the first time any East European dance group had come to London since the war. The only problem: we needed to raise some money. I was persuaded to cobble together some £5,000 – a colossal sum in those days. But Peter and Leon were brimming with confidence that we were all bound to make money on the project.

That May of 1952 the dancers, fifty strong, arrived at the Cambridge Theatre in the West End for a whole month, billed as 'The Year's Most Colourful & Romantic Show', and so indeed it was. A good-looking lot, beautiful girls with open faces and proud and virile males – the best of Serbia – they were an instant success. Their energy and sheer joie de vivre were boundless. The dance critics raved; Lord Beaverbrook invited the whole ensemble down to his private domain at Cherkley Court in Surrey; chic socialite members of London's émigré Yugoslav community endeavoured to seduce them, males and females. Together with the fierce Olga, I had the invidious role, late at night, of rounding them all up. Claude flew over from Berlin for the first night. I basked in their reflected glory and went night after night, provided I wasn't on the *Telegraph* graveyard shift. The only trouble was, that May happened to be one of the hottest on record. People simply didn't want to go to the theatre; they stayed away, out in the country or snogging in the park. After the initial surge, the box-office take dwindled. Daubeny Presentations lost money; I lost my shirt.

Before I could attend the final night, say *dovidenja* and thank-you to the boys and girls at the Cambridge, something unexpected had cropped up in my own professional life. One day Pawley, the Foreign editor, had come into the news room and enquired baldly: 'Hands up anyone who speaks German? Reggie Steed's having a nervous breakdown in Berlin, and needs a number two. Any offers?'

Slowly, and rashly, I put up my hand. No one else did. I had done a year's O-level in German at school, aged 15, that was all – but I hoped it might be enough with a bit of swotting up. Anything to get out of the dreaded newsroom.

'Good,' said Pawley. 'Come along with me.'

And before I could modify my claims to prowess in German, I was on my way to Berlin. The worrying thing, slightly, was that no one at No. 135 who knew Steed had much good to say about him: 'a difficult fellow', they all warned.

7

GERMANY: FROM OUR
OWN CORRESPONDENT

Otto John at a press conference in East Berlin, 20 July 1954. (Topfoto)

Compared with Paris ... [Bonn is] cruel and unnatural punishment.

US Ambassador David Bruce

As of May 1952, what had once been Bismarck's, and later Hitler's, proud German Reich, lay partitioned between East and West. West Germany was divided into three zones: British, American, and a smaller French zone. To the East lay the Soviet Zone, which contained an encircled Berlin, which in turn was split into four sectors run by the wartime Allies. Since 1949 the Western zones had largely operated as one unit, the Federal Republic with its provisional capital in Bonn, headed by the redoubtable Dr Konrad Adenauer.

On 26 May 1952 the Foreign Ministers of the United States, Britain and France signed in Bonn the historic documents that would lead to full independence – and rearmament – for Western Germany's Federal Republic. They were known in the West as the Bonn Conventions, but by the Soviets and their East German satellite as the General War Pact. That was a warning of what lay ahead. Immediately the Soviet Zone government announced retaliatory measures. A 'death strip' was established along the whole 500-mile length of the interzonal frontier, from the Baltic to the Czech frontier, totally cutting off all traffic between East and West. Forerunner of the grim Berlin Wall, within the death strip all houses, trees and obstacles were levelled, the ground mined and wooden control towers with searchlights and machine guns constructed at regular intervals. On the one interzonal autobahn that linked West Germany with Berlin, via Helmstedt, all Western military patrols were suddenly forbidden access. Telephone cables were severed, while the Soviets presented the Allies with a £7 million invoice – the largest telephone bill in history to date – for accumulated past use of cables running through their zone. Though set deep in the Soviet Zone, through the end-of-war agreements at Yalta and Potsdam, Berlin's three Allied sectors were tenuously linked to the West by three air corridors and that one autobahn, to which the Western 'occupation' powers were allowed full rights of access – in theory.

Suddenly, in aggressive reaction to the 'General War Pact', in Berlin itself armed Russian troops moved in to occupy three small enclaves that belonged to the Allied sectors on the periphery of the city. Were these measures preliminary to a complete close-down of the city – something Stalin had attempted in 1948, defeated only by the astonishing Berlin Airlift organized by the Allies? It began to look like it.

This was the scene I headed for. At full speed in a Healey, a powerful but lethal sports car which, bankrupting myself, I had bought on leaving Cambridge, I tore across Belgium (or rather rumbled across pavé roads – there was no motorway), and then roared up the West German autobahn. It was exhilarating to be able to cruise at over 100 mph on empty roads, to be challenged by the vainglorious German Porsches of the day and leave them standing. I passed through the Helmstedt checkpoint, manned by squat Soviet troops with tommy-guns, then raced through East Germany – enemy territory – with mounting excitement. Was I not about to become a real-life foreign correspondent, envy of every hack in the *DT* newsroom? Driving through Cologne, I had been stunned by the destruction – still, eight years after the last bombs had been dropped, a wasteland of rubble, with only the sombre, blackened cathedral standing undamaged in the middle. It was worse than I had ever imagined. But nothing – not even wartime newsreels – had quite prepared me for Berlin, the mile upon mile of deserted blocks of heaped-up rubble. The worst areas of the City of London were nothing by comparison. Did we really do this? Had it really been essential to winning the war?

I reached the *Daily Telegraph* office on Berlin's Fehrbelliner Platz, smugly confident that I had set up a speed record from the Channel. My new boss, Reggie Steed, did indeed look like a man on the verge of a nervous breakdown. His eyes were red-rimmed with fatigue. There was no greeting, no congratulation on my speed record, only 'Why did you take so long to get here?' The steaming Healey outside, hallmark of a spoilt young layabout, seemed only to distress him. No sooner had I taken my jacket off than he said, 'I want you to take over monitoring the East German radio.' I mumbled that the dialect was unfamiliar to me, but the cat was out of the bag. 'You have no German?' I thought the beleaguered Steed really might begin eating his desk. There were instant calls to Foreign Editor Pawley: 'You've sent me someone who's totally useless, can't speak German ...' I pleaded; Pawley temporised. Eventually I was permitted to stay, on probation, to take on the most menial jobs (which, *inter alia*, meant the evening shift every day). It was hardly a promising prelude to becoming the Great Foreign Correspondent.

Going into the Berlin Press Club for the first time was almost as daunting as entering the Coldstream Officers' Mess as a fresh ensign, but I had the good fortune to make almost instantly some excellent friends – notably Charles Wheeler of the BBC and Rachel Terry, wife of the *Sunday Times* correspondent Antony Terry.* Both, sympathetic to my treatment by Steed, took me by the hand, helped me immeasurably and became lifelong friends. They tried to explain Steed. A grammar-school boy, he had come to Dresden before the war with aspirations to becoming an opera singer. He couldn't make it, so he was picked up by the ace reporter on the German scene, Sefton Delmer, who gave him a menial job on the *Daily Express.* Delmer made a hobby of sadism, finding out the weaknesses of colleagues and sticking the pin in. He bullied and exploited Reggie, having realised just how vulnerable and dependent he was. Steed had now developed into a talented, and dedicated veteran journalist, but he had collected every imaginable chip on both shoulders. For him a junior who was ex-Brigade of Guards and a Cambridge graduate was insufferable – and the Healey was the last straw. 'Now Reggie will pass on the Delmer treatment to you,' warned Rachel. But what options did I have? Understanding Steed's background was not to make our relationship much easier.

One of my first assignments was to be sent over to East Berlin, to cover a speech made by Kim Il-Sung, the North Korean leader, at the monstrous Palace of Culture. Among 10,000 Communist worshippers, I appeared to be the only Westerner there. (Was this how Steed intended to get rid of me?) At regular intervals during the interminable speeches, there were shouts of 'Auf!', and all leaped to their feet to applaud with slow rhythmic

* As Sarah Gainham, Rachel later became a novelist of repute, author *inter alia* of *Night Falls on the City* (1967).

clapping, the sort that a flop first night gets on Broadway. I did not see why I should clap too, so I remained seated, in face of much muttering and scowling. I imagined this was how a Nuremberg Rally must have been. Mass emotion is a terrifying thing, and after about the tenth 'auf' I began to wonder if my nerves would hold to the end. They did – just. But it was all very frightening, to realise that between the Volkspalast and Japan there was just one great monolithic bloc of the Dictatorship of the Proletariat. I was glad to get back to Fehrbelliner Platz.

As a small counterjab to the Soviet measures, the British had decided to seal off the Soviet Zone radio headquarters, which, as one of the many anomalies of the division of Berlin, was still housed in a building in the British Sector – whence it poured out vilification against the British and the West at large. Inside the blockaded Rundfunkhaus was a dedicated Communist, the chief commentator Karl-Eduard von Schnitzler, an interesting figure whom Steed had known while involved in 'black' broadcasting* during the war. The building was surrounded by the Royal Scots, who had run up barbed-wire barricades. From inside the Rundfunkhaus the bored troops were bombarded with Communist marching songs, interspersed with propaganda harangues. No one was allowed in. I would be sent to bait Herr von Schnitzler with sandwiches, while Steed – developing a curious kind of friendship with Schnitzler – regularly telephoned to ask how supplies were holding out. Schnitzler would reply defiantly, 'We shall stay here half an hour longer than your troops will stay when our comrades from the East come to liberate us.'

In May 1952, it looked as if that might indeed be any minute now. At the barricades, I got into conversation with a disgruntled musician carrying a cello case. Every morning he came down to take up his place in the radio orchestra, and every morning a kilted soldier barred his way. He was not interested in politics. 'I am a German and an artist, and I think you and the Russians are being equally childish,' he said and stalked away. That was the Cold War. After a week of siege the Russians withdrew from the seized enclaves, the Berlin crisis simmered down. I was despatched to Bonn, to live out my probation there, which meant principally manning the *DT*'s main office on the night shift.

---

* A special BBC service which affected to emanate from the Resistance in the Reich.

Bonn, a sleepy Rhineland town, home of Beethoven and with a noble university (and a disgusting climate which seemed to accumulate all the gases of the Ruhr, giving you a hangover most mornings when you awoke), had been senselessly bombed in the last stages of the war. Now, in the early 1950s, because – it was said – of its convenience to the Federal Chancellor, Dr Konrad Adenauer, who lived just across the Rhine in his beloved rose garden at Rhöndorf, it became the capital of Federal Germany. Suddenly Bonn found itself having to house all the apparatus of government, the Allied High Commissions, the Corps Diplomatique and, of course, the press. Whole cantonments sprang up; British diplomats were housed in dreary uniform dwellings in what became known as Mig Allee. The important, zealously fought-for status symbol was how many loos each possessed: one for a third secretary, two for a second secretary and so on. The foreign press were herded together in jerry-built offices called the Bundespressehaus, adjacent to the equally new Bundestag or parliament. From behind the flimsy partition walls emerged a babel of voices. The *Daily Telegraph* office was so small that there was barely room for Steed, our Berliner secretary (the supremely effective and long-suffering, Fräulein Klinke), myself and three elderly typewriters. When our Rumanian Volksdeutsch stringer, Carol Schmidt, came in with the latest gossip, someone had to stand to make room for his solidly built frame.

The apartments where married journalists lived were equally flimsy *Neubauten*. At regular intervals Steed was infuriated, his rage mixed with perhaps a certain libidinous envy, by the Italian correspondent of *Il Tempo*, the unique and splendidly misnamed Sandro Paternostro, who lived three doors down the hall but whose love-making (invariably accompanied, like Dudley Moore in *10*, by Ravel's *Bolero*) pulsated through the whole *Neubau*. Sandro was a diminutive Sicilian with disproportionately large hands, which – on whatever subject he was articulating, whether it was the economy or Adenauer's latest reshuffle – would appear to be delineating some part of the female anatomy. Like many small Latins, Sandro had an incurable passion for large, blonde Teutonic Brünnhildes. As the Brünnhildes grew larger, so Ravel grew fortissimo. Steed would come into the office next day, pale with indignation, and take it out on me or Klinke.

On the dreary screen of Bonn, Sandro and his adventures afforded a constant and merry distraction. His father was a leading lawyer for the Mafia in Palermo (with a name like Paternostro, how could he not be?), one of his clients being an eminent tailor who could only pay his fees in suits. These were promptly shipped to Sandro in Bonn where he would appear among the soberly clad locals in amazing varieties of shot silk and electric pinstripes. No *capo* could have done better. Sandro drove around in a vast pink Studebaker, with a large woolly dog seated on his lap so that – since Sandro's eyes could barely be seen above the dashboard – terrified burghers of Bonn thought they were about to be mown down by a demented canine.

As a journalist Sandro was kindness itself to me, always prepared to share a story in order to snub Steed. His rapportage was, however, imaginative – to put it mildly. One day he took me, plus the daughters of the French and British High Commissioners respectively, to interview a gypsy sorceress in the Eifel hills, whose advice – he claimed – was sought by half the Adenauer Cabinet. There we found a fearsomely grubby Madame Arcati, in a caravan complete with crystal ball and flea-ridden monkey angling its sore red bottom towards the client. Swiftly she dealt with the two girls, electrifying Liz, the Brit, by telling her how many abortions her highly respectable mother had had. Then came Sandro, who wanted to know what would be the future of Trieste – Yugoslav or Italian? – which was then the big issue in Italy. She gazed intensely into the crystal ball, then asked, 'Is Trieste blonde or brunette?' Resourcefully Sandro nevertheless managed to sculpt from it a front-page scoop in *Il Tempo*, with the headline 'Adenauer's Soothsayer Says: Trieste Will Remain Italian'. In this, at least, history was to prove Sandro perfectly correct.

One day Sandro came up to me outside the Bundespressehaus with an unusually conspiratorial expression. 'Alistair, I have an exciting proposition for you!' It turned out that at the famous Resi Bar, a huge dance hall in the American Sector in Berlin, the telephonist was about to give notice so that she could get married. A vacancy was thus created. The Resi was famed both as a place of pick-ups and assignations and for its vigorous spy traffic, with some twenty-seven assorted intelligence agencies vying for information to please their various masters. Each table of the Resi had a number on it, a telephone and access to a pneumatic tube. So if you fancied a lady at another table, you could instantly ring or send a saucy billet-doux in a pneumatic capsule. It was no less ideal, of course, for the transmission of spy messages, which was then West Berlin's main industry. And every single message passed via this one telephonist! The potential was enormous. 'Signor Bonefaccio of Italian intelligence has made an offer, and she's working for me too. But she's expensive. We need a third partner – how about the *Daily Telegraph* joining in?' asked Sandro. It sounded all a bit like buying one leg of a racehorse. 'I'll have to run it past Reggie. I'm not sure he'll like it.' That turned out to be the under-statement of the age: 'Horne, that's the most irresponsible thing I've ever heard of. The *Daily Telegraph* – "The paper you can trust"? How could you even think of it.' (Sandro later became a famous TV presenter in Italy; aged seventy-six he married a soubrette forty years his junior, but died in London two years later.)

I was sent back to writing paragraphs of utter banality, about the death of an old German general or construction of the new (hideous shoebox) British Embassy in Bonn. How would I ever break out as a Malcolm Muggeridge or Sefton Delmer? Steed would never trust me with any serious story. Meanwhile I spent dreary evening after dreary evening manning the office till eleven o'clock, reading through the turgid Deutsche Presse-Agentur reports (certainly good for my German). It was my fault, fibbing about my German. That beastly language was the problem. Three times a week I would attend sessions with an arrogant old pedant at the University, Professor Dr Paul Menzerath, who declared at the outset, 'Compared to German, you English have a very poor language – ony 50,000 words. German has 250,000 *echte Wörter* – and you will need to learn every one.' My friends urged me to find a *dictionnaire dormante*, but how was I to find such a creature when night after night I was condemned to that poky little office in the Bundespressehaus?

Generously, Fräulein Klinke tried to get me together with her pretty opposite number, Gisela, who worked for Karl Robson on the old *News Chronicle*. But Gisela was a tough, upwardly mobile little number who snubbed me painfully; anyway her English was too good. Then one evening I spotted a willowy blonde leaving the United Press office just down the hall. Ursula, otherwise 'Usshi', was also working on the late shift. I gave her a lift home several times; swiftly we became lovers. Lithe and lissom, she was enthusiastic, with few inhibitions, and seemed experienced for one so young. (She wouldn't tell me her age.) My linguistic abilities improved by leaps and bounds, far the nicest way to learn a language. Only, they weren't exactly the cadences of Goethe I was learning. Frowning deeply, Herr Doktor Menzerath at Bonn would sort me out during the day, Usshi in the post-work hours of night. Then Usshi was transferred to UP's Frankfurt office. Ten years later we met again, in Cologne. She had become the mistress of an up-and-coming architect. She looked prosperous, a gorgeous young woman in the bloom of youth. Curiosity prompted me to ask, 'Truly, how old were you in those days?' She chuckled: 'When we met, not quite sixteen!' Oh Lord!

The work, apart from the constant acidulous discouragement of Steed (it took the best part of a year to get on to a 'Reggie' and 'Alistair' basis), was absorbing. It seems hard now to think of dull, Swiss-like Federal Germany being the focus of exciting news. But, day after day, even on the laconic pages of the *Daily Telegraph*, our tiny outstation in Bonn–Berlin 'led the paper' (the approved jargon on the mysterious Fifth Floor). We were truly at the centre of the storm. Nothing demonstrated this better than a small sign in Russian at the east end of the Bonn bridge over the Rhine, which politely informed members of the overwhelmingly powerful Red Army that their personnel were not permitted to cross the river. That was just about all there was to keep out Stalin's Mongol hordes, apart from a handful of under-strength US and British brigades. (Much of the rest remained committed in faraway Korea.) How often, in the prevailing context of the mutual fears of the Cold War, did we go to bed half expecting to see Soviet tanks in the streets of boring Bonn next morning! Of course we had the hydrogen bomb, but would we dare to use it, now that Stalin also had his? That was the issue which eclipsed all others.

While from East Germany the Soviets kept up a barrage of threats, in Bonn everything that summer of 1952 focused on signature of the so-called Contractual Agreements. These aimed at nothing less than giving West Germany full independence and the right to rearm, within a carefully chaperoned European Army. All the animosities of the past war, the American threats to turn Germany into a rural wasteland occupied for a hundred years, the devastation of the Allied bombing, the century of

Franco-German belligerence, were to be obliterated overnight. Washington and London desperately needed German soldiers, those supermen whom they had been battling only seven years previously, to stand between them and the Russians. It was as simple as that. Argument over ratification of the Agreements raged back and forth over the next two years, in and out of the Bundestag, in London, in Washington and particularly in Paris, where the French still had too-vivid memories of *feldgrau* soldiers on the Champs-Elysées. Many Germans, too, were fiercely opposed. The discussions revealed a deep nervousness, almost neurosis, at every level of German life. One of the first things I learned about the Germans: they were absolutely not the stolid, disciplined and phlegmatic people I had always somehow imagined; they were profoundly prey to the deepest emotion.

While the great issues raged round my head, however, my inadequacies and Steed's hostility often landed me with jobs of little consequence, such as tracking down five English schoolgirls who had gone missing during a holiday jaunt on the Rhine. Sometimes I wished I was back in the exciting, smoke-laden newsroom at No. 135 or in the Punch Tavern. I missed my chums there. Yet gradually I made new friends, Germans as well as press colleagues. While few could compete with Sandro Paternostro for sheer entertainment value, the foreign press were an interesting and diverse group. The most reliable journalist was the Hon. Terence Prittie, who had spent six years as a prisoner of war, escaped numerous times and ended up in Colditz. Terence always referred to the Germans as the 'gremlins', yet no one reported the German scene with greater accuracy or sensitivity. Here was a conundrum; perhaps a third of the British correspondents, and a similar proportion among the PR staff at the British High Commission, had been POWs – and they were among the best. Many had married Germans. Why? If I had spent my youth in Colditz I think I would want to get as far away from the land of Goethe as possible, for ever. Was it some form of Stockholm Syndrome which kept them there?

My closest friend was Ian Fraser, chief of Reuters, who was two or three years older than me. A remarkable linguist, and with a brilliant (if sometimes arrogant) mind, Ian was wasted in Bonn, cast up on the shore for years by a disingenuous boss who was always offering him the 'top job' but never coming through. Eventually he left to pursue a meteoric career in the City with Warburgs and Lazards and finally as head of Rolls-Royce. Disliking dear Reggie even more than most of our colleagues, he was a generous friend to me, introducing me to people in every walk of German life, sharing stories and helping in every way. Fighting his way up through Italy in the Scots Guards, he had, I knew, won an MC, yet it wasn't until the end of his life when he published, in his memoirs, one of the most remarkable accounts of what the Second World War in Italy was really like for a platoon commander, that I learned just what he had gone through. Ian had one particular obsession – spies. Cigarette dangling from the corner of his mouth, looking down his nose – a Fraser speciality – he would declaim, 'Every journalist here is a spy, for one or other of the agencies, all working against each other. Except me. You're a spy, aren't you?'

'No,' I was able to protest, then.

'But you were?'

'Only when I was in the army.'

'Oh, well – once a spy always a spy. They'll get you, you'll see!'

I had little enough spare time, and little indeed on which to spend the £18 a week (plus modest expenses) which the *Telegraph*, paid me. I found a two-room apartment on Godesbergerstrasse, let by a charming (and broad-minded) war widow named Frau Holland. When I revisited it in the 1990s the side-street had been renamed Werner von Braunstrasse, after the genius who invented the V-2 that nearly got me in Guy's Hospital and who later helped develop the US moon rocketry. Frau Holland's house shook every time the main Rheingold express passed, but I was of an age not to be concerned. In downtown Bonn there was one seedy nightclub, the Tabu, and a couple of tolerable restaurants. Mostly I ate out, often in the Bundeshaus restaurant, a good place for picking up stories. For better food, and often better company, I went to the French Club in Bad Godesberg. Run by the French High Commission for its employees, one would often meet Willy Brandt there, the future Socialist Chancellor – who was later to be ruined by a spy scandal but was then a mere deputy. Willy, who had blotted his copybook with the German nationalists for having sided with the Norwegian Resistance during the war (though that was to be the foundation of his political popularity with the left), particularly enjoyed the French Club because he could escape from his compatriots and all the heavy earnestness of Bonn politics. Also he was a great bon vivant and an excellent drinking companion, with a considerable appetite for the pretty young French secretaries to be found eating there.

And it was here that one of those rare happy confluences of business and pleasure led me to my first scoop on Bonn's stony road. Somewhere along the line that summer I made the acquaintance of a jolly Marseillaise secretary who walked with the most eye-catching wiggle of her *fesses*. She did nothing to help my German, but in bed was a tornado of garlic-generated frenzy, leaving me covered with bruises and scratches. She was an unfailingly cheerful soul, until one day in August 1952 I found her in the Club looking uncharacteristically glum. 'I've had a terrible day.'

'Why?'

'Well, you know my boss was a deportee in the war, in fact a slave-labourer in the Nazi arms industry. Now he's just heard that the Allies – you British and the Americans – are going to hand back to Herr Krupp all the factories they took away from him after the war.'

She took me into her office and showed me some highly classified documents. Steed was away on holiday. I rushed home and did some urgent telephoning. I spoke to the various PR reps at the UK and US offices, playing one off against the other, until I squeezed all the details out of them. The British were shamefaced, and evasive, the Americans rather less so ('Well, how can you expect us to encourage the Germans to rearm, as our ally, when their generals are still in prison and their leading arms manufacturers are expropriated?'). The French, as expected, were seething. For the man in the street everywhere the name Krupp had become a synonym for German beastliness; it fitted conveniently into a newspaper headline, and was one of three German names – together with Hitler and the Kaiser – to be known universally. However you pronounced it, the word 'Krupp' sounded like the explosion of a shell. To the French it was Krupp arms that had ravaged France three times in a century. It was heavy Krupp mortars that had bombarded Paris in 1870. In 1918, it was a monster Krupp gun, 'Long Max' (erroneously nicknamed 'Big Bertha' by the Allies, after the Krupp heiress), which had shelled Paris from a range of 75 miles. In 1944 it had been Tiger tanks built by Krupp that brewed up our Shermans by the hundred in Normandy, and spearheaded the Ardennes offensive. Krupp had even built the first U-boats in 1914. In Germany, however, Krupp conveyed largely the opposite: it was the nonpareil of industrial excellence, always the best of employers and, historically, a special case.

In bald terms, the new deal signified that Alfried Krupp, the forty-six-old playboy heir who had been sentenced in the post-Nuremberg trials to twelve years' imprisonment for crimes against humanity, would once more become the richest man in Europe. Even though partially broken up, Firma Krupp would resume its role at the head of German industrial combines. My story got headlines in the *Telegraph*; in Fleet Street parlance, we had it all to ourselves, and it ran and ran. Congratulatory messages flowed in from the Fifth Floor. Reggie returned from holiday in a fury; why hadn't he got the story? I was tempted to crow, 'Contacts, contacts, old boy!' but curbed my tongue. Anyway, in London's eyes I had made my name at last.

As soon as I could I went up to grisly, bomb-shattered Essen to look at the heart of Krupps. Destruction from the numerous Allied raids was still dreadful – scores of wrecked buildings with their girders bent and twisted by fire had been left standing amid the acres of rubble. Working in the wreckage were employees with intense, over-worked faces, the colour of that German asparagus grown underground. There was a lot of pent-up resentment. The Krupp directors treated me with the worst kind of German condescension. I felt they were laughing up their sleeves. When I asked where the Tiger works had stood, I was shown a workers' latrine adjacent to the demolished plant. When I asked about 'Big Bertha', I was given figures on locomotive production. If Krupp was planning any new German conquest of Europe, it was plain that it would be with washing-machines and earth-moving equipment, not with tanks and guns. I visited the Villa Hügel, family home of the Krupp dynasty – affectionately nick-named 'Kanonenberg'. Now no longer inhabited by the family, it was an appalling place, built in Wagnerian style, totally bereft of any charm or taste. Even the dining-room dresser incorporated a serving hatch that somehow managed to suggest an open-hearth furnace. One wondered what kind of grim souls, out of Thomas Mann, had inhabited this house.

Apart from improving my image on the Fifth Floor, the Krupp saga unexpectedly opened exciting new vistas in Germany for me. Contacts

I made in the Ruhr helped me to carve a niche for myself reporting on German industrial recovery, and on the *Wirtschaftswunder* or 'Economic Miracle' launched by Professor Ludwig Erhard, the Economics Minister – all of which bored Steed. Now that I was relatively fluent in German, I learned all about Bessemer Converters, explored steel foundries and Hamburg's new dockyards, went down ultra-modern coalmines and paid several visits to the greatest success story of them all: Dr Nordhoff's Volkswagen works at Wolfsburg. I found it fascinating to observe this phoenix arising from the ashes. At the same time, it was deeply depressing to note by comparison the lethargy prevailing in my own country. Visiting sales reps from top British companies would repeatedly come out to Germany, equipped with brochures in English only, not speaking a word of German themselves and seeming to spend their time boozing on expense accounts with their fellow countrymen. Only a very few British enterprises had their own residents locally.

Apart from that sign on the Rhine bridge at Bonn, as of the early 1950s there seemed to be, chiefly, one other dyke holding back the Soviet hordes: a stern old German with a face like an Amerindian (he had suffered severe facial injuries in a car accident in 1917), Dr Konrad Adenauer. Today, outside Germany, Adenauer is a largely forgotten figure, but I wonder if we appreciate just what he achieved, not just for Germany but for the West as a whole. Adenauer himself would probably have claimed that his greatest single contribution to his country was the sealing of amity with France, through the person of de Gaulle. But, to me, living through his early years in Bonn, his most outstanding feat was to restore tranquillity, to repair the nerves of a shattered and thoroughly neurotic nation.

It would be hard to conceive of a more uncomfortable inheritance than to be legal successor to a regime responsible for the most lethal war and the most monstrous crimes in history. This is what Konrad Adenauer and the new Federal Government inherited, and it embraced issues that were constantly at the forefront of our minds in the Bundespressehaus. One of the earliest bills to be passed through the Federal Parliament was the Israel Reparations Scheme, to help Israel assimilate the floods of Jewish refugees that were the consequence of Nazi persecution. Following a unanimous vote, the Bundestag rose and stood in silence as a gesture of abhorrence at the crimes of the past. Initially, however, the German offer of reconciliation met an icy response in Israel, and the signing ceremony had to be planned to avoid Jewish delegates having to shake hands with their German opposite numbers. How could one begin to quantify what the Jews had suffered at the hands of Hitler? But at least it was a start in contrition and seemed to indicate which way Adenauer's Germany was pointing.

One uncomfortable legacy Adenauer inherited from the war was the aftermath of the Nuremberg War Crimes trials, and German attitudes that prevailed to what many considered 'Justice of the Victors'. It was also a regular issue in the columns of the *Daily Telegraph*. While I was there, two leading Wehrmacht Field-Marshals serving long sentences, Kesselring and Manstein, were released on health grounds; Manstein was to survive another twenty years. Reactions to their release in the British press, including the *Telegraph*, were acrimonious. It did occur to me at the time, however, that it was unrealistic of the Allies to think of forming a new, and effective, German army – if that was what they wanted – while at the same time pursuing retribution from members of the former Wehrmacht.

Some individual cases merited more sympathy than others. There was the case, for instance, of two simple ex-sergeants – Hans Kuehn and Wilhelm Kappe, who were 'sprung' from serving twenty year sentences for killing shot-down Canadian airmen. The charges were that, on leave from the Russian front, the two had returned to find their homes in the Ruhr a sea of fire, following a recent bombing raid. Crowds were clustering round a shot-down allied air crew; the two sergeants, enraged by what they had seen, went and killed the wounded men with hammers. A brutal crime, but, given the circumstances, not beyond comprehension. Meanwhile, like several others at the time, the two escaped prisoners, extensively helped by the local population, disappeared underground. Their case was strongly supported in much of the West German press, and I found it hard to be totally out of sympathy with them. All of us ex-soldiers knew of cases where enemy prisoners had been shot, or similar war crimes, committed by Allied forces in the heat of battle.

Much of the early birth pains of Adenauer's Federal German Republic revolved around efforts to create a new, and respectable, German army. The foreign press was watching intently in the wings. Then, in November

1952, an upheaval occurred within the so-called Amt Blank,* a government agency supposedly responsible for relations with the Allied occupying forces but discreetly planning the rebuilding of German military
strength. The upheaval was sparked by the dramatic resignation of two
distinguished former Wehrmacht officers. One of them was called Axel
von dem Bussche. The two feared that the school of *Kommiss*, of hard-
line Prussian discipline, might be gaining ground among those charged
with developing the structure and philosophy of the new Bundeswehr.
Understandably, the direction the new West German forces, only seven
years after that cataclysmic day of May 1945, would be likely to assume
was of paramount concern to the foreign press. It was the extraordinary
background of the thirty-two-year-old Freiherr von dem Bussche which
brought the dispute far greater publicity than it would otherwise have
had. As a young much decorated major, Bussche had committed himself
to a heroic, suicidal one-man plot to kill Hitler.

Bussche held a press conference to explain to the outside world the
principles lying behind his resignation. I wrote in a despatch shortly
afterwards:

> His tall, distinguished figure with its heavy limp became a familiar and
> impressive sight in Bonn. There was something about his almost quixotic
> idealism that made him strike one as the very epitome of Hölderlin's
> 'inwardly torn' German. He seemed an anachronistic survival of a breed
> nearly extinct as a result of two wars and the massacre which followed the
> '20th of July', the best of the German nobility that opposed Hitler.

In 1943, almost a year before the bomb plot of 20 July 1944 led by Colonel
Klaus Schenck von Stauffenberg, Axel, then a highly decorated regular
army officer aged twenty-four, volunteered to model a new army overcoat
before the Führer. In the pockets of the coat were hand-grenades which
he would detonate, thereby killing both himself and Hitler. With his
extraordinary sixth sense, Hitler cancelled the demonstration. Axel
screwed up his courage for a second attempt, but by a million-to-one
chance the overcoat was destroyed in an RAF air raid. The raid was,
ironically, to save both Hitler's and Bussche's life. The demonstration was

---

* Named after its chief, a trade union official called Theodor Blank.

now fixed to take place at Christmas, only for Axel to be recalled suddenly to his regiment on the Russian front. A few days later he was severely wounded, resulting in the amputation of his leg. The long hospitalisation which followed isolated him from the conspirators in the abortive Stauffenberg plot, and thereby undoubtedly saved his life.

Perhaps in 1952 we all exaggerated the Amt Blank episode and its importance to Germany, nervous as it was. But its influence on the future Bundeswehr is still detectable today, Certainly Axel's significance, what he stood for and had been prepared to die for, was lost on none of us. Through his resignation in that year, I got to know Axel and his enchanting Irish wife, Camilla, and they were to become two of my dearest friends. At first it was not an easy friendship. For a start, immensely tall, his physical presence was rather overpowering. Perhaps, though only six years his junior, I was too young. Also I could not help viewing him with considerable awe. Memories of the war were still close at hand for both of us, and I was to him as a junior captain to a most distinguished battalion commander, who had (before he had turned his mind to killing Hitler) been awarded the Ritterkreuz, the equivalent of our VC, in the Battle of France in 1940. In this one greatly damaged torso, and possibly even more damaged psyche, resided the whole agonising story of the courageous, but failed, plots to rid the world of Adolf Hitler.

He used to remark, 'Our only fault is to have survived.' It was a sentiment with which I could identify. Through surviving he had somehow crossed over a frontier into a land of which the rest of us could have no conception. It was, I often used to fear in later years, this unbridgeable frontier, this inevitable setting of himself aside from the rest of the world, which never ceased to mark, and torment, Axel. But, of all the people I got to know during those years in Germany, he was by far and away the most imposing. Though also possessed of a marvellous black sense of humour – what Germans call *Galgenhumor* – he was, quite simply, the bravest man I would ever meet.

8

FOOTSOLDIERS IN THE COLD WAR

Berlin, March 1953. On the death of Stalin, Soviet officers rapidly quit BRIXMIS party.
The host, Brigadier Claude Dewhurst, is facing the camera on right.

My first year as 'Our Own Correspondent' in Bonn ended with a minor boob which, on a paper that so prided itself (then) on meticulous accuracy, could have led to the sack – had it not been for the glimmer of a reputation that Krupp had bestowed on me. One of my more tedious jobs was to relay the snow reports from Garmisch-Partenkirchen to the sports page for skiers. Unfortunately, arithmetic never being my forte, I managed to render metres as feet by mistake. It was a particularly lean year for snow in the alps, and the German resorts were gratified to find a flow of *Telegraph* readers streaming in their direction. There followed angry letters to the paper and an 'inquest on the Fifth Floor'. A painful correction had to be printed.

But all this receded into the background in the new year of 1953 when the British High Commissioner, Sir Ivone Kirkpatrick, ordered the arrest of seven neo-Nazis in their beds, including their leader a Dr Werner Naumann. Then aged forty-three, Naumann in his early thirties had been second-in-command to Dr Goebbels in Hitler's Propaganda Ministry; two of those seized at the same time included former Gauleiters of Hamburg and of Salzburg. The charges alleged that they were plotting to seize power in the Federal Republic. The arrests hit the West German press with the force of a blockbuster: it was shocking that there might be a serious plot afoot to bring back a Nazi regime, and it was no less shocking that the Occupation Authorities could effect the arrests without liaising with the German civil authorities – and at a time when the Federal Republic was already so far down the road to independence. Why couldn't the British trust the Germans to do the job? Adenauer, informed only hours before the arrests, was deeply affronted. A man of brilliant intellect, Kirkpatrick had strong personal motives for his action; he had been a

young diplomat in Berlin before the war and had witnessed the Nazi
seizure of power. Never again!

It was soon apparent that Kirkpatrick had seriously overreacted. Three
months later, on April Fool's Day, the seven neo-Nazis were handed over
to the German authorities (at the 'request' of Dr Adenauer). They were
subsequently released for lack of evidence and then disappeared from
view. Piqued by their unsympathetic rapportage, Kirkpatrick never spoke
to the British press corps again. It was a thoroughly silly episode, but
spoke volumes for the deep distrust that still existed eight years after the
war had ended.

The Naumann affair brought scurrying over from London the portentous Sefton Delmer, or 'Tom' as his acolytes and friends liked to call
him. Lord Beaverbrook's ace reporter, Delmer epitomised the crusading
knight that was the logo of the then *Daily Express*. Of Australian extraction, he was a massive and menacing figure who spoke perfect German,
from his days when he had been Reggie Steed's boss in pre-war Nazi
Germany, and had a wide range of sources and informants. He ate suspected neo-Nazis for breakfast, and at his approach Kirkpatrick's amiable
press officers on the British High Commission ran for cover. Steed, too,
became all of a twitter and – to display his present rise to grandeur on a
par with his former boss – put on a special soirée for him. In advance he
filled me in on Delmer's sadistic technique of casting a spider's web
around his victims, as I'd been told when I first arrived in Berlin. It
consisted of studying what their particular fears and weaknesses were,
and then exploiting them. Typical, Steed recalled, was the story of a
German-Jewish refugee who had fled to France. The reason for his flight,
Delmer discovered, was that in the early 1930s, the man had been involved
in a fracas in the Saar with Nazi stormtroopers. Injured, he woke up in
hospital with a battered Nazi in the next-door bed. Pulling out the
chamber-pot from under the bed, he brained him, and then fled. Delmer
took the refugee on a tour of eastern France, then – as they approached
the German frontier – declared, 'Why, the Saar's just over there. Let's go
and have a look!', putting his foot down on the accelerator. So convincing
was Delmer's performance that the refugee began to gibber with fear, and
for the rest of the time Delmer had the wretched man totally in his power.

The Steed soirée was a painful affair. As Steed's ultra-refeened wife

Evelyn rushed around with canapés and sweet Rhine wine, it began with an opera recital by Reggie. He then produced his favourite reminiscence of how, when Delmer had reported news of the Reichstag Fire – one of the seminal events in Hitler's rise to power – the sub-ed at the *Express* had blandly enquired, 'How many fire engines?' At that point the guest of honour, announced that he had some film of pre-war Germany he wanted to show. When the film began he said, 'Now here's a keen young reporter about to make his name ...' On the screen there appeared a thoroughly harassed Reggie, in a grubby mac, endeavouring to get interviews with Jews who were lined up to receive their yellow stars – and being repeatedly brushed away. There were suppressed giggles; Steed was deeply, and indelibly, humiliated. So much for 'my friend Tom'. It was a dreadfully embarrassing episode and made me want to put a sympathetic arm out to Reggie – but, if anything, it only made him more prickly. Meanwhile Delmer, with dexterity and resourcefulness, set about producing a series of front-page scoops exposing Nazis under every bed in the Federal Republic. The wake he left made relations of the resident British journalists with both Bonn government officials and the British High Commission that much tougher. Many years later after the fall of the Berlin Wall, the discovery of some fairly convincing documents from the files of the East German secret police, the Stasi, suggested that Delmer may himself have been on the payroll of the KGB. I was not surprised.

At the beginning of March 1953, came the world-shaking news that the Red Dictator, Stalin, had died. Who was going to be his heir? Clearly a power struggle was being waged inside the Kremlin. There was the greatest apprehension, universally, as to what would happen next. Then in Germany an RAF Lincoln bomber, with its seven crew members, was shot down over the interzonal frontier, followed by a US fighter shot down by MiGs 15 miles inside the American Zone. Cold fear gripped us in Bonn. Did these acts mean that the unknown new men in the Kremlin were about to make the long-feared lunge into West Germany, a repeat of Korea? We now know that the Soviets never had any such intention, but we had no means of learning that at the time. One good reason for more and better espionage?

A few weeks later news came out of a major Soviet spy-ring smashed in West Germany. Accompanied with much excited trumpeting, the CIA then produced before the Bonn press corps the first major Russian army deserter to defect since Stalin's death. A fairly rough specimen, he did not immediately seize the imagination. Asked why he had defected, he claimed 'political oppression'. When questioned further, he revealed that he had been 'oppressed' by his sergeant-major; one day he could bear it no longer, so he picked up his 'oppressor' and sat him on the red-hot stove in the barrack-room. 'From that moment on the political oppression became intolerable, and I had to flee.' Collapse of one red-faced CIA handler.

But this was, supremely, the age of the Great Game, of espionage and dirty tricks, and the pitch it was played on was Germany. It was the age of joint MI6 and CIA tunnels tapping Soviet cables under East Berlin, of KGB kidnappings in West Berlin, of huge MI6 apparatuses in Wahnerheide, near Cologne, of even larger CIA set-ups in Frankfurt and Munich, and of all those intelligence agencies spying and eavesdropping on each other. Prominent in Berlin was my old boss from Cairo days, Claude Dewhurst, eccentric as ever, but now a brigadier in charge of the highly secret BRIXMIS mission to the Soviets, which had the overt – and unique – role of spying on events inside East Germany. Claude now had an XK Jaguar, so fast that it enabled him to pop up at any point in East Germany before the ponderous Soviet communications system could get out a warning.

Progressively, from the death of Stalin, it became apparent that trouble was brewing in East Germany. In June 1953 a demonstration by angry workers on the great empty bombed site of Potsdamer Platz, adjacent to West Berlin, flared up into a major riot, the first since Stalin had clamped down his Iron Curtain on Eastern Europe. Communist Party offices were sacked, and government files hurled out of windows. For a few brief intoxicating hours it looked as if freedom was going to come back to East Berlin. The riots spread across the Soviet Zone. Then, with brutal force the Red Army intervened – just as it would do in the Budapest uprising of three years later. T-34 tanks charged recklessly on to the Potsdamer Platz, grinding young Berliners under their tracks. The most memorable image of that day, *der Aufstand*, as it came to be known, was of a defiant young Berliner hurling a rock at a Russian tank. In the *Telegraph* office in Bonn, meanwhile, it transpired, against all probability, that Reggie now had a hot girlfriend in Berlin, which provided extra incentive for his presence there. I was delighted, because I could be my own master in Bonn.

In September Dr Adenauer's Germany went to the polls in its first federal election since 1949. Its results were awaited across the world as a test of just how reliable democracy was in West Germany. At the one extreme, there were the neo-Nazis – Werner Naumann and his friends having just been released – and on the other side, the Communists. On election day I drove up to the Ruhr with my good friend on the *Daily Mail*, Ken Ames DFC, to look at the voters. As usual on these occasions, he had with him a little black logbook of his wartime bombing operations: '... Gelsenkirchen, 10 October '43;/Bochum, 10 June '43 – and again on 15 July, and [12] August' and so it ran on. The debris and the gutted houses were still there. Ken became quiet. He never travelled without his old logbook, to remind him which of these pulverised cities he had bombed. There was hardly a city in the Ruhr that didn't bear Ken's mark. Twice, three times over. It never ceased to haunt him; years later he committed suicide. There were many, like him, who – questioning just how little the indiscriminate mayhem did to hasten the end of the war – ended as psychological wrecks from deeply troubled consciences.

Turnout figures in the elections revealed that an extraordinary 86.2 per cent of the electorate had voted. The Communists and neo-Nazis had won respectively only 2.2 and 1.1 per cent of the votes, which meant that neither would have deputies in the new Bundestag, while the Social Democrats had polled little more than half as many votes as Adenauer's ruling Christian Democrat Party. Led by the uncharismatic Erich Ollenhauer, the Socialists were knocked sideways. The results constituted a huge personal triumph for the old Chancellor, whose calm consistency had won the day, but also they were a reassuring tribute to the solidity now of democracy in the free half of Germany.

With the 1953 election victory, the return of Dr Adenauer and his plumply owl-like Minister of Economics, Professor Ludwig Erhard, marked a new take-off in the German *Wirtschaftswunder*. As I wrote warningly in the *Telegraph*, again and again, those indolent British exporters were going to have to look seriously to their laurels; all across the world the West Germans were moving in, grabbing traditional British markets – as often as not by default. It was all very depressing. At home

German was booming as never before. I had two yardsticks: one was my garage man, Herr Rademacher. When I arrived in Bonn, he and his mistress were a fairly forlorn, scraggy couple operating out of a lean-to of corrugated iron, but they inflated visibly with prosperity. Soon Herr R could barely get under the Healey to carry out repairs, then he was moving into larger and plusher surroundings. When I returned to Bonn some years later, Rademacher IG had become one of the leading industrial companies in Bonn. Then there was the Bundestag itself: during the summer recess a side-wall had to come down so that the chamber could be expanded laterally in order to allow seats to be each 5 centimetres wider to encompass the new girth of deputies. What clearer statement of prosperity could there be than that? Meanwhile I too cashed in, now that my German was stronger, taking a part-time job translating for a Bonn government propaganda journal called *Deutsche Korrespondenz*, earning the handsome sum of 1 Deutschmark a hundred words. It was incredibly boring, but it provided a welcome supplement to the £18 a week the *Telegraph* paid. And I was about to get married, and would need every penny I could scrape up.

I had fallen seriously in love. Renira had just returned from Malta, where her father had been the Admiral Commanding, and was living in London. We met on a blind date while I was on leave from Bonn. Aged twenty-three, she had been running her father's house in Malta with greatest efficiency and charm. A honey blonde with a Botticelli mouth, she had an utterly sweet nature, and I was instantly smitten. After six years, the spooks of Jo were laid to rest. We conducted a lightning court-ship, almost by remote control. We got engaged, in Germany, at the 9th Lancers' Coronation Ball of May 1953, and were married that November. Leaving Frau Holland and Godesbergerstrasse, I found a simple but agreeable one-bedroom flat at 38 Rüdigerstrasse, at Mehlem on the west bank of the Rhine. It looked out over the Lorelei's romantic Drachenfels (Dragon's Rock). We got to know by name all the Rhine barges as they chugged upstream, beating against the powerful current, before they came flying back down from Lake Constance a week or so later. That winter of 1953–4, as the leaders of the world wrestled frostily and point-lessly at the Four-Power Conference in Berlin over the future of Germany, for the first time in goodness knows how many centuries the mighty river froze over. The foolhardy could skate, or slide, from one side to the other. Then the ice broke up, with a sound like the creaking of a thousand wooden ships.

It provided an exciting backdrop to what was happening in Berlin; and it was a pleasant and happy place to start on a marriage. Our landlord was a genial Rhinelander, Herr Stottrop from Bottrop, who had a habit of proudly hanging from the front door foxes he'd shot up in the Eifel hills. On the floors above were two German families constantly at (verbal) war with each other – petty-bourgeois Catholic Rhinelanders and Lutheran *Flüchtlinge* (refugees) who had lost everything in East Prussia. It said, I thought, a lot about the much vaunted unity of the Germans. It was not an easy time for Renira, speaking no German and having no friends in the area. Nevertheless, she managed superbly and uncomplainingly. We had a good life there, on Rüdigerstrasse. For the best part of a year it was a happy, fulfilling time. Even Reggie seemed unusually benevolent.

Before Renira and I had met, as a palliative to the heavy boredom of Bonn, I took to making weekend excursions to Brussels, some three hours' drive away. There my old friend from SIME days, Michael Wrigley, was doing his first stint as an undercover MI6 officer within the British Embassy. There were some interesting people in the Embassy, among them the distinguished war hero George Jellicoe and – as air attaché – Group Captain Peter Townsend, in a state of exile from England, nursing a patently broken heart from his love affair with Princess Margaret. On one of my trips to Brussels, I found Maurice, now a senior figure in SIS, quite unexpectedly there too. It was obviously not just a pleasure trip. He took me aside and asked me if I would do something for the 'Office'. It involved helping out in the Great Game from Bonn, working to counter Soviet penetration, but also in effect spying against the West German government. In essence, we had three valuable assets (as they would be called today) in Bonn, but their handler was retiring to emigrate to Canada. Would I take them over? Why couldn't someone from the huge MI6 apparatus at Wahneheide do it, I asked? Because, explained Maurice, under secret provisions of the Bonn Treaties 'we're no longer allowed to spy on our new allies – through operatives inside Germany. But, as a journalist, you have perfect cover, and you'll be run from Brussels.' What about the *Telegraph*? I demurred. 'We'll talk to Pawley [the foreign editor]. He was a wartime colonel in intelligence with SHAEF, and he's very cooperative. There won't be a problem.'

I wasn't entirely happy about spying on the West Germans. Weren't they about to be our allies? But Maurice was persuasive. Less than eight years after the war, we still didn't really know which way the cookie was going to crumble; all this Delmer stuff, maybe it wasn't all smoke without fire? Then, what was the actual state of Soviet penetration in Bonn? Once Adenauer got full independence, it would be very difficult to know what was really going on inside the Bonn government, so it was considered prudent to keep existing networks warm, not to wind them up. Also there were one or two eminent Bonn politicians whose connections with the Soviets were widely suspect. I thought about it, and agreed, somewhat reluctantly. However, with the hot war only so recently ended and the Cold War raging, wasn't it almost a loyal Briton's duty? I set forth with names and instructions, plus a superbly crafted suitcase with a false bottom (fabricated by the Mayfair Trunk Company, in a little shop off Shepherd Market, which had supplied SOE agents with similar wares during the war) for carrying documents and cash back and forth across the frontier into Belgium or Holland. Two of my agents, X and Z, were to receive money; Y did it for love of Britain. All were to have generous Christmas presents, carefully selected – for the *Ehefrauen*, the wives. My three assets were very different personalities. All worked in sensitive posts in various Bonn ministries. X was an intellectual in the *Auswärtigesamt* (or Foreign Office), and both he and his wife knew they were suffering from terminal tuberculosis. Y was partly in it because he really enjoyed the game, and affected to love everything about Britain. With quite excessive concern about security, he would insist on meeting in a pub up in the Siebengebirge hills (of which the Drachenfels was one), far from Bonn; he would carry a copy of the London *Times* in his overcoat pocket: if it was upside down that would mean he wanted to abort the meeting.

Z was an unattractive personality, the least likeable of my three, and I did not entirely trust him. But he was capable of producing the most valuable material. Perhaps because he had the most to lose, he was also the most nervous. We would meet deep in a wood, our cars nose to tail, engines running, and he would almost fling his harvest of documents into my car, then take off. On one occasion, a forester drove into view. Z was thrown into a major panic, reversed and nearly bogged down his Mercedes, then roared off at top speed. I thought I had lost him for good. Then, some days later, he made contact again, to claim that what had most freaked him out was not fear of being exposed as a spy but – under the prevailing draconian federal laws – finding himself accused of meeting an Englishman in a wood for unnatural purposes. As in all intelligence work, there was always close at hand the burlesque and the ridiculous.

What bound all three agents together was a flattering belief in the power for good of British secret intelligence. Had we been caught, they would not have been shot, as would have been their certain fate on the other side of the interzonal frontier, under the tender mercies of Markus Wolf's Stasi. But they would have been dismissed and sentenced to substantial terms of imprisonment. I, on the other hand – if caught with the Mayfair Trunk Company's incriminating suitcase – could have escaped, pleading journalistic activities, though I would probably have been expelled from Germany, disavowed by the FO certainly and sacked by my newspaper, in mock indignation, my journalistic career wrecked. So was it worth while? Much of the secret information that came my way was helpfully complementary to what I was able to garner as a journalist. In essence, it offered confirmation that the Federal Republic, though it was certainly no unqualified friend of Britain's, was not up to dirty tricks, was not being run, or undermined, by dangerous old Nazis with evil intentions – however nasty a past some of its servants had had. More difficult to assess was the level of Soviet penetration. In sieve-like Bonn, Willy Brandt was to discover this when he became chancellor – and it was to destroy him. I left Bonn with little doubt that one of his top associates, Herbert Wehner, who was high on my watch list, had never left the Communist payroll. History suggests that I passed on the right warnings there.

It was certainly not easy to keep separate the two strands of my life – as the cynical Philby managed, for so long and so skilfully. And was I performing any kind of useful service? Maurice seemed to be appreciative. As with so much intelligence information, one could only hope that the whole was worth more than the visible sum of the parts. When I discussed the matter with my friend and colleague Tim Garton Ash of

St Antony's College, Oxford, following publication of his brilliant memoir about the Stasi's watch on his activities, *The File*,* he was visibly shocked, deeming the whole thing unethical, if not immoral. But we were different generations: to us veterans the Second World War had been very close, and the Cold War was a very real thing – around us every day, its implications highly alarming. There was, I suppose, too, an element of Buchanesque patriotism, in those days. I doubt I convinced Tim. Over the years since, however, episodes like the Cuban Missiles Crisis in 1962 and the intelligence mess and duplicity that saw the launch of the Iraq War in 2003, regularly persuade me of how good secret intelligence can save lives, if not avert wars. Better safe than sorry. Washington may yet have to learn this.

My humble contribution to the Cold War was, however, but child's play compared with two big episodes of the Great Game that burst on us in 1954. In Frankfurt, in the American Zone, there existed a shadowy group of Ukrainian émigré dissidents, the NTS – backed, like many such bodies, by the CIA for its work in running agents into the Soviet Ukraine. Evidently its operations had attracted the attention of the KGB, which had come to regard it as the most effective and dangerous of the irredentist groups being operated inside the Soviet Union. One day there was a knock on the door of the apartment in Frankfurt where lived the chief of the NTS, a Dr George Okolovich. He opened it on Captain Nikolai Khokhlov, a senior operative of SMERSH, charged with special killings and sabotage abroad. With him were two members of the East German Stasi, both veterans of the Spanish Civil War. Khokhlov himself was distinguished for having assassinated a German gauleiter during the wartime occupation of Russia.

The three men came equipped with a formidable and ingenious armoury of weapons that would have challenged the imagination of James Bond's Q. These included a miniature pistol firing bullets tipped with cyanide, which made less noise than 'the snap of a finger'. Even more diabolical was a packet of Lucky Strike, in which each cigarette had been converted into a tiny pistol firing a poisoned dart containing enough cyanide to kill ten people. When Okolovich opened the door, Khokhlov

---

* First published by Random House in 1997.

announced that his mission was to assassinate him and then slip away back to East Germany. But he then threw his arms around the neck of the man he had been sent to kill, declaring – amid floods of very Russian tears – that he could not do it. His wife, back in Moscow, had dissuaded him; if he returned with Okolovich's blood on his hands she would not have him back. It is a scene straight out of Dostoyevsky. Okolovich then led Khokhlov and his team to the CIA, who took them under their wing.

A few weeks later, Dr Truschnovich, head of the NTS in Berlin, was kidnapped and disappeared into oblivion. The MVD was trying to find out what had happened to Khokhlov and his mission. So the CIA decided to produce Khokhlov at a major press conference at the US High Commission in Bonn, together with his armoury of weapons. It was a breathtaking production; nothing like it had been seen since the war. At first, recalling the CIA's debacle over the 'politically oppressed' defector of the previous year, there was considerable doubt. Up on the platform the two men, slight bespectacled figures, the experienced killer and his intended victim, looked for all the world like a pair of harmless bank clerks. As we hacks rushed back to our offices (the story made full front-page coverage on the *DT*), the real human drama began. It was an outstanding CIA coup in the Great Game (very privately I couldn't help recording the contrast between the stakes here and my rendezvous with German civil servants in dank woods). But Khokhlov had apparently been persuaded by his CIA handlers that they could get his wife, somehow, out of Moscow. When he attempted to ring her apartment, there was no reply. The line had been cut. She was never seen again – sentenced to five years in the Gulag in punishment for her husband's defection. The wretched Khokhlov, feeling utterly betrayed, had a breakdown. Okolovich, wisely, went into hiding. Khokhlov died of a heart attack in 2007, safely in California, but constantly in fear of assassination.

It was an extraordinary episode. As the *Telegraph* leader declared at the time, if Conan Doyle had written such a story 'he would have been asked to limit his imagination to the plausible'. The episode had its fallout. The lines from London began to hum as the foreign manager of the *Sunday Times*, one Ian Fleming, badgered his man in Bonn, my chum Antony Terry, for every detail of Khokhlov; James Bond was born a short while later. Subsequently firebrands within the Office, like my old friend

Wrigley, pressed for similar operations to get rid of traitors like Philby
and Blake whose double-agent activities had caused the deaths of so many
brave British agents. But, so Wrigley later remarked (as reported in a
surprisingly forthright *Times* obituary), 'The trouble was the buggers had
no balls!'

Three months later the opposition, the East Germans, rallied to
pull off what seemed like the most outstanding coup in Germany's
Great Game to date. The head of Dr Adenauer's MI5 (the Bundes-
verfassungsschutz), Dr Otto John, defected one night to East Berlin.
Before I had set off from London for Bonn in 1952, I had asked Maurice
for any useful contacts. He replied with the name of Otto John, adding,
'He's a good friend of ours.' I looked at him questioningly, but he averted
my gaze. During the war John had worked for Lufthansa in Berlin and
been involved with the anti-Hitler plotters. He was not highly regarded
by other members of the Resistance because he had taken few risks; also
he gave evidence at the War Crimes Trials against Field Marshal von
Manstein, who was still venerated by most of the former Wehrmacht.

So, returning to Germany after the war, John had few friends. He was
a lonely, unhappy man. When I first went to see him in his office in
Cologne I found a youngish, good-looking, typical north German, blond
with clear blue eyes. He had a wife, but I felt he could easily be bisexual.
I wondered if he had been – or possibly still was – on Maurice's payroll
He was very friendly and forthcoming. We met several times, and I came
to like him, but felt there was some deep inner disharmony that I couldn't
quite fathom. Clearly he was not easy in his relationship with Adenauer,
and spoke glumly about the presence in his entourage of certain unre-
constructed former Nazis, notably the all-powerful State Secretary, Hans
Globke, whose name had been linked with preparation of Hitler's infamous race laws. Globke wanted John out, and soon. Otto felt that there
were moves afoot to have his organisation sidelined in favour of the
more aggressive intelligence agency run by a wartime Abwehr operative,
General Gehlen, in Frankfurt, now under powerful US influence.

We didn't see each other for a month or two; in view of the work I was
undertaking for Maurice, I felt I had to be particularly circumspect in my
dealings with Otto. Then, on the evening of 20 July 1954, the bombshell
burst. That day was the tenth anniversary of the Stauffenberg bomb plot

against Hitler. In Berlin, there had been particularly sombre com-
memorations marking it and the whole epic of the Resistance against
Hitler. Otto John attended. He was observed to be in a very emotional
state during the ceremonies at the Bendlerstrasse. That evening he never
returned to the hotel where he and his wife were staying. A few days later
he came over the air, his voice strained and hesitant, broadcasting from
East Berlin. He declared that he had taken this fateful step because he saw
Germany 'in danger of being divided forever', and went on: 'in the Federal
Republic ... I have been slandered continuously in my office by Nazis
who are reappearing everywhere in political and public life'.

It was a cataclysmic statement, aimed in particular at Adenauer's State
Secretary Dr Globke, who had been John's only direct access to the Chancellor as well as his enemy. Bonn reeled in confusion, in a state not far
from hysteria. From Berlin Reggie Steed wrote in a front-page column
that the Stasi, 'by getting hold of Dr John, has brought off by far its
greatest coup since the war'. It seemed hardly an exaggeration. I wrote at
the time that I was left feeling 'morally winded'. Otto was someone whom
I had liked personally, and respected for the courageous role he had played
against Hitler. Also he was a very big piece on the chessboard of the Great
Game. Was there something horribly wrong with the Western ethos? His
defection filled us with self-doubt.

Slowly the waters closed over Otto John's head. Eighteen months later, an
extraordinary thing happened. Having been spirited all the way to southern
Russia, suddenly one day in December 1955, John ambled back into West
Berlin, aided by a Danish journalist. It was unprecedented. No important
defector, or abductee, had ever done this before. *Twice through the Lines* he
labelled his subsequent memoir.* He handed himself over to the federal
authorities, wanting to clear his name and have his story heard. He was
promptly arrested, treated with harshness as a common traitor, and sentenced to four years' imprisonment. Both at the trial and in his book he
insisted that he had been drugged and abducted by the KGB, but there
remained – and still remain – many unanswered questions.

I still think of it as the greatest mystery of my life. At various intervals
after his release from prison, Otto would ring me up and reappear in

* Published by Macmillan in 1972.

England, beseeching me to help reopen his case. Bitterly he denied that he had ever handed any secrets to the Stasi or the KGB; he had never committed treason. He was a broken, tragic man, obviously with a drink problem, but desperate to clear his name before he died in 1997. His story was just too improbable. I suspect that, under intolerable mental pressures, he simply broke down after that gruelling tenth-anniversary commemoration of the 20 July bomb plot. However you read his story, perhaps he was its last, tragic victim.

As far as the British in Germany were concerned, they also had their problems – minor as well as major – of moving from occupiers to allies. Montgomery's orders forbidding 'fratting' with Germans had not survived long after the war. But in spring 1953 I had an outraged call from a friend in a Cavalry regiment. He complained that the pompous Commanding Officer of a Guards Regiment had specifically requested them not to bring German guests to the ball that was to follow a local horse show. There was deep outrage, and distress – many of the officers had German girlfriends, while half the horses entered were German, as were several of the prizes presented. Rashly I wrote a piece of two or three sentences in 'Peterborough', the *Telegraph* gossip column, little realising the storm it would stir up. Early next morning I was telephoned by the new High Commissioner, Sir Derek Hoyer-Millar, the agreeably laid-back foreign official who had just succeeded the peppery Kirkpatrick. He had been woken up by an irate Prime Minister, Winston Churchill, no less, who had read Peterborough with his morning tea and was outraged. In the best Churchillian style, he bellowed down the telephone, 'This is dishgrasheful, they are our allies... Germans will be invited to the ball.' The fat was truly in the fire. For several years I was ostracised by my fellow ex-Guardsmen, but I survived, and Germans were invited to the ball. Unfortunately, however, there were too many such examples of stupid prejudices that should have begun to dwindle a decade after the end of hostilities.

What was going on in Germany all around me continued to fascinate, but I was beginning to realise that I was in a dead-end in Bonn. Relations with Steed had progressively improved, especially under Renira's diplomatic touch. Yet still I remained his dogsbody, getting the secondary assignments, provoking jealous tirades if ever I seemed to usurp his role as bureau chief. And Renira became pregnant. There would be no room in sweet Rüdigerstrasse, and understandably Renira wanted the baby to be born in England. Over weekends and in my spare time, I started writing a book about contemporary Germany. Beginning with the extraordinary story of the House of Krupp, to my agreeable surprise it flowed easily. If it succeeded, I supposed it might furnish a ticket to get out of Bonn. I sent bits of it to a literary agent, Osyth Leeston of A. M. Heath. Osyth and her colleagues liked what they saw and sent me to a series of publishers. The first, the great house of Collins, had a snooty editor called Mark Bonham-Carter, who turned it down with the words, 'My dear fellow, the British are ostriches. They really don't want to know that the Germans still exist.' After several other rebuffs, Osyth finally found a small firm, Max Parrish, which accepted it. I returned to Bonn, elated. Renira was wonderfully supportive.

Then trouble started. I should have foreseen it. Steed hit the roof: 'How dare you? I'm bureau chief. If anyone should be writing a book, it should be me.'

'But you're not writing it!'

Of course, he was right. It was sheer cheek on my part. I should have asked his say-so in the first place – but then inevitably he would have refused and there would have been a row anyway. Steed rang up Pawley to complain. Noncommittal, anything for peace as always, Pawley's reply was, 'Well, can't stop him. As long as he doesn't neglect his *DT* work.' Steed ensured that there was no shortage of tasks; meanwhile he hardly spoke to me. It was a rough time, anyway: the French – after many months dithering – had just rejected the Bonn Treaties. Bonn was in an uproar, and we were once again leading the *Telegraph* with our rapportage. After a series of sessions up to the wee hours in the office, I had just gone to bed after midnight when the night-editor rang. He wanted to know what time the Rheingold Express would arrive in London – Lady Pamela Berry, the all-powerful daughter-in-law of the *DT*'s owner, had two au-pairs on it. I exploded: why couldn't she ring up enquiries at Victoria? My intemperate language was reported unfavourably on the Fifth Floor. Steed capitalised on the event, on top of other complaints. I found myself summoned to London. It was a court-martial. The option offered was to return, manifestly under a cloud, to that dread smoke-filled newsroom. In effect, it meant the sack. I resigned, and went back to Bonn to a pregnant wife, a half-completed book and no job.

There was worse to come. We packed up Rüdigerstrasse, sadly; we had been happy there. We said our goodbyes. I had to tell Maurice what had happened; my three assets were put on ice. It pained me having to hand back the Mayfair Trunks suitcase – such a brilliant piece of equipment. There was one last piece of admin. I remembered I had tucked away four $100 notes which I had bought (illegally) several years ago from an MI6 contact of Jimmy Brodie's. The US dollar was still an object of great value, going up as the pound went down, and I had been keeping these notes for a rainy day, for a future trip to the US. The day before leaving Germany I thought it might be safer to transfer them into American Express travellers' cheques, so I went up to the exchange bureau in the American High Commission and did just that.

I was packing up the car shortly afterwards when I heard the crunch of gravel outside the garage. I looked up and there were two pairs of long black-leather Stiefel boots, each with a German policeman inside, looking extremely menacing. For a moment I felt as an escapee from Colditz might have felt during the war. My immediate and greatest worry was that one of my secret assets had been caught, with all the serious complications that that would have involved. But no: the policemen were on the track of counterfeiters. Those four $100 notes were forgeries. Where had I obtained them? It sounded most unconvincing when I said, 'In a bar, in London, three or four years ago.' And I couldn't identify the source. What made it look blacker still was that similar notes, probably off the same forger's press, had recently surfaced elsewhere in Germany. It was a remarkable coincidence. Any moment they would start turning the house upside down, looking for the printing press. Fortunately, as an Allied journalist I was still nominally attached to the British High Commission. The chief of the press department, Michael Robb (to whom I'd only just said goodbye a few hours previously), was a tremendous help. He sent the Polizisten packing, but warned me that I would still have to explain myself to the British authorities on my return to England.

And that was how I left Germany – on hardly a more cheerful or encouraging note than when I had joined Reggie Steed in Berlin nearly three years previously. It was autumn 1954.

9
AUTHOR, AUTHOR

October 1958. Mid Canada Radar Line, Labrador. (AH, centre, with survival kit.)

> The journalist is the historian of the moment.
>
> Albert Camus

So there I was, cast up on a frost-bitten coastline. Returning to it in the autumn of 1954, England seemed scarcely more friendly than it had at Liverpool during that air-raid just eleven years previously, and my morale was no higher. It wasn't till I had left the *Telegraph* that I fully understood what an outstandingly honest newspaper it was, justly famed for its accuracy and fairness and unbeaten in terms of foreign rapportage, with a rare, clear-cut distinction between rapportage and comment. Today's 'hacking' skullduggery would have been unheard of. It was also a good ship that was fun to be aboard. Sadly, when one left, like last week's news story, one was swiftly forgotten. I was to miss it, miss my friends and, not least, miss the buzz of being at the centre of world affairs as one was as a foreign correspondent. Every time I heard newsvendors shouting 'Paper!' I felt a pang.

Now I was jobless, with nowhere to live. Renira was cheerfully stalwart and supportive, amid all the adversities. We found and rented a two-bedroom flat off Sloane Avenue. Camilla was born that November of 1954 in a Dickensian nursing home so full of bugs that our Jewish gynaecologist would not allow any baby boys he brought into the world to be circumcised there. Against a ferocious barrage of wails in the next room (Camilla always could make herself heard) I set to finishing my book on Germany, at forced-march speed. One of our first visitors was a gentleman with highly polished black shoes from the Fraud Squad. He was deeply suspicious of my story: 'So you bought the dollars off an intelligence services employee, a friend of a friend, in a bar, you say? Where and when? What was his name?'

I couldn't provide a satisfactory answer to any of these questions, certainly couldn't mention the name of the MI6 operative, and I knew that the light-footed Brodie, even if I could track him down, would not be a helpful witness. Suddenly I was confronted with the grim realisation that, contrary to the usual principle in English law, if you are charged with the 'uttering of forged notes' the burden of proof rests with you. Things looked bad. After nearly an hour the detective put away his note book with the menacing words, 'You'll be hearing from us shortly.' I never did, but I wonder to this day if somewhere in Scotland Yard there lurks a black mark against my name. For years each time I entered the States I half expected to be turned back as a felon.

Early in 1955 *Back into Power: A Report on the New Germany* came out. At Max Parrish, my two editors Stephen England and Stephen Freud had done a good job; it sold at the handsome price of 18s 6d in hardback. A first encouragement came in an unexpected letter from Hugh Trevor-Roper, the notoriously crusty author of the classic *The Last Days of Hitler*: 'I hope you will not think me presumptuous if I write to tell you how good I think that your book *Back into Power* is. I have read it with such pleasure and such advantage to myself. I have written a review of it for the *Sunday Times*, but I cannot be sure they will print it; you know how chancy these things are …'

That Sunday I bought the papers and crept off, in terror, into Hyde Park to hide my embarrassment at the mauling I expected. To my astonishment, I found a great slab of a review in the *Observer* by Alan Bullock, already the established authority on Hitler: 'This is journalism at its best,' I read, 'in the tradition of the great foreign correspondents of the 1930s. Not pretending to be history, but retelling with all the liveliness of the born reporter, and without prejudice, as remarkable a story as any in the post-war decade.' And there, in the *Sunday Times*, was Trevor-Roper, regarded as one of the top experts on Germany: 'Here, and nowhere else, can one study the whole complex history of Germany, East and West, in the last ten years. He is wonderfully well informed in detail, judicious and accurate …'

In ensuing days I was even lauded by the mighty *Times* as 'a shrewd political analyst', while the *Financial Times* greeted 'one of the most important books on Germany during the post-war period'.

Yah-boo to Reggie Steed! I had made it. What reviews! Every door in Fleet Street and in publishing would now surely open, clamouring for me. But, no, it was not to be. There were no instant follow-ups, nor ideas, whether from newspaper, publisher or literary agent. Like the Yugoslav dancers, the book may have been a critical success, but it was certainly not a commercial one. Mark Bonham-Carter had been quite right. It never reprinted, but was published in the US, by Fred Praeger. And pride goeth before destruction. That October I received a letter from a solicitor that made my bones shake.

Lord Russell of Liverpool (a former Deputy Judge Advocate General, no less) was suing me for libel. It was my first and, touch wood, last encounter of this sort. Admittedly, in my book I had been as rude as I could be about the noble lord, condemning his short history of Nazi war crimes *Scourge of the Swastika*, published the previous year, as 'a crude catalogue of horrors'. My main objection, though I expressed strong reservations about prevailing German attitudes to war crimes, was that Russell's book was 'just the sort of thing which will definitely not amend the German outlook ... To the intelligent German, this book coming many years after the event, appeared solely as the mischievous work of a man with a personal grudge intended to weight the scales against German rearmament ...'

It was of course rash to attack in such virulent terms so distinguished a lawyer, much decorated in the Great War. His son, Jock Russell MC, was also a good friend of mine. Lord Russell was furious and sued, not for my attack on his book but picking out the one sentence which I in my youthful naivety had thought perfectly innocuous. I had described him in a footnote as having been 'forced' to resign as DJAG by the Lord Chancellor when his book came out. He was able to claim that, no, he had been offered a choice. Nervously I consulted a QC, the famous Helenus 'Buster' Milmo, who – bolstered by an intense personal dislike of Russell – urged me to fight. He declared, 'If you win, you'll sell a lot of copies of your book. If you lose, ditto. But I think you'll win. At worst it'll cost you a couple of hundred quid.'

A couple of hundred quid – those were the days! I agreed. But, alas, Max Parrish chose to settle. Buster was furious. 'Bloody craven publishers' was the mildest of his imprecations. But Max Parrish was a small firm, with modest funds, so I had to capitulate. Russell was decent enough to demand no damages, but I was made to publish a grovelling apology – on the back page of the newspaper which had just sacked me. Buster's last words to me were: 'In future, dear boy, try very hard never to libel a lawyer – they always know better!' It was lapidary advice, which I have never ignored.

Meanwhile I was trying my hand at freelance journalism. Apart from selling a few articles on Germany to prestigious but ill-paying magazines like the redoubtable Lady Rhondda's *Time and Tide*, there were just no takers for all that hard-won expertise I had mustered working out in Bonn. A faintly acid letter came back from Colin Coote at the *Daily Telegraph*: 'Dear Mr Horne . . . I do not think that it would be possible to commission any articles from you which would not tread on the toes of our staff correspondent . . .' Then, one day, Cyrus Brooks, the head of A. M. Heath, came up with a proposition: with my knowledge of German, how about translating a German bestseller by Robert Jungk about the development of the atom bomb? The result was a translation, much slaved over, which was by no means alpha-plus, given that half the technical terms in nuclear physics were unfamiliar to me even in English. Jungk, fluent in English, and something of a control-freak, read every comma of it, howled in pain and pressed Gollancz (the British publisher) to reject it.

The bitter pill was that Cyrus Brooks took Jungk's and Gollancz's side, not mine. Here, for the first time, I came up against one of the fundamental problems of author–literary-agent relations. An agent is retained by the author, yet when the chips are down a powerful publisher, to whom the agent may be keen to sell a score or more authors, has to be a more important client to mollify than a hapless author, especially if he is a beginner. Here was a second lesson on the literary front that I would not forget in a hurry. I've often wondered since whether it wouldn't be a fairer deal for publishers to share agents' fees with the poor author.

I hunted around for a book to write. Still with a penchant for anything that flew, the tragic story of the de Havilland Comet grabbed my imagination. The Comet was the first jet airliner to fly and was quite simply the most beautiful commercial plane ever produced. Years ahead of its time, and way in advance of its US competitors, with all their resources, it seemed an extraordinary testimony to British know-how at a time when the country's industry was just emerging from the doldrums of Socialism. Patriotic to the hilt, the *Telegraph* in Bonn (and it had become my

particular baby) unreservedly supported the British aircraft manufacturers in the competition, against the Americans, to sell the first generation of jet airliners to the newly recreated *Lufthansa*. Renira and I flew
in it on our honeymoon to Morocco in November 1953. Compared with
the noisy, bumpy, low-flying piston planes of the past, it was breathtakingly quiet, floating silently at 30,000 feet. It flew as fast as today's jets,
and you could balance a threepenny bit on edge on the table inside it. It
was a magical experience. But we were providentially lucky. Like Icarus,
this beautiful bird flew too high. Maybe the Comet was just too advanced,
beyond the capabilities of the industry. A few months later (January '54)
there was one appalling disaster, followed only weeks later by another,
when two Comets disintegrated high over the sea. Contrary to *Telegraph*
usage, planes could explode in mid-air. Among those on board the first
was a distinguished historian of the Second World War, Chester Wilmot.

As both planes blew up close to the time of Khokhlov's terrifying
revelations of SMERSH activities, several of us Bonn correspondents
(myself included) strongly suspected sabotage. From the start, however,
de Havilland rejected that thesis, suspecting a fault in the design of this
revolutionary plane. In an amazing operation never before attempted,
they pieced together fragments dredged up from the Mediterranean
seabed, over 70 per cent of the plane's fragments. Then they 'tested to
destruction' a new model. After months while all Comets were grounded,
they announced the conclusion – metal fatigue around the windows had
caused the two planes to burst like paper bags. It was an honourable
admission; but it was to prove, in effect, the end of any serious challenge
by a British manufacturer to US dominance in world aviation. 'Comet
had pushed "the state-of-the-art" beyond its limits,' declared aviation
critics years later. According to John 'Cats Eyes'* Cunningham, de Havilland's top test pilot, representatives from American manufacturers such
as Boeing and Douglas admitted privately, 'that if it hadn't been for our
problems, it would have happened to one of them'.

Within the year, however, a restructured test model called Comet 3 took
to the skies, and de Havillands invited me to accompany – and chat up –

* He had gained the nickname, as well as DSO and two bars, DFC and bar, during the war for
his numerous victories over the Luftwaffe as a night-fighter pilot.

a top-level delegation of Germans, potential customers from the future Lufthansa, on a special demonstration flight at Hatfield. Apart from the two crashes, the odds against British enterprise had already lengthened with a sub-plot traceable back to the Second World War. One of the key figures in the new Lufthansa was a certain Dr Kreipe. He had a brother who was a general commanding the German Occupation in Crete. In a brilliant *coup de main* pulled off by the legendary Paddy Leigh Fermor, the general was kidnapped and whisked off into POW camp for the rest of the war. Treated with utmost courtesy by Paddy, the general became an Anglophile; not so his brother, who regarded the kidnap as a family humiliation and made known his disfavour for any deal in aircraft with the wicked British. When I related this tale to Paddy many years later, his normally ebullient exprerssion turned glum. I changed the subject.

Nevertheless, on the day of the demonstration, de Havilland (from an airfield that had produced the Mosquito, one of the deadliest British planes that smashed up the Luftwaffe) rolled out the red carpet for the Germans, plying the distinguished guests with the best (German) wines. Then we took off, on a loop down to Bristol and back, with former Group Captain Cunningham at the controls. With twenty kills to his credit he had shot down more German bombers than any other single RAF night fighter. There must have been several old Luftwaffe hands aboard that day, and I wondered what their thoughts might have been as they filed past 'Cats Eyes' standing by the cockpit. It was Cunningham's day, however it was certainly not de Havillands'. Predictably, it was a magical flight, smooth as cream; but – as soon as the beautiful bird reached altitude, equally predictably the Rhenish wine had its effect. The distinguished guests trooped to the rear of the plane – but de Havillands had omitted to put a loo on this particular test model. In its place there was a great coil of rope (what on earth was it doing there?) As we touched down again, instead of pausing to thank the smiling, expectant hosts for the fabulous day they had enjoyed, there was a stampede of embarrassed, bladder-bursting, cross Germans heading for the nearest comfort station.

A few weeks later Lufthansa bought Boeings. I do not believe the inspirational British aircraft industry ever recovered from the failure to market the beautiful Comet. That small episode at Hatfield has remained with me ever since, as a sadly emblematic occasion; the memory of that coiled rope in the back of the Comet returns whenever I read stories of the awful, arrogant, Little England gaffes of British banks or commercial enterprises. It still makes one want to weep. Meanwhile, for me, though I always thought it an exciting, and brave, story deserving of a book, that day at Hatfield put an end to *my* Comet project. For whatever reason, de Havilland were uncooperative; they simply did not want to discuss the Comet in the media, or in any way open their files. A few years later the firm, for all its pioneering renown, was bought out, and passed into history.

I too, was beginning to feel 'time's wingèd chariot' running me down. I had now passed thirty. To underline the message, my father-in-law, a bluff admiral, remarked to me forthrightly, 'Well, what are you going to do now? After all, you're over the hill now, let's face it!' Like many of his contemporaries, he never felt that writing, let alone journalism, was quite a proper profession. But 'over the top' at thirty! A certain desperation moved in, and I now tried a totally different professional tack and embarked on a six-month apprenticeship at the august house of Robert Fleming, investment bankers of Crosby Square in the City of London. I was truly sorry when my stretch in the analysts' back-room was up. Perhaps I could have stayed on and made a career at Flemings – in which case I would now be a very rich man, but maybe not necessarily a satisfied one. Instead, in April 1956, Renira and I set off on a mammoth, four-month trip across the US. It wasn't easy on £100 each, which is what the annual travel allowance had been increased to, and we were painfully aware of cadging off hospitable Americans.

By plane, train and Greyhound bus we travelled the country 'from sea to shining sea' and saw a lot in the middle. We started with my oldest friend, Bill Buckley. Bill and Pat were living in the lovely house they were to inhabit all their married lives together, at Wallack's Point in Stamford on Long Island Sound. Graduating from Yale a few years earlier Bill had caused an uproar across the country (and made his name) with his first book, *God and Man at Yale*, which attacked what he construed to be the misguided Liberalism he found there. The political and philosophical health of the nation continued to concern him; he had espoused McCarthy, but later distanced himself from the senator's excesses; and the previous year he had started his own magazine, *National Review*. It was a courageous venture, as Bill declared memorably at the time, to 'stand athwart history, yelling stop.'

While we were in New York, through publisher Fred Praeger I appeared on radio on the *Barry Gray Show*, compered by an anchorman who knew little of the world outside the Bronx. To twelve million New Yorkers, I was introduced as 'a South African back from fighting the Mau-Mau in Rhodesia. He has just published a book on Germany, called *The Return of the Nazis* ...' Afterwards Praeger's lieutenant, a gloomy man called Morton Puner, suddenly leaned towards me and said, almost apologetically, 'Tell me, do you find New York terribly Jewish?' Puner's question, coming from a very Jewish New Yorker, was certainly a conversation-stopper. I recalled that time in Boston, nine years previously when I had been so disagreeably assailed about Britain's role in Palestine. Since then my own thinking and emotions about Palestine, the Middle East and the Jews had swung some 180 degrees, and most, not just many, of my closest friends were Jewish.

The next stop was Washington, DC, where I met my old friend from Bonn days, Axel von dem Bussche, now working in the West German Embassy. Once an unsmiling figure of high seriousness, Axel was now possessed with a new carefree gaiety. Since he had been living in the US, 'For the first time I feel free from all that has happened in Europe over the past twenty years. Can you understand what I mean?' I thought I could. It was, after all, the boom-time of the American Dream. Under Ike nothing could go wrong: an attitude which was reflected in an observation I had picked up on the on American's fundamental sense of impatience: 'We don't like standing in line. We won't wait to be served in shops either while the girl rearranges the stock or tidies her hair.'

From Washington we spent a week exploring the Civil War battlefields of Virginia, which rekindled the spark of fascination with military history first ignited by my star wartime teacher at Millbrook, New York, Henry Callard. Then, via Detroit and the Grand Canyon, we crossed to that sink of iniquity, Las Vegas, and on to Los Angeles – which we both hated – and then to San Francisco and the Napa Valley, where the wine industry was in its infancy (and anyway no American drank wine in those days). We began to wend our way homewards, exhausted but inspirited, making a grand detour into Canada, at Vancouver in the west and New Brunswick in the east where I had last been as an aspirant airman in 1943. We spent our final days in Martha's Vineyard. There, on South Beach, I lay listening to the prolonged hiss of the water drawing back down the sand into the green maw of the next wave – dreaming of a world that seemed to have not a single care to upset its reveries.

But we returned to a Britain in deep turmoil, and grievously divided, over Suez. Britain and France had invaded Egypt in response to President Nasser's nationalisation of the Canal. At the time fearful of the implications of Nasser opening the door of the Middle East to the Soviets – to 'Soviet penetration', the enemy I had been trying to fight on the banks of that very Canal just ten years previously – I supported intervention. Unfortunately, the United States was deeply hostile. Like the rest of us, I did not know the truth about the shameful act of secret collusion between Britain, France and Israel. In the years since 1956, I have lectured and participated in seminars countless times on both sides of the Atlantic on Suez, and it still puzzles and appals me how Britain and America, those two wartime, and natural, allies, could have got so out of sync with each other as they did over Suez.

In distress at the way Britain and the US had fallen out, and in some anger at the promiscuous knocking of America in which many British commentators were indulging, I sat down to write *The Land is Bright*.* It was a book I had not intended to write before our travels. When it came out, in 1958, the reviews were as discouraging as those of *Back into Power* had been encouraging. Since Suez many reviewers had become hostile to the very notion of America. One said maybe the Land was a bit too Bright, the author's smile a bit 'too fixed'. Even my former *Telegraph* colleague, Perry Worsthorne, gave the book a splash of acid: 'I am not quite sure what mood will make me turn' to it, he wrote. It sold miserably. But I was not unproud of it. It said some of the things about America I wanted to say, and it helped correct some of the vicious sniping by British writers – from J. B. Priestley down – that was painfully rife at the time.

At this point two new factors had entered my life. The first was a new

* I borrowed the title from Arthur Hugh Clough's lines made famous by Churchill in the Second World War:

> In front the sun climbs slow, how slowly,
> But westward, look, the land is bright.

literary agent. Ever since the Jungk debacle, A. M. Heath and I had felt mutually disaffected. It was the beginning of a pilgrim's progress which led me in and out of the doors of several agents. Ursula Winant, the progenitor of Winant, Towers, was my second. Ulie, as she was known, was the sister-in-law of my old friend Phil Goodhart MP. Never married, she lived for her authors, who were her surrogate children. On her recommendation I left Max Parrish and went to an upmarket publisher, Macmillan and Co. This move, the second of the two new developments in my life, was to prove a career-changing one.

When I arrived in 1958 the venerable House of Macmillan resided in St Martin's Street, in a stately Victorian building now long since disappeared. It was exactly how one imagined an old-fashioned London publisher should be. You ascended a grand staircase of pickled walnut, hung with the vaguely threatening, certainly awe-inspiring portraits of the hirsute Scottish ancestors and eminent past authors such as Kipling, Hardy, Wells and Yeats. With 'Mr Harold' away being prime minister, over the house at that time presided his elder brother, 'Mr Dan'. A desiccated figure who hobbled about on feet that appeared to have no toes attached, Mr Dan had the appearance of an ascetic, yet was reputed to be quite a lad, with a sprinkling of illegits here and there. Did I ever imagine, as I climbed the portentous staircase, that in two decades' time I would be invited to write the official biography of the former Primer Minister, Chairman Harold? Certainly not.

My contact was H. R. 'Rache' Lovat Dickson. Rache, as I was invited to call him after a while, was a tall, spare Canadian, inordinately good-looking (which he possibly knew), a Torontonian very much of the old school, deep-dyed in the bonds of loyalty to the Old Country but highly sensitive to any hint of condescension from its denizens. My idea, that I should write a book about Canada – a compendium of history, geography, politics and culture – appealed greatly to him. I was commissioned, with an advance of £250, reinforced with a further $500 (Canadian) from John Gray, head of the sister firm in Toronto. I went home wildly excited.

In July 1958, from a parking lot in Boston, Massachusetts, Renira and I picked up an ancient monster Chrysler belonging to Bill Buckley's Canadian brother-in-law. The rental fee was to drive it for him to his home in Vancouver. After taking it by ferry to Nova Scotia, at the eastern end of Canada, Renira and I motored from there steadily westwards until we hit Vancouver, 8,000 miles later. Renira then flew home, and I took off into the High North to spend two months exploring. All in all, I covered nearly 20,000 miles, by car, scooter, plane, helicopter, bus, train, gas-truck, snowmobile, boat and horse, but no dog-sled. I reckoned I had seen more of Canada than most Canadians ever would.

'Why did you visit Canada, Mr Behan?' the famously alcoholic Irishman was once asked, to which he is supposed to have replied, 'I saw a picture at the airport saying "Drink Canada Dry" – so I thought I would come here and try.'

'Acá nada' (There's nothing here), the first Spanish explorer to reach these immense tracts of emptiness is alleged to have complained. Rather worryingly, Canadians repeatedly said to me, 'Don't you find we're an awfully dull country?' During a bibulous evening, in Ottawa, the provincial capital of the world's second largest country, Nick Monsarrat, author of the classic *The Cruel Sea*, confessed that he had gone there in pursuit of silence – but he wasn't bored. When you burst out of the forests east of Winnipeg into the prairies, which leave you feeling as exposed and naked as a gopher for the next thousand miles, it isn't exactly dull, just overwhelming. In Jasper National Park, I had my duffel bag (it reeked, enticingly, of trout that we'd illegally poached that day) wrested off me by a 500-pound black bear. I lost that argument, but it wasn't exactly a dull one.

Back in Europe, laden with material, I sat down and wrote *Canada and the Canadians* with a great deal of affection and respect. It was not expected to be a bestseller, and it wasn't. Rache Lovat Dickson, the loyal Canadian, thought it 'splendid'. We now entered on to a first-name basis; there was no more 'Dear Mr Horne'. Reviewers were polite, apart from W. H. Smith who, in their trade magazine, selected the jacket as one of the year's worst. I was wounded; it came from one of the best photographs I ever took, of two slope-shouldered grain elevators standing in the empty prairie with the Rockies in the background. As a whole, the British probably thought the book as dull as the Canadians deemed themselves to be.

On my way home via New York, I spent a night with Bill Buckley at Wallack's Point. We discussed our work in hand; I had *Canada and the Canadians*, he had *Up from Liberalism*. Neither was destined to be our sparkiest book, but one evening after vast consumption of wine one of us said to the other, 'Why don't we rent a chalet in Switzerland, write together in the mornings and ski in the afternoons?' And so we did. Having solemnly promised the Buckleys – notably the rather demanding Pat – that I would find a wonderful chalet for mid-January 1959, there were some anxious moments when I got back to London. It was already November, and there were no offers. Then one day I was invited round to see some photographs by a quiet smallish man with a moustache. He was Major Pat Reid MC, the first POW to escape from Colditz and make it safely to Switzerland, in 1942. The chalet he was showing us, the Bärgsunne, had been an MI6 property during the war, where escaped POWs were hidden out of reach of Swiss internment until they could be found flights via Portugal back to freedom. While waiting in Switzerland himself, Pat had met an affluent American lady, a Miss Cabot no less. They got married, and after the war returned to Switzerland and bought the Bärgsunne. It was a romantic story, but so was the chalet itself. At 4,000 feet, it sat high up above the little hamlet of Saanenmöser, in the Bernese Oberland, which in itself (as well as boasting the prettiest railway station in Switzerland) marked the watershed between Zweisimmen and the Gstaad valley. In 1959 Gstaad was still a simple, exquisitely pretty ski-town. We couldn't resist.

The view from the Bärgsunne was unforgettable. To the right the early-morning light bathed the jagged peaks of the Gummflüh and Rüblihorn, on the left in the far distance the evening light landed on the mighty Jungfrau and sinister Eiger.

The first time we stayed there was a magical time. We had our children with us, Camilla and Za (who had been born in 1957), and there was seven-year old Christo Buckley, the future novelist. We learned to ski properly, thereby launching into a passionate love-affair for both Bill and myself that would last until our respective knees gave out. From those days I can still remember the unremitting joy of the diamonds in the air after a really cold night, the crinkly feeling in the nostrils, the seductive hiss of skis on virgin powder snow. After a month of almost unblemished sunshine, the Buckleys left us. Enamoured of the life, the Family Horne booked the chalet for a further month, then another – and so on until we had spent nearly two-thirds of a year there. At the end of summer, we drove in our tiny Morris Minor Traveller down to Dalmatia, to renew my old acquaintances of eight years previously. (The Healey had long since been sold to meet the costs of joblessness.)

After writing, and dabbling around, in such a diversity of books, the course that led me to the next one, *The Price of Glory*, was a complex one.

While completing *Canada* at the Bärgsunne, I began to read voraciously about the First World War. Born seven years after that conflict ended, I grew up in an atmosphere deeply affected, indeed infected, by it. I could never forget the solemnity of Armistice Day, the procession through our house of widows or unmarried women who had all lost their men; and the men with staring eyes still suffering from shell-shock. The story of that terrible war repelled and fascinated me. In the course of 1959, two books particularly impressed me. One, just published, *In Flanders Fields*, by an American, Leon Wolff, told of the agony of the British Army in the vain Passchendaele offensives of 1917 and the incompetence of the directing generals; a second was *Gallipoli* (published in 1956) by Alan Moorehead, who had made his name as one of the top war correspondents of the Second World War. He knew what war was really like, and I still rate his book one of the best battle histories I have ever read. I had met Moorehead briefly in London the previous year, and he gave me a useful piece of advice. As one of many diffuse projects, I was toying with the idea of writing a history of the Middle East – a subject that continued to engage me. Moorehead said, 'Don't. Too diffuse – that would be like using a shotgun. Use a rifle instead, pick one event, one battle – like Gallipoli – and then spread out from there.'

I constantly endeavour to remember that good advice, though not always successfully. After reading Wolff and Moorehead, I sat down to fill in the whole background of 1914–18 with Basil Liddell Hart's *The Real War*. At a *Spectator* party shortly after publication of *Back into Power* I had been introduced to this tall, strange-looking figure who resembled a maribou stork. The 'Guru of Medmenham', as he later became known, had followed up by writing me a charming, congratulatory note about *Back into Power*, and there began a copious correspondence, and a friendship that lasted the rest of his life. *The Real War* impressed me deeply, with its incisive understanding of the issues and personalities involved.

Living in that perpetual haven of peace and prosperity, Switzerland, with the Korean War nearly ten years behind us, I began thinking back to my time as foreign correspondent in Bonn. In the ruins all around me was the all too tangible legacy of the last bout of that Franco-German rivalry which had lain at the roots of the First World War. Now that relations between France and Germany had already taken a sudden miraculous turn for the better, I began to think of a book which traced the lethal course of these relations over the preceding century. Given that war has a curious way of crystallising the more peaceful trends of history, my notion (much influenced by the writings of Liddell Hart) was to weave the book around three great Franco-German battles. I chose Sedan 1870, Verdun 1916, and Sedan – again – 1940. All had taken place in that one blood-sodden corner of eastern France, just a few miles apart. Each had been decisive in wider historical contexts than its own war.

Another new friendship, in fact two, profoundly influenced my ultimate choice – and, indeed, more than that. Francis Huré was a talented diplomat in the French Embassy in London. His wife, Jacqueline, a passionate Corsican with flashing black eyes, was descended from 'Madame Mère', the mother of Napoleon. In her twenties, she had been caught working for the Resistance in Paris and had been sent to the concentration camp at Ravensbrück. Unlike most, she survived, and was liberated in 1945 by a young French diplomat who had been despatched by de Gaulle to Moscow, to move westwards with the Red Army, rescuing French deportees in the camps as they went – Francis Huré. In the late 1950s, the Hurés' life in London was, refreshingly, rather more bohemian than diplomatic. They lived and loved life to the utmost; at 1 Neville Terrace, they ran one of the most lively salons in contemporary London. At one such lunch, I vividly remember sitting opposite the Duchess of Argyll, who halfway through the meal turned to Frau von Braun, wife of the German Minister, and said quite openly, 'Siggy is so attractive. Would you mind if I went to bed with him?' I don't recall Frau von Braun's response, but the Duchess went to bed with Siggy anyway, thereby launching the scandal in which Braun was ultimately nominated, among ninety other candidates, as co-respondent in the famous Argyll divorce case.*

---

* The ardent Sigismund von Braun was brother to Werner, the V-2 designer, whose rocketry in the US was currently encountering technical problems. A German joke going the rounds at the time ran: 'What is the difference between the two von Braun brothers?' Answer: 'The one cannot get up, the other cannot get down.'

Through the windows opened by the Hurés began the preoccupation with France and French history that was to dominate the next three to four decades of my writing life. They took great interest in my projected study of Franco-German conflict, but urged me to concentrate on Verdun. There, Francis insisted, 'you can find the key to everything that's happened to France'. I came to realise that this was no exaggeration, and, appropriately, I dedicated *The Price of Glory* to Francis and Jacqueline.

The following year we returned to the Bärgsunne, and in the spring of 1960 I drove out there via Verdun, accompanied by Venetia Pollock. Venetia, sister-in-law of my old SIME comrade-in-arms Michael Wrigley, had been a friend since Cambridge days. She was currently working as a reader for the publishers Secker and Warburg, but for the next twenty-five years would be a kind of special editorial adviser to me. Her letters, copious and handwritten, often fiercely critical, were classics of their kind. She was invariably right, and I listened to her – most of the time. On a preliminary reconnaissance of the unforgettably grim battlefields of Verdun, she was seized by the place almost as much as I was, and would continue to be on many subsequent revisits.

Between the Battle of the Marne in 1914 and Ludendorff's last-gasp assault in March 1918, the attack on Verdun on 21 February 1916 was the only time the Germans would assume the offensive on the Western Front. It had supposedly a limited objective: not to capture Verdun, but to 'bleed white' the French Army by forcing it to fight for this linchpin of its defences, this pride of France, the strongest fortress on earth, the Gibraltar-cum-Singapore of the Great War. Caught horribly unprepared, having denuded the forts of most of their guns, the French Army would suffer more than 400,000 casualties; the attacking Germans, supported by an unprecedented weight of artillery on a front only 15 miles wide, were to lose almost as many.

In the ten months that it lasted, the Battle of Verdun was to gain its sombre repute as the worst battle in history. A German miscalculation of enormous proportions, it would end in one of the most glorious victories in all France's history, yet its unbearable cost would lead her down the road to defeat a generation later. Britain, endeavouring to relieve the pressure on Verdun, attacked prematurely on the Somme that July; her new armies on that first terrible day alone would suffer 60,000 casualties. What was peculiar to Verdun was the concentration of artillery fire over an area not much larger than New York's Central Park. The majority of those who died never saw the enemy. For the benefit of the historian, another unique feature where it differed from the amorphous character of the fighting on the British sector of the Somme, or round Pas-schendaele, was that much of the action centred round massive forts, like Douaumont and Vaux, which accorded the battle an historical backbone that enabled one to follow its course with some clarity.

Throughout 1960 I made repeated pilgrimages to Verdun, exploring every inch of the battlefields. On one occasion I was accompanied by a friend serving in a British cavalry regiment, Major Christopher Diggle, who studied the topography with a professional eye. In the woods the sinister, cratered terrain were covered with wild lilies-of-the-valley. We made a good friend of the French army chaplain at the gruesome Ossuaire, which housed the bones of hundreds of thousands of unknown soldiers, and I would go with Commandant Homant on his walks around the battlefield looking for remains rootled up by the wild boar. Seldom would we return without a tibia or a jawbone, or the holed steel helmet of a long-forgotten German soldier. Once out by myself, I got horribly lost amid the young forestry belts that had been planted to cover the poisonous shell-fields, where nothing else would grow – and where, poignantly, no birds sang. Panic gripped me; I ran and ran. Though I have never seen a ghost in my life, I felt I was being pursued by an army of them. I stumbled back to my car in a state of total exhaustion and shock.

In Paris, at the Services Historiques de l'Armée located out at the grim Château de Vincennes, where Napoleon had the poor young Duc d'Enghien executed, I was helped by a genial French brigadier general, de Cossé-Brissac. He would take me into the room of 'sleeping flags', colours of defunct regiments, with tears in his eyes, tears of the memory of what 'la gloire', so often gained, lost and betrayed, had meant to his generation of Second World War French soldiers. De Cossé-Brissac presented me with a complete set of the French official history of the First World War, which filled the whole of the back of my Morris Traveller, the volumes' weight keeping it firmly on the snowy roads between Switzerland and the

UK. He set me up at a small reading room, the BDIC,* at 5 Rue Auguste Vacquerie, just behind the Etoile. There I worked day after day on published *récits* of the battle, living in a modest hotel nearby.

At the German archives in Freiburg they were equally helpful. Then, on one of my trips out to Paris, in July 1960, Verdun nearly claimed yet one more body. I had yet another car smash, the cause never resolved, and I ended up in a clinic in Le Touquet. Finally I had all my material and settled down to writing, in a rotating summer-house (to which my children took great pleasure giving a powerful push from time to time) at our cottage in West Sussex. No other book moved me as much in the writing as *The Price of Glory* did, as I recounted the suffering, the superhuman sacrifices, the tragic heroism, the folly and the waste of it all. There were times when I wept at the typewriter.

By April 1961 I was able to send a synopsis and a sample chapter to Macmillans. Rache was enthusiastic; he was sure it was 'going to be a first-class book'. So too was Venetia. Basil Liddell Hart, whom I had approached for guidance, was outstandingly supportive, remarking when I sent him a full draft that 'As a contribution to history it more than fulfilled my expectations.' 'Brilliantly written,' wrote Field Marshal Montgomery in a jacket puff; 'almost like a historical novel – except that it is true.' The reviews were heartening too. A. J. P. Taylor said, 'He has a splendid gift for depicting individuals from generals down to fighting men ...'

American reviewers liked it too. Leon Wolff in the *New York Times* generously rated it 'a masterpiece'. But I was not altogether lucky in my adopted country. The book came out amid a New York press strike; the review in one distinguished journal simply read '*The Price of Glory* is $5.95.' Nor did I fare much better with my next book, *The Fall of Paris*. Reaching the top of the short list for the Book-of-the-Month Club, which assured vast sales, it was pipped to the post at the last minute by Louis Auchincloss's stunning novel, *The Rector of Justin*.

Nevertheless, many doors now opened. *The Price of Glory* was translated in more than a dozen countries, from Finland to Israel, and notably in France. Penguin put it into paperback, and – going into many editions – has kept it there for nearly fifty years. Hollywood offered an option but

* The Bibliothèque de Documentation Internationale Contemporaine.

never exercised it, perhaps on realisation of how many extras would be required. Old warriors wrote to me, one or two in anger, meetings were arranged, and many fascinating discussions followed. From tranquil Oxford there came two letters from an unknown don, John Bayley (he was the husband of Iris Murdoch). In the second he wrote, in a tight academic hand: 'You may remember I wrote you a fan letter about *The Price of Glory*. I can now happily (if complacently) disclose that I was able to do more than just admire it, as I am on the Hawthornden Prize Committee and I put your book up ... we all agreed to give it the prize.' The Hawthornden Prize! With it came a lunch at the Ritz and a cheque for £100, but it was the oldest and most prestigious literary prize there was at that time. Awarded for 'a work of imaginative literature', hitherto it had been won almost exclusively for poetry and fiction. Siegfried Sassoon, Evelyn Waugh, Robert Graves, Graham Greene had won it, so had Ted Hughes for poetry. I was in noble company, and felt proud to the point of folly.

The ghosts continue to linger at Verdun, as I discovered on many subsequent trips to lecture there. Nearly a century later, the birds may have finally come back, but the casualties never let up. As late as 1975, three young Germans were wounded by an exploding 1916 shell. This, however, was as nothing compared to what it did, spiritually and morally, to the 1940 generation of Frenchmen, as I would try to show in a later book (*To Lose a Battle*). I was deeply struck by a remark made by a Frenchman, Jean Dutourd – infuriated by the failure of that 1940 generation of his countrymen – in his 1957 book *The Taxis of the Marne*: 'War is less costly than servitude ... the choice is always between Verdun and Dachau.' I quoted that many times. When (in spring 2002, on the eve of the second Iraq war) I last produced it before a group of twenty-four US generals on the glacis of Douaumont, the leader – General (four star) Montgomery C. Meigs, then commanding the US Army in Europe, reacted indignantly. 'No, no, no,' he cried. 'There has to be another way. Verdun was no way to fight a war.' He was, of course, dead right. It was as a simple narrative historian that I was writing *The Price of Glory*. I was not a Liddell Hart. I could see clearly that Verdun was no way to fight the First World War, but was it for me to come up with an alternative, an 'indirect approach', such as Basil had urged over so many years in the inter-war period? I am certain of one thing: though the Verduns of the Second World War were fought out of sight on the Eastern Front, no Western nation today could fight as did the French defenders in 1916. As Second-Lieutenant Raymond Jubert declared, before he was killed on that murderous field: 'They will not be able to make us do it again another day ...'

10

FRANCO-GERMAN CONFLICTS

Clockwise from left: Francis and Jaqueline Huré; Jany ('Pocahontas') Minvielle and Pat Buckley in Gstaad; Venetia Pollock on her last holiday abroad.

By way of R&R after publication of *The Price of Glory*, Renira and I set off on holiday to Turkey, to stay with Francis and Jacqueline Huré. Francis was now Minister, number two in the French Embassy. Typically they refused to live in the grand official residence in Istanbul; instead they were living in an old wooden stable building which belonged to the Embassy up the Bosphorus at Tarabya. The hooting and tooting of the small craft that passed incessantly by reminded me of that unforgettable first sight in summer 1947. After breakfast we would jump off the quay into the cool waters of the Bosphorus, and drift along with the 5-knot current coming out of the Black Sea, to climb out on the quay half a mile further down. In the evenings, all dressed up, black tie and all, Francis would roar us across in his rubber bombard dinghy to dine, covered in spray, at some exquisite wooden *yali* across the water.

After a couple of weeks, Francis and Jacqueline were intending to set off to drive round the Mediterranean, to end up at their holiday home in Corsica's Cap Corse. Would we join them? The first segment of the journey, from Istanbul across the Greek isthmus, via Salonika, was the part the Communist guerrillas had denied to Brodie and me six years previously. Eagerly we said 'yes'. It was to prove a most memorable trip. Francis had his own agenda: to canvass various colleagues in their Mediterranean holiday homes to change post so that he and Jacqueline could leave Istanbul, which he considered a dead end. It was in vain, nevertheless, a few years later, Francis was to re-emerge as de Gaulle's Ambassador to Golda Meir in Israel in the wake of the 'Six-Day War.'

Though much recuperated by our trip, writing *The Price of Glory* had left me feeling mentally wrung out. Often, at night, Verdun would revisit me. Nonetheless, bolstered by the Hurés' enthusiasm, I started right away on the next project. Although Verdun had come to occupy the full screen, sticking to my original project I sensed I would now be drawn back to the Franco-Prussian War of 1870–1, launched by Emperor Louis-Napoleon against Bismarck's Prussia. It was to become in effect the first panel of a triptych. Originally the focus was to be the 1870 Battle of Sedan. It soon dawned upon me, however, that by the time Louis-Napoleon reached Sedan at the head of his battered armies, the French never had a chance, the issue having been decided, militarily, elsewhere. All that actually happened at Sedan was the ultimate humiliation of the regime, abdication of its head and collapse of the Second Empire. It was in Paris, whose brave citizens refused to capitulate, determined to resist protracted and brutal siege by the Prussians and their allies from other German states, that the supreme drama took place. At Paris France had a chance, admittedly a slim one, if not of actually winning the war against Bismarck, then at least of gaining less harsh terms in the peace that followed. However, what was lost at Paris, by France, in 1871, was more than just a battle. Victory against the French encouraged the German states to unite and create the German Empire – a development fateful for the future of the entire world. In Louis XIV's haughty Versailles, in the room dedicated 'à toutes les Gloires de la France'. Germany's unification was followed by the seizure of Alsace-Lorraine and laid a train of powder leading directly to 1914 and Verdun, and, ultimately, to Hitler and the defeat of 1940. Take away Paris 1870–1, and there would have been no First and Second World Wars.

Writing about the Siege of Paris then confronted me with a further problem. How should I separate it from the infinitely more horrible civil war that followed, when the workers rose up after the Germans' departure and created their own Commune, or city council, and were besieged by (French) government forces? The two Sieges could not be treated in isolation from each other. The moving-staircase clanked forward once again, and I found myself confronted by the Commune of Paris as the more portentous of the two events. Without the lessons and legends derived from the failed Commune, there might well have been no successful Bolshevik Revolution in 1917, and its influence behind another French disaster – that of 1940 – was to become increasingly clear. In historical terms, I came to see the two Sieges conjointly as proving to be one of the seminal events of the ensuing century, and not just for France.

I plunged into the story with zest, starting work in 1962, finishing in February 1965 and publishing that October. *The Fall of Paris: The Siege and the Commune 1870–71* was to prove one of the most pleasurable books I ever wrote. True, there was suffering, there was tragedy, but it was not so unrelieved as 1916, and was leavened by colour and humour. The ingredients were hard to beat. Setting the scene, I loved writing about the frivolity and extravagances of the Second Empire. So much of the published material came from Olympian hands; there were writers like Maupassant and Daudet, Flaubert and Gautier, Zola and Verlaine, Labouchère and Elihu Washburne, Thiers and Karl Marx, not to mention the ubiquitous Edmond Goncourt and that priapic old master of bombast, Victor Hugo. And then, perhaps first of all, there was the leading lady herself: Paris. Choosing weekends when the streets (in the 1960s) were empty, I got to know almost every inch of the city, including its least fashionable faubourgs, corners like Père Lachaise and Belleville. I learned a lot about that unique breed, the Parisian, from the crusty concierges (now mostly supplanted by impersonal press-buttons) to the *midinette* who steals your taxi with the sweetest of smiles.

A personal windfall enhanced my task. I advertised in various US and British journals, questing after unpublished sources. A most exciting surprise came from an elderly spinster, retired from running a sweetshop in Stockport in Lancashire. With great trust, Miss Edwina Child sent me the diaries and lovingly preserved letters of her father, Edwin Child, who – as a highly perceptive twenty-year-old – had not only witnessed both Sieges but had actually served in the Paris National Guard. Coming from a neutral the Child papers provided an incredibly rich vein of information.

Research in Paris, however, had its downside. The antiquated Bibliothèque Nationale in the IIe Arrondissement, where most of the published material resided, was a nightmare to work in. For economy and ease of access I stayed in crummy hotels in the quartier, the business section, empty and gloomy at night. I didn't have many Parisian friends. It was a lonely time until I discovered, or was discovered by, Walter Goetz. A Berlin Jew who had escaped from Berlin with his parents on the advent of Hitler, Walter was quintessentially cosmopolitan. He knew everybody in five different countries (his friend, Romain Gary, wrote in one of his books that 'everybody is linked by Walter Goetz'; and so it was). Blessed with a multiplicity of artistic talents, he had achieved considerable success as a landscape painter, but chucked it, feeling that he would never be good enough. He switched to newspaper cartoons, where he gained fame for his invention of 'Colonel Up and Mr Down' in the *Daily Express*. During the war his knowledge of German and Germany brought him to work with Sefton Delmer's team on 'black propaganda' and 'Soldatensende' Calais. In the 1950s he moved to Paris, and later took up being an art dealer, where he developed an unerring eye for knowing at a glance whether a canvas was 'right' or 'wrong'. He seldom made a mistake and became partner with the legendary Dudley Tooth. Whenever Dudley wanted to impress a particularly grand client, he would say, 'I've just got my Paris office on the line.' Often the Paris office would be Walter in his bath, alone or accompanied, splashing away with his lethal deuxième empire metal telephone in hand. Given the vagaries of the Paris telephone system in those days, it seems a miracle that he was never electrocuted.

Walter had just gone through a particularly bad period when I met him, having lost two wives and (recently) a mistress. So we fell into each other's arms; I liked to think we were good for each other. Whenever alone in Paris, I would now stay in his creaky apartment on the 5th floor of 86 Rue du Bac. Walter was a generous and kindly host, and it was revitalising to come back after a gruelling day at the archives to hear his anecdotage, and hobnob with his friends like Pierre Daninos and Sam White, as well as the procession of glamorous girls that flowed through No. 86. Walter's friendship made work on *The Fall of Paris* infinitely more agreeable.

Among the *galère* at No. 86, I particularly remember Romain Gary, whose books came to intrigue me. Sometime in the 1960s Romain and his turbulent *ménage à trois* moved into the once quiet by-water of the Rue du Bac, just up the road from Walter. He and his relentless *vie de bohème* fascinated us both. One day Walter stalked Romain, catching him entering a jeweller where he was trying on a pair of earrings in front of a mirror. 'Ha, gotcha,' cried a triumphant Walter: 'Who are they for?' 'Why, for me of course, moi-même; I love earrings!' Though I only met him a few times Romain was something of a natural hero to me: the man of action who, for de Gaulle in the war, had won every available gong flying on 25 separate ops, losing crew after crew; the novelist who with *The Roots of Heaven* (that eloquent plea, so in advance of its time, to save the elephants of Africa) wrote one of the novels I would most like to have written; the autobiographer who, allowing generously for the fantasising, in *Promesse de l'Aube* produced one of the timeless classics of the second half of the twentieth century.

When I first met Romain, *chez* Walter, he had the look of the untamed Tartar from the steppes, coupled with Jewish blood. That was how he was, and how he appeared on the jacket of his famous novel *Lady L*. He was then married (unhappily) to the English writer, Lesley Blanch. The last time I saw him, only a few years later, then married (very unhappily) to Jean Seberg, he looked more like an ageing Einstein, weighed down with all the problems of relativity. I couldn't see the point of Seberg; apart from the Jeanne d'Arc gamine haircut she seemed to have little but the attributes of a Midwestern small-town girl, contributing nothing through dinner but a (pretty) pout. What was the mutual attraction, aside from pure, unadulterated sex? They divorced in 1970. Seberg, falling into the drugs and depression trap that opens before many a young American woman in Paris, inadequately equipped for life there, took an overdose in 1980. Romain, plagued with obsessions of waning virility, never got over it, and shot himself the following year.

Meanwhile in London, at Macmillans, there had been great changes. Robert Yeatman, the keen young editor, badly incapacited with polio, who had worked on *Canada* and part of *The Price of Glory*, had departed for W. H. Smith, and Rache had retired. In their place entered two new figures, Alan Maclean and Caroline Hobhouse. Alan's career in the Foreign Office had been blighted by the defection to Moscow (in 1951) of Donald, the elder brother he worshipped – indeed it had seared his soul and driven him to the bottle. He had been rescued, first by the publisher Billy Collins, then – by Harold Macmillan. Though it was not without the occasional hiccup, for the next two and a half decades I flourished, with the happiest of relationships, under the Maclean–Hobhouse team (in today's kaleidoscopic, ever changing world, most authors consider themselves fortunate if an editor sees them through one book).

The reviewers of *The Fall of Paris* were once again surprisingly benevolent. Richard Cobb, Oxford's leading historian of France, said it was 'likely to be the definitive account . . . his narrative is clear, gripping, fast moving and agreeable', while A. J. P. Taylor, though not uncritical, gave me one priceless pat on the back that I have prized ever since: 'Alistair Horne has one incomparable gift as a historian. He can narrate.' (An 'historian' the great AJP had called me! I have often reflected when it is that a 'writer of history' – as I designated myself – graduated to become a full-fledged 'historian'. Was it as a caterpillar emerging from the chrysalis a beauteous butterfly? Or was it like the inflationary semantics where 'rat-catchers' became 'rodent-officers' and tarts became 'models', 'escorts' and even 'starlets'? To me an historian was ever a learned figure at Oxbridge, who actually taught. In my own eyes I remained a 'writer of history'.) In the States my towering rival, Barbara Tuchman, delighted me by calling me an 'historian' too and adding, 'he is honest, meticulous, consistently interesting and readable, with an eye for the colorful and informative detail, the telling picture and dramatic episode . . .'

Though suffering, again, somewhat from battle fatigue, I had already started thinking about the third leg of the French trilogy, about Sedan 1940. Then several things intervened to sidetrack me, few of them entirely good. The first came in the form of an invitation from the BBC to participate, as scriptwriter and adviser, in its television series *The Great War*. I was principally to do Verdun, and America's entry into the war in 1917. Still in black and white (which certainly enhanced the sombre reality of the history it was depicting), and running to some twenty-five episodes which filled screens weekly for half a year, it came to be one of the milestones in the history of the Corporation. But, for most of the writers engaged, it was sheer hell. These included eminences like Correlli Barnett and John Terraine, the biographer of Haig. Disagreements on strategy and personalities were lively, sometimes volcanic. I recall one occasion in a taxi when 'Bill' Correlli Barnett, a feisty Irishman , actually climbed out in mid-journey enraged by the current debate. But it was nothing as compared with what went on inside the 'Beeb', run – it seemed – by an excess of virtuosos, frequently on the verge of breakdown and constantly changing their minds or stabbing each other (and ourselves) in the back. Over it all, as supreme arbitrator in case of unbreakable deadlock, was a deity called Grace Wyndham-Goldie, frequently invoked, but whom none of us (I think) ever met.

Such was the discord, many of us writers often doubted whether the series would ever be completed. Miraculously, it was; we hacks had a first showing on 22 May 1964. Even more miraculous was the historical integrity of the whole – deservedly, it won every award and universal praise. To mark the centenary of the Paris Commune in 1971, I made a further film with the BBC, one of the first of its full-length chronicles in colour, which became an illustrated book called *The Terrible Year.* That was a happier experience, partly because the work was done mostly on-site, away from the intrigues of Wood Lane, and I had an inspired woman producer, Julia Cave. The result was good. But, because that first major flirtation with television and its lords-and-masters had been so disagreeable, I tended to stay away from the small screen thereafter – which I have no double was a serious professional and strategic miscalculation.

About the same time as *The Great War* series, another blandishment came at me from Doubleday publishers in New York. Would I do a book for them in a new history series, on the British Empire at its peak at the time of Queen Victoria's Diamond Jubilee? The working title would be 'High Tide of Empire' and the advance a beguilingly generous $15,000. I liked the idea. I had become a bit jaded with French strife, fed up with the apparent inability of my New York publishers to do better saleswise, and felt that 1940 could wait a year or two. I signed a contract with Doubleday, and spent a year amassing material. Then disaster struck. One day in February 1965 I supped in London with an American agent, Julian Bach, who had been after me; when I asked him, casually, what brought him to London, he replied he had come to see one of his favourite authors, James Morris, who was writing a book, *Pax Britannica*, on the British Empire in its heyday – and for Doubleday, no less. The more Julian told me about it, the more I realised that James and I were writing if not exactly the same book, then something very similar. James, a wiry, energetic man, an ex-soldier and the *Times* correspondent who had courageously accompanied the Hillary Everest Expedition in 1953, was an old friend. I rang him. We met. He confirmed all my fears. The plot worsened; from correspondence James showed me it was plain that Doubleday, or at least one of their senior editors, had known about James's book, which was already under contract with Faber and Faber in London at the time they were signing me up, without communicating the knowledge to me.

It would have been foolish of me to take on a competitor as skilled as James, already well into his book. So I had wasted a whole year's work. I wrote to Doubleday, putting the whole saga to them in no uncertain terms; I was pulling out: under the circumstances, in no way did I feel it incumbent on me to refund their advance. The transatlantic correspondence became acrimonious. Doubleday threatened court action. James, bless his heart, immediately promised to back me at any such hearing and fly to New York at his own expense. The stress of fighting one of the world's richest and most powerful publishers was painfully distracting. Eventually a face-saving deal was patched up. But the whole episode had lasted nearly four years, a waste of many precious writing days. It was a singularly insalubrious affair and, to me, an illustration of just how small-minded a big publisher could be. James's *Pax Britannica* appeared to acclaim in 1968. Not unlike my own trilogy, his original book grew into three – the last, *Farewell the Trumpets*, not appearing until 1978.

I was glad to get back to work on Sedan 1940. I divided it into two parts: the essentially political run-up to war, from the Peace Treaty of Versailles in 1919 (roughly where *The Price of Glory* had left off); and the disastrous six weeks' military campaign of 1940. It was the story of a great nation, victorious in 1919, reduced to the lowest depths of defeat and degradation within a generation. I tried to describe at length the stages of the bitter inter-war period when France tore herself to pieces (unhelped by her allies) just as Hitler was building up the most powerful military machine of all time. I found two baleful influences at work within France, traceable back to my earlier books. The Commune of 1871 and the bitter mystique it left behind it helped me understand the divisions in France that brought the nation to the brink of civil war by the 1930s, just when the threat of the new Germany was at its highest. The Nazi–Soviet Non-Aggression Pact of August 1939 came as a last blow, leaving at least half of France opposed to the coming war. The second influence was the demoralising realisation that the heroism and bloodletting of that victory at Verdun had been in vain. I found it pervading all French anti-war literature of 1919–40, just as it pervaded strategic military thought in the form of the Maginot Line mentality.

These were the influences that destroyed the will of France to fight; in 1939 she entered the war with both hands tied. The notion that the French

Army was 'rotten' from top to bottom was deeply unfair to the brave *poilus* at the front. Some units were rotten, but the fact that the French suffered nearly 100,000 battle deaths alone during the six-week campaign surely indicates that many, like the heroic young cadets of Saint-Cyr, or in fierce engagements unrecorded by history, fought back with bitter courage. Not for the first or last time in history, the French Army could claim to have been *trahi* by the politicians back at base. Just as in 1870, the war was lost not on the border at Sedan, but back in Paris.

For research I made my way back to the Service Historique at spooky old Vincennes, where my old friend General de Cossé-Brissac had since retired, and to the library in the Rue Auguste Vacquerie. But, such was the speed with which the 1940 Blitzkrieg had moved, there was a telling paucity of French documentation. Regiments just didn't have time to record what was happening to them. What was rather shocking (and hardly made me popular in Gaullist France) was my discovery that de Gaulle had fudged his own seminal critique of modern warfare, *Vers l'armée de métier*: he had inserted after the war, *ex post facto*, a crucial passage on the importance of airpower.

In fact, I discovered much of my material across the Rhine, in Stuttgart's excellent Bibliothek für Zeitgeschichte and the Bundesarchiv. It was pleasant to be working in Germany again, among meticulous German scholars. There I had the extraordinary good fortune to chance on Rommel's original hand-annotated maps for his 7th Panzer Division. Back in Medmenham, Basil Liddell Hart (who had never seen them himself) was enthralled by the discovery. It was under his broad wings that I did much of my research, in his archive at States House, surrounded by his signed portraits of Wehrmacht generals who had taken on board his message about the future of armoured warfare when ours alas had not. Puffing away at his pipe, while his long-suffering wife Kathleen poured us cups of tea, he could be abrasive in his criticisms of one's views and writings, but his files and his memory were voluminous and priceless. He was outstandingly generous with his time.

Then, too, unlike my two previous books, there was a wealth of first-hand witnesses, men still in mid-life, such as Air Chief Marshal Sir Arthur 'Ugly' Barrett, who had commanded the RAF in France throughout the campaign, and my friend from Bonn days, Axel von dem Bussche, who had been a lieutenant in the vanguard of the attack on 10 May. In 1940, before he devoted himself to the elimination of Hitler, Axel saw that campaign as the battle against the traditional enemy, France, and revenge for the evils imposed by Versailles, almost as a holy crusade. It was a 'good war', and they fought it with a zest lacking on the other side. He recalled how in those hot May days, when they never saw a dead German, his footsore men had taken to wheeling their weapons along in commandeered prams. It all seemed 'like a jolly picnic'. Then, fighting his way down to the River Meuse, his arm raised in the act of lobbing a grenade, he saw 'a frightened Annamite face taking aim at close range'. The bullet removed his right thumb, and him from the campaign. The episode won him one of the top Wehrmacht decorations. Meanwhile in Paris Nancy Mitford brought me together with her faithless lover, Gaston Palewski, who had fought through the campaign in the French Air force. Waving his arms with Polish vigour, he expounded on how absurd it was that those stupid Germans should have won in 1940: 'After all, we had more tanks, and better tanks.' At that point Nancy, become somewhat bored with the conversation, interjected with blue-eyed innocence a priceless verdict: 'But wasn't the trouble that the poor darlings kept them in their garages?' Harsh, but could anyone think of a better one-liner on what went wrong in the Battle of France, at least on a military level?

Though in a far lower key, the time of writing what came to be called *To Lose a Battle** was also one of change for me. We moved house. Hitherto I had worked in a partitioned part of our drawing room in a small house behind Harrods, with three articulate children aboard and little privacy. For a while I sought a remedy to the working arrangements by renting a room in a nearby house at £4 per week. Then we bought a stately house in the Boltons, for what seemed a terrifying sum in those days, £37,500, and split it in two.

For the first time I had a palatial, sound-proof office all to myself. (Looking back on those far-off days, I cannot believe the relative affluence in which many of us lived!) As a researcher specifically helping read up on the Siege and the Commune I had Michael Wheeler-Booth, who later

---

* The title came from de Gaulle's majestic proclamation of 22 June 1940: 'France has lost a battle, but she has not lost the war.'

became clerk to the House of Lords and a knight. He was replaced for 1940 by Peter Bradley, a schoolmasterly figure of Pickwickian appearance and diligent precision.

Even more fundamental was a shift of publishers in the US. Both Ulie Winant and her New York co-agent, Monica McCall, had become increasingly disillusioned by the sales performance of St Martin's Press (a Macmillan subsidiary) on the previous two books. They urged me to move. There appeared to be many contenders who wanted to take me on, so I flew to the States to meet them. Two, Alan Williams of Viking and Ash Green of Knopf, who were to remain the old guard of American publishers, strangely enough were both to become my publishers in later years, but sadly not for this book. On Monica's recommendation, the field narrowed to two venerable and highly successful publishers in Boston, Houghton Mifflin and Little, Brown. There seemed little between them; it was a searingly hot day, unusual for Boston, so I settled for the firm which had air-conditioning, Little, Brown, on the simple assumption that this would indicate a go-ahead attitude to publishing. It was a terrible error. In the first instance, Little, Brown took too literally my desire to have an American edition tailor-made for the US market, and an eager young girl hot from college was set to work. With an excess of zeal she filled the Macmillan MS with red ink, altering commas to semi-colons and vice versa, and generally making such a mess that we had to fly her to London to take them all out again under Macmillan's supervision. Failing one target date after another, the whole editorial process was a nightmare.

Finally I lost the support of the senior editor, Harry Sions, who had first welcomed me aboard with egregious enthusiasm. It was partly my fault. In November 1968 I reviewed, less than favourably, a book called *The Arms of Krupp* by William Manchester, the biographer of John F. Kennedy. The Krupps were a thoroughly nasty lot, whose weaponry had cost so many Allied lives in two world wars, but – recalling my exposé back in 1952 which had boosted my career as a foreign correspondent – I felt needled that this 900-page book should be so packed with errors and so laced with old-style anti-Germanism. Originally headed 'A Load of Old Krupp' (the genteel *New York Times* toned it down), my review provoked some lively controversy, in which I was supported by the eminent Christopher Lehmann-Haupt in the *Daily Book Review*.

Unfortunately the book's editor was Harry Sions, Manchester was one of his favourite authors, and he took my review very personally. Little, Brown went to the extent (and cost) of buying a whole-page ad in the *Times*, challenging the reviews in an attempt to boost the book. I could have wished they had lavished similar care and expense upon *To Lose a Battle*. As it was, the whole episode spelled the final doom of any Bostonian enthusiasm. Judiciously Monica McCall placed my next books with the delightful Alan Williams, one of the most professional publishers I ever came across, at Viking.

On publication of *To Lose a Battle* (never one of my favourite titles) in 1969, once again reviews were more than friendly. Up to the time of writing, various publishers have kept the trilogy consistently in print over some four decades. Along with the others, *To Lose a Battle* was translated into a dozen different languages, and it brought in a bundle of correspondence. From Germany came a number of letters from veterans of the campaign. One wrote, in literal English: 'I greet book with only my highest esteem for your correct, exciting, provided with many interesting details, valuable account.' From an old acquaintance of mine from Bonn days, General Hasso von Manteuffel, who led the German offensive in the Ardennes of 1944, came a courteous rebuke (backed by others) for describing the elite Grosses Deutschland formation as an SS division. I apologised; nevertheless, Manteuffel graciously described it as an 'outstanding' book. From France, comments were understandably muted; as my publisher Sven Nielsen noted, it was difficult to promote a book in France about a period that remained 'very painful'. In Israel, where *To Lose a Battle* was translated into Hebrew by the Army Publishing House – but not until 1971 – it had perhaps the most far-reaching consequence, as will be seen later.

It was 1969. Renira and I had finally achieved our long-pursued dream: a house and rolling acres high up at the top end of Wiltshire in Membury. I look back at the purchase price with amazement: £113,000, at an auction which was over about as quickly as if one had been buying a £200 painting at Christie's, bought us a house and five cottages and 350 acres of (not quite) prime Wiltshire, a price that in today's crazy property values would just about secure a croft in the Outer Hebrides. For the first time in our married lives, we were wildly over-housed. From Membury one could gaze out over more than 20 miles uninterrupted by any other house, to Salisbury Plain. In my folly, I thought I could run a small cattle farm, support myself financially and write at the same time. It had sounded an ideal combination. After all, my hero Peter Fleming seemed to have achieved it. But when I told him about Membury, he looked at me in shocked disbelief: 'You must be out of your mind! It's utterly and totally impossible! You're in the middle of a crucial chapter, and suddenly the stockman comes and tells you a heifer has died of some mysterious disease. That's the end of your chapter. You'll see.'

I did, over a period of some dozen taxing (in every sense) years. I discovered I was not designed to be a so-called gentleman-farmer like Peter. Shades of Old Testament Job, twice our small herd was wiped out by brucellosis. Our one and only bull proved to be a hermaphrodite. Meanwhile, too, after completion of the trilogy, a ten-year slog, I was now totally burnt out. I had no new book project in mind, I badly needed a break. For me, it wasn't quite like the emotions suffered by the Goncourts, when they wrote: 'Our novel is finished ... It is strange how, once a thing is done, it no longer grips your emotions ... It is a feeling similar to that which follows coition; your work arouses nothing in you but boredom, indifference, and disgust.' But I did feel an intense lassitude. After nearly ten years' work I had finished the Franco-German trilogy. And what next? There were distractions, not always praiseworthy ones.

One day, out of the blue, came a brief note from my friend James Morris. He wrote 'I don't know if you have heard of the queer goings-on in my life, but if you have and they don't worry you, do have lunch with me when I am next in London.' I had heard nothing, but rang my agent, Ulie. She was coy, but murmured something about James having become a woman. 'Don't be silly!' I exclaimed. Eventually we made a date in Bath. When I arrived at our rendezvous, I had to cruise round looking for a parking-space. Suddenly I espied a stately country dame in a tweed skirt, with James's unmistakably frizzy hair. So I entered partially forewarned. In the other corner of the restaurant, it so happened, were a party of chums from the Garrick, too busy in their own chatter to notice anything, but the Italian waiter did, murmuring slyly the whole time, 'Would Madame care for another glass of wine?'

However, when the initial shock wore off, I quickly realised that the tweedy lady sitting opposite was still the same dear, sweet-natured, humorous James. He had all his life wanted to be a woman. There was absolutely nothing sexual about it; he just wanted to spend his life in the company of women, as a woman. He was, so to speak, still in mid-stream, awaiting the summons to go to Casablanca for the final, definitive set of operations. James/Jan confided he had written the last part of his recent book (*that* book!) in India, in 'drag'. 'I had no problems – just a few cheeky Indians.' So we parted, wishing each other all the best, with a somewhat raspy embrace; it all seemed perfectly natural. James/Jan went to live in his/her beloved Wales, with his former wife and lifelong best friend, Elizabeth, continuing to write those exquisite books. But somehow, dare one say it, I often felt James wrote rather better than Jan. When we next met I taxed her about the differences; she replied, perhaps half teasing, 'I don't think I drive quite as well as I used to!'

Meanwhile there was also developing what became one of the most fulfilling components of my whole life. I had become much involved in authors' rights, such as the struggle for Public Lending Right (PLR). That had a very slow beginning. I recall one particularly dismal demo that we – the Society of Authors – had launched against the then Labour Minister for the Arts, a dreary man with a bedraggled beard that made him look like some Neapolitan wharf-rat, later to become Lord Jenkins of Putney. He seemed to have little interest in the problems of contemporary literature, and such was the apathy of authors towards their own affairs, our half-hearted demo barely managed to fill one of the small islands in Belgrave Square opposite the Minister's office. What a feeble, internecine lot we authors were, collectively! As Bernard Shaw once remarked, 'To fight for authors' rights, you need to wear a back-plate as well as a breast-plate.' Fortunately, however, under the inspired and energetic leadership of Michael Holroyd and Antonia Fraser, the campaign ensured that PLR ultimately entered the statute books. They should both be beatified. The campaign added to my personal realisation of just how difficult and costly it was for young authors to get a foot on the first rung of the ladder.

About this time, in 1969, my concern over the plight of authors was sharpened when I was invited to join the management committee of the Royal Literary Fund, an august body which since 1790 had been disbursing charitable funds to needy authors. I was to serve on it for some twenty years. Beneficiaries of the RLF had ranged from Samuel Taylor Coleridge and Chateaubriand to Joseph Conrad, James Joyce and D. H. Lawrence. We would meet on Wednesdays once a month, in the comfortable surroundings of the Garrick Club. But the cases that came before us made anything but comfortable reading; a norm might be a divorced writer living in penury, with a mistress suffering from terminal cancer, and an autistic child, while he struggled to keep writing: then the boiler explodes. That would be the last straw. From funds bequeathed by successful authors like Somerset Maugham, we could afford to give him £500 to replace the boiler. That somehow would set him on the road to gainful productivity again. Cases like this constituted the bottom end of the scale.

What truly horrified one was the number of literary grandees, of household names, who – after a lifetime of dedication – found themselves forced to appeal for our help; or, embarrassed to do so, came to our notice only through the intervention of friends. Two whose names, and whose hardships, stunned me when they came up were Angus Wilson, a worthy recipient of the James Tait Black Memorial Prize, later knighted for services to literature, and V. S. Pritchett, Companion of Honour. Victor, always cheerful despite his penury, was still writing prolifically in his nineties, having published some fifty books. We helped them both. When I came on board the RLF, £500 for that new boiler was almost the limit to which our beneficence would stretch. Then, suddenly, in 2001 a bequest from the A. A. Milne (Winnie the Pooh) estate, via Walt Disney Inc., of some $60 million changed everything. The RLF could hardly find enough indigent authors to consume their generosity!

A happy story, but still the hardship of many struggling authors lives with us. I had learned for myself how much much tougher it was for non-fiction writers like me, burdened with the extra costs of research. Even in the 1960s, research (including travel and research assistants) for our kind of books could be prohibitively expensive. It had taken me three books before I published one (*The Price of Glory*) that could have begun to offer anything like a living wage, and that had been, in a modest way, a bestseller. How, then, could a young, unknown historian or biographer even begin? What talents might be lost for ever, because of a simple lack of opportunity, or else drained off abroad, a common phenomenon in the 1960s? What I felt was needed was a kind of kick-starter to help provide a worthwhile author with either the time or the cash (they amount to roughly the same thing) in which to write a specific book.

It so happened that, by 1968–9, the publication of my Franco-German trilogy had left me in a rare state of literary affluence. So for the best part of a year I hunted around, testing the water, plaguing friends, colleagues and publishers for advice and help, and looking for a vessel to contain my idea and which I might be able to fund from my own earnings. I must have made myself a perfect pest; those initial letters and responses fill half a box-file. Reading through the responses now, I hear voices from a distant past, none of them reproachful, most of them encouraging and helpful. Generally they thought the idea had merits; but how and where to put it into effect? I approached the Arts Council, UNESCO, my old college at Cambridge, Jesus, and the Society of Authors. None of them could quite come up with what I wanted. The Society of Authors, an admirable but underfunded institution, came closest, and we were on the verge of negotiating a trust deed.

Then, early in 1969, there came a response to one of my letters from John Bayley, of St Catherine's, Oxford, the English don who six years previously had proposed *The Price of Glory* for the Hawthornden Prize. Since then we had become friends – though I was often disconcerted on the telephone, taking Iris Murdoch's deep, rather masculine voice to be John's, and his gentle falsetto to be that of the great and, to me, rather daunting novelist. After putting forward several names in his letter, he came up with 'A bigger gun, Raymond Carr, former colleague of mine, now Warden of St Antony's College'. Only recently founded, St Antony's, it transpired, held particular significance for John, who had been one of its first fellows: it had been the launching-pad from which he had conducted his dedicated suit of Iris in adjacent St Anne's College.

I had known Raymond, tangentially, when he had been a somewhat reprobate don tutoring various friends of mine in history, and well nicknamed 'the Soul of All Fellows'. He had taken over, from Bill Deakin, as warden of St Antony's only the year before, but already was leaving his stamp on it.* Raymond was one of the last of the true Oxford eccentrics,

---

* As a nonagenarian, Raymond would be regularly heard to proclaim that he was the only warden never to have committed adultery. It was a challenging claim that none would question.

and his rich brand of eccentricity greatly appealed to me. One of the world's leading Spanish historians, he somehow managed to combine an imposing erudition with living it up wildly, foxhunting with playing the clarinet, trumpet and tenor-sax. Students, who thrived under his tuition, would recall addressing a rather green-hued face resting on the floor at a tutorial – Raymond believing that hangovers could best be cured with the feet raised higher than the brain. Not infrequently he would return to Oxford at the beginning of term with his arm in a sling, having fallen off his horse hunting on Exmoor. While warden of an Oxford college, he had absolutely no inhibitions about working as a barman in Stockholm, when funds ran low. But beneath the raffish surface of Raymond lay great wisdom, humanity and flair. He did not always convey the appearance of a kindly man, but an element of generosity came bubbling out from his rather unusual philosophy as a reviewer: never take on a book if you're going to slam it. 'Think of the poor sod who wrote it, all that bloody effort,' he would proclaim.

We had our first meeting in March 1969 and Raymond instantly took up my idea. He refined it and modified it, and made it work. Most significantly, he railroaded his Governing Body into allocating a matching sum from the College's Ford Foundation Funds, thereby doubling the modest commitment I was able to make, which I topped up from time to time with various prize moneys. There was an initial problem over the title. Raymond wanted it to bear my name; I demurred. He insisted: 'As your reputation grows, old boy, it'll bring fresh kudos to the Fellowship.'

So the Alistair Horne Fellowship was born. In those early days, we also managed to lure three publishers (one of them Macmillans) into backing our first years financially. This was an invaluable pump-primer, and the publishers thereby gained prior knowledge of projects on offer publishing, several books from both the accepted and rejected candidates which might not otherwise have seen the light of day. The Fellowship, as a result, was able to offer initially between £1,200 and £2,000 per annum. It was a shoestring – barely ever enough to be able to compete with average university stipends. It was to be awarded, as a rule, for one author per year. Limited as the financial inducement might be, the biggest attraction was to prove to be the associated attachment to the unique and eclectic body of St Antony's. Entirely postgraduate, with half of its students from overseas, then and now the College offered an especially stimulating multinational and multidisciplinary environment.

For those crucial kick-off years, 1969–70, our first selections proved about as good as they possibly could be. Tim Clark came from Essex University as a young history of art lecturer, and for a modest pittance he produced not one but two excellent books: *The Absolute Bourgeois: Artists and Politics in France 1848–1851* and *Image of the People: Gustave Courbet and the 1848 Revolution.* Both were provocatively left-of-centre in the political approach; this seemed not altogether inappropriate, as St Antony's, with its strong Russian and East European Centre, was under regular attack from Moscow as 'that well-known nest of right-wing spies'. Quite unintentionally, the balance was somewhat redressed by our next Fellow, Norman Davies, whose *White Eagle, Red Star: The Polish–Soviet War 1919–1920* had little of comfort to say about aggressive Soviet foreign policy in the Leninist era. Both followed up with most distinguished academic and writing careers. Norman Davies, through his works on Poland, went on to receive all the top honours that country could bestow.

Apart from the perennial problem of finance, each academic year we would face the concern of whether we were reaching the candidates we wanted. Occasionally we advertised, but by and large the best applicants came to us by word of mouth. As John Bayley had told me, Raymond knew everyone, from the great and the good to down-and-out students with a touch of unsung genius. Over its first eighteen years while he was Warden, the Fellowship owed everything to him. Some applicants brought their own share of eccentricity. There was Alan Davidson, for instance, who took even Raymond aback at interview. In answer to the conventional question 'Do you intend to spend time in the College?' his reply was: 'As a matter of fact, Warden, I was going to ask you about that. You see, I live on a barge, and it's leaking, so I wondered if you'd mind my putting it up on blocks in the quad?' The college rejected the barge, but he got the Fellowship and went on to write a classic, *The Oxford Companion to Food.* Some years later Alan went on to win Europe's most lucrative prize, the Netherlands' Erasmus Award, worth £150,000. (Sadly, he died only a few months later.)

We had applicants ranging from their twenties to their seventies; apart from the manifest needs we were trying to address, there were refugees from matrimony, or those trying to break an alcohol problem. One Fellow, Robert Kee, took twenty years to complete his biography of Parnell – but finally presented us with a winner in the shape of *The Laurel and Ivy* (1993). He was kind enough to write that only the Fellowship had kept his project going.

The Fellowship has survived into its fifth decade. Raymond's successors – Sir Ralf (later Lord) Dahrendorf, Sir Marrack Goulding and Professor Margaret MacMillan – have all been enthusiastic supporters, and each a delight to work with. I have been privileged to get to know almost all the Fellows; many became good friends, and I benefited a lot from their work and knowledge, learning about areas that ranged far beyond my own horizon. I look back on it all as just about the most rewarding enterprise of my life. Not least was the incidental privilege, which I hugely appreciated, of being elected an honorary fellow of St Antony's – probably the most exciting college in Britain – with all the *richesses* it had to offer.

11

THIS YEAR IN JERUSALEM

Past Fellows convene to mark the 25th anniversary of the Alistair Horne Fellowship at St Antony's, Oxford. (Sheelin and AH on bottom step.)

Palestine is the cement that holds the Arab world together, or it is the explosive that blows it apart.

Yasser Arafat

The Arab–Israeli Six Day War of 1967 took most of us in Britain by surprise. True, there had been rumblings in the Middle East and a great deal of sabre-rattling from Nasser – but, since Suez in 1956, when had there not been? Few thought it would come to war, and no one had anticipated the brilliant lightning success of the Israeli campaign. For me, working away on my trilogy about Franco-German battles and wars, by 1967 Israel was far from being at the front of my mind. When I had left Jerusalem with my demob suit in summer 1947, to the accompaniment of Irgun bombings – which included the revolting murder by Menachim Begin's men of our two Field Security sergeants, their dead bodies booby-trapped – I had been committedly anti-Israel. Over the ensuing twenty years, with the brutal threats and pan-Arabism of Nasser, the recurrent displays of Arab venality and incompetence, and infant Israel's heroic showing in the 1948 war and later in the Suez debacle of 1956, the rancour of 1946–47 had dissipated; my feelings had progressively swung round. As the attacks of the fellahin guerrillas escalated in the run-up to the Six Day War, I had come to see David Ben-Gurion's and Golda Meir's Israel as a decent, embattled and endangered bastion of democracy surrounded by vicious foes intent on wiping her out.

The first news bulletins on the Six Day War suggested that Israel had acted just in time to nip in the bud an overwhelming attack on her, concerted by Egypt, Jordan and Syria – in effect all her surrounding Arab neighbours, now far better armed (by Soviet Russia) than they had been in 1948 and 1956. That Israel might – in effect – have committed a pre-emptive Pearl Harbor was not apparent then. The opening reports of the Israeli Air Force successes against a sleepy Egyptian Air Force, its Soviet MiG-21s wiped out on the ground, were exhilarating. Nevertheless, the contest looked horribly like David and Goliath – but could David win this time? As the Arabs mobilised their hugely preponderant forces on three sides of Israel, with their powerful Soviet patron growling in the background, with America bogged down and humiliated in Vietnam, the situation looked mortally dangerous, indeed one-sided. And might Russia come in, turning Cold War into hot war?

As that grim, frightening first week of June progressed, watching it hour by hour on the BBC, I felt that brave little Israel really had her back to the wall. Explaining why there was a sudden dearth of taxis on London streets, a Jewish taxi-driver told me that many of his mates had left to drive ambulances. Though without an ounce of Jewish blood, I too felt drawn in. I made up my mind that I would go to offer my services to the Israeli Embassy. But within the week it was all over. David had triumphed over all the enemies of Israel, winning an Old Testament victory of Samsonian scale. Sinai, the Golan Heights and the whole of the West Bank had been occupied. Israel looked safe – at least temporarily.

In retrospect, I think that I would not have been much use driving around in the Mitla Pass or on the Golan Heights. But, as the dust settled in the Middle East, my literary agent, Ulie Winant, wrote to tell me that the publishing house of the Israeli Defence Forces had offered to buy Hebrew language rights to *The Price of Glory* – for $50. She explained that the IDF, uniquely, had its own publishing house which selected books on military history that it felt might be of particular value to Israeli defence policy. I accepted, pleased and flattered, though puzzled. For the life of me, I could not see what relevance Verdun, history's most static of all grinding battles, had for an army which had just won one of the most brilliant feats of manoeuvre. Shortly after a contract was signed, there arrived an invitation from Israel to come and speak on the book.

I was doubly enticed because our dearest French friends, Francis and Jacqueline Huré, had just been appointed to run de Gaulle's Embassy there. It also happened that I was committed to go to Australia to inspect a sheep-station enterprise, into which, in a syndicate, I had disastrously ventured, and – and at the same time – to lecture on another book (*The Fall of Paris*). So in early 1969 Renira and I decided to take the Oz opportunity and fly round the world westwards (the sensible way), taking in Mexico, Australia, Thailand, Cambodia and (I alone) Israel on the way home.

Thus there were various interludes on the way to Israel. In Mexico we stayed with our Ambassador, a genially hospitable, engaging and faintly piratical figure called Peter Hope (nicknamed 'Pedro Esperanza'), an old friend from Bonn days who had – a rare exception – performed the voyage from MI6 to the 'proper' FO. After all his kindness, as we took leave to fly down to Merida, our host said: 'Now there's something I want you to do for me, in return. I'm putting you in the charge of our Honorary Consul in Merida, and when you leave him I want you to send me in a candid report; we're somewhat worried, there are reports that he's gone a bit "tropo".'

We arrived at Merida in a tropical rainstorm. After about half an hour a battered Ford Popular, minus door handles, appeared, driven by the HC himself. In the belting rain he let us in with a screw-driver, apologising: 'Terrible place, Merida, you know; they even steal the door handles.' That afternoon we were bidden to take tea. Except for the very Mexican patio, it was all entirely English – cake stand, doilies, tea urn and all – nothing 'tropo' about the HC, clearly reports were exaggerated. We sat making desultory conversation with Mrs HC about the weather, and Harold Wilson. Suddenly there was a grunting and a snuffling from the under-growth in the patio and an enormous crocodile heaved himself up the stairs, to take up a position between my legs and the cake stand, with one rheumy and hungry eye fixed on each. I raised my feet as high as I decently could without upsetting the tea party; but the consul and his lady paid no attention as she fed the crocodile choice goodies from the cake stand. Afterwards she asked me if I would kindly help him back to his lair: 'he's very elderly, you see, and a bit gone in the back legs.' I reported back to the ambassador, gently, that all was well down in Merida, provided you took tea cautiously with the HC.

I loved Mexico, but I didn't much fancy the Land of Oz. Perhaps it was lack of imagination on my part. In Sydney I was irritated – possibly like Dickens in 1842 America – by the pressure to admire everything: 'Don't you think our new Opera House is just wonderful?' Rashly after a while I responded that it would be fine if they'd only take away that load of old Meccano behind it. 'What, you don't like our Bridge!' I soon realised that the Aussie sense of humour was something one could not take liberties with. At the other end of Australia, Perth was delightful, though it imparted the strange sensation of having nothing but desert behind and nothing in front but the empty ocean, and little to the north or south. Two hundred miles north lay the 'styetion' we had all clubbed together to buy – hundreds of infertile acres bought at rock-bottom prices, but a blissful natural reserve for the kangaroos and emus that knocked down the fencing, and for the myriads of gallahs and sulphur-crested cockatoos that stripped off the insulation on the roof of the homestead. From the happy-go-lucky manager (shortly to be sacked) I learned a key Aussie phrase: 'She be roight on the die, mite!' When you heard that, you knew it never would be. After going out with the dawn to help remove murderous barbed seeds from the eyes of our underprivileged-looking sheep, replacing the eyeball before sitting down to breakfast, and smearing tar on the wounds caused by clumsy electric wool-shearers, I decided I was never designed to be a sheep-farmer. We sold our share as fast as we could.

On to Thailand, my first visit, to stay with Michael and Phillida Wrigley. Michael, my very old friend from intelligence days in SIME, who had moved on to MI6, was now completing a remarkable stint of twelve years as our man in Bangkok. He loved the Far East, and the Thais in particular, but possibly he loved racing even more. One day shortly after his arrival in Bangkok the Chief Steward of the race track was found trussed up and very dead in the boot of his car. Unhesitatingly Mike took over this perilous job, making himself esteemed and feared in the Thai racing world, but also providing himself with the most perfect cover for his intelligence activities. During the Vietnam War, Bangkok was an all-important listening post.

After the hubbub of Bangkok, Phnom Penh was an oasis of tranquillity. Cambodia's tiny capital was the nearest thing one could imagine to Babar's Celesteville – a paragon of a French colonial town, red roofs, white walls, bougainvillea and palm trees, inhabited by tiny, smiling and gentle people. Their, and its, very gentleness made the horrifying eruption of the Khmer Rouge and Pol Pot in so few years' time – that irrational, murderous revolt of the peasantry against the urban elite like something out of the dark age – seem all the more inconceivable. I think often of our sweet-faced, diminutive guide round Phnom Penh, a town-dweller to the core, and wonder on which heap of grinning skulls in the Killing Fields his ended up – or might he possibly have become one of the execution squads? Knowledge of those crimes – genocide on a scale which, as a percentage of the population, dwarfed anything perpetrated by Hitler or Stalin – deters me from wanting ever to return to that smiling country again. What terrible truths might lie concealed behind those sweet smiles? Already while we were there came sounds of gunfire close in the jungle.

From Cambodia, Renira flew directly home. I went on to Israel, excited, but with some foreboding. Would I be received like the Germans return-ing to Paris after 1945, who came bringing unpopular memories of the occupying power? I need have had no such apprehension. The Israelis were warmly welcoming. The country as a whole was still on a tremendous high in the wake of the triumphs of 1967. None of the problems that were to plague the Middle East within a few years were yet manifest. My first impression was of an extraordinary effervescence of morale; secondly, of how everybody in this, then, tightly well-integrated little country knew everything about everybody else and what they did and, indeed, instantly everything about the visiting former British intelligence officer. Mossad then was omniscient and ubiquitous. Frequently I would be introduced on the lecture circuit, with a not-unfriendly smile, as one 'who, as a young British Army officer, did his best to prevent Israel being born'. Because Israel was such a tightly knit country, it was also dead easy to find, and meet, anyone one wanted. As a writer of history, it was an event to be able to sit in the warm, peaceful autumn sun of the Negev, discussing the details of the shocking King David Hotel bomb of July 1946 with a *Ha' aretz* journalist who claimed to have been the sole survivor of the operation that had struck such a deadly blow against British intelligence in Palestine, and killed so many.

As planned, I stayed with Francis and Jacqueline Huré in the Embassy Residence. Just as in Turkey, their previous post, they had eschewed the official lodgings, so in Israel they chose to live in Old Jaffa, one of the Arab cities which the conquering Israelis had seized in 1948. From their charming old house I went to Jerusalem to revisit old haunts, as well as to lecture and conduct interviews: the imposing YMCA building, where I used to stay when it was a British Officers' Mess; the King David, once more a grand hotel, all its 1946 wounds long vanished. In his office as the indestructible and everlasting Mayor of Jerusalem, a historic site in himself, I found Teddy Kollek. We reminisced cheerfully about how, in SIME days, he used to visit Maurice Oldfield in his Cairo office, to swap information. As ever, Kollek was ebullient and optimistic, dreaming of a Greater Jerusalem where Jews and Arabs would intermingle and go about their business freely, under Israeli control of course – at least 'provisionally', whatever that might mean. Israel's leading expert on the Arab world, Professor Yehoshafat 'Fati' Harkabi, almost uniquely, was much less sanguine; the Arabs, he was convinced, would never give up, never accept peace until the last Israeli was driven into the sea. The security Israel had just won herself would not last long.

Certainly Jerusalem now resembled much more a polyglot, multi-ethnic city like New York than when I had left twenty-two years before. The new mix was exciting. There was the new influx of dark Sephardic Jews, refugees from the Maghreb (the big Jewish community in Algeria), the Yemen and Iraq. The Sephardis were already beginning to outnumber the old predominantly Ashkenazi settlers, the original *sabra*s, primarily from the European diaspora. With them they brought other priorities, new fears, new hatreds – of Arabs, not of Germans or Russians. Returning from Jerusalem, I had a manic taxi-driver, smelling like a goat and scaring me to death as he swung round the hairpins of Israel's most lethal road, but I was unable to communicate in any language to ask him to slow down. Finally, after one hair-raising swerve, I uttered – I don't know why – a searing expletive in Spanish. This Jehu smiled – he came from Spanish Morocco. In Spanish, I managed to get him to take a kindlier interest in my welfare.

All over what used to be 'my' Palestine, there were ghosts, moments of déjà vu. Perhaps the most extraordinary was visiting IDF Headquarters in Tel Aviv. Immediately I recognised it to be the old 6th Airborne Division compound. The barbed wire, the sentry posts, nothing had changed. As I approached the entrance, the living image of a Guards sergeant-major, complete with handlebar moustache, quivering salute and earth-shaking stamp, came leaping out at me. I rubbed my eyes. The clock seemed to have stood still. Why was he saluting me like that? 'Sir, still always recognise a Guardsman when I see one!' It transpired that in the last years of the Mandate he had been a locally recruited sergeant with a Guards unit, and had then joined the new IDF. Old habits die hard. Even the Israeli police uniform had a curiously British look about it. On several occasions in 1969 I met middle-aged or elderly Israelis who admitted with pride that they had once served with the British forces. Some even went so far as to admit that, as crisis followed crisis, and war followed war, the years of the Mandate had come to seem a kind of golden age. How strange it was, after all the passion, hatred and violence that I recalled!

Inside the compound the Israeli Chief of Staff, General Chaim Bar-Lev, greeted me most affably and made some obliging remarks about *The Price of Glory*. I thanked him, then put my puzzlement to him: why on earth they had bought it? What had the Western Front, 1916, got to do with their remarkable, modern style of highly mobile warfare? He replied: 'When you go down to our lines on the Suez Canal, you will see why. The Egyptians are shelling us night and day, and we are losing two or three men each week, which Israel with its tiny population just can't afford. The sanctity of life is very fundamental to us. So we want to explore which side got it right at Verdun – the Germans or the French.'

He was to be proved right. In the event, the IDF plumped for the model the Germans came to adopt along their Hindenburg Line on the Western Front, which I had described in *The Price of Glory*. Along their defences on the Suez Canal, the Israelis dug deep, but held their forward positions lightly – emulating the Kaiser's armies in 1917. Thus when the Egyptians attacked with total surprise in October 1973, they came close to overwhelming the Israeli positions, and possibly only the fact that the IDF had made the right appreciation of the lessons of the Western Front in the First World War enabled Israel to survive. It is seldom given for military historians to influence the course of events on the battlefield. In Israel, in the early struggles of 1948 and 1956, it had happened when leaders like Moshe Dayan and Yigal Allon benefited from their reading of Basil Liddell Hart and his strategy of the 'indirect approach', so that day at IDF HQ I felt much honoured to be allowed to follow modestly in the footsteps of my old guru.

Shortly after this visit to IDF HQ, I had a dramatic and rather more disturbing encounter with high Israeli brass. Francis and Jacqueline had been invited to a soirée at the prestigious Weizmann Institute at Rehovot, under the aegis of Charles Clore. They kindly took me along. In the course

of the evening, I found myself in a small group around General Ezer
Weizman, nephew of Israel's first President, Chaim Weizmann (Ezer spelt
his name differently), and hero of the Six Day War in which he had been
architect of the decisive air campaign. A wartime pilot in the RAF, well
over 6 foot tall and broad to match, Weizman was a striking figure. With
his blue Ashkenazi eyes and cropped fair hair he could almost have
passed – unfortunate parallel though this might seem – for a 1940s Luftwaffe ace. He was formidably self-confident to the point of arrogance.
With him in the group was a young brigadier called Rehavam 'Gandhi'
Ze'evi, in uniform with rolled-up shirtsleeves, casually lolling full length
on a sofa and contributing nonchalantly to the conversation. (I remembered his chisel-jawed face well, and was shocked when I saw his photograph accompanying the news of his assassination thirty-two years later.)*
Also in the group was a one-time IDF chief of intelligence, a dapper and
quieter figure with an English military moustache, a former major in the
British Army at Arnhem and son of a Dublin rabbi, Chaim Herzog. Both
he and Ezer Weizman were later to become presidents of Israel.

Slightly looking down their noses, it was either Weizman or Ze'evi who
asked me, 'Well, you're a military historian, so what do you make of our
great victory?' I replied that I thought it one of the most exciting, almost
Old Testament, victories of our time, then added, perhaps rashly, that
I was not quite sure, however, how Israel could now win the peace. They
pushed me to explain myself. I suggested that maybe Israel had one year
in which to use the vital bargaining counter of the Occupied Territories.
Weizman, backed by Ze'evi, exploded: 'We don't need to be lectured by
you Limey armchair strategists!'

Weizman was then well known for his short fuse, and there followed a
shockingly racist diatribe about the lessons of the Six Day War. 'We won',
declared Weizman, 'because blacks [that is, Egyptians] can't fly. Their
reactions are altogether too slow. Even our blacks' – I raised my eyebrows;
what he meant, he explained, was the Yemeni Sephardis – 'can't be taught.

---

* Ze'evi, always a right-winger, became Minister of Tourism under Ariel Sharon and was
assassinated by the Popular Front for the Liberation of Palestine in a hotel in Jerusalem on 17
October 2001. He was then leader of Moledet (Fatherland), a far-right party which advocated the
mass expulsion of Arabs from the West Bank and Gaza.

They're only good for cannon fodder, for the infantry.' I was appalled. Could I really be hearing a Jew from Israel say this? The conversation became increasingly heated, with Weizman and Ze'evi uniting against me. Fortunately the fourth member of the group, Chaim Herzog, very gently poured oil on the waters and separated us. But I never forgot the episode – nor, I discovered a few years later when we met again in London, did Chaim Herzog. (As an afternote to this story, personal tragedy brought about a sea-change in Weizman's philosophy. In the Yom Kippur War of 1973, his son was severely wounded in the head, and from that moment Weizman was transmuted from being arch-hawk to super-dove.)

Then, in the brutal spring of 2002, the circle took another turn. Just before the Israelis launched their March offensive into the West Bank, Mark Sullivan, the late Basil Liddell Hart's stepson who studies the Israeli press, sent me this quote from *Ha'aretz*: 'Sharon has said recently that on his bedside table he has a copy of Alistair Horne's definitive history of the Algerian war, *A Savage War of Peace*. One can only wonder what he'll learn from it.' Following the *Ha'aretz* revelation, Sharon infuriated the French for having boasted that, if he had been in charge in France during the Algerian War, he would have won it. But it was hard to see any message of comfort for Sharon. As far his bedside reading goes, the only advice might be – don't follow the French example. Don't misread the lessons of Algeria.

I spent my forty-fourth birthday at Affikim, one of the oldest and biggest kibbutzim, located close to the Jordan and its confluence with the Yarmuk. Affikim was a small empire in itself, with sawmills and furniture plants, citrus plantations and a stud. Riding out one morning, we stopped to raid the orchard – and can there be anything more delicious than a pink grapefruit, warmed by the sun, straight off the tree? Yet in this idyll menace was never far away. Regularly since the 1967 war Affikim had come under fire from nearby Syrian Katyusha rockets, so the children's communal dormitories had chutes down into bomb-proof cellars, where they could be posted, like parcels, the moment there was hint of an attack. Just across the Jordan, in the Yarmuk hills where I had jeeped about so merrily in 1946, with the naked eye one could see dug-in Jordanian tanks, their gun barrels pointing threateningly in our direction. Almost every night there was the sound of sporadic firing, not too distant. One evening a friendly kibbutznik told me, proudly, how, under the Mandate, he had served with the last real British cavalry unit in Palestine. Assuming that, like every other Brit he had ever met, I knew all about horses, he invited me to help take his mare to the stallion next morning. Both were fine beasts, but blindingly white – perfect targets for a nasty-minded, unsporting gunner in one of those tanks just across the Jordan. As I hung on to the wildly thrusting stallion, I wondered nervously if horses took as long as a well-adjusted human male. Suddenly, in seconds, it was all over. I asked the ex-cavalryman whether the horses were as nervous as I was; he roared with laughter 'No, it's always like that – poor things!'

From Affikim I was taken up to the Golan Heights, scene of some of the fiercest fighting in 1967 before the Israelis, with great courage, wrested this imposing strategic feature from the Syrians. We passed abandoned Syrian vehicles and a burnt-out old Russian T-34, still with a nasty smell in the turret, and I reflected on what hellish terrain it must have been for the attacking force. Quneitra, the former Syrian centre on this bleak, windswept plateau on the way to Damascus, was still deserted, its shops gutted, left just as they had been by one or other looting army two years previously, now in the midst of a kind of deserted no man's land. Returning down towards the Sea of Galilee, alias Tiberias, I stood on the brink of the Heights, looking down at an Israeli farmer on a tractor hundreds of feet below. It made one appreciate just how imperative to tiny Israel's security were vital strategic places like the Golan Heights, and – recalling the encounter at the Weizmann Institute – how hard it was going to be for Israel ever to be persuaded to abandon crucial territory won in 1967. What guarantees in exchange would suffice? At the same time I wondered just how long it would be before the Arabs would somehow find a way round their present humiliation. (Two and a half decades later, and after yet another war, I was drinking passable white wine grown by the industrious Israelis in vineyards set up on those same contested slopes. What would ever make them move? And would there ever be peace if they didn't?)

My last trip in Israel in 1969 was to the hellish Gaza Strip, the desperately over-populated coastal zone (most of its inhabitants are Arab refugees) for which neither Egypt nor Jordan wanted responsibility or stewardship. It has remained imprinted in my memory ever since as one of the most wretched places on God's earth. Even in 1969, Gaza was seething with discontent, with shootings and explosions a daily occurrence. In a small and inconspicuous car I had rented for the occasion, I went to see for myself – accompanied by an understandably grumpy IDF lieutenant, who told me he was still, officially, on his honeymoon. Casually he laid his Uzi sub-machine gun on the back seat, then asked me to roll up the windows. It was very hot and there was no air-conditioning, so I asked him why. 'In case they throw a hand-grenade at us. There's a good chance that it'll bounce off the window, instead of exploding inside.' He looked increasingly unhappy as we drove round Gaza, confronted by a sea of sullen Arab faces. I felt sorry for him, and thought I ought to do my best not to spoil his honeymoon. A few minutes after we had passed through a crowded market place, there was a sharp explosion behind us. Israeli police were soon on the spot and, as we returned, I saw the scorch-mark of a grenade blast on the road over which we had just passed. An ambulance was arriving to collect the wounded. In deference to the honeymooner, I cut the trip short and headed back out of this breeding ground for terrorists.

I left the Hurés, and Israel, exhilarated and impressed, but at the same time deeply worried. I had experienced what was a heroic time for the Israelis, but I was certain that in the swings of Jewish destiny there would be tears to come. History would, alas, prove that in my encounter with Ezer Weizman, my judgement wasn't entirely wrong.

12

SMALL EARTHQUAKE

'Commandante Pepe' (left) in 1971, eighteen months before he was killed following the
Pinochet Coup; Bill Buckley and AH in Swizterland, 1972.

In any case, we had a devilish good time.

Comte de Fleury

In those quiescent, essentially fallow years between major efforts, 1969–
71, I ran off two short, heavily illustrated, books: *Death of a Generation*,
about the murderous years of 1915–16 on the Western Front, and *The
Terrible Year: The Paris Commune 1871*, a centenary work based on the
film made for the BBC. I also found myself reviewing more and more,
chiefly for Anthony Curtis, literary editor of the *Financial Times* and,
later, of the new *Sunday Telegraph*. But I never found it light work.
I couldn't, as some did, write an honourable review having read the
wrapper, the first ten pages and the last five, with a quick check of the
index; just in case one was mentioned. I envied Antonia Fraser, who with
disarming modesty claimed that her principal skill was her ability to read
down the centre of a page and yet remember every word on that page. A
serious, 1,000-word review would take me as much as two to three
working days. So I tried to restrict myself to books that particularly
interested me or where I felt I had some expertise.

As a book reviewer, I tried to take the line of Raymond Carr, whose
doctrine was, simply, that if some poor sod has taken the trouble to write
a book, you must find good things to say about it or else not review it at
all. Consequently, in all the several hundred book reviews I've written,
I can recall only one book which I wholeheartedly damned. That was the
memoirs of the first woman head of MI5, Stella Rimington; not only was
it a deplorably bad book, it was a disgrace – given her position – that it
had been allowed into print. Secret intelligence should remain secret.
Nevertheless, such is the vanity of authors (myself included) that even a
mildly critical sentence or two can raise hackles. David Pryce-Jones
wouldn't speak to me for years because I suggested that his book on Paris
under the Occupation, though commendable, could have been a more

intensive study; the late Anthony Sampson, one of the dearest of friends, was cool for a lengthy period because of minor reservations I had expressed on his book *The Arms Bazaar*. Two biographies of de Gaulle, neither first rate, got me into social trouble; the wife of the author of the first, an ex-ambassador, gave me hell through two courses at a dinner in the French Embassy; the author of the second, an over-inflated Labour peer, resolutely turned his back on my wife, innocent of all grievance, throughout another dinner party. Such are the tiger traps, on top of all the labour involved in reviewing – for which one is usually paid a pittance. But if you don't review *them*, they won't review *you*.

By no means, however, was life all work. A Sunday painter of extremely modest talent myself, I had always been attracted by modern art, and in the 1960s I began collecting Contemporary British. My partner in crime was a young woman doctor, Jean Shanks, who had set up her own one-woman pathology practice, which she eventually turned into the biggest private pathology business in Western Europe, employing over a hundred staff. She was a collector too, and I very much shared her taste. Over a lunch hour, or at a *vernissage* in the evening, we would go hunting – the 1960s were a marvellous time to buy. You could get a Lucian Freud for £625, as I did. We both kept to strict and modest budgets, never more than a few hundred for any single painting. Both our houses filled with acquisitions, till there was no wall-space left. So we moved.

I got to know the artists. The single most original British talent I found, a true and sometimes impenetrable genius, and equally eccentric, was Edward Burra. A frail figure, suffering from an early age with rheumatoid arthritis, Burra lived with his sister in East Sussex. One day in the 1930s he announced that he was just going down to the bottom of garden. Never having travelled before, he reappeared some nine months later having been all over the world, including to New York, where in louche bars and nightclubs he painted some of his most famous early works. There was almost always a touch of the sinister, the unfathomable, in even his most joyous landscapes. I bought two of his amazing works. Then, when he died in 1976, to my delight he left me his 'last palette'. A scruffy painter, like that other Briton of unique vision, Stanley Spencer, the 'palette' consisted of the back of an old envelope, and some child's watercolour brushes. It was from this that he had composed some of the greatest English works of our times.

In this restless, brutalised age, one tends to forget just how good the good life was in the so-called Swinging Sixties in Britain. You could afford to send three children to good schools without facing bankruptcy. Travel was cheap, skiing was cheap and the slopes were empty. There was a social and sexual revolution afoot. The Pill, and easy sex had swept away the principles of those wartime days, when you were supposed not to sleep with a girl until you were officially engaged. And how we now revelled in this new freedom – going to Annabel's, the Berkeley Square nightclub opened in 1963, and nuzzling each other's wives, and making assignations. It all seemed so harmless, falling in and out of love, meeting in the discreet little bistros that were springing up all over London where you could happily lunch on £7 or £8 for two. Where were we heading? Byron knew the answer: 'Let us have wine and women, mirth and laughter, Sermons and soda water the day after.' Divorce lawyers made hay.

Nevertheless, it was not all fun, those Sixties and Seventies. There were sad times as well. At the beginning of 1970 my old guru, Captain Basil Liddell Hart, the Seer of Medmenham, died. I owed him a lot. He gave me a kick-start in thinking about military history. There he sat, in his den above the Thames, surrounded by the photographs, signed with suitably unctuous inscriptions, of the foreign generals who had benefited from his teaching, and helped their countries to win wars. A true prophet-without-honour: while Hitler's apostles of Blitzkrieg were studying up on the 'Indirect Approach' to smash Poland and France, only the bovine British staff of the 1930s had stood aloof. Sometimes irascible, often incomprehensible as he struggled to light his determinedly resistant pipe while carrying on a conversation at the same time, he was never inaccessible, backed up so loyally by his long-suffering wife Kathleen. As is often the case with many original thinkers, posterity has not been entirely kind to Basil. The hooters and nippers, as Thomas Beecham would have dubbed them, have been at work. But to me, his reputation and his friendship still stand on a special plinth. He made us all think.

In the autumn of 1970, Bill Buckley arrived in England. We had never lost touch, seeing each other – here or there – at least twice a year. Since those days of a decade back, when we had shared the Bärgsunne, Bill's star had soared dramatically. From being a lone voice in the conservative wilderness, maverick founder of a magazine, *National Review*, that was read only by conservative loyalists and intellectuals, he had become a national figure in the USA whose hand everybody on a plane or a train wanted to press. Almost as a joke, he had let his name be put forward in the New York City mayoral race of 1965 against a Democrat candidate, Abraham Beame, and a liberal Republican, John Lindsay. Instantly Bill's eloquence, his biting sense of irony and above all his unquenchable sense of humour took over the headlines. Americans love someone with an offbeat wit (there have not been many in US politics through the ages), but what particularly endeared him to the New York electorate was one piece of repartee, which remains engraved in all reference books of Americana: when asked by a journalist what he would do first if he won, quick as a flash he riposted, 'Demand a recount.' Overnight he became a household name from coast to coast. He came to be regarded not as a maverick but as a serious figure, the philosopher, the voice and the moving spirit of conservative protest against the liberal sclerosis of both parties.

While all this was going on in Bill's life, he never ceased to be my oldest and dearest friend, a true chum in need and a generous godfather to my daughter Camilla. We could always switch on where we had left off, with never a split or a row in a lifetime of buddydom, despite our occasional political and ethical divergences and despite the vagaries of my disorderly life. (Maybe it was the geographical distance which guaranteed that!) As anyone interviewed on his 'Firing Line' could testify, Bill was not all sweetness and light. But on the big things, such as opposition to Soviet Communism, we were not divided. With joyous regularity, we would meet to ski, and write, in Switzerland (and, once, in the bottomless snows of Alta, Utah). After our sojourn at the Bärgsunne in 1959, Bill and Pat had fallen in love with the exquisite medieval Château de Rougemont, fifteen minutes away down in the valley. They would rent it, every year for two months from mid-January to mid-March. Bill had an inflexible regime; he would arrive, with no idea what he was going to write; then, two months later to the day, he would return to Connecticut with a finished book (usually a novel about the all-American hero he had invented, Blackford Oakes), as well as having written his weekly syndicated column. His daily schedule was just as ritualistic: writing, accompanied by a Bach cantata or Ella Fitzgerald, all morning; a quick lunch, then skiing till 4 p.m.; then more writing, drinks, chat and dinner, then painting, in the basement atelier he had created around a ping-pong table. His talents varied immensely. Harpsichordist, sailor, skier – all these Bill shone at, but on the whole painting proved more elusive. His enthusiasm was nonetheless boundless, and no dinner guest was ever excused from joining in; there were canvases by Charlie Chaplin, James Mason, Teddy Kennedy and Jackie Onassis, one signed by that most redoubtable of English literary Dames, Rebecca West, with the inscription: 'Bill, why do you make me do this? I love you much too much. Rebecca.'

But the uncontested *grand maître* among us was David Niven. A true professional among us amateur paint-slingers, he was also one of nature's funniest men and a born raconteur. With it went an unquenchable zest for life. He could make a tale out of any humdrum incident. The stories never ceased to flow. In 1972 had just published his runaway bestseller, *The Moon's a Balloon* (with engaging modesty, he signed my copy, 'From David, the amateur, to Alistair, the pro'). But what an amateur! Hitherto never much more than a B-actor in Hollywood, though he had starred in many excellent movies, *The Moon* made him world famous.

In the cellar of his chalet in nearby Château d'Oex he had constructed a cosy *Stübli* or sitting room, encased in murals of a bullfight which David had painted himself, with great competence. There, evening after evening, we would booze together and watch Laurel and Hardy movies on David's ancient projector. Before I met David I had never had any particular affection for the two English funny men, but David, the truly professional comedian, adored them, and his rippling laughter was so commandingly infectious that you fell about too. Always the perfect courtier, he was most generous in the way he instinctively spread his expertise for all to enjoy. He would cross the floor, abandoning a princess or a filmstar, to entertain one or other of my then gauche teenage daughters. They certainly never forgot him.

But, like the clown of tradition, David's capacity for laughter was tinged by a lot of sadness on the home front, always well concealed. He had never got over the tragic, accidental death in a fall of his first wife, Primmie. His second, Hjördis, a once beautiful Swedish model, could not keep up with David's fireworks; she took to the bottle and became increasingly morose. David suffered, but if he ever complained he made a joke of it. Then illness struck, of the very worst kind. He had just arrived in the mountains from presenting some film award or other in Hollywood, and jokingly complained to us that something had gone wrong with his voice, making him sound like 'a constipated parrot'. The voice got worse; finally he was diagnosed with Lou Gehrig's disease, or motor neurone disease. He slowly wasted away, progressively unable to speak with that electric voice which had enchanted so many, an utterly miserable end that lasted some eighteen months.

In those far-off days at Rougemont a stream of notables, some more eccentric than others, flowed through the hospitable château, where Bill would invariably follow his regime of writing in the morning, skiing in the afternoon. There was the famous liberal economist, J. K. Galbraith, 6 foot 8 inches tall, a fearsomely improbable figure on the ski-slopes; in his old-fashioned, baggy ski-pants it always looked as if he had at least two knees on each leg. You didn't share a T-bar ski-tow with him more than once. Happily Ken gave up before the snows got him. His relationship with Bill (I even think I may have introduced them back in the early 1960s), strained at first because of their acute political differences, became a deeply affectionate one. To the day of Ken's death in 2006 aged ninety-seven, Bill would religiously trot off to Cambridge, Massachusetts, almost every week to visit the seer of the 'Affluent Society'.

Once, disastrously, David Niven brought the octogenarian Marc Chagall to dinner – on a solemn Buckley promise that he would *not* be invited down to the atelier after dinner. Bill must have forgotten. On rising from dinner, David was appalled to hear the aged genius being urged to 'come see our paintings'. But Chagall won; standing mute in front of an early Buckley he was heard to mutter, 'Oh, the poor paint!'

One evening a handsome young Greek with flashing black eyes entered our lives. According to Taki's recollection, I was sitting in the bar of the Gstaad Palace Hotel, nursing a dislocated shoulder and the accompanying ill humour, and I made his acquaintance by slinging a heavy glass ashtray into the midst of a party of Greek carousers (Taki of course was one of them) who were singing Italian *fascisti* songs. It landed with deadly accuracy, scattering all their drinks, and they had come over with aggressive intent. When he saw that the perpetrator was only a Brit with one arm,

Taki's innate sense of chivalry took over; I was spared a going-over, and we became friends. The following night at the château he said to me earnestly, 'I want to become a Hemingway – how do I start? Seriously.'

He was always great company, generous to a fault, but neither Bill nor I could quite take him seriously then: playboy, born with silver spoon, Wimbledon tennist, karate black belt, expert skier, sexual athlete, his English was in some default (he spoke, *con brio*, of 'meandering a woman into bed'; snootily, I pointed out that it was an intransitive verb). I told him that his way ahead lay in becoming (as I had) a foreign correspondent, thinking we would hear no more about it. But he went one, if not several, better than my suggestion: he became a fearless war correspondent, and then established himself as 'High Life' correspondent of the *Spectator*, never missing a week, decade on decade, to file his libel-defying pieces.

Like a classical gladiator, Taki, red in tooth and limb, went on to fight many battles, heedless of danger. To my amazement, only rarely did the libel lawyers corner him in his record-setting run with the *Speccie*. I admired his courage, and his belief in personal honour and good manners. For all his alleged obsession with extreme youth, as far as my own daughters were concerned – like the great and irresistible David – he was ever the *chevalier sans peur et sans reproche*. Most times we shared the same hates (though not the same likes, or loves); his targets, his enemies, were mine (though not invariably). He conquered English, superbly well. I urged him really to become a Hemingway, to write a substantial book – a history of the Hellenes' heroic war in the Epirus against the Italians in 1940. He didn't. Then, foolishly, in 1984 he got caught with a packet of dope in his pocket at Heathrow. He went to prison for three months. Though disapproving, Bill remained his loyalest supporter, helping him hugely to reinvent and re-establish himself on leaving Pentonville. In return, Taki's affection and loyalty to Bill and Pat remained peerless. Then, out of Pentonville, came that serious book, *Nothing to Declare*. To my mind it is one of the best ever written about prison life; certainly his account of his experiences would by itself keep me out of the slammer.*

* Years later, I was passing through the Customs channel at Heathrow when a voice behind whispered: 'Hey, Al – would you mind taking a small packet through for me?' It was Taki, at his irrepressible, unrepentant worst.

Rougemont thus helped ensure that Bill's arrival in England in the autumn of 1970 was part of a pattern in our continuing friendship. But there was a new element this time. I had been spending time at St Antony's. All the talk was about the elections in Chile. For the first time that most enlightened country had elected a radical left-wing government, headed by Dr Salvador Allende, with the tiniest of majorities. There were a number of Chilean postgrad students at the College, many of them from the Catholic University in Santiago, and most of them were horrified by what Allende was already doing at home. For the most part, they weren't right- or left-wingers, just intensely patriotic Chileans who cared deeply. Allende, they claimed, was opening the doors to the extreme, revolutionary left. His economic reforms would bankrupt the country, and the extremists, backed by Castro and Moscow, would move in. I became drawn into these postgrads' discussions, fascinated by what was going on. Outside St Antony's no one in England seemed to know anything, or care.

Bill and I talked about Chile; I passed on all that I had been hearing in Oxford. Unexpectedly he said, 'You know, I'm going there in January – on a special information mission for President Nixon. Why don't you come along?' With minimum hesitation, I agreed. I set to vigorously brushing up my Spanish, which I had learned in a passionate love affair with Andalusia a few years before. I boned up on Chilean politics. I called in to see Maurice (by then Deputy to 'C' in MI6; he became 'C' himself in 1973). He was closely interested in Soviet activities in Latin America. Things looked bad, he thought: we could be seeing the beginning of a major new Soviet gambit in the Cold War. If the Russians were to establish a foothold in mainland South America, it would be truly alarming.

Quite independently of Maurice, I made contact with an interesting writer called Brian Crozier, an expert on Franco and Iberian matters. He was currently running a syndicated features service called Forum World Features and would be be interested in anything I could file from Latin America. I ended by sending him nearly a dozen pieces, which were then published across the world. It was no secret that FWF received CIA funding, but so what? So did that most prestigious journal, *Encounter*. I could never understand all the fuss. The US never had any equivalent to the British Council, so here its function was partly fulfilled within the vast embrace of CIA headquarters at Langley. All I know is that not a single word of any piece I wrote for either FWF or for *Encounter* was ever chopped or altered in any way.

I arrived in New York to join up with Bill at the beginning of January 1971. Allende had been established in power for just over two months. He was already moving at an astonishing rate, considering he had come to power by a margin of only 39,000 votes, propelling Chile powerfully leftwards and towards the Soviet bloc. In all my many visits to the US, I do not remember finding morale so low. The unwinnable war in Vietnam was biting ever deeper; indeed it was clear that South American countries were moving to the left for that very reason – that the US was losing in Vietnam.

We flew first to Colombia, a ravishing, baffling country of charming people, speaking exquisite Spanish, and yet riven by the most appalling, endemic violence. We then moved on to Peru. The moment we left the airport at Lima, the horror – the sight and smell – of the *callampas*, the world's worst shanty slums, hit us. Experience of this horror made it easier in later years to understand the rationale behind the Sendero Luminoso revolutionaries.

I was glad to go on up to Cuzco and Machu Picchu, pure tourism and pleasure. But Bill was restless; he was no sightseer, and constantly wanted to move on. At the ruins I wandered off by myself. From high up on mighty Huayna Picchu I spotted a tiny figure hunched over his inseparable portable typewriter. Excellent! The mood of this unique lost world had finally got to him. I crept down, peered over his shoulder and read: he was writing a column on Clare Luce and the legalisation of abortion.

Then it was south to Chile. On our first morning we set off down to the coast from Santiago, to see the great poet, Pablo Neruda. Accompanying us were Selden Rodman, American translator of Neruda, and a Chilean journalist friend of his, Nena Ossa. With a magical, silvery laugh Nena stole our hearts – Bill's and mine – at once. The quintessential Chilena, and one of Chile's leading women journalists, she was an outspoken opponent of Allende and his policies. She was to become the nexus of our trip to Chile, and a lifelong friend to both of us.

As we approached Neruda's lair at Isla Negra, Nena warned us that she was not going in, but would 'hide on the floor of the car'. She had recently written a satirical article on the Communist bard, for which she had dug up an old poem of his:

> If you are born a fool in Romania
> you follow a fool's career ...
> But if you are born a fool in Chile
> soon they will make you an ambassador.

Neruda was about to be appointed Allende's ambassador to Paris. He had no telephone, therefore Rodman had not been able to warn him of our visit. We had obviously not chosen a good moment. The great poet was affable enough, but his afternoon was filled up with official appointments and briefings with new poets. Nevertheless, Rodman persisted. We were taken on a tour of the property, which contained little to indicate the dedicated, lifelong Marxist-Leninist, winner of the Stalin Prize and (later that year) the Nobel Prize for Literature. It was, in fact, positively bourgeois. The house was crammed with beachcombers' bric-a-brac: ships' figureheads, bottles containing crucifixes, model Eiffel Towers, Indian masks and a bidet painted with roses. The bare joists were inscribed with lines from Neruda's favourite poets (other than himself); some seemed rather mundane. There was a bar clad with bottle ends and split bamboo. In our brief snatches of conversation he neither said nor did anything to dispel the stockbroker image. I came away disconcerted, disappointed and rather wishing that I hadn't met him. But then who would expect the ethereal spring-song of the thrush to burst from such a drab-coloured bird? To me Neruda's poetry remains sublime.

But it was Allende we had come to study. Under a policy of agrarian reform about as radical as anything seen in Eastern Europe, Chilean *latifundos* or plantations were being taken over, often through illegal *tomas* (takeovers) by semi-guerrilla groups of the MIR (the Revolutionary Left Movement). On flimsy excuses of financial irregularity, smaller as well as larger firms were being expropriated by the insertion of government proxies, and there had been soaring wage increases. The powerful US copper companies, which – representing an investment of almost $1,000 million – formed the backbone to the Chilean economy, were being nationalised; Washington was retaliating by blocking Chilean credits.

Meanwhile, in the media, the principal opponents to Allende's Marxist experiment were being effectively silenced by a combination of officially orchestrated strikes, financial pressure on their advertising revenues and rank intimidation. Agustín Edwards, the owner of *El Mercurio*, the oldest newspaper in all the Hispanic world, an honest and most honourable journal, which led the vanguard of opposition to Allende, felt it necessary to flee to Connecticut for his own safety.

For the next few days Bill and I flew around Santiago, interviewing government officials, trades unionists and journalists. It was exhausting, but exciting. Daily, Nena telephoned to enquire cheerily, 'Are you still alive?' We went up to the University, to meet a remarkable figure called Claudio Veliz, director of its Institute of International Affairs. Barely forty, Veliz was already something of an institution himself, having attended Harvard, the Sorbonne and the London School of Economics – not to mention St Antony's, Oxford, whence came my introduction – and he was a champion swimmer and skier to boot. Originally well left of centre, he had backed Allende at the 1970 elections, but was rapidly changing his mind. His black beard bristling with rage, he said, 'Look, I have to get out of this bloody place. Let's drive up into the mountains and talk.' We drove furiously, up and up. The view over Santiago and towards the Andes was incredible. But not for Veliz. His beloved university was being politicised, wrecked before his very eyes, by the student supporters of the MIR. 'You know, we're all getting what visitors to Germany in the early Hitler days used to call the *deutscher Blick* – that look over the shoulder to see who may be listening.' A few weeks after our conversation, Veliz arrived at the University one day to discover he had been locked out, his door screwed shut. *Mirista* students had simply moved in and taken over the building. Veliz left for Australia, and a distinguished international career – like thousands of refugees from Allende's Chile, never to return.

Almost as one watched Santiago was becoming polarised – into exultation and euphoria on the one hand, deepest gloom on the other. Bill likened the euphoria to the mood of 1917 Russia that John Reed described in his classic account, *Ten Days that Shook the World*. For Chile's sake, I hoped he was wrong, but certainly the confrontation was hotting up daily. To my simple, English, conservative mind, it seemed alarming what Allende and his zealots were doing to this relatively prosperous country. But it was a fascinating time for a historian of war and revolution. Bill, moving – as all his life – in overdrive, took off for Rio and homewards, to report to the White House. I decided to stay on; I wanted to see more.

It was quite clear that centre-stage was not Santiago, or La Moneda Palace where the *compañero presidente* sat, but down in the countryside far to the south. There the *reforma agraria* was really biting. Hundreds of thousands of acres of farm and forestry properties were being *tomado*, expropriated, either legally or illegally. Although real poverty was nowhere as desperate in Chile as elsewhere in South America, land hunger had long been a gnawing evil. When Allende's predecessor, the Liberal Eduardo Frei, came to power in 1984, between 2 and 5 per cent of land-owners possessed an estimated 75 per cent of the land, much of which was inefficiently farmed. Under Frei's reform laws, properties of more than 200 acres could be expropriated. With the advent of Allende his new Minister of Agriculture, a Cuban-trained apparatchik named Jacques Chonchol – whose love for the *latifundistas* was about as warm as Stalin's for the kulaks – made it clear at once that he intended to accelerate Frei's programme out of all recognition. But for the young firebrands of the MIR things were still not moving nearly fast enough.

At El Arrayan, up in the foothills of the Andes, I sought out a good-looking young sociologist-turned-journalist called Pablo Hunneus. Pol-itically a Frei-liberal, he was deeply disturbed by what he had discovered. He had a list of at least eighty-six *fundos*, embracing an area of 400,000 acres (it later turned out to be several times that amount) that had already been *tomado* by the MIR and its allies in the two southern provinces of Cautin and Valdivia alone – the breadbasket of Chile. Groups of them were being led by a mysterious figure known as 'Comandante Pepe', who – a little like the free-booter Strelnikov in *Doctor Zhivago* – was roaming the countryside at will, carrying out *tomas* and setting up revolutionary committees wherever he went. Pablo described how he had found Pepe up in the wild mountain country close to the Argentine frontier. On the map it looked forbidding country. He reckoned the aim of Pepe's *miristas* was to create a *foco* (guerrilla base), in case of a coup by the Chilean right wing. Meanwhile property owners were beginning to import machine guns from over the border. The situation looked menacing. The Allende government had been enraged by Hunneus's articles in *La Prensa*, and

formally declared that Comandante Pepe was a figment of his imagination.

What was strange (and rather deplorable) was that, apart from
Hunneus, no member of the vast corps of national and international
press tumbling over themselves in the bars of Santiago had taken the
trouble to get off their hunkers and go down south to have a look at what
might be the big story in Chile. I decided to do just that, and managed to
persuade Nena to come with me. It was the happiest idea I ever had;
she knew everyone, and every door – government, opposition and even
miristal – flew open at the sound of her laugh. We went first to Temuco,
the local capital some 500 miles south of Santiago, a wooden town where
it never stops raining, and then headed north-east towards Liquiñe in the
heart of Pepe's *foco*. The perfect cone of Villarica volcano had a constant
wreath of cloud and perhaps smoke around it. These Andean foothills of
silent lakes and rich green mountains were astonishingly empty, with a
certain tranquillity in the villages; no weekend villas or restaurants, no
Coca-Cola signs – only an occasional farm, an ox cart with wooden
wheels, *campesinos* on horseback, bat-like in their copious black *mantas*
that almost enveloped the horses as well, all smiles and quiet courtesy.
We passed more and more MIR slogans, promising revolution. Eventually
we reached dense forest and jungle country close to the Argentine frontier.
The whole neighbourhood exuded a miasma of neglect, of slow death.
Eventually we came upon a roughly painted sign:

CARRANCO

TERRITORIO LIBERADO

This was the area where Hunneus claimed to have met the elusive Comandante. Rough-looking guards directed us on to another camp called
Trafún. This time the men on the barricades were rather more menacing;
one was fingering a revolver barely concealed beneath a blue shirt. One
was on crutches, nursing a leg-wound. What did the *compañero* want?
With something of a dry mouth I told Blue Shirt that I was an English
historian, that I was touring Chile studying a great moment of social
history (true). The lady was my interpreter. I remembered that I had with
me among my papers in the car the jacket for *The Terrible Year*, my latest
book on the Paris Commune. Somewhat disingenuously, I implied that

I was a sympathising historian of the Commune. That opened the door. Hosts of *miristas* appeared, at their head a smallish man dressed predominantly in black: black trilby, black leather jacket with a ruff collar, black knee-boots, black hair, black moustache, lively black eyes and freckles, his tight jeans held together with a string, a large automatic and Bowie knife slung from a rawhide belt. He looked every boy's image of a Latin American outlaw.

Yes, he was the legendary Comandante Pepe. With him was a pretty girl – brown eyes, poor complexion – whom he introduced as Valentina. Speaking with nervous rapidity Pepe explained that he was not a Cubano as some of the opposition papers were suggesting. His real name José Gregorio Liendo, he was twenty-six and (as might have been expected) of petty-bourgeois origin, his father a dairy-worker. He was a student at Valdivia University – the great hothouse centre for the MIR – and had spent four years working on the local *campesinos*. His number two, Valentina, also of bourgeois origins, had been sent to school in Maryland, USA, and had returned to join the MIR out of impatience with President Frei's reform. She was twenty-three. We moved up into the house of the absent owner, a Señor Kunstmann, which had been seized by the MIR. It was a modest working-farmer's dwelling, with very few traces of luxury. I asked Pepe and Valentina if they were now living there. 'No. We have allotted it to the *campesinos* who live in Trafún. We are sleeping on the floor in their houses, like them, so as to share their lives fully.'

Pepe uncorked a bottle of Señor Kunstmann's wine for us, but none of the *miristas* would join us. 'We have given it up. Alcoholism is such a problem up here and we must set an example,' they explained primly. We discussed the *reforma agraria*. 'Remember,' said Pepe, 'for centuries a minority has abused the majority in this country, and now it is the turn of the majority to abuse the minority, and there is bound to be injustice in the process.' They expressed impatience with the slow speed of Allende's reforms. Valentina was a red-hot pedantic doctrinaire, totally sincere and dedicated, but seeming to regard the *campesinos* as little more than political symbols in the struggle for Marxist victory. Her only concession to femininity was a touch of mascara on her eyelashes. Pepe, on the other hand, was a romantic of considerable attraction and charm, such as Latin America seems to specialise in. He manifested a deep human involvement with the *campesinos*. In a war, I would like to have had him with me. We discussed bourgeois versus Marxist truth. Pepe insisted that the Paris Commune had been provoked by economic injustice. After a lengthy dialogue Pepe confronted me: 'Do I have the impression that you are not a Marxist?'

'You could be right!'

Then, almost in a whisper: 'But if you were a Chilean of my age, you would be with us, wouldn't you?'

'Quite possibly.' (But as a half-baked romantic, not as a Marxist, I thought to myself.)

Things developed on a free and easy basis, and Pepe did not seem to be worried by my dialectical shortcomings; but I worried about Valentina – definitely the more dangerous of the species. I could see her pulling a trigger without compunction. Pepe urged us to stay the night – 'so we can *concientizar* you!' It was already dark. I asked Pepe about the future. He said, 'Historically there is bound to be a counter-reaction against the Allende government, a right-wing coup.' Several times he repeated with chilling emphasis, 'Civil war in Chile is inevitable.'

Next day, we left the *fundo* on a battered truck. There were women and children clinging to it on every side. Their exhilaration was unmistakable, as was the impact that Pepe and his *miristas* made on the *campesinos*. There was something most engaging about him. As we bade adios to Pepe he said cheerfully, 'When you get back to Europe don't forget to put a flower on the grave of Karl Marx for me! And please greet my good friend Jacques Chonchol when you see him. He was here two weeks ago.' A few days later we returned to Temuco for an interview set up with Chonchol himself. I questioned the minister about his strategy of land reform. Trained in Cuba, like many a theoretical ideologue he had never worked the land himself. He said he had a simple formula: 'If a proprietor tells me he employs thirteen people, I tell him that's far too few, you must multiply by ten.' (Not surprisingly, the unhappy landlord now employing 130 bodies could not afford the wage bill and had to sell up, or simply move out.) When we arrived at the delicate issue of the MIR and the illegal *tomas*, I enquired, 'And what about this Comandante Pepe?' Looking me straight in the eye, the Minister of Agriculture replied: 'All an invention of the press. I doubt if this Pepe exists. Even if he does he has little significance.'*

I could not help remembering Pepe's parting remark:

'Please greet my good friend Jacques Chonchol when you see him. He was here two weeks ago.'

In retrospect, I suppose it was highly irresponsible to take the risks we did, sticking our heads in the lion's den at Trafún. Certainly it was unfair of me to have exposed Nena to such danger; she, after all, had to live there. It was only a month since the British ambassador in Uruguay had been hijacked by the Tupamaros, blood-brothers of the MIR. It was far from certain that he would be found alive – in fact he was, eight months later. We returned to Santiago. All over the city I noted the unfinished buildings, the projects that recalled the socialist planning in Tito's Belgrade of two decades previously. Runaway inflation was beginning; within a year this once modestly prosperous economy, its agriculture ruined by Chonchol and the MIR, would be buying chickens from France, with badly needed credits. More and more of the middle classes that Chile needed were leaving the country. The latest joke was 'Los cobardos se van, los tontos quedan' (The cowards are leaving, the fools remain). Nena was no fool, but – Chilena to the core – she would never leave her native soil. I too was leaving, for Bolivia and home, and felt more than a bit of a coward, deserting this attractive country in whose problems I had become so unexpectedly involved.

Bolivia had its charms, eccentricities and challenges. In the mid-nineteenth century, following a (well-deserved) slight to the British Ambassador, Queen Victoria was said to have ordered Palmerston simply to 'wipe it from the map'. In La Paz one would be shown a lamp-post, always garlanded with flowers, from which a president had been hanged not so long before. British politicians should visit the site and take note. The hotel I stayed in caught fire, but, because of the lack of oxygen at 13,000 feet, the blaze quietly died out. Two days later, returning from the famous carnival at Oruro, the bus I was in was hijacked by left-wing students armed with Kalashnikovs. After a few ugly moments, they were

---

* On 21 September 1973 Pepe was reported captured with seventeen of his men; two weeks later the London *Times* announced his execution.

bought off with $1 a head per passenger. Later, in Colombia, I had a narrow escape from a mob surging through Bogotá. Fleeing back to the safety of my hotel, I watched from the top floor as the army herded the demonstrators, with no little brutality, into the adjacent bull ring. Over the next twenty-four hours, a combination of hunger, boredom and hailstones the size of golf balls completed the job of pacification.

That was my farewell to South America, with all its violence, hopelessness and courage, its passion for colour and music at any price, the lovable irrationalism of its people (which Marquez and Vargas Llosa capture so well), the uplifting gaiety and the heart-rending poverty.

13

A SAVAGE WAR OF PEACE

1980, Birch Grove. Harold Macmillan enjoys a joke.
(Wish I could remember what it was!)

I know what helps them go on living: that wave of hope the morning brings with it, that light which gives the illusion that even death is vanquished and that nothing in this world exists but the sun, the cries of children, and the beauty of the sky.

Jules Roy, *The War in Algeria*

In the spring of 1971, the Great Adventure over, I returned home to England. But I had brought Latin America back in my luggage. Everything smelt of it. The music of quena, charanga and guitarra was constantly tintinnabulating in my ears. I finished off the articles promised for Brian Crozier and Mel Lasky and tried to turn back to that never-to-be-finished novel. I couldn't. Chile was too much with me, as things went from bad to worse there. I hadn't intended writing a book about it, but suddenly I knew I had to. The title was unmissable: 'Small Earthquake in Chile; Not Many Killed' had won the prize for the most boring newspaper headline in a 1930s competition set by the humorist Claude Cockburn. Chile then was a small, faraway country of which we knew little. And now, in the other sense of the caption, under Allende Chile had been struck by a *terremoto* off the Richter scale, its tremors reaching out to strike the rest of the world. In New York, my new American publisher, Tom Guinsburg of Viking, and his outstanding, lovable editor-in-chief, Alan Williams, instantly expressed an interest. At home, the other Alan – Maclean – at Macmillans was more resistant. 'Of course we'll publish anything you write' was the gist of what he said, 'but be warned: you and we won't make any money out of it.' Macmillans didn't really try to sell the book, but I had indeed been warned. I wrote it with gusto, and some passion, in less than a year.

Small Earthquake in Chile came out in Britain in September 1972. It was exactly one year before the brutal Pinochet coup which killed the brave but misguided little *compañero presidente*, and ushered in sixteen grim years for a Chile ostracised by the grown-up world. Predictably, the book was either half ignored by the provincial-minded British press or savaged by the radical chic, the left-of-centre for whom Allende was (and remains) a folk-hero of Che Guevara's stature. Hugh O'Shaughnessy in the *Financial Times* dismissed it in one paragraph, observing that £4 'seemed a steep price to pay for this view of South America'. Curiously enough, the most perceptive and unbiased review was that of Richard Gott, self-proclaimed Marxist/Maoist, later exposed as a KGB operative; in the *New Statesman*, while disagreeing with most of what I wrote ('many of his judgments hopelessly off key'), he generously allowed that I had been 'remarkably free from venom or rancour'. Writing with that lofty capacity to be wise before the event, in July 1973 the *New York Times* (Norman Gall) pooh-poohed my predictions of a military coup. Two months later Pinochet was bombing La Moneda.

As well as blowing his own head off, Allende had already shot himself (and Chile) in both feet. The Pinochet coup would have happened regardless of whatever feeble contributions were made by the wicked CIA. Chile deserved neither Allende nor Pinochet; without Allende and his follies there would have been no Pinochet. If anything, the passage of time makes Allende look a great deal worse, and more dangerous, than he did in 1971. Material emanating from the KGB files after *glasnost*, notably the remarkable Mitrokhin Archive,* indicates that if Allende was not actually a fully paid-up agent of Andropov's machinery, he was the next closest thing.

Miserable at what was happening in her beloved Chile, and finding it more and more difficult to write for the opposition press, Nena arrived penniless in England. She set about taking a degree in art history at the Victoria and Albert Museum, from which she graduated with the highest distinction. Returning to Chile, she got herself appointed director of Santiago's National Art Gallery. Never losing touch, she remains close to all of us. Momentarily I disappointed her, by declining to be associated with a new Anglo-Chilean Society, intended to improve relations with Pinochet's Chile. Shocked by reports of the continuing excesses of Pinochet, I was reluctant to join a body from which I felt I would almost certainly end by resigning.

---

* Christopher Andrew and Vasili Mitrokhin, *The Mitrokhin Archive II: The KGB and the World* (Allen Lane, 2005).

In October 1972 I received a letter from Harold Macmillan. Having spent the previous nine years fretting in the wilderness, after his prostate had forced him to resign prematurely, and resentfully, as prime minister, he had taken over the family publishing firm. He ran it with flair and gusto, writing his own prolific memoirs at the same time. He had just read *Small Earthquake*, not at all his scene but, he wrote engagingly, 'You are quite right, none of us in Britain knows anything about South America and I must plead guilty to the general ignorance. Your book gives a fascinating picture of an extraordinary scene.' I was invited to call in and speak to Mr Harold. It was our first meeting. Sitting behind his publisher's desk, now in the rather nasty modern boxy Macmillan offices in Little Essex Street, he put me in mind of a wounded old lion at bay, and I noted his hooded, shrewd but not unkindly eyes. I had not a thought that this would turn out to be the first of many meetings, that it would be a landmark leading in a few years' time to a quite unexpected sea-change in my literary and professional life. Like a benevolent headmaster, he questioned the professional wisdom of writing about Latin America, before adding, 'Do go back to France, dear boy. You write about it so well. It's your subject, you've got it all to yourself. How about Louis Philippe and the Bourgeois monarchy?' I mumbled something about wanting to get on with my novel. Supermac, as the cartoonist Vicky had dubbed him, looked disappointed, even disbelieving.

We met a second time. He had something much more positive to propose: would I think of writing about the Algerian War (which had ended ten years previously)? He explained: 'When de Gaulle came to power and I was prime minister, so often all our difficulties seemed to stem from that one word – Algeria. That was a seminal event in our times, and you, with your background of modern French history, I know you could do it.' My objections that I was not strong on the Algerian, on the Arab background, that it might be too soon to write, were waved aside. 'Do it before we're all dead, and the facts are forgotten,' he urged me. He for one seemed to have forgotten little; old age had not dimmed his remarkable recall of detail and dialogue. The conversation ranged, with superb parallels and admirable relevance, from the first Roman Republic to Cromwell's Commonwealth, to the advantages of ministerial rule from the Great Houses of England – but always back to de Gaulle and his

Algerian nightmare. He spoke of de Gaulle generally with a mixture of deep admiration and irritation. He seemed obsessed by the General's cap measurement. 'Winston, you know, with his great big head could think both backwards and forwards in time, but de Gaulle with that little pinhead of his could only look backwards, to Louis XIV. But he was one of the bravest men I ever knew.'

I went away, promising I would think hard about it, and I did. Algeria had always fascinated me. During all those months I had spent in Paris researching the Franco-German trilogy, the war there had been rumbling on; I was in Paris in January 1960 when 'Barricades Week' broke out in Algiers. The European settlers, or *pieds noirs*, were in revolt against de Gaulle, and in the French Army the elite paras were openly siding with them. For the first time the French press had begun using the ugly word 'insurgents', menacingly evocative of Franco and the Spanish Civil War. Momentarily it had looked as if the still-fragile structure of de Gaulle's Fifth Republic might crack. Then the General delivered one of his magical appeals, and the crisis of Barricades Week dissolved like a puff of smoke.

What most vividly remains in my mind of those tense days in Paris was the passionate involvement of members of the foreign press. Beyond the excitement of events and professional detachment, they agonised over France's dilemma and, during de Gaulle's television appearance, tears of emotion were brought to more than one otherwise steely eye. I also happened to be in France on two other occasions when events in Algeria threatened the very existence of the Republic – in May 1958, when de Gaulle was brought to power, and again in April 1961, the latter the most dangerous of all when ancient Sherman tanks were rolled out on to the Place de la Concorde to guard against a possible coup by the paras mounted from Algiers. Each episode seemed to me, in retrospect, to bear a curious resemblance to the essential rhythm of other great crises in modern French history, whether in 1870, 1916 or even 1940: a headlong rush to the brink of disaster, or even beyond it, followed by an astounding recovery and eventually leading to a reflowering of the creative energies and brilliance that are the essence of France.

I had kept copious notes and cuttings as the war in Algeria ground on, so I ended doing what 'Mr Harold' proposed. After some intensive preliminary reading from a gigantic list, I prepared to go to Algeria in the spring of 1973. I fired off letters in all directions, not least to every surviving French prime minister. All were surprisingly receptive. But first there was a painful problem to face. No fewer than four times I had encountered a competitor writing the same book as I was. Worst of all had been the affray with Doubleday and James Morris. Now I learned that Anthony Nutting was already doing Algeria. A former Tory minister who in his thirties had been a golden boy, Sir Anthony Nutting had been Eden's heir apparent: he might well have ended up leading the Tory Party, but Suez – and his very honourable resignation – had sunk him. We met in the Garrick Club to discuss the problem. He looked ravaged, utterly destroyed; he had ruined his own career. I felt desperately sorry for him, and prepared to make way; after all, with his close links with the Arab world, he would probably do the Algerian side of the story better than I possibly could. It was a painful conversation. At one point I glanced over his shoulder, my eye catching a mischievous sculpture, one of the Garrick's theatrical relics, of two nude women spanking each other's bottoms. To try to lighten the atmosphere, I drew Nutting's attention to it. Nothing would educe even the slightest smile. Looking haunted he said he would withdraw. 'You go ahead and do it.' I felt really bad, as if I had removed the lifebelt of a drowning man.

Was I biting off more than I could chew? Realisation of the sheer intricacy of the material, far more complex and diffuse than any campaign, or subject, that I had tackled before, scared me. Between 1954 and 1962, the Algerian War had lasted twice as long as the First World War. There was also a convoluted background going back to 1827, when the Dey of Algiers, in striking the French Consul with his fly-whisk, had provided an expansionist-minded French king, Charles X, the last of the Bourbons, with an excuse to occupy the lawless but rich territories of Algeria. By 1954, there were nine million Algerians, with a soaring birthrate, to one million *pieds noirs*. But statistics on landownership and annual earnings told another story, showing that Algerians of European origin possessed economic strength out of all proportion to their numbers. All this provided the essential backdrop to the revolt that began on 1 November 1954. This was the year that France had suffered a crushing defeat at Vietnam's Dien Bien Phu, which alerted Algerian colonial troops who had witnessed it to just how vulnerable France might be in Algeria too.

What in France is called the Algerian War and in Algeria the Revolution was one of the last and most historically important of the grand-style colonial wars, in the strictest sense of the term. Many a Frenchman, especially the *pieds noirs* of Algeria, waged the war in the belief that they were shouldering the 'white man's burden'. Many a French para gave his life heroically, assured that he was defending a bastion of Western civilisation, and the bogey slogan of 'the Soviet fleet at Mers-el-Kébir' retained its force right up to the last days of *la presénce française*. The struggle was undeniably and horribly savage, bringing death to an esti- mated one million Muslim Algerians and the expulsion from their homes of approximately the same number of European settlers. If the one side practised unspeakable mutilations, the other tortured, and, once it took hold, there seemed no halting the spread of violence. As at a certain moment in the Battle of Verdun in 1916, it appeared to me as if events had escaped all human control; so often, in Algeria, the essential tragedy was heightened by the feeling that – with a little more magnanimity, a little more trust, moderation and compassion – the worst might have been avoided.

Important as it was in the history of France, for Algerians the Revolu- tion obviously meant far more. War, said General de Gaulle, 'gives birth and brings death to nations'. To Algeria it brought birth. But, during that war, more was involved than simply the issue of whether nine million Muslims should gain their independence or not. The war itself was enacted in a complex fashion on several levels. Not merely one but several revolutions were actually taking place, not least a profound social revolu- tion going on within the framework of Algerian Muslim society, and, on the French side, revolutions first by the army and later by the far-right Organisation Armée Secrète (OAS) against the political authority of France. There was also the tug-of-war for the soul of Algeria as fought externally on the rostrum of the United Nations and the platforms of the Third World, and in the councils of both Western and Eastern blocs. The sheer length of the war resulted in a huge cast of characters constantly appearing, disappearing and reappearing, and its multiple levels of action were often out of phase with each other. All of this presented a canvas of daunting size, one lacking in any obvious single focus or climax, until perhaps the arrival of de Gaulle in 1958.

In the spring of 1973, accompanied by Renira and, for part of the way, by a friend, Patricia, I started my exploration at Zéralda on the coast just west of Algiers, not far from where the French had landed in 1830. We stayed, initially, in a new hotel where the Boumedienne government was, allegedly, beginning to encourage tourism. But it was plain that the Algerians, though they badly needed the foreign currency, didn't much like tourists, or foreigners of any sort. 'Nous autres algériens, nous ne sommes pas de tout serviables [good servants],' one Algerian diplomat explained to me, as if any explanation were necessary. The atmosphere was all a little reminiscent of life behind the Iron Curtain: strange, unclubbable people, ravishing country! At Zéralda, under umbrella pines cooing with doves, there still existed the remnants of typically French barracks, bearing such faded lettering as 'Poste de Commandement' that the Algerians had not yet got around to effacing. Like many other relics of the 130-year *présence française* that I visited elsewhere in Algeria, Zéralda was permeated with ghosts. But although it was barely more than a decade since the last *pied noir* had left, somehow those ghosts seemed to belong already to almost as remote a past as the ruins left behind by the Roman conquerors. A short distance down the beautiful, unspoiled coast lie the ancient Roman ruins of Tipasa. There are few more idyllic spots in the entire Mediterranean, and it provoked from that great French humanist, Albert Camus, one of his most eloquent and nostalgic essays. Writing in those tranquil pre-war days of colonial Algeria, Camus – in some ways the typical *pied noir* – described euphorically how he had experienced there 'the happy lassitude of a wedding day with the world'. Lapped by a peacock-coloured sea, Tipasa remains an absinthe-perfumed paradise of expressionist colours.

Five years after Camus wrote these words, when Algeria was occupied by the Allies in the Second World War, General Charles de Gaulle and Harold Macmillan, then Churchill's plenipotentiary in Algiers, spent an historic afternoon together amid the joys of Camus' Tipasa. Macmillan (so he recorded in his memoirs) had bathed naked, but de Gaulle – always ram-rod correct and conscious of his dignity – sat bolt upright on a rock in full uniform under the Algerian summer sun. Little could de Gaulle have realised then just how closely his own future was going to be linked to the fate of Algeria.

When I first discovered Tipasa in 1973, it moved me almost as strongly as it had Camus. Revisiting it twelve years later, I was still able to find the small memorial to Camus that bears the now worn quotation from his works: 'Glory consists of the ability to love without measure.' In a way the ageing obelisk stands as a memorial to all the heartbreak, savagery and bitterness of the Algerian War. The glory that colonial France once created in Algeria has passed into limbo, and the gently peaceful beauty of Tipasa casts a deceptive cloak over a much more ferocious past. For it was on a sunny beach close by that French women and children, as well as men, were machine-gunned as they bathed, by freedom-fighters of the Algerian FLN (Front de Libération Nationale). At Zéralda itself, Algerian suspects died in a French torture camp; and it was from barracks in this same Zéralda that rebel units of French paras launched a nearly successful coup against President de Gaulle's Fifth Republic in April 1961.

From Roman Tipasa, we drove in an East-European-built Renault up to snow-covered (in May) Atlas peaks. Here the road disappeared terrifyingly in a landslide. After some hair-raising reversing, we continued through the ravishing broom-covered mountains of Kabylia, where the Berber douars sit atop razor-backed ridges to protect them from the foes of countless past wars, down into the hostile gorges of the Aurès where the first spark of FLN revolt ignited in 1954, and beyond into the endless sands of the Sahara. On my second trip, in Algiers, led by agile young Algerians and stifling a terror of heights, I leaped from rooftop to rooftop across the narrow streets of the Casbah to study how Algerian 'freedom fighters' had escaped from the deadly net thrown round them by the paras in the renowned Battle of Algiers in 1957. I was taken to places in the nigh-impenetrable *bled* or outback that had remained FLN strongholds almost throughout the war.

Exploring this breathtakingly beautiful but hard country helped me understand one or two simple and extremely basic facts. One was that most of it was guerrilla country par excellence, and a nightmare terrain for a conventional army fighting a defensive war. If it testified to the staggering endurance of the FLN *djoundi*, equipped with primitive weapons and suffering under appalling conditions, so it did to the remarkable achievements of the French Army which – in military terms alone – had virtually won the fighting war by 1960. The second thing I learned –

as I toured through the once prosperous farms of the Mitidja with their acacias and vines that looked as if they might have been lifted from Languedoc – was why the *pieds noirs* had struggled so stubbornly to keep hold of this exigent demi-paradise, the only homeland most of them knew, just as the Algerians had fought with such ferocity to regain it. And, by their lights, what a marvellous country they had made of it. Some *pieds noirs* families had been rooted there for three or four generations, since the emigrations that followed France's defeat in the Franco-Prussian War of 1871, and they had led the good life. The main squares of the once prosperous towns and villages of the Mitidja, surrounded by well-pollarded plane trees (and containing the inevitable, graceless monument *aux morts*) would almost invariably boast a highly ornate bandstand where, every Sunday, the band of the local garrison would endeavour to distract the *indigènes* from their lack of more worldly privileges with rousing martial music. The life and pleasures of the *pieds noirs* were those of the true Mediterranean being: the old women knitting and gossiping on shaded park benches, the men arguing and storytelling over the long-drawn-out pastis outside the bistros; the protracted silence of the siesta; then the awakening in the cool of the evening, the games of boule in dusty squares, under trees crammed with revivified and chattering birds.

The good life they enjoyed depended on the cheap labour of the under-class, of Algerians. Yet not all *pieds noirs* experienced such comfort: there were the *petits blancs*, who lived in close juxtaposition to, and economic competition with, the Algerians – by whom they felt constantly threat-ened. Slum suburbs like Algiers' Bab-el-Oued were so heavily impreg-nated with Spanish blood that their inhabitants were known collectively as the 'Hernandez-and-Perez'. They had been the most vociferous sup-porters of Algérie Française. And they were passionate Mediterranean people, capable of great fury and fanaticism. They did everything to excess, as witness Camus' classical study *L'Etranger*, about a man who, dazed by the sun, kills for no reason: excessive exuberance, excessive hospitality, excessive affection and excessive hate. Under the implacable sun the *pied noir* married young and was burnt out young. As Louis Joxe, the man chosen by de Gaulle to negotiate the withdrawal from Algeria, remarked to me: 'L'Algérie montait à la tête.' Often the *pieds noirs* showed contempt for the native Algerian that shocked soldiers from Metropolitan

France. At a court hearing, for example, when a judge asked, 'Are there any other witnesses?', the reply was 'Yes, five – two men and three Arabs.' Or again: 'It was an Arab, but dressed like a person.'

On the other hand, so strongly had the new, Algerian inhabitants of those farms and cities imposed their imprint (not least in uprooting, according to Muslim law, the vines that had once made Algeria's agronomy rich) that, by 1973, it was impossible to think of Algeria being anything but a totally Muslim, Arabo-Berber society. Nevertheless, all the tokens of destruction of those eight terrible years had not been removed. Along the main roads, like rows of neatly felled trees, the power pylons still lay where they had been blasted by the FLN, and frequently one had to bounce one's way across rocky fords where destroyed bridges had not yet been replaced. Everywhere I saw the empty shells of farmhouses, barns and homesteads, sometimes whole villages. Memories had blurred as to who was responsible for each separate tragedy: was it an isolated *pied noir* farm destroyed by the *fellagha*, or a Muslim *douar* razed by the French Army in reprisal? On their broken walls, superimposed upon each other like the strata of archaeological diggings, the rival war slogans remained clearly legible:

ALGÉRIE FRANÇAISE!!

F.L.N.

'Everything fades', says Camus, quoting a cemetery inscription, 'save memory.' Returning to Algeria in October, intent on carrying out a mass of interviews, I found this particularly true of Algerian participants in the war. Everywhere I heard the expression 'The page is turned.' Either my interlocutors really had forgotten details or they didn't wish to remember them. Prevalent too was the *deutscher Blick*, the nervous look over the shoulder. Too many old comrades, FLN leaders, had been liquidated by their rivals. I was received with formal courtesy, interest and hospitality; nevertheless, there were those wouldn't see me and those who couldn't. Vital informants would not return my calls (even supposing I could get through on the rickety Algerian telephone system). Or, having made a date, they would not turn up. Or they would ask me to veil their utterances with impenetrable anonymity. Or they simply had terrible memories. Ben Bella, one of the founders of the FLN revolt and independent Algeria's first president, was hidden away under house arrest. Ugly rumour (later proved utterly false) had it that his tongue had been torn out.

Some, however – and often those with apparently most to fear – were surprisingly forthcoming. In a marvellously Palmerstonian, elder-statesman's letter, Harold Macmillan had written to both President Bourguiba of Tunisia and Boumedienne requesting they see me. There were other problems that demanded sympathetic understanding. There were no organised archives, understandably. On the purely military level, the style of guerrilla warfare was such that, with the FLN constantly on the move, few men in the field had either the time or circumstances to keep coherent journals. And, it must be remembered, many were illiterate. Unlike the Yugoslav Partisan War of 1942–5, with its rich literature, there was no centralised command. Many of the records that would normally have found their way into the archives of the new state were (so Algerian officials claim) either destroyed or 'removed' in the last desperate days of the OAS. Under the pressures of creating a new state the work of collating the archives that exist was also not very far advanced.

The high walls that surround the houses in Algeria, the delightful courtyards concealed in total privacy behind squalid exteriors in the Casbah, hint at an Algerian characteristic that also did not ease the path of an historian. This natural instinct for secretiveness, developed over the five generations of French suzerainty, was further heightened to the point where few inklings leaked out during the eight years of clandestine warfare of the many internal splits that repeatedly threatened to rive the FLN leadership. It was no less difficult to discover the truth of such divisions a decade later. Compounded with secretiveness there also remained some degree of apprehension. The factionalism of the Revolution continued long after independence in 1962, and as late as 1967 there was an abortive coup against Boumedienne. Two of the founders of the revolt against France, Krim and Khider, had been mysteriously murdered in exile in Europe. Apart from Ben Bella, several other former revolutionary leaders were hiding nervously abroad beyond the reach of Boumedienne. Though Algeria in 1973 was not a police state on the Soviet model, it was an authoritarian regime, and the risk of a fall from grace could be incalculable. There was, additionally, a more general factor in that the Arab tradition holds a concept of history that is rather different from the

European. It rates altogether lower priority, insofar as the essential fatalism of religious teaching suggests that man is strictly limited in his capacity to shape his destiny. Thus there is a tendency to write off the past,
relegating its events – whether they occurred yesterday or in AD 600 – to
the same vast limbo.

When I returned to Algeria, via Tunisia, in October 1973, I was fortified
by an assignment from my old friend, Tom Pocock, now travel editor of
the *Evening Standard*, to write some articles for him. Here began an
extremely agreeable and sometimes remunerative tangent to my literary
career – travel-writing – which over the next three decades would take
me to all corners of the globe. But I ran into immediate bad luck. The
Yom Kippur or Ramadan War had broken out, and that was the only
conflict many of my interviewees could think about. In Carthage, I spent
an hour with that ebullient paternalist President Bourguiba, much of
which was devoted to a discussion of which maquette of him on a prancing
horse would be most appropriate for the central square of Tunis, followed
by a tirade on how the war on Israel could go on 'for a thousand years'.
Although the interview was supposedly off the record, it appeared on
all the television screens of Tunisia that night. Next, my tape-recorder,
together with the tape of the Bourguiba interview, disappeared mysteriously. Attached to me as dragoman-interpreter was a disastrous
figure – he might have been invented by Graham Greene – appropriately
called Monsieur Trikki. Whenever a key rendezvous was in the offing,
Monsieur Trikki would somehow arrange to have the car not start or
blow a bald tyre at high speed, or he would start a fight in a post office
resulting in a lengthy police intervention, or he would simply not appear
at all. He also had an engaging habit of only telling one what he thought
one would like to hear. We visited a Bedouin encampment where the
inhabitants were patently seized by inhospitality verging on the murderous, and when teasingly I asked Monsieur Trikki to translate their
abuse, he answered, 'They are saying, "Greetings, welcome to the foreigners to our homes."'

In a thoroughly neurotic Algiers I found myself seemingly labelled,
somewhere down in the lower echelons of Boumedienne's secret police,
as an 'Israeli spy'. An improbable guise, but I was followed regularly,
my luggage searched daily. (Appreciating that the Algerians might be a

rougher bunch than Tito's UDBA in 1950, I forebore from deploying the admonitory mousetrap.) I hovered for financially ruinous days in the Hôtel Saint-George – where, a brass plaque recalls, General Eisenhower had set up his Allied Headquarters in 1942 – waiting for the interview with President Boumedienne. Repeatedly it was promised for tomorrow: 'Bukra, bukra.' Little could I know that in fact he was out of town, on a crisis tour of Moscow, Riyadh and other points east in an endeavour to save Egypt's chestnuts on the Suez front. As a sop, I was sent his 'inter-preter', a glamorous Delilah with kohl-blacked eyes like a tigress, who was clearly very close to the President. Chaperoned by three heavies, we dined one night in a French restaurant with a traditional paper tablecloth. She asked me, conversationally, what my view was of the situation on the Egyptian Sinai front. Not a word about Sadat's debacle there had yet appeared in the Algerian press.

As it happened, I had been able to follow its course through copies of *Le Monde* available in the French Embassy. Meanwhile, eighteen months previously, the Israeli Defence Forces publishing house had translated my *To Lose a Battle: France 1940*. Suddenly I woke up one day to the fact that the course of war, up till then running against Israel, had changed dramatically. An Israeli column, headed by a dashing fair-haired young general called Ariel Sharon, had crossed the Suez Canal, striking on the hinge of two enemy armies, and had fanned out behind them, destroying their communications as it went. Within days Israel had turned defeat into yet another historic victory. The more I studied Israeli operations on the Canal, the more I realised how closely they resembled the Manstein Plan which had shattered the French Army in its crossing of the River Meuse in 1940 – and which I had described in great detail in *To Lose a Battle*. It was ironic that a Jewish army should have resorted to the strategy of one of Hitler's generals to win a war, nevertheless. Yet, in an encounter a few months later in London, I put it to Chaim Herzog, my guardian angel that night in 1969, future President of Israel. With a smile he replied, 'Yes, I happen to know Arik Sharon is very grateful to you. You should be getting a medal!'

To impress Boumedienne's seductive emissary, I rashly sketched out a map of operations on the bistro's tablecloth. As we left, out of the corner of my eye, and to my considerable alarm, I saw the tigress carefully folding it up and concealing it in her hand bag, no doubt to be presented in the Presidium the following morning – product of the interrogation of an 'Israeli spy'.

That decided me. It was clearly time to cut my losses and get out, without hanging around to see the invisible Boumedienne. I called for my bill at the Saint-George the next day. When it was presented to me, I blanched: because of the grotesquely high rate of exchange, the sum demanded was gigantic. I could see all my advance for the book and the *Evening Standard* fees disappearing. Then, just as I was reaching for my travellers' cheques, a sinister leather-clad motorcyclist roared up and snatched the cheque book out of my hand. He had orders from the Presidency that on no account was I to pay. I protested. I rang the British Embassy: I was being bought off, how could my professional standing permit me to accept? The Embassy official was rattled: no, it was 'not a nunc dimittis, and we would be very embarrassed were you to refuse . . . Please accept – and go quietly.'

If the gods had not altogether smiled upon me in sunny Algeria, it was – most unexpectedly – quite the opposite in wintry France. The exciting thing about the French is that you never get what you expect; if you expect a red carpet, you get kicked in the crotch; if you expect the worst, you can get a red carpet and all the warmth and generosity in the world. The official papers from the Gouvernement Général housed at the University of Aix were still closed, so I had to depend largely on published material and orals. Yet, in Paris in February 1974, I encountered endless goodwill. In my démarches I received only one turn-down – from Simone de Beauvoir, whose writing I admired unreservedly, in inverse ratio to her political acumen, but who had been a focal figure in the whole anti-war movement. On a fragment of squared paper, apparently ripped out of a child's *cahier de mathématiques* she responded with the following:

Cher Alistair Horne

   I have written in *La Force des choses* all my recollections on the Algerian War. The best is for you to refer to it.

   Avec mes meilleurs sentiments

      S. de Beauvoir

Since then I have tried resolutely never to brush off any aspirant author seeking to tap into my modest recollections.

There were two other factors. First of all, to my extreme surprise, apart from Mme de Beauvior, I found almost universally, in all directions, more than just a willingness to talk, in fact a positive need. Because I was not French, it was as if I were the confessional priest, or the shrink's couch. Here I realised I had a positive advantage in being an outsider, not another Frenchman who might be critical or condemning. I found myself stumbling on an *embarras de richesses*. Everybody (or almost everybody) wanted to talk – and talk. Torturers confessed how, through exigency, they had come to torture. Ex-OAS killers revealed why and how they had killed. Those who had opposed the war with all their hearts confessed how they had crossed the frontiers of treason to do so. Senior generals who had rebelled against de Gaulle spoke of their years in prison with the unashamedness of old lags. Former members of de Gaulle's intimate entourage discussed with painstaking honesty his motives for ending the war.

Secondly, I found some remarkable allies. One was a French author, Yves Courrière, who between 1968 and 1971 had written a four-volume popular study of the war; he was exceptionally generous with his source material. Then there was Christopher Ewart-Biggs, currently the Minister at the British Embassy in Paris. With his monocle (he had lost an eye at El Alamein) and protruding teeth that made him look somewhat like a pressed flower, Christopher's very Bertie Wooster appearance belied the most acute brain. As a much loved former consul in Algiers, he was a fund of information and contacts.*

Perhaps above all others, however, were a couple at the heart of the Paris left-wing Establishment. Jany Minvielle was a spirited Bordelaise whom Bill Buckley and I had met skiing, at a nocturnal *flambeau* in Gstaad. He nicknamed her Pocahontas, because of the long pigtail which flowed behind her on the slopes. We immediately became warm friends. With no children of her own, Pocahontas was to be a kind of fairy

* Two years later, as newly appointed ambassador to Dublin, Christopher was murdered by an IRA bomb at the age of only fifty-four. It was the end of a brilliant career and a charming personality.

godmother, a true *marraine*, to all my daughters in turn when they were in Paris. Now she and her much older husband, Gérard, a veteran Socialist, who spoke like a machine gun with an accent from Les Landes that required an interpreter and was then *questeur* in charge of finances (or number three in the pecking order of the Senate), opened every door – not only on the left but also among the so-called 'fallen angels' of the OAS.

Gérard invited me to a sumptuous lunch at the Senate, Marie de Médicis' resplendent Palais Luxembourg. I told him I was working out at Nanterre University, where all the books and records of the BDIC (formerly in the cosy and accessible Rue Auguste Vacquerie) had been transferred. Nanterre, ultra left-wing, had been the birthplace of the 1968 riots which nearly brought down de Gaulle. It didn't seem to have improved much, covered as it was with layer upon layer of revolutionary graffiti. Gérard, the veteran Socialist, wrinkled his nose in horror: 'Mais, ça c'est abominable! C'est *très socialiste* ... et c'est un désert gastronomique! Mon pauvre! You can't work there!' The thought clearly distressed him all through the rest of the meal, then he said, 'Come upstairs. I'll introduce you to Monsieur Bécarud, the bibliothécaire. You give him a list of what you need, he'll order it all sent from Nanterre and you can work here. Or you can take it back home, and send it back eventually.'

I could hardly believe my luck. No more revo graffiti, no more stale sandwiches out of a machine! Could one conceive of some stray French writer in London or Washington being accorded similar privileges at the House of Lords or the stuffy Library of Congress? So for several weeks that winter of 1974, while at home the miners-versus-Heath struggle was tearing Britain to pieces, I worked away *en luxe* beneath the vast Rubens murals acquired by Marie de Médicis. Loaned a flat on the tip of the Île Saint-Louis by my friend Michael Edwards, perhaps the most enviable location in all Europe, with the frosty morning sun rising exactly along the Quai de Bourbon, I relished the sheer beauty of my surroundings.

Partly through doors opened by the endlessly helpful Gérard, I interviewed no fewer than five ex-premiers who had been in office at the time of the war: there was Georges Bidault, Michel Debré, Antoine Pinay (how they had come and gone!) and Guy Mollet, 'the Man of Suez', who declared he would refuse to talk about that episode, then discussed it for forty-five minutes, and who flattered me by talking throughout in French without once revealing that he was also a professor of English. But my hero was always Pierre Mendès-France, the Sephardic Jew with the face of a pessimistic toreador, who had got France out of Indo-China, but fell when endeavouring to wean Norman five-year-olds from Calvados to milk. Looking deathly ill but still superbly articulate, surely the most intelligent and fascinating man of the Fourth Republic, he was the only one who (had he survived in office) might have prevented the endless tragedy of the war. There was also the fervid intellectual, Jacques Soustelle,* who concluded our conversation on the way to the Assemblée at terrifying speed in a Mini, talking all the way with both hands off the wheel; and there was the brave little ethnologist Germaine Tillion, who had survived Ravensbrück and still held a regular salon for deportees at her house, and who – with Camus – had fought so hard for a liberal, third-force solution in Algeria. She would reach her hundredth birthday.

Then, among the military, there was General Jacques Massu, still every inch the tough front-line soldier, not quite so big as I had expected, but with a face like one of those Swiss bears carved out of wood. Refusing either to deny that his paras had resorted to torture in Algeria or to condemn its use, he was exactly what you saw, the honest and borné para, but loyal (to de Gaulle) to a fault. In contrast Raoul Salan, the complex figure nicknamed the Mandarin, the former C-in-C who ended up as leader of the outlawed OAS in revolt against de Gaulle, his silver hair alternately tinted yellow and mauve, was as devious as they come. Surrounded by orientalia from the Indo-China which had infatuated him and so many other French officers of his generation, he spoke quite unaffectedly of his leadership of the OAS and his ensuing years in prison.

Jany, who knew everyone, had one most remarkable friend, a Madame Gardes, who owned the fashionable restaurant, Les Ministères, in the Rue du Bac, which had been a hub of the Résistance in World War II. Her son, Colonel Jean Gardes, a slight figure who looked deceptively like Stan Laurel, was a much decorated Para hero, one of the Algérie Française

---

* Courageous wartime Gaullist, distinguished anthropologist and forward-looking Governor-General appointed by Mendès-France, and one of the principals who helped de Gaulle to power in 1958.

'colonels' of Algiers who had led the putsch for de Gaulle, and then turned against him. Sentenced to death in absentia when the Challe putsch collapsed, Jean took off to Argentina – there, until he was pardoned, he made a living selling champagne and pâté from recipes learned from his mother. Colonel Gardes was a most helpful source.

The leader of the 1961 revolt, General Maurice Challe, a thoroughly decent airman who had won the British DSO in the Second World War, was perhaps the most tragically admirable of all the principal actors of the war. He had revolted because he felt de Gaulle had forced him to betray promises he had made to his Algerian *barkis* loyal to France. Though he had been pardoned in 1968, the French security services never left him alone. At our last meeting, his voice now reduced to a painful whisper after a throat-cancer operation, he told me how his office was constantly being 'burgled' but nothing stolen. 'De drôle!' I exclaimed. Something strangely similar had happened to me in London recently: with surprising alacrity the CID had homed in on my 'Algerian connection'. He replied, 'Et voilà!' For the last time he declared, in a hoarse voice that obviously pained him, and with emotion, 'Je ne regrette rien, except having failed.'

At the other end of the scale of 'Fallen Angels', was a *pied noir* doctor, one of the most frighteningly nasty men I ever met. Currently with a prosperous practice in the 15ème, he had been the OAS Chief of Operations. Till the early hours one night, supported by several unsavoury former colleagues, he boasted of his 'opérations ponctuelles', of how, in the morning, he would tend and repair 'my parishioners'; then go out at night and 'blow off a few legs of bounoums'.

I was also received by François Mitterrand, then out of power as leader of the Socialist Party. He had been a key figure in the early days of the war as Mendès-France's hard-line Minister of the Interior, who had uncompromisingly declared, 'Algérie c'est la France!' and 'The only possible negotiation is war.' They were not statements he liked to be reminded of. As leader of the left in 1974. I met him in a newly acquired house of haut-bourgeois elegance in the Rue de Bièvre, the equivalent of London's Chelsea. As it was being done up, he asked if I would mind if we sat in the dining room. Every once in a while the swing-door connected to the kitchen would move disquietingly. With thoughts of OAS thugs I had met pervading my consciousness, it made me feel uneasy. Then I looked down to see a tiny dachshund trying to push it open. Clad in a tartan gilet, it was the quintessence of Parisian haute bourgeoisie – curiously incongruous for the leader of the new Front Populaire.

Studying the Algerian War, horrors and torture were never far away. Details of excesses, on either side, sickened the stomach. What stuck in my mind most of all was the terrible scourge of torture and its evil consequences, which are still with us today as perniciously as ever, as the war in Iraq has demonstrated with such force. Because of the slow speed of media coverage in those days, details of abuses committed by the French Army, methods of interrogation employed that had been condemned under the Nazi Occupation, took a long time to emerge. But when they did the consequences were seismic, both in Metropolitan France and in the world at large. It could be said with no exaggeration that, although Massu may have won the Battle of Algiers with the use of intelligence gained from torture, it almost certainly lost France the war. 'In war opinion is nine parts in ten,' observed Jonathan Swift.

Not excessively squeamish, I was stunned when ex-Governor-General Lacoste gripped my thigh, to assure me that the paras who had inflicted the gégène a little higher up the anatomy were but 'jeunes gens sportifs', and that the torture hadn't really hurt. Among the leading figures whom I really admired was Maître Teitgen, former Prefect of Algiers. He was informed by the Algiers police that they had intelligence of a powerful bomb which could have caused appalling casualties. Could they put a suspect to 'the question'? Himself a deportee in the Second World War, Teitgen told me he had refused: 'I trembled the whole afternoon. Finally the bomb did not go off. Thank God I was right. Because if you once get into the torture business, you're lost ... All our so-called civilisation is covered with a varnish. Scratch it, and underneath you find fear. When you see the throats of your copains slit, then the varnish disappears.'

How applicable this remains to the dilemmas facing the West in the war on terror today! From the Inquisition to the Gestapo and the Battle of Algiers, history teaches us that, in the production of reliable intelligence, regardless of the moral issue, torture is counter-productive and should *never* be resorted to. In passing, one might also note France's painful discovery that, fifty years on, many former torturers in the armed services were having to resort to psychiatric counselling. The inflicters of torture as well as their victims remain grievously impaired.

So finally I got down to the writing, in England. All in all it was to take about three years – not so long given the quantity of material I had had to accumulate. In sleepless despair I remember rewriting the preface five times. It was still wrong, and my publishers, Macmillans, agreed. I appealed to them for help, then one day I intercepted an internal memorandum from one editor to another: 'A. H. should rewrite the opening on a much more personal note, explaining why he came to write the book (and "Macmillans told me to do so" will not be acceptable!).' By the end of 1977 the book was ready for publication, over 600 pages of it, the longest and most complex book I had ever written, perhaps ever would write. I said farewell to it with mixed feelings.

Had I managed to produce anything new, and of lasting value? It was hard to associate one's feeling too closely either with the expelled *pieds noirs* or with the victorious Algerians, who generally seemed to me a cruel, unappealing people with none of the charm of their Tunisian or Moroccan neighbours. There were parts of the book which I could not bear to read again, and I resolutely set my face against including among the illustrations any of the countless atrocity photographs of tortured Algerians, or European children with their throats slit, or Algerians with their noses cut off by other Algerians. Had my own views been modified in the course of the work? I suppose I did to some extent review my previously much more critical appreciation of General de Gaulle, as a result of the role he played in the Algerian War. One of the great difficulties that biographers of *le grand Charles* perennially face is in appraising him as one person; there were too many different de Gaulles.

Above all else, however, I know for one thing that I came out with a stronger conviction than before as to the fundamental wickedness of *torture* of all kinds, and its feckless counter-productivity. I was left, also, with a deep sense of pessimism at the intrinsic failures of West European Society which had been highlighted by the Algerian war. Could it all have ended differently? Was there any time when moderation might have prevailed? Looking back on it now I doubt whether any permanent settlement could have been achieved which would not have led eventually to the expulsion, or at best, to the emigration of the whole European minority.

I have seldom known a publisher come up with a good title; but, as the manuscript went into print in London, Alan Maclean and Caro Hobhouse between them came up with a winner, a natural: *A Savage War of Peace* derived from Kipling's

> Take up the White Man's burden
> The savage wars of peace –
> Fill full the mouth of Famine
> And bid the sickness cease.

It would be hard to think of a more savage war, and one arising at a time of general peace. I didn't hesitate a second. Equally it seemed only natural and fair that I should dedicate the book to them, my co-editors, who had provided so much support throughout, and indeed so loyally over all the books of the trilogy. At the same time, I had been sustained and encouraged by Harold Macmillan, who had really sowed the original seed. Though he was nearly eighty when I started my research, he read the book three times – in typescript, in proof, and the finished work, coming up with numerous thoughts and suggestions. On publication, he sent me a letter that would have warmed any author's heart:

'I have now read *A Savage War of Peace, Algeria 1954–62* carefully and slowly – as my now fading eyesight demands.

It is a masterpiece. You have marshalled a very complicated story and divided it up and presented it in such a way that it reads almost like a novel – a sort of historical Tolstoy. Then there are vast numbers of characters again like Tolstoy who emerge very clearly in their different types.

Finally the main and rather tragic figure of de Gaulle is beautifully presented. Altogether I must congratulate you on the best thing you have ever done.

Then came the reviews; once again they were generous to a fault. 'A work of great beauty and insight,' said the wonderfully eccentric Richard Cobb of Oxford (who was to become a new mentor in my life) in the *New Statesman*. In the *New York Times* John Leonard declared, 'Alistair Horne has a terrible story to tell, and he has done so in a splendid book.' Privately from the US, Bill Buckley wrote: 'if I had written such a book as this, to say nothing of the other three, I would, simply, consider that my life's work is done. And retire to the farm?' But perhaps most reassuring were critiques that I received from French writers. *Le Figaro* said, 'Such is the incomparable value of this book as a study of the Algerian War that one will no longer to be able to talk, or write, any more without referring to it.'

Conspicuously absent, however, were any critiques from the Arab world. To this day, despite numerous nibbles from Algeria, I have never managed to find an Arab-language publisher. And, once again, with publication, troubles began – as they always did. In October 1977, Caro Hobhouse was writing to me about 'emergency measures to deal with those orders which are delayed because of our warehouse problems'. What this in effect meant was that Macmillan warehouses had elected to go on strike just in time for the Christmas rush. I found myself replying acidly:

> to be extremely blunt, as I told you the other day, Macmillans among booksellers does have – and has had for a considerable time – a mediocre reputation for delivery of books. It is therefore *very* disheartening to produce what is acclaimed to be a very big book, attain the absolutely first rate editorial support which one has long associated with Macmillans ... only to discover that through a 'hiccough' or something worse down the supply line, books are simply not there to be sold ...

Then, on top of all that, the man in charge of PR, a post that tended to be filled and refilled by a sequence of ex-debutantes or old lags who had failed in other departments, turned out to have a serious health problem. (I was made to recall the disconsolate author of many years past who once accused Macmillans of being 'not publishers but secreters of books', noting the impressive array of tomes by eminent authors on their shelves, he added: 'but do you also *sell* them?') In terms of profitability, it was brought home to me that *A Savage War* would be most unlikely to have proved 'worthwhile'. With all that foreign research and interviews alone swallowing up one-fifth of a not ungenerous publisher's advance, once other costs and tax had been deducted I would be extremely lucky if the four years' work earned me as much as a typist's wage. Could one afford to attempt such an undertaking ever again? Could one afford a publishing house like Macmillans?

My happy relations with the firm took a distinctly cool turn. Then, suddenly, *A Savage War* sprang something utterly unforeseen.

14

SUPERMAC

'The time has come,' the Walrus said, 'To talk of many things:'

Richard Cole's cartoon published in the *Daily Telegraph*,
on the publication of *Macmillan*, vol. 1.

'It is the duty of Her Majesty's government neither to flap nor to falter.'
Harold Macmillan

That supreme opportunist, Otto von Bismarck, once remarked of a states-man: 'if ever in the events around him he hears the sweep of the mantle of God, then he must jump up and catch at its hem'. Perhaps the same might equally apply to lesser mortals – like us authors. Paraphrasing the same thought, Harold Macmillan was to remark to me later, 'Things never turn out quite how you expect, dear boy – but never miss an opportunity ...'

Following publication of *A Savage War* in the US, in the spring of 1978, I was lecturing at the Royal Military College of Canada at Kingston, Ontario. There I made a new friend, a young major of engaging modesty in the USAF called Jon Reynolds. Right at the beginning of the Vietnam War Jon had been shot down over the North in his fighter-bomber. He had endured eight long years as a prisoner of war, much of it in solitary confinement, under far worse conditions than our POWs had suffered, for a far shorter time, in Colditz in the Second World War. With no books or any other form of distraction in solitary he had somehow kept his mind from destruction by learning Spanish through tap-tapping on the pipes in Morse code with a neighbouring Hispanic. In the course of those lost eight years his fiancée, Emilee, had given him up for dead and married another. When he finally returned, she divorced her then husband, married Jon and had two children – and, as they say, lived happily ever after. Retired from operational flying, he was currently teaching history at the USAAF College in Colorado Springs, and would become a lasting friend.

On my departure from Kingston, almost casually he threw an invitation to me, to come and speak to his air force cadets in Colorado Springs: 'We can't pay much – but do you like skiing?' I shouted, yes I did, but knew nothing about skiing in the Rockies. 'You wait!' Little could I foresee what a joyous new opening in life was about to unfold.

I moved on, down the Hudson, to hold a seminar at West Point. In that austere setting which had produced most of America's great soldiers, I was somewhat dismayed to find the first two rows at my lecture were mostly fast asleep before I had even opened my mouth. I asked one afterwards why.

'Sir, it's the jogging, Sir.'

'Why do you jog, then?

'Sir, to get away from being yelled at, Sir!'

It seemed a reasonable response, though not an encouragement to a visiting lecturer.

It was somewhere between Kingston and West Point that a yet more earth-shaking invitation than Jon Reynolds' landed on me. A cable reached me from Alan Maclean at Macmillans. It requested me not to accept any new writing commitment while in the US, but to ring back ASAP – and collect! That, from the firm of Scottish crofters, renowned for their parsimony, had to imply something of far-reaching significance. What a mystery! As soon as I could, I rang. Would I, Alan asked, think of taking on the official biography of Harold Macmillan? Would I come to see him as soon as I returned and meanwhile keep it quiet? I gasped: what possible qualification did I have? At Little Essex Street, when I got back to London, there were beaming smiles. The story was that the editors of Macmillans had, for some time, collectively been pressing Mr Harold, now a spry eighty-four, to appoint an official biographer. Referring to his own six-volume work (published, of course, by his firm) he responded that he felt no need or inclination; then, approached again shortly after publication of *A Savage War of Peace*, he had relented – with the proviso 'if Alistair Horne would do it?'

I reeled with the honour – and my own inadequacy. Very privately I consulted friends: Bill Buckley was hugely positive: 'Go for it, Al!' My revered old headmaster, Ed Pulling, with those icy Atlantic-blue eyes, administered a cold shock of realism: '"Who's Harold Macmillan?" Americans will ask. A lot of work, and it won't sell here!' But, back in England, Warden Raymond Carr was most forceful: 'Good God! Of course you can't refuse. If you do, I'll write it!'

Yet, still, I more than hesitated. The offer seemed unbelievably flat-tering. But I had never attempted a biography before – certainly not of a living subject – and I had written virtually nothing on any British subject. Finally it was agreed that I should go down to Macmillan's Sussex home, Birch Grove, so that subject and biographer could 'look at each other'. As we walked round and round the garden, lovingly laid out by his redoubt-able American mother, Nellie Macmillan, and improved by Dorothy, his wife, exchanging politesses about flowers that bloom in August, I began to realise that he was just about as diffident as I was. I recall making some flip remark about my knowing all too little about British party politics, and not even being sure that I was a very good Tory. He replied, 'Nor was I, dear boy!' How could I resist? The ice was broken. We went into the house, and there began ten of the most rewarding (though demanding) years of my life.

The undertaking provided for one mid-sized book, taking three years maximum. Little did I suspect that my subject, who already looked frail, would live another eight years, or that the book would explode into two blockbusters. I didn't regret that decade's work, but had I been endowed with foreknowledge I doubt I would have had the energy to go ahead. The terms were generous. All his copious papers and his own remarkable store of recollections were put at my disposal. The only one major limi-tation was that nothing should appear in his lifetime – a condition designed to rid us both of inhibitions. 'That will make it easier for both of us, dear boy.' The relationship was a curious one. Boswell once claimed (though it could possibly be said he was pleading a special case) that 'nobody can write the life of a man, but those who have eaten and drunk and lived in social intercourse with him'. That great chronicler of contemporary America, Tom Wolfe, believed that writers 'should spend days if not weeks with their subject'. I did. Few biographers of eminent contemporary figures have the enviable good fortune to have access to the memory of their victim during his lifetime. (I did have such access again, some twenty-five years later, with Henry Kissinger). But the project also had its disadvantages: in the sheer weight of material amassed, in the checking and cross-checking involved, and – not least – in having to resist falling totally under the spell of one of the most fascinating political figures of the twentieth century, not known as the 'old magician' and the 'actor-manager' for nothing.

We would work often three days at a stretch at Birch Grove, an uncomfortable and bitingly cold neo-Georgian house (supposedly the biggest private house built in Britain during the Depression years of the 1920s). The sessions, which usually exhausted me more than the octogenarian Supermac, involved recording on tape the career of 'this strange, very buttoned-up person', as he liked to describe himself, trying to probe into the many corners left uncovered, or unexplained, by his own voluminous but impersonal memoirs. As we wandered round the shrubberies and borders of Birch Grove that first day, he remarked, 'I think gardens should be divided, so you can't see everything at once.' Later I came to recognise the unspoken parallel. Despite the showman exterior, acquired over the years of public life, he was by nature private and deeply reluctant to talk about anything bordering on the personal. My hardest task was always to drag him out of his own corner, to winkle the ever wily politician out of his protective shell. After one particularly arduous session (I think it was over Suez), he jokingly introduced me to neighbours as 'a cross between Boswell and Torquemada'.

To Pamela Egremont, the widow of John Wyndham, his aide-de-camp and close friend for many years, he was Proteus – the figure of Greek mythology capable of constantly changing his guise in bewildering fashion: 'One moment you had a salmon in your hand, the next it was a horse.' Few men could have been more constituted of paradoxes than Harold Macmillan; it was what gave him his charm and mischief as a brilliant conversationalist, and made him an enticing (but elusive) subject for a biographer. Every thought was followed by an afterthought, or two. What looked like white turned out to be black. He was a tease, he loved to *épater les bourgeois* with a remark that he did not really mean – or perhaps only half meant. Once when I remonstrated with him over what appeared to be excessive flippancy in the wrong context, he riposted: 'It's very important not to have a rigid distinction between what's flippant and what is serious.' It was, I thought at the time, something of a key to his whole style of government, as well as to his challengingly complex personality.

In conversation, his commentary on famous contemporaries was always vivid, often acrid, but usually coming down on the side of charity. When I asked him why he kept out of his published memoirs (greatly to their loss, and in marked contrast with later political diarists such as Richard Crossman) the more barbed comments of his unpublished diaries, he replied that such remarks made in the irritation of the moment never represented a considered view. (He added, typically, as an after-thought: 'Also, I wasn't a publisher for nothing. Libel's expensive!') But, equally, it seemed to reflect a fundamental kindliness. When he talked, there would be lots of mischief, some penetrating insights, occasionally anger, but never enduring malice. Obligingly, he supplied me with pithy one-liners on political associates, family and friends alike whom he felt I should see. On Katie Macmillan, wife of his only son, Maurice, occa-sionally given to over-dramatisation: 'Now Katie's Welsh, you know. If a blackbird lands on the lawn out there, she'll run in and cry, "Harold, come quickly! There are five thousand blackbirds on the lawn." Welsh, you know ...' On grandson Alex: 'Should have been a politician. His father [Maurice] was much too nice. But Alex is a shit, like me!' On former Prime Minister Ted Heath: 'Hengist and Horsa were very dull men. They colonised Kent [I began to wonder if the old boy was beginning to lose it]. Since then the Men of Kent, how shall I put it, have been rather boring ... But Ted Heath was a first-class Chief Whip.' On Anthony Head, Minister of Defence at the time of Suez: 'Cavalryman. Salt of the earth, but language of the stables.' When I interviewed Head, the first minister I found uninhibited enough to talk about the Suez operation, he summed up events: 'No bloody good. All that heave-ho, and then no orgasm at the end. No bloody good.' Language of the stables!

What ended up as the first volume of my biography took Harold Macmillan through his childhood, Oxford and his five wounds in the trenches of Flanders, his start as a publisher and entry into politics, the long wilderness years of the 1920s and 1930s, and the near break-up of his marriage to the Duke of Devonshire's daughter, the Second World War, and fulfilment at last as Churchill's envoy in North Africa, followed by the frustrations of six years in opposition in Clement Attlee's post-war Britain. The volume culminated with the Suez debacle of 1956, which was to bring Macmillan, at an age when most men are thinking of retirement, to 10 Downing Street. Volume two covered the seven years of his premiership, and the unexpectedly eventful two and a half decades of his life that remained after his precipitate resignation in 1963.

The web of any biography must be composed of a multiplicity of strands. Here there was a superabundance. Apart from the stacks of documents in what he called the Muniments Room, interviews with contemporaries and books written by them, there were Macmillan's own letters to his mother from the front in the First World War, and his diaries, those written in the form of letters to his wife Dorothy when he was sent to the Mediterranean as Churchill's resident minister in 1942 (which were published virtually *in toto* in 1984), and those covering the years, from 1950 to his resignation in 1963 (which were then still unpublished). Arthur Ponsonby, son and biographer of the great Victorian courtier Sir Henry Ponsonby, once observed that diaries were 'better than novels, more accurate than histories, and even at times more dramatic than plays'. This certainly could be said of the 1950–63 Macmillan diaries. Far more lively than his autobiography, they were outspoken, biting and occasionally savage. His comments on bêtes noires like Prime Minister John Diefen-baker of Canada, or Chancellor Konrad Adenauer of West Germany, sometimes even on President John F. Kennedy (for whom he had great esteem and personal affection), could be blistering. Then, on top of all this material, when Macmillan finally left office, to the considerable embarrassment of the Cabinet Secretary, he took with him more copies of classified official documents than any of his predecessors. I would get repeated, and somewhat menacing, calls from the Cabinet Offices to have them cleared, which I ignored.

It was all gruelling hard work, but I genuinely came to look forward eagerly to the visits, to the flow of wisdom, merriment and comments on every aspect of life that accompanied our meals. I also liked to think that perhaps all those visits to Birch Grove might have contributed something to the lonely life of a former prime minister who had so long outlived his contemporaries. Beyond the innate sadness of an empty home that had once rung with the voices of children, Birch Grove never struck me as a happy place. It was too full of ghosts. In a place of honour in the library, where they had worked together during his visit in 1963, there was the rocking-chair, still draped with its plaid rug, bought specially for Presi-dent Kennedy. The whole house was kept open, just as it was when

Dorothy had died, for the occasional weekend visit by the family, but it was largely unheated and such was the winter cold that anyone not of crofter stock would surely have died of hypothermia. Strangely for a countryman, Macmillan made no concessions in his clothing. I hardly ever saw him wear anything but a thin City suit, of double-breasted grey chalky-stripe, and a much darned pullover. He seemed to own only two ties: the Old Etonian and the Brigade of Guards. Until his daughter-in-law Katie moved in in 1980, by some curious inter-family financial arrangement Harold Macmillan 'leased' only his study commanding the front door – where he would spend most of his day reading – and his 'fortress'.

To reach the fortress (it disappeared in Katie Macmillan's reconstruction of Birch Grove in 1981) you had to steer between the gents' cloakroom and the game-larder, then up a narrow staircase with a partition flimsily built ('So as to get the coffin down easily!' he would explain with typical black humour). It consisted of a spartan two-room suite, reminiscent of a boys' prep school, or perhaps the modest accommodation above the Beefsteak Club, of which he was so fond. No modern cook-general would have dreamed of living there. On the wall of the tiny sitting/dining room were two prints of Bad Godesberg (despite his cool relations with Adenauer and his ambivalent opinion of the Germans), presented respectively by Konrad Adenauer and Willy Brandt. No one else actually slept in the great empty house where he passed the nights disquietingly alone. Lunch, which would be prepared by one of two elderly devoted retainers, consisted – winter and summer – of cold ham, undressed salad and cheese, with an occasional treat of 'plum pie just for you, dear boy, as you never get enough to eat here!'

The frugality of his life always struck me as being incongruous for an ex-prime minister, and indeed for an affluent publisher. Yet he obviously felt that it was in keeping with the spartan background of the family, an attitude reinforced by an exaggerated conviction of personal impoverishment not untypical of someone of his age – 'rags to riches, and back again, in four generations, that'll be our story!' The one conspicuous exception to this regime was the regular bottle of champagne (in fact, one or more 'thirds', given him by friends), the 'duke's son-in-law' obverse side of the crofter coin, but for which a suitable excuse had to be found:

'I'm feeling rather poorly this morning,' or 'We must drink to that brave young woman, Mrs T' (after the 1979 election), or simply reciting with gusto his favourite lines of Belloc:

> Beneath an equatorial sky
> You must consume it or you die;
> And stern indomitable men
> Have told me, time and time again,
> 'The nuisance of the tropics is
> The sheer necessity of fizz.'

Though 'tropical' was one adjective that could never be used about Birch Grove, the door jamb rippled like corrugated iron where – because his hand had been weakened by a German bullet – Macmillan had opened countless thirds of 'fizz'. When it began to flow, so did the conversation.

In addition to the voluminous tapes I recorded more or less formally with Macmillan, I kept a file, marvellously rich, of what I chose to call 'Table Talk'. It comprised conversation on an infinite range of subjects during meals, walking round the gardens or chatting late into the night over a bottle of whisky, times when 'Uncle Harold' was at his best, when his imagination soared and when a tape-recorder would have been intrusive or bad form. Trying to emulate Boswell, I jotted down this Table Talk as soon as I decently could afterwards, while the memory was still fresh. He was at his compelling best at meals up in the fortress or late in the evening (he was the total owl and could keep any audience up till two in the morning) – the random marginalia, the witty anecdotes on contemporaries, the acute commentaries on the day's events interlaced with the mighty sweeps of historical analogy. He was, I suppose, the last survivor of the great conversationalists from a bygone era.

Out of curiosity, I once listed some two dozen topics of conversation covered in the course of one visit. They ranged from the origin of the Guards' tall bearskins – should these have been worn instead of steel helmets in the First World War, given that riflemen always aim high? Hardy versus Kipling as stylists, and decadence in Hellenistic literature, to the Anopheles mosquito in sixth-century Italy, the explicitness of sex in the modern novel – would *Jude the Obscure* be considered shocking now – and wasn't *Vanity Fair* in fact more daring than *For Whom the Bell*

Tolls? problems of publishing in Nigeria. Then, finally, with much hilarity and numerous living examples, he would expatiate on the difference between a 'cad' and a 'bounder'. 'In war,' he explained, 'a bounder is a chap who goes to the Front, wins the VC, then seduces his colonel's wife. But a cad seduces his colonel's wife and never goes near the Front. Women can be cads, though curiously enough I don't think ever bounders. Have you ever known a female bounder?' (Reflecting, privately, on the great personal tragedy which so shaped Macmillan's own life, his wife Dorothy's protracted affair with his friend and colleague Bob Boothby, I felt she would in fact have rated as a bounder, Boothby, unmistakably, as a cad.)

It seemed to me that one of the things that kept Macmillan alive in his last years, two decades after he had left Number 10, was this vivid, often passionate, interest in almost every aspect of *la condition humaine*, a boon granted to few octogenarians. Within a few minutes, despite the more than thirty years between us, I used to feel as if I were talking to a contemporary, but one of rare intellectual agility. In everything his sense of humour was unfailing, and of a particular quality. Often black, it also derived a special delight from the ridiculous. A few days after the murder in Ireland of Mountbatten, I made one of my visits to Birch Grove. On the table by his armchair was a new white bell-button: 'Don't touch it, dear boy, I'm only to ring after I've been blown up, and then the police will come in ten minutes – isn't that thoughtful of them?' The police had also asked him to give up his regular post-prandial snooze in an isolated summer-house, but one sunny day he insisted on going out to it. Waving aside my remonstrances, he said with a mischievous chuckle, 'If you hear a big bang, that'll mean you can then publish your book, dear boy!'

His own favourite yardsticks were whether something, or somebody, was 'fun' or a 'bore'. The Cuban Missiles Crisis was 'a bit of a bore'; running the country was 'fun', and anybody who worked with him at Number 10 would testify to just how much more fun the Macmillan regime was than any of its successors.

I came to realise that the famous façade of unflappability was, however, somewhat cultivated. Underneath the sharp wit and the love of fun was a great gulf – especially in later years – of loneliness and melancholia. It was an aspect of the Black Dog, the recurrent depression to which he had been a prey throughout his life, and from which Celts notably are alleged to suffer. 'I felt it very badly at Eton,' he admitted, 'and I used to get it when in office, then I'd go to Birch Grove for two days, by myself, read Jane Austen. My wife understood. I didn't want to see people ... it was seasonal ... makes you inward-looking, isolated. External things like Profumo never really worried me. It was just the inside feeling that something awful and unknown was about to happen – or, sometimes, a great exhilaration.'

As a fellow sufferer, I understood what he was saying all too well; maybe my own affliction also helped me to understand his complex personality. Beneath the melancholia, there was also a deep-seated fatalism about life in general. Macmillan's declared philosophy was: 'Take it as it comes. It never turns out as you expect ... I never hoped to be PM – of course dear old Rab [Butler] did!' (Did he not?) This fatalism sometimes seemed at odds with his strong religious beliefs. He used to tell with relish the story about Clementine Churchill reproaching Winston for non-churchgoing. 'Ah, you, my dear Clemmy', replied Winston, 'are like a great pillar: you support the church from the inside! But I am like a flying buttress: I support it from outside!' When I suggested to Macmillan that he was more pillar than buttress, he said, 'Yes, I suppose so. I go to Communion as long as I still can. At home in the house, I reach for the Bible whenever I can. I still find religion a great help.' As he declared, when we were on Bill Buckley's television show *Firing Line* in New York in 1980, 'If you don't believe in God, all you have to believe in is decency ... decency is very good. Better decent than indecent. But I don't think it's enough.' He fundamentally believed in both God and decency.

Out of the many, possibly hundreds, of requests I made for interview I received only two notable rebuffs. One was from Clarissa Avon, widow of Macmillan's predecessor, Anthony Eden. Even before I had written a single word or committed myself in any way, she declined to see me on the grounds that I was 'in the enemy camp'. I don't know whether she ever read the book, but she maintained her antagonism to the end. It was an insight into the implacable if not ferocious loyalty of widows, which keeps old animosities alive. Another who did read the book, and was bitterly hostile, was Lady Butler, widow of Rab, Macmillan's defeated rival for the premiership.

The other major rebuff came from Ted Heath, who – changing his mind twice – refused to talk to me because anything he said might detract from his own memoirs. I was angered, and told him so – not because of any affront to me, but as official biographer I felt that his old chief, to whom after all he owed his own subsequent career, deserved better. Heath was the only one of five surviving ex-PMs I did not see. My meeting with Margaret Thatcher I remember most vividly. It was shortly after she had taken over, and she was generous enough to give me nearly an hour, largely devoted to the principles of conservatism. The interview took place in her office in the House of Commons, which, with its decor of pickled-oak panelling, was reminiscent of the study of a prep-school headmaster. We sat at a small table; at the other end of the room sat her attentive parliamentary private secretary, Ian Gow (later murdered by the IRA). She had been up all night in the Commons (on, I think, the Rhodesia Bill), and clearly the light from the table lamp was straining her eyes. I pressed the switch, which prompted a great 'harrumph' from Ian at the other end of the room, as if to warn that this was improper behaviour. But the Prime Minister's response was to lay her hand on my offending arm and say, most engagingly, 'Oh, thank you.' I often thought of this charmingly feminine gesture whenever mention was made of Mitterrand's famous observation, that she had 'the eyes of Caligula, and the mouth of Marilyn Monroe'. However fierce she might be, she was unmistakably all woman – which may have accounted for her attraction to good-looking bounders like Alan Clark and Cecil Parkinson.

Equally generous with his time was 'the other Harold', Wilson. Puffing away at his renowned red pipe, he seemed to have something on his mind as I took my leave.

'May I just ask you this?' he said. 'Is it true you're not to publish in his lifetime?'

'Yes, it is.'

'Extraordinary! I would never permit anyone to write a book about me that I couldn't see.'

It was, I thought, a revealing remark. Of the ex-PMs, the two I particularly liked were Alec Douglas-Home and 'Sunny Jim' Callaghan, both defeated in their different contexts. Home, 'the 14th Earl', truly the *parfait gentilhomme*, always the most modest and unresentful of men, was I felt also the most underrated of Tory leaders. For all the hullabaloo over his succession, I could always understand Macmillan's preference for him over the 'wet' Rab or the unpredictable Quintin Hailsham. One eminence who, for all his brilliance, I did not take to was Enoch Powell. (Macmillan, as he once confessed, had had Powell's institutional place at the coffin-shaped Cabinet table shifted: 'I couldn't stand those mad yellow eyes glaring at me across the way.') Apart from his dreadful halitosis, Powell the classical scholar upstaged me by quoting from ancient Greek, then observing, 'But of course you wouldn't know Greek.' However, while I was recovering from the gibe, he produced a quotation from Goethe, in incorrect German. A rare coincidence, I happened to know the allusion, and vengefully put him right. Those yellow eyes glared.

On the other hand, researching Macmillan did have what one might call spin-offs, in the way of new acquaintances. There was the feisty Julian Amery, Macmillan's son-in-law; the engagingly eccentric David Ormsby-Gore, a brilliant choice as ambassador to the Court of JFK, but who sadly died in a car accident; Peter Carrington, Foreign Secretary while I was at work, and who was to remain a lasting friend (and, later, neighbour); and, in America, Jackie Onassis and Arthur and Alexandra Schlesinger. One very old friendship, from Cambridge days, that was further cemented by the book was that with Philip Goodhart. A long-time Tory MP, he obligingly took on the task of reading the MS for political howlers. I couldn't have done it without him; his pithy comments, classics in themselves ('You have said this before, and you will say it again, and it's wrong', filled a whole filing box. Meanwhile, over the ten years a new cast moved into my literary life. Alan Maclean, after twenty (mostly happy) years as my editor, retired from Macmillans and was replaced by Nicky Byam Shaw, who proved a tower of strength and support, especially in adverse days. So too did Michael Sissons, of A. D. Peters, who became my literary agent in succession to Curtis Brown. Ulie Winant, who had represented me for fifteen long years, had died just before I began work on *A Savage War*. She was irreplaceable.

There were other sad losses. Serena Booker, a brilliant young woman whose parents had educated all three of my daughters and who had worked as a tireless researcher (as well as great morale-booster) for four years, was brutally murdered while on holiday in Thailand in 1982. Then Venetia Pollock, another brilliant woman, quite simply the best (external) editor in the business as well as a lifelong friend, was stricken with cancer halfway through the labour of editing a long and complicated manuscript. The deprivation of her encouragement, and enthusiasm, was almost irreparable. (But Peter James, who would meticulously edit another five books for me, happily took over.) Finally, Andrew Harding, to whom the dedication of this book I had long promised, who shared some aspects of the subject's life – Eton, Oxford, wartime Grenadier Guards – and whose inestimable support over three decades as family lawyer had made all my books possible, died after a courageous struggle against illness, just before I was able to tell him that his book was finally ready to appear. And, in midstream, I went through the agonies and stresses of divorce.

In terms of sheer consumption of time, however, the most troublesome topic I had to deal with in the book, and the one most hurtful of all to Harold Macmillan personally, concerned his supposed complicity in handing back to Stalin in 1945 Cossack prisoners of war who had fought for Germany. Raised chiefly by Nikolai Tolstoy, the allegations were unsparing in calumny, culminating in innuendoes that went so far as to imply that Macmillan himself had been in the thrall of the KGB, although Tolstoy later expressed regret for these slurs. By nature a compassionate man, these charges hurt him deeply – more deeply than he would let on. Friends urged him (as I did) to sue for defamation, but it was not in his character. However, having seen, later, what the court case would do to his fellow accused Lord Aldington, despite his being vindicated with damages of £1.5 million (still the highest ever recorded, though not a penny of it was ever paid), it seemed unlikely that Macmillan, at ninety, could physically have withstood prolonged cross-examination in a witness box. Instead he rolled himself into a ball like a hedgehog where a younger and lesser man might have been tempted to riposte. While his assailants could press their attack in the certainty that there would be no danger of a comeback, he believed that, in the fullness of time and when seen in its proper historical context, the record would vindicate him. It did. But what, in retrospect, still seems extraordinary was how so many intelligent people supported Tolstoy in his allegations, and even bailed him out when the courts closed in.

While I felt indignant on Macmillan's behalf, I also felt indignant on my own account. At one point, uniquely, I found myself being threatened with libel by both contestants, Tolstoy and Aldington. It was not only the work involved (much of it put in by Serena), which came to equal, in hours and days, at least half of that first volume, but it was also being wrongfooted, insofar as my own sympathies lay otherwise totally with the traduced Cossacks, in their terrible fate at the hands of Stalin. It was there that Tolstoy's anger should have been concentrated, not against an old man of ninety, whose involvement had been only marginal.

Troublesome and unpleasant as the Tolstoy issue was, the story of Dorothy and her lifelong affair with Bob Boothby, Macmillan's friend and parliamentary colleague, was even more painful for this intensely private man. Boothby, whom I spoke to twice, was an inveterate liar, ambisexual and wildly indiscreet, but with the charm of the devil. The affair must have caused Macmillan immeasurable pain. I didn't approach the subject with enthusiasm, let alone any prurient sense, though the media, and not least the BBC who should have known better, would never leave it alone. But I felt it had to be tackled. The main reason was the effect it had had on his political career. His close friend Pamela Egremont regarded the betrayal as 'the grit in the oyster'. Without it, would he have had the incentive to reach for the heights of his profession? The fault lay largely, I always felt, through his inability, indeed aversion, to coping with sexual peccadilloes. Here the wound dealt by Boothby was unmistakable; Macmillan simply did not want to know. Jack Profumo, who later became a good friend, and whom I greatly respected for the selfless way in which he atoned for his misdemeanour (a pretty modest one by contemporary political standards), once assured me that 'if Harold himself had asked me, I couldn't have lied.' But Harold didn't, and couldn't.

When I finally summoned up the courage to ask Macmillan about Dorothy and Boothby, in the library at Birch Grove, he declared emphatically, with what was demonstrably still a great deal of pain, 'I never loved anyone but her. On her side, there were transient things – unimportant. What counts are the fundamentals. I had everything from her, owed her everything. She filled my life, I thought in everything I did of her. We were very close. I told her I'd never let her go – it would have been disastrous . . . a hopeless fellow. In the way women do, she said it was my fault. But what's physical love compared to things you share, interests, children? But it took a lot out of me, physically.' I left it there. In 1958 Macmillan introduced his ground-breaking Life Peerages Act. At the time a hereditary peer, Viscount Esher, remarked with wit: 'It looks as though the House of Commons will retain the aces and kings, and send up to the House of Lords the queens and knaves!' With what many saw as deep cynicism, Macmillan had nominated as the first of his new Life Peers his tormentor Bob Boothby, an appointment thereby seeming to fulfil Esher's prediction with some accuracy.

To me, in retrospect, Harold Macmillan always represented an essentially tragic figure, within the classical definition. There was the heartbreak of his marriage, the 'Grand Designs' attempted, never quite consummated; but, perhaps the most poignant of all, his departure from office as a result of a prostate illness – to realise subsequently that resignation had been unnecessary after all. There followed twenty-three years of what he called 'life after death', of frustration in the political wilderness, watching as the beloved country which he had led for seven definitive years seemed to fall apart. But it wasn't all darkness and gloom. On 10 February 1984 'Uncle Harold' celebrated his ninetieth birthday. This was a joyous occasion at Birch Grove, a remarkable mix of 200 of the great and the good, prime ministers, friends, family, secretaries from the family firm and Birch Grove estate workers, all bearing immense goodwill and warmth. It was more like a coming-of-age party – even the police guards were in the best of humour. It also happened to be the day of the death of the Soviet Union's sinister KGB Premier, Yuri Andropov. In an aside as he accepted the presents and good wishes of his guests, Macmillan remarked to me, in his best black humour: 'And wasn't it thoughtful of Mr Andropov to choose today!' That same day, the Queen was 'graciously pleased to approve' the bestowal of an earldom (of Stockton, his old constituency) upon him, something he had long resisted.

He was soon making use of it, making himself felt, in the House of Lords. First there was the maiden speech. Coinciding with the miners' strike which was ravaging the country, it drew tears to the eyes of the most hardened with his reference to the courage of the miners in two world wars. By any standard, it was a tour de force, as good in its way as anything anyone present had ever heard him produce in the Commons in his heyday, and an outstanding triumph of mind over matter; for thirty-two minutes he had spoken without a note, and without a slip or a falter. Next came his much quoted speech about 'selling the family silver', a direct attack on Thatcherism – which was less well received by the Party faithful. It also was his last performance.

Then, in 1986, after suffering pleurisy and shingles, he seemed to be going downhill rapidly. His blindness now made it painfully difficult for him even to see to eat. Often the old sparks would fly, but much of the time he seemed prey to a new form of dejection – the dejection of the losing struggle against old age and its indignities. In the spring of that year, it took a supreme effort for him to get through the degree-giving ceremony at Oxford for King Juan Carlos (he had been Chancellor of the University since 1960). But it was too much for him. On returning to Birch Grove, he was laid low again with pleurisy, 'the old man's undertaker' as doctors used to call it, and for several weeks his life was despaired of. That November, Macmillan paid what was to be his final visit to his beloved Oxford, to attend a Feast at St Edmund Hall. The following night he dined quietly with his biographer. It was the last time we were to meet. He was visibly exhausted, suffering recognisably from the Black Dog. It was distressing to see him, though he perked up in the course of the evening, reminiscing about his first schooldays at Oxford's Summer Fields at the turn of the century. I knew I would never see him again. On 29 December, after a very brief illness, he died, only a few weeks short of his ninety-third birthday. Some of the family felt that, dejected and unable to console himself by reading, he had simply died of boredom. Life was no longer fun.

According to his grandson, Alexander, he had nevertheless kept his wits to the end, and his last words were: 'I think I will go to sleep now.'

'Supermac' was buried, quietly, alongside Dorothy and Sarah, in the small parish churchyard of Horsted Keynes near Birch Grove, under a severe block of square granite, that then bore the simplest inscription:

DOROTHY MACMILLAN
1900–1966
SARAH MACMILLAN
1930–1970
HAROLD MACMILLAN
1894–1986

15

REDISCOVERING AMERICA

1989, Boston, 'Firing Line' on Macmillan II. Left to right: Bill Buckley,
Arthur Schlesinger Jr, Professor J. K. Galbraith and AH.

'When the curtain falls, the best thing an actor can do is go away.'

Harold Macmillan

One of the incidental consequences of the Macmillan biography was a serious return to the US. More or less out of the blue came an invitation to take a year as visiting scholar at the Woodrow Wilson Center in Washington, DC. The purpose was to enable me to research the Eisenhower and Kennedy papers that related to Macmillan. I felt some trepidation; it was a big chunk of life, as well as being the first time I had lived over a prolonged period in the States since my enforced wartime sojourn. Would I be disenchanted with all that I had come so to love in the challenging 1940s? In fact it was to prove one of the most rewarding years of my life. I would miss the children and home, but it was also a time when our marriage was faltering. I welcomed the space. Best of all, it provided opportunities for taking up with old friends again, as well as making many new ones.

I arrived in Washington amid the spectacular fall colours of 1980. There was a dry crunch to the leaves and a zip in the air, despite the deep gloom in the city at large. Trees were festooned with yellow ribbons, symbol of the continuing nightmare of the US Embassy hostages held by the mad mullahs in Iran, and the regime of dreary, hapless Jimmy Carter was crumbling to its inconsequential end – the well-meaning peanut-farmer from Georgia, who looked a bit like one of his own dried peanuts. The zip was in the air because an election was pending.

The Woodrow Wilson offered no accommodation, but my old friend Barny Howard (then living in New York State) came up with the goods – a whole comfortable house out in the Chevy Chase outskirts of Washington, for which a friend of his wanted a house-sitter. With it went a lovely black maid called Mary, straight out of *Gone with the Wind*.

The Wilson Center was then located on the top floors of the Old Castle

Building of the Smithsonian Institute, with its crimson bricks a legendary Washington landmark. A unique testament to the beneficence of that eighteenth-century illegitimate son of an English duke, James Smithson, with a passion for the young America (which he never visited), it had grown to become the hub of the world's greatest accretion of culture, and now consisted of a score of famed museums, such as the fabulous Air and Space Museum. The Center itself was a cheerfully matey, faintly chaotic place which brought together a rare combination of talents from all over the world. It reminded me often of St Antony's, Oxford. I was made to feel at home at once. The boss was Dr Jim Billington, who appeared the quintessence of the preppy, collegiate American (Princeton, Harvard and Balliol; he was later to earn the *Guinness Book of Records* distinction of being the first Rhodes Scholar to have a Rhodes daughter). An original thinker and a Russian scholar of distinction, he was shortly to become Librarian of Congress, a post of immense – and untranslatable – grandeur in the US Establishment; no mere keeper of books, in the Washington pecking-order, it was only a peck or two inferior to the President. His second-in-command was Prosser Gifford, whose somewhat deranged-sounding laugh in the corridors would presage an administrative problem of immense and insoluble proportions. My particular friend among the hierarchy was Sam Wells, the gently erudite head of the Securities Program.

There were some thirty of us Visiting Scholars. An eclectic lot, we would meet for convivial salad lunches at a long table surrounded by the book-filled cases of the Library. There was Ariel Dorfman, a far-left refugee from Pinochet's Chile. Ariel and I had vigorous arguments about Salvador Allende, but as we parted he proffered a generous invitation: 'When I get back to Chile, whatever happens, you'll come back as my friend.' But Pinochet hung on for another eight years, and Ariel never did go back. Instead he wrote his world-famous, searing play *Death of a Maiden* and took up a teaching job at Duke, North Carolina. Then there was Ariel's fellow South American – an utterly different Latino, Mario Vargas Llosa, the Peruvian novelist, of flashing eyes and legendary sex-appeal, who was working on his sombre book *The War of the End of the World.** He must have been the first novelist to come to the Center; later

* He won the Nobel Prize for Literature in 2010.

he ran for president of Peru. Mario became a particular chum. When it was time for him to return home, his was a farewell gift of true friendship: 'Alistair, I'd like you to have my office. It's the only one in the Smithsonian with a bed in it – they think, as a Latino, I have to have a daily siesta!' Gratefully I declined, reckoning that social life in Washington offered enough danger and distraction from work already. Instead, I took over the office atop one of the Smithsonian's landmark Victorian towers, from an American who suffered from vertigo and who jibbed at the perilous circular iron staircase. It was quite eccentrically unique: 16 feet high and only 8 feet square, just room for a desk, with tall Gothic windows on each side, thus commanding the whole of Washington: to the front, the White House; to the left, the Washington Memorial; to the right, the Capitol. I felt as if I were lord of the whole of this extraordinarily beautiful, vibrant city.

It was all very spoiling. On the Mall, within easy walk of the Smith-sonian, lay the world's greatest concentration of art and artefacts. Often after lunch I would take time off to stroll across to the National (Mellon) Gallery and look at a dozen pictures, or to its brand-new, sharp-edged sister, Pei's East Wing, or to the Hirshhorn sculpture museum just next door to my office; or to its neighbour, the stunning Air and Space Museum. I came to realise that Washington was really just an overgrown small village, and more or less a single-economy village at that. If you were working in the Mall, in government or media-related employment, then – at least in 1980 – every door was open to you. But if you weren't on that inner track, you might as well be living in Hoboken. And at least in its small, cosy, warmly beating heart of Georgetown, everybody knew who you were, and not only what you were doing but almost what you were about to do. It was often said, sardonically, of the nation's capital that it was 'government by leak'. Chatter, chatter, gossip, gossip; how did anyone ever keep a secret here? At one grand soirée in the Corcoran Gallery, I observed one of the matriarchs of DC pointing interestedly in my direction and clearly asking my hostess, Ambassador 'Lucky' Roose-velt, 'Who's that?' Lucky relayed teasingly: 'Oh, she just wanted to know, "Is that the new spare man?"' Certainly in this city disproportionately inhabited by widows, female journalists, high-powered women executives

and Congressmen's aides, a 'new spare man' did have commodity value.
The telephone rang a lot.

The problem was how to get any work done at all. I made flying trips
up to the Kennedy Library in Boston, to look at Kennedy–Macmillan
papers there, to the Mudd Library in Princeton for Eisenhower documents, and all over the place to interview survivors of the Macmillan
years. At the Woodrow Wilson, I was given a bright young research
student, Neil Robinson, who devilled for me in the forbidding, mile-long
tunnels of the Library of Congress. Yet, excellent as he was, his labours
tended to increase the work; the best researcher in the world tends to do
that. The problem also lay in the nature of the Center itself. It seemed to
be the eye of the storm, the very focus of the focus of the world. Visiting
academics would zoom in on you and issue an invitation to their university; one of these, Roger Louis, with the polished face of a baby – who
was later to find fame as the great expert on the latter-day British Empire
(and gain a CBE in recognition of his work) – introduced himself one
day and thereby opened up to me the whole great new world of the
University of Texas at Austin.

Meanwhile there was huge, real excitement gripping Washington.
Ronald Reagan and the Wild West had come to town. A Californian, a
Hollywood B-movie actor and conservative had won the presidential
election. Poor Carter with his furrowed brow, exhausted by his inability
to delegate so much as the stamping of an envelope, and his defeated
team had been swept out by the new wind from the west. As a final insult
to his feeble efforts, the Iranian captors had finally let his people go. The
American hostages were coming home, an apparent gift-offering to the
new, no-nonsense man from the west. Washington was suddenly filled
with breezy Californians, bringing with them that old frontier sense of
American can-doism, and optimism. There were parties, and fireworks,
all over town – except in Georgetown where the affluent liberal hostesses
put up the shutters, and in the offices of the *Washington Post*, where there
was much rending of clothes. Up in New York, Bill Buckley was quietly
triumphant. After twenty-five years the *National Review*, the magazine he
had founded and run against the odds, had got its candidate – a champion
against rampant liberalism – into the White House. Even Ronald Reagan

himself would be the first to admit that, without the labours of WFB Jr and his acolytes on *NR*, he would never have made it.

There was no mistaking that new breeze blowing in DC. All anyone could talk about was 'transition' (with a short 'a'). Coincidentally, and at the same time as the Californians, my subject Harold Macmillan came to town. Then eighty-six, he was visiting – not as a distinguished ex-prime minister – but as a travelling salesman for the family firm, flogging the (hideously expensive) *New Grove Dictionary of Music and Musicians*. It was on this trip that Bill had him on his *Firing Line* programme in New York and invited me to participate as 'moderator'. I thought that that was something to do with the Scottish Kirk and wasn't quite sure what was expected of me. In the event, practically nothing: the two giants of political conservatism – the ultra and the moderate – held the floor, and the audience, without any help from the biographer. Then the old lion came on down to Washington. As is their wont, his American hosts had visibly exhausted him. Nonetheless when Nicko and Mary Henderson, the diplomatic hosts of the epoch, threw a gala dinner for him at the British Embassy he grabbed the affections of his audience by commencing his remarks with touching modesty: 'I am nobody, I represent nothing', before embarking on a stunning *tour d'horizon*.

The next night, the Woodrow Wilson put on a special jamboree for him, dining among all the artefacts downstairs in the Old Castle Building. Generously, Jim Billington asked me to act as co-host. Among the eminences of DC, I found myself sitting between Robert McNamara (Defense Secretary to Presidents Kennedy and Johnson) and Henry Kissinger – the first time I had met either. Kissinger turned to me as Macmillan rose, and said – in that Central European growl that I was to come to know so well two decades later: 'Is ze old man all right? He looks as if he's going to die!' 'Supermac' did indeed look terrible, exhausted by all the lionising. But I assured Dr K that, no, he always looked like that before he spoke, but afterwards – tension released – he would undergo a complete rejuvenation and keep everyone up into the small hours. I was right. He began with an old chestnut (I winced with apprehension): 'As Adam said to Eve, when they were expelled from the Garden of Eden, "My dear, we live in times of ... [calculated pause] transition [with the short 'a']."' The audience roared with appreciation: the old master had them in his hands – he could do no wrong. When questions came, someone ineptly asked: 'Mr Macmillan, what do you think the Russians are doing in Afghanistan?' 'Well, I don't suppose they've gone there for the winter sports, do you?' More roars of applause. At the end of a triumphant evening, my famous neighbour turned to me and admitted: 'You vere right – he survived. He was great.' I thought no more about our encounter; then, taking me by surprise came an invitation from the Kissingers for dinner. It marked the beginning of a long but sporadic acquaintance, culminating in what Dr K himself might have dubbed 'unattended consequences'.

Meanwhile, my work on the biography went on steadily but very slowly. One of the greatest coups I had was to discover a correspondence between Macmillan and Jacqueline Kennedy following the assassination of JFK. There were intimate and deeply moving letters, almost father to daughter in tone, between two lonely, bereaved people – with a gap of three decades between them. They said so much about the 'special relationship' between JKF and Harold Macmillan that I was burning to use them in volume two of my biography. To my considerable surprise, considering the very personal nature of the letters, and her own sense of privacy, Jackie Onassis gave me unhesitating permission to quote them, with only one very small excision (a slighting reference to de Gaulle). Our correspondence brought me into social contact with her, and (through Arthur and Alexandra Schlesinger) I met her several times up in New York. I liked her a lot, not least for that open smile – though occasionally it was a haunted smile (or was it more hunted? hunted by the media, who for years had never left her alone).

At the time of departure from Washington of the defeated Jimmy Carter, up in New York she invited me round for a drink to her apartment on upper Fifth Avenue. As we watched the scene of Carter's farewell on television, she was clearly so moved by it and all that leaving the White House had signified for her during those terrible days of November 1963 that she poured tonic, instead of soda, into my whisky, and I remember her saying, with feeling, 'Just imagine – giving up *all that*, to return to The Plains, Georgia!'

One day soon after the Reagan team had taken over, I was taken to lunch with the famous Bob Woodward and Carl Bernstein, the darlings and terrors of the Georgetown opinion-makers. How many journos have had A-films made about them, played by Hollywood's prize actors (Robert Redford and Dustin Hoffman in *All the President's Men*)? How many, since Emile Zola, could lay claim to having brought down a government, as their Watergate reports brought down Richard Nixon in 1974? They struck me as supremely arrogant men, and I was never able to rid myself of the feeling that they were the most overrated hacks in America, who had just had phenomenal good luck, just happening to be in the right place, at the right time – and, above all, with the right source, the mysterious 'Deep Throat'. That lunch remains etched in my memory. Seated at the Woodward round table were half-a-dozen eager young acolytes from the *Post*. Addressing them with the bored languour and self-satisfaction of a Middle Eastern potentate, the host challenged them: 'Well, guys, we've got Reagan now. So what's going to be the next scandal? Any ideas?' The acolytes remained eager but uninspired. None could come up with an idea.

Then, with the remorseless speed of Grecian tragedy, the Furies hit the *Post* – amidships. The previous September, a bright young journalist called Janet Cooke had published a heart-rending story, entitled 'Jimmy's World'. It recounted the life of an eight-year-old boy who had allegedly fallen victim to the thriving heroin trade which had the low-income neighbourhoods of Washington in its thrall. Cooke was awarded the prestigious Pulitzer Prize for her story. But, shortly after the Woodward lunch, Cooke was revealed as a fraud, her 'Jimmy's World' a complete fabrication. The *Post* looped-the-loop in its dismay and self-flagellation. Day after day, page after page, fresh exhalations of mea culpa were exuded. It was if the *Post*, because of Watergate, had set itself up in a kind of cocoon of divinity, beyond the ken of mere mortal newsmen. An American TV producer explained to me, 'You mustn't forget Americans need to wash their dirty linen in public.' Nevertheless, none but a newspaper that had grown far too big for its breeches could have behaved quite this way. It was all faintly repellant. Meanwhile, the divine duo were not seen around the salons of Georgetown for a time.

Little more than two months after Reagan's triumphal inauguration, I returned to the Woodrow Wilson one afternoon after lunching out. People, 'scholars' and secretaries were huddled in gloom – and alarm almost amounting to panic – around the television. 'The President's been shot!' It was impossible to believe. 'Please God, not again!' I exclaimed to myself. Miraculously the septuagenarian survived, all the time cracking jokes while on the hospital stretcher, which would endear him to the hearts of the nation in a remarkable way. Once recovered, the Gipper's popularity soared. To an outsider it was heartening to see this President, who evoked the very epitome of American optimism, bring America out of its post-Vietnam, post-Watergate, post-Carter hangover.

For me one of the particular joys of my months in Washington in 1980–1 was the opportunity to take up with all the friends and surrogate family from those far-off wartime days. Judy Shinkle would fly in from St Louis for a weekend, to stir things up; the Breese family lived on an exquisite old farm at Accokeek, in sight of DC down the Potomac; and there was Lucky Roosevelt (wife of my old friend, Archie, former chief of the CIA in London) to introduce me to *le tout* Georgetown. (Lucky lived up to her sobriquet. One day she printed an article in the journal she wrote for, headed 'Let's Stop Knocking Nancy', defending the new First Lady, who was currently being savaged by Washington hackery. The next day she was invited to tea at the White House – and left as Chief of Protocol, a high-ranking job she held for the next seven years during which Reagan was in power.) Then, when Dick Pipes was appointed Reagan's adviser on Soviet affairs, he and Irene moved down from Harvard. Dick reckoned he had arrived in the inner Palace circle when he was given an office in the Old State building with a view of the White House: 'If you don't look on to the White House,' he explained, 'you're going nowhere.' He did, and was to become chief architect to Reagan's hard-line policy that was eventually to bring down the 'Evil Empire.'

There was one sad interlude. Together with Eric Stevenson, a classmate with me at Millbrook School, we went to Baltimore to see our old history teacher, Henry Callard, who was in hospital paralysed by a stroke. Henry was the greatest teacher in my life; it was he who made me see history in human terms, and made me want – eventually – to write it. From his hospital bed he seemed to take in what we said to him, smiling the sweet smile we all remembered and loved. But he could not speak a single word. It was painful to see this extraordinary, articulate man stricken dumb.

Jim Billington and my masters at the Woodrow Wilson were

marvellously tolerant of the travels I indulged in while working on their time. Through my new friend Roger Louis, I went to lecture at the University of Texas in Austin, and sampled the delights of the Lone Star State, and in April 1981, towards the end of my scholarship, I was invited to speak at Stanford, California, and at the Navy School down the coast at Monterey. It provided a happy opportunity for one last tryst with Bill Buckley en route – at the magical ski resort of Alta, a short drive up from Utah's Salt Lake City, for deep, deep powder snow, the best the world has to offer. As I was flying west, Bill was heading east from San Francisco. There a young woman, less enthusiastic about Reagan than he was, had thrown a cream pie in his face.

It was one of those rare interludes in a friendship that was lifelong. Apart from the custard-pie incident, Bill was in high spirits. He was elated by the way 'his' man, and personal friend of many years standing, was shaping up in the White House. His own latest 'Blackford Oakes' thriller, *Marco Polo, If You Can*, where the dashing hero is shot down in a U-2 spy plane over the Soviet Union, was also taking shape well. At Alta the snow (which seldom ceases) comes dried out across the Salt Lake desert, so that it falls like fluffy, bottomless powder, and is world-renowned as one of the great deep-snow experiences. One famous slope, called High Rustler, is so steep that you feel you are about to plunge down the chimney of the Alta Lodge. On a previous visit, I was lucky to have a Mormon bishop (Utah being the Mormon state) with ten children and the gentlest of bedside manners as my ski guide. He taught me at least one valuable lesson: 'When skiing in trees, look at the holes, not the trees – then you'll hit them.' That may have saved me many painful entanglements and splinters. Now, in spring-time Alta there was a lazy atmosphere of approaching *fin de saison*. The sun burned down. We plunged and soared all day, to exhaustion. In the evening we discussed our respective books and the performance of the Reagan government.

After that short joyous visit to Alta in May – before the Washington summer heat struck – suddenly it was all over. The months in the US had rushed by. In one sense the very personal experiment of rediscovering America had gone supremely well. In terms of work I left feeling fulfilled, and I had had an immense amount of fun, being reunited with old friends and with my surrogate wartime family. But, in another sense, it was disquieting. There were too many sad goodbyes. The umbilical cord – the tugs of dual attachments that continued to afflict me through so much of my life – was as firmly attached as ever. Like Axel von dem Bussche, I always felt at ease on that side of the Atlantic; I sensed I could always relate to Americans, to the warmth, the sense of humour, the optimism and the wider values. Perhaps it remained, still, an unattainable illusion. The other side of the hill. But the duality, the divisiveness of the Doppelgänger, persisted, would always persist. There would even be moments when, with Richard Hannay in that first paragraph of *The Thirty-Nine Steps*, I shared a feeling that 'you have got into the wrong ditch, my friend, and you had better climb out'.

I returned home from the US with a huge mass of semi-digested matter – a great deal more work to do on Macmillan – and some massive personal decisions to face. It was good to be back, and to see the girls again. But my marriage was in disarray. I now knew I wanted to separate from Renira. It was, of course, primarily my fault. But, in the abstract, divorce is surely a hellish institution. A neighbour at Membury, who had been through the mill, warned me that it was going to be 'worse than you can possibly ever imagine'. He was dead right. People took sides; old friends disappeared, as did one's capital. Despite his devout Catholicism and instinctive hatred of divorce – as well as his affection for Renira – Bill was one who unhesitatingly stuck by me. At the time of my worst despair, a year or two later, in Switzerland he stunned me with the gift of an exquisite gold watch, engraved with a personal message – in no way a prize for misdemeanour, but simply an affirmation of an unbreakable friendship.

We sold up Membury, and all its memories, which took three years. It was a horrible time, and a financially destructive one. For several years I shuttled around, from rented digs to rented digs. My Macmillan papers were all over the place. It was during this period that my wonderful researcher Serena Booker was murdered in Thailand. She was irreplaceable. There were so many changes in the editorial set-up at Macmillans, with my MSS being passed from hand to hand, that I got close to dropping the whole massive Macmillan project in despair. Perhaps it was a sense that I owed something to old Supermac that at least partly kept me going.

I dilate on all these personal details to explain why, in part, the project took so long to complete – another six years. When *Macmillan* (grown from one medium-sized book into two thick ones) did finally come out in Britain, volume one in 1988 and volume two the following year, the reviewers were once again surpassing kind. I could hardly credit my good luck, and I was especially pleased to read the verdict of Roy Jenkins, himself a biographer, in the *Observer*: 'one of the most compelling pieces of biographical narrative that I have read for a long time. I simply bounded through it.' For all the cautions of my old American headmaster, Ed Pulling, the US press proved to be hardly less generous, even though the pre-PM Macmillan could not have been a star figure. In the *Washington Post* David Cannadine wrote, 'Macmillan was essentially an artist in politics, and in Alistair Horne he has found an artist in biography. The result is the most completely satisfying life yet written of any 20th-century British statesman.' Both in Britain and in the US each volume made the bestseller list, and stayed there for a respectable period. Of course, inevitably, there were dissenting views. The egregious Lord Lambton (I had written in volume two that Macmillan had been dead right to sack him, as a loose cannon, from the government) wrote with cheery malice in the *Spectator* that 'Horne was the only person known to have been seduced by Harold Macmillan.'

When it was all over, I couldn't help feeling a great emptiness. After each big book, I had always suffered a certain flatness, but somehow this time it was different. Apart from being a prodigious task, which led, directly, to nothing further, there had been too many milestones along the way, of which my divorce was the most distressing. My one-time boss and guru, to whom I owed so much, Maurice Oldfield, had died of cancer just weeks before I returned from Washington. I felt miserable that I had not seen him during the last period of his illness. It had been a pathetically sad ending to a brilliant career, hastened I suspect by the calumny which had overtaken him. He had been pressed by Margaret Thatcher to take on an arduous job in Northern Ireland too soon after he had retired, burned out, from being 'C' at MI6, and was outed, perhaps in a honey-trap, in a sordid homosexual encounter. The press made hay. He was traduced by *soi-disant* friends who had made their reputations on the back of Maurice's friendship and indiscreet tip-offs over the years. If

Maurice had a failing it was that, for a super-spy, he was just too trusting.

Then, undeniably, when he died I missed the old actor-manager immensely. I missed our sessions in freezing Birch Grove, missed our lunches with the cold chicken and thirds of champagne, the after-dinner, whisky-and-soda chats deep into the night. I missed the sparky conversation, and the courageous sadness of a lonely old man. Most of all, I missed being able to ring him up, at each new development on the world scene, and hear his comment, at once wise and funny, and supremely tuned in. Perhaps Lord Lambton was right: I had grown very fond of him. That had certainly not made the writing of a critical, warts-and-all biography any the easier. But I felt, too, that I had learned a lot from him, not least some ability to speak publicly without deadening terror – the tricks that he in his turn had learned first hand from Lloyd George; and maybe I had gained a few insights into how the strange world of the British Establishment operated. I just hoped, as biographer, that I had been honest and had done him justice. He deserved it.

Since Macmillan died there have been two plays devoted to him, a number of TV programmes, and two new full-length biographies, a level of attention lavished on few other recent British prime ministers save Winston Churchill. My biography was perhaps fortunate in being published in the Thatcher era, at a time when the current prime minister's unpopularity boosted popular affection for the old master from what seemed like a happier age. But in subsequent years the private image of the grouse-moor and the dated plus-fours returned, obliterating the very considerable statesman that lay within. Then, in our sex-obsessed age, it was the story of Dorothy and Boothby which rose to the fore. In 1995 the BBC invited me to collaborate on a major documentary about Macmillan which promised to have serious intent. At the eleventh hour, the producer announced a shift of emphasis – 'to liven it up'. Instead of 'Macmillan' its title would be 'The Macmillans'. My heart sank; I knew exactly what that would mean. Sure enough, three-quarters of it was devoted to rehashing the Boothby saga; names one might have thought worth a mention, such as Eisenhower and Kruschev, were omitted. I protested; but in vain. It was the Beeb at its ratings-seeking worst.

Twenty years after my official biography was published, a distinguished biographer who had already written admirable studies on such Tory

grandees as Selwyn Lloyd, Douglas Home and Eden, D. R. Thorpe, produced a new and meticulously sourced life of Macmillan, *Supermac*, in
2010. It was due time for a reappraisal. Though obviously I had no
influence on the contents, I have to confess an interest in that Thorpe had
previously been an Alistair Horne Fellow at St Antony's while writing his
authorised biography of Eden. Inevitably, we had different slants, and
time had enabled him to produce much new material; but fundamentally
we agreed: 'his survival in history is assured,' says Thorpe. One survivor
of his cabinet, Lord Carrington, still held him to have been 'one of the
great Prime Ministers of the twentieth century'. I like to think he was
right. But what gratified me beyond all else was Thorpe's ability to go
even further than I could at the time to clear Macmillan totally of those
disgraceful accusations of his responsibility for the repatriation of the
Russians in 1945. They caused him great anguish in his last years, and it
was not until three years after his death that, with the pulverising verdict
of the Aldington v. Tolstoy libel trial of 1989, an all-embracing judgment
could be made.

16

A BUNDLE FROM BRITAIN

La Moneda, Chile. Interviewing General Pinochet in 1987.
(Note the all-concealing sheaf of papers.)

Creative people should avoid being psycho-analysed as long as their intimate miseries do not impair their creativeness.

Arthur Koestler, 'The Yogi and the Commissar'

While I was writing the Macmillan biography, there were some irresistible literary temptations that came along to eat up my working day. In 1982 I was surprised and thrilled to be invited to give the Lees Knowles Lectures, for the following year, a series of four at Trinity College, Cambridge, the most prestigious that lay open to a military historian. Among the galaxy that had been invited over the years since it was founded in 1915 were such giants as Basil Liddell Hart, John Buchan, Fitzroy Maclean, Field Marshals Wavell, Harding, Slim, and Carver and Professor Michael Howard. It was monumentally flattering and simply not to be refused, even though I was now moving gradually away from being a main-line military historian. As my subject, I was allowed to choose 'The French Army and Politics, 1870–1970', drawn from the four books I had written on French military matters. In turn it would become a short book with the same title.*

The lectures at Trinity were well attended, by both students and dons, as well as outside experts. By way of intro, as an unforgiving Scot, I couldn't quite resist exacting a modest revenge by retelling my first encounter in this most august of colleges, when, in 1947, appearing in uniform, hot out of the army, I had been turned down by the Senior Tutor with the outrageous advice: 'Since you were in the Brigade of Guards, may I suggest you try Magdalene on snob value!' The lectures also had an unexpected spin-off. I was invited to London, Ontario, to represent them at the University of Western Ontario as one of the series of Joanne Goodman Lectures, established in memory of a young girl tragically killed in an automobile accident while a student. My fee, in essence, was a week's helicopter skiing in the Bugaboos of British Columbia. It

---

* Published by Macmillans in Britain and by Peter Bedrick in the US.

was good to be back in Canada – though the students derided me when I appeared lugging a pair of skis, given that Ontario has to be just about the flattest part of the country. But, knowing where I was going, I had the last laugh, and the most exciting week in the snows of my entire life.

From London, Ontario, I flew west over the endless prairies where Renira and I had driven all those years before, to Calgary at the base of the Rockies. Thence, meeting up with the ski group, I was flown by helicopter deep into the untracked British Columbia mountains. The Bugaboos camp was so far from civilisation that my transistor could not pick up a single station. We were a diffuse group of about forty, including only six women, the majority Germans or Californians; I was the only Brit. We divided into four classes: I, sensibly, opted to be in the bottom class. The top comprised four Olympic skiers, who were a joy to watch as they wedeled effortlessly down the virgin slopes, without apparently making the least check to their speed. One of them was Willy Bogner, the ski-wear designer, film producer and stunt-man for ski scenes in James Bond movies. A quiet, shy man, Willy's life had been clouded with tragedy when, in the 1960s, his fiancée 'Barbi' Henneberger – together with the US Olympic skier Buddy Werner – was swept away by an avalanche at St Moritz, as a horrified Willy was actually filming them from an adjacent slope. We spent the first hours in the Bugaboos paired off each with a 'buddy', doing avalanche drill with Skadi transceivers, designed to locate a victim under an avalanche. I was not encouraged to find that my 'buddy', Joan, was constantly searching in the opposite direction to the Skadi.

The next morning, a six-minute vertiginous flight in the chopper whirled our group – trembling with anticipation – up over turquoise crevasses that lay like sharks' jaws in the glacier below and painfully close to the cruel razor-sharp Bugaboo Spires. Then the rotor note changed to a whop, whop, whop and we settled on a peak made invisible by the spume of snow it threw up. We clambered out into the unknown, as the chopper immediately took off again. As the spume dissipated, we were left to ogle a mountain snowscape of incredible beauty, the size of an empty Switzerland, beneath our feet – nothing but silence, solitude and beauty. Skis on, and we found ourselves gliding, floating silently down endless untracked slopes of perfect pitch and vast widths all to ourselves. It seemed impossible not to get a perfect rhythm, and a new incredible bounce at every turn. One run that day was called, appropriately, Seventh Heaven, another Grandpa's Orgasm; each seemed to stretch for ever, laps of two, three miles with pauses dictated, not by the mountain, but by lack of puff. We began to think we were incredibly good. At a picnic lunch (brought in by helicopter) we toasted each other in apple juice. (Alcohol was banned, for good reasons. Some years before, two skiers, after too good a lunch, fell upside-down into a deep 'tree-hole' and died, suffocated in their own vomit.) At the bottom of each run, there was no pause. Immediately the chopper was there, to take us up to the top again, like some relentless conveyor belt. It was all hurry, hurry, belts on, belts off, get out! – one of the least appealing features of heli-skiing. By the end of the week I was amazed to discover that I had skied 100,000 vertical feet – equal to four Everests. Goodness knows how many Everests the Bogner group had notched up. For days I walked like Petrushka, with paralysing stiffness.

It marked, literally, the peak of my skiing life – from then on (a bad pun) it was downhill all the way. Ten years later, ill health forced me to give it all up. How I regretted it! I still dream of the Bugaboos some nights. But, in those last years, I also learned a new awareness of the mountains, and of the dangers that lurk around every corner or cornice. I observed, all too close for comfort, two vast avalanches, and saw great firs in Utah 2 feet thick snapped off like bamboo canes, and realised the damage they could cause – and with what frivolous ease they could be set off. Moving at up to 200 mph, they would turn a human body into hamburger; worse still was the slow death from suffocation, upside down with arms pinioned by snow like concrete. The last few ski articles I wrote were largely devoted to cautionary utterances about avalanches. I visited the Swiss Institute for Avalanche Research high above Davos, and what I learned there left me ashen-faced. People had been killed in an avalanche no higher than the slope of a roof, and often the victims were the most experienced skiers, like the fiancée of Willy Bogner. One young guide I knew died in snow 'not deeper than a table'. I came away from the Avalanche Centre like an old mother-hen, my own skiing made immeasurably more cautious, with a new respect for the mountains and what snow can do – as well as a new topic that would fill my ski columns for years.

I was travelling a lot, much of it made possible by travel-writing. Given particularly the brevity (and the need for accuracy) it imposed, it wasn't always the easiest of literary formats, but – apart from the financial support it provided – like painting, travel-writing was a marvellous means of focusing the mind's eye and memory on things and places experienced. Thanks to my kind patrons, over the years I managed to visit and write about destinations as various as Tunisia and Leningrad, Salamanca and the Silk Route, Krakow, Peru and Cuba.

In 1987 I went back to Chile, to have a happy reunion in Santiago with Nena, and for a most important meeting which Nena had managed to set up. It was at 7 a.m., in La Moneda. General Pinochet's office in the grim, grey palace was situated very close to the room where Allende had met his death, probably by suicide, in September 1973. The scars caused by the Chilean Air Force rockets fired during the coup, with remarkable accuracy, still showed around the windows of La Moneda. It was guarded by tough-looking *carabineros* with sub-machine guns. Only the previous year Pinochet had narrowly escaped an assassination attempt.

If not actually the first, I was certainly one of the very few gringo journalists or writers to whom the dictator had granted an interview. The opening came partly through the influence of Nena, and my *Small Earthquake in Chile* (published in 1972, the year before Pinochet had seized power), and partly through *A Savage War of Peace*, which Pinochet had read in the Spanish edition. He also knew that I would be writing up the interview in the *Sunday Telegraph*, for whom it would be something of a scoop.

The general was shorter than I expected, and dressed in an elegantly tailored civilian suit of shiny silk. He was courteous, affable and relaxed, and looked well for a man of seventy-two, despite current rumours about his health. His office was furnished in a comfortably unmilitary style; we sat in armchairs, there was a crucifix and a book of poetry open on a reading stand by his side. Instead of the allotted twenty minutes, I was with him for forty-five. He spoke in a low voice, staccato, spiced with military usage, and in that most difficult Chilean variety of Spanish, so that I was grateful to be accompanied by a good interpreter.

An obliging reference to *A Savage War* presented me with a heaven-sent opening. Rushing in, I observed that the French Army had indeed won the Battle of Algiers, but only by resort to torture, and that that had cost them the war through the revulsion of public opinion at home. Why had Chile not shown more concern about its public image? If there were to be a renewal of terrorism in the future, could his government guarantee that it would meet it without the unacceptably harsh measures of the past, specifically torture? There was a pause, during which I half expected to be ejected by the *carabineros*. But Pinochet riposted: 'Do the Communists, do the Cubans, recognise human rights?' I remarked, rather piously, that surely the West had to set higher standards. Then, looking me straight in the eye, he declared, 'In Chile, there has not been torture.' I recall a silence in the room, I looked up at the ceiling, his entourage looked down at their feet.

We then moved on to less controversial matters like Chile's economic success story (which continues to this day to be the envy of her Latin American neighbours). He admired Mrs Thatcher: 'It is comforting to know that our successes are being repeated in other countries.' Throughout the interview, he repeatedly showed himself haunted by an ageing caudillo's fears of *après moi*. He was determined that Chile would never return to the bad old days of Allende, and that she should never again allow herself to be endangered by Marxist totalitarianism. We turned to the forthcoming elections, the first since Allende came to power in 1970. Pinochet had said he would submit himself to a simple plebiscite. If he lost in 1988, he assured me, he would then withdraw as a candidate in the presidential elections the following year. In Chile, and certainly abroad, the general view then was that, if Pinochet did lose in 1988, he would somehow fudge the results to stay in power.

What if the Communists tried to disrupt the elections with violence, I asked? At this point, I thought I heard him say, and the interpreter translate: 'We will reject every harsh measure, and, whatever happens, we will not torture again.' At least this is what I recall writing in my notes (maddeningly my own tape-recorder had stalled); but, later, on my return to London, this revealing slip-up was omitted from the official Chilean transcript, and a spokesman qualified the President's remarks by explaining that torture had never been an instrument of government policy: 'If there had been excesses, these would have been made known to the judiciary.' My attention was drawn to the number of policemen against whom charges of such excesses had been filed recently.

To give him credit where it was due, after the ensuing plebiscite Pinochet did exactly what he promised he would do and stepped down. Thirteen years later Pinochet came to London, only to be arrested and imprisoned for several months at the whim of a maverick Spanish judge (disgracefully, in my opinion). Unlike Margaret Thatcher, Lord Lamont and others, though invited I declined to go and see him. I found his record of torture too odious; and what would I have to say to him?

In winter 1974, the Heath government was tottering, the unions were winning, we had a three-day week: it seemed as if Britain was on the brink of collapse. In the midst of all this gloom and doom, Renira and I were invited to a prenup party in which we all had to dress up as 1917 Russians. Given that one could almost hear the tumbrils lining up outside, I found the whole ambience depressingly unsuitable. But I sat next to a very beautiful young woman whom I had never met before. I was instantly captivated by a smile that would have thawed the snows of Everest, let alone the freeze-up outside. Her eyes twinkled with merriment. She was a talented painter, and – I later discovered – had a unique capacity for surrounding herself with nature, and a deep harmony with it. She also loved dogs, just as much as I did. There was a tinge of gold or pale apricot in her complexion. With Irish strongly in her genes went some subtlety of thought, but it never conflicted with her dominant honesty, or capacity for giving affection and love. Though punctuality, I was to discover, was not one of her talents, time taken on preparing to go out was usually well spent. She always looked marvellous. When she entered the room, the world became a sunnier place; it still does. Thirteen years later Sheelin and I got married.

My divorce came through in 1984, but there was a minefield yet to be traversed – as my neighbour had warned me, deadlier than either Renira or I could have foreseen. It wasn't till the end of 1987 that Sheelin and I felt able to take the plunge. Our good American friends, Dick and Irene Pipes, had a lovely house on a promontory in faraway Tortola in the British Virgin Islands, where we had once stayed, and they suggested we might come there, to tie the knot, discreetly and out of sight. We came for Christmas, a feast which, as Jews, they did not celebrate, but they thoughtfully found a small Christmas tree to place in our room. My solicitor, exploring diligently, assured me that marriage in Tortola would stick; it was after all a Crown Colony (he even encouraged me by discovering the telegraphic address of the Governor to be 'HE VIRILE'). The deed required various complex steps: first, going down to the tiny capital, Road Town, to buy $100 of stamps* with pretty doves on them from the Post Office, presumably to avoid all possibility of graft. We then crossed the street to the imposingly named Attorney General's Office, where a friendly lady took our passports and the stamps and gave me solemn forms to sign. These we had to take to Miss Rabstatt, the Registrar, at the other end of town.

Our friends, the Pipeses, were thrilled to hear the name of the officiating Registrar, Sidney Jacobs: 'with a name like that, he has to be Jewish, a Rabbi – so you're going to become one of us: congratulations!'

We experienced some difficulty in tracking down our minister, the Rev. Sidney Jacobs, who turned out to be a chocolate-brown Grenadian, but the wedding eventually took place on 30 December on the Pipeses' veranda. It was a brief but touching ceremony, and I was terrified of dropping the ring through the wooden decking, to be carried away by some large Caribbean rat lurking beneath. There was a jolly wedding party of sixteen, champagne and chopped liver (a favourite of our hosts). The Reverend confided that it was the first wedding he had done. In his nervousness he got the details on the marriage certificate wrong, transposing our respective ages and professions. Perhaps, after all, we were never properly married. Afterwards he handed me a packet of papers, our passports and a plastic bag tied up in an elegant bow. It contained a warning about AIDS, a pamphlet about herpes, a packet of condoms and a 'best wishes' card.

One of our biggest challenges had been the need to find a house, somewhere that all our children and future grandchildren, could look upon, at least in part, as home. Somewhere in the country, not too far from London, and facing south-west, to catch the fugitive English sun. Our requirements were exacting, so for the best part of five years we hunted in vain. Our catchment area was roughly Wiltshire and Glosucestershire, where each of us had lived formerly. Month after month

* The US dollar is the official currency in the British Virgin Isles.

nothing came up; our spirits began to sink. Then, in the summer of 1987 I went away on a lecture tour, and returned to ask Sheelin casually, 'Any houses?' 'Not really. Oh, there's one, but it's not in the area we want – a vicarage in a village called Turville, near Henley. But it's rather pretty – maybe worth looking at.' I responded, with penetrating realism: 'Looks to me like a very expensive cottage.'

We went to see the Old Vicarage. I was smitten, little appreciating that Sheelin had already gone to see it with her mum, had fallen in love and set her heart on it. There followed some agonising bidding – *in absentia*, because I was then lecturing at Verdun. We won, though at the time it seemed a bit like Verdun itself, a Pyrrhic victory. I had to pay a dreadfully high price; then, when it came to payment, funded by selling stocks and shares, the markets collapsed on 'Black Monday', 19 October 1987. We have been recovering ever since. Only three days before, the Great Storm uprooted a magnificent chestnut splendidly sited in the field in front of the house. Then, in order to convert a battered barn into the glorious library where I work, I had to sell the beloved Lucian Freud I had purchased for £625 in the 1960s. Nevertheless, as I write these words, we have lived in the Old Vicarage for over two decades, mostly in bliss, and longer than either of us had tenanted any previous house.

But what can one write, without resort to hyperbole, about the prettiest house in the prettiest village in what remains of bucolic Britain, a village already exposed to media gaze by being the location for *The Vicar of Dibley*? The outstanding virtue of Turville, though it is only 45 miles from the metropolis, was and remains its tranquillity. Someone once remarked, in either derision or envy, that on a weekday you could hear the hollyhocks grow. Then, at weekends and Bank Holidays especially, the village explodes with hikers, centred on the charming, unspoilt pub, the Bull and Butcher, with cars parked all the way from it to the bluebell woods. But, hidden away in the Old Vicarage, looking inwards upon our tiny empire, one was blissfully unaware of all the hubbub. The most intrusive noise was – in spring – the croaking of a million frogs come, from nowhere, to copulate in our pond, and risk being gobbled up, two at a time, by a predatory blue heron.

Shortly after we moved in, there arrived on our doorstep, as if borne in by some magical Welsh Red Dragon, a lady with smiling rosy cheeks as round as any delicious apple. In answer to an ad for a housekeeper, Gaynor Griffiths from Swansea, her husband Paul and four-year-old boy David came to live in our tiny cottage and keep us in order. She has stayed all these years. The Griffiths family became an integral part of Turville life, while Gaynor made it possible for us to go on our extended travels abroad, for me to write a dozen more books in spoiling calm, for Sheelin to paint, and for our successive dogs – Bumble, Bertie and Georgie – to thrive in pampered love. In a score of years, she must be the only person I've never exchanged a cross word with.

But, even in Paradise there has to be a worm in the apple. Or, as Henry Kissinger would jest, 'inside every silver lining there's a cloud'. Soon after we arrived in Turville we were to learn, painfully, how fiercely minor controversies, what the French would call a *querelle de clocher*, can escalate, poisoning the atmosphere for years. The *querelle de clocher* in idyllic Turville arose over the usage of a deserted village school which a faction (mainly of outsiders, it has to be said) wanted to resurrect as a holiday home for inner-city children during the summer. It wasn't going to affect us in the Old Vicarage, as we were out of sight and out of earshot, but half the village strongly opposed the idea. Notably there were the residents of School Close, in two-bed bungalows, for whom undisturbed peace during their summer holidays was at a premium. They felt the noise and nuisance factor in a confine which had no more space than a tiny asphalt yard, would be intolerable. We sympathised with them, and supported them. It was a warm-hearted idea, but with its lack of facilities Turville School seemed quite the wrong place for a summer camp. I personally thought the building would be much better utilised if converted into three or four starter homes at low rents, which were seriously lacking in the neighbourhood.

Perhaps rashly I allowed myself to become appointed as the local scribe, even more rashly accepting an invitation from the *Daily Mail* to air the dispute. It opened the door to the national media, and it was just the kind of story they love. We, the 'antis' were seriously outgunned, dubbed 'child-haters', and Turville damned, in an *Evening Standard* headline, as the 'village with no place for children'. Eventually, as these things do, an acceptable compromise was reached, not, however, before a large amount of poison had flowed. John Mortimer, one of the leaders of the project who lived well outside the village, never spoke to me again. But we found we had many lasting friendships within the village. Altogether it was an unhappy story, but there are times when one has to take a stand, as in the miserable Tolstoy affair, even at the risk of unpopularity. It was costly, in professional as well as personal terms. I reckon all the lobbying, the stresses and strains of the Battle of Turville cost me the equivalent of a whole book in terms of effort. Reaching a crescendo in 1994, it came at a time when I was having to concentrate on completing my book, *The Lonely Leader*, in time for the fiftieth anniversary of D-Day, and I missed all-important deadlines.

Beloved Turville went back to listening to the hollyhocks grow. There is a lot of unspoken love and affection in this village; with bonds of genuine affection where people truly look after their neighbours in adversity. After twenty-four years, it is still a wonderful place to call home.

It was in the pastoral setting of Turville that I at last allowed the shiny technology of computers to enter my life. My education had begun at the Woodrow Wilson in 1980–1 when a fellow visiting scholar offered to give a lecture on computerisation. It was, he asserted, the ineluctable future for all writers. He began, somewhat pedantically, by explaining the binary system, whereby the world was reduced into a series of figures, either 0 or 1. I returned in uncomprehending scepticism to my beloved thirty-year-old portable Olympic typewriter and its grubby carbons. But at about the same time I was coming under pressure from Bill Buckley, now hunched over his new toy called a Kaypro and, as ever, insistent that I should share his joy. To gratify him, I discarded the Olympic for an electric typewriter. I instantly hated its imperious clatter. Later I tried one of Alan Sugar's Amstrads, but couldn't bear it.

I could trace my snail-like evolution in terms of secretaries/PAs. Reflecting on over five decades of dependency on a series of wonderful, uncomplaining, loyal women, who would laboriously retype my messy manuscripts and letters, and decipher my illegible writing, I regularly send up a prayer of thanks and gratitude. First, in the 1950s, came Peta Thorp, half Indian with one kidney, and a smokaholic. I would ply her with tapes off a state-of-the-art Grundig, weighing almost as much as the Olympic. Then came Teresa Girouard, conscientious to a fault, who worked with me on *The Fall of Paris*. Next, for some thirteen happy years, came Denny Nicol. Another smokaholic, wafting a permanent aroma of the substance ahead of her, she couldn't spell; but it didn't matter, she was such fun to work with. Denny was followed by Serena Booker, who was more researcher than secretary, chaotic in her dizzy disorganisation, but a superb assistant. After her terrible murder I had Helen Whitten, who stayed with me for over five years and saw out the Macmillan epic, and was first rate. Helen too tried to coax me towards the unappealing Amstrad, then – one day in the late 1980s – she came in with a look of Archimedes, having discovered the miracle of the fax machine. I bought one, and couldn't believe the hi-tech joy it brought into my life (now, two decades on, it has all but joined the ranks of collectibles, along with my old Olympia).

Helen moved on, and was replaced by the conscientious, tennis-playing Anne Whatmore, who in her spare time worked for the Samaritans. At various intervals we would discuss, inconsequentially, following the Buckley example and 'going computerised', but never quite got round to it. Then, one day at the end of July 1990, when I rang her I got her young son instead: 'You didn't know? My mother's twin brother was the MP who's just been murdered by the IRA.' I didn't know. It was all over the news that day: Ian Gow, Margaret Thatcher's parliamentary private secretary, an acquaintance over the years who had been present at my long interview with Thatcher in 1979 had been blown up by a car bomb, outside his home. Strong personality though she was, I sensed that if anyone needed Samaritan help then it was her. All I could do was propose a distraction; we would both buy an Apple (recommended to me by a nerd friend as the 'idiot-friendly system'). The two of us set off on a course out at Swiss Cottage. It was agony, like learning a complicated new language at an advanced age. However, it opened up a whole new world and perhaps extended my writing life by another decade or so. Bill had been quite right: gone was the fatigue of carbons and footnotes, and the perennial fear of losing an entire manuscript.

The first book I wrote on my computer was *A Bundle from Britain*, which I conceived as a great big thank-you to America, following my second return after that spell at the Woodrow Wilson in 1981. It was the bread-and-butter letter that I had been meaning to write for many years. As I tried to retell in the story, in July 1940, on my widower father's unilateral decision, I was one of the hundreds of British schoolchildren who were shipped off – reluctant, but protests unheeded – to America. After the Fall of France that grim summer, the aim was to preserve us children, for posterity, from the clutches of Adolf Hitler.

A Bundle from Britain (the only book, incidentally, where I have ever hit on the title before a word was written) was originally to be published to coincide with the fiftieth anniversary of that red-letter month of July 1940, when I first touched down on American soil. Then it was rescheduled for Pearl Harbor day, and finally for the anniversary of my return to England in 1943. In the jargon of my exasperated publishers, the date had 'slipped a bit'. The reason for this slippage was that, as with almost all my other books, the end product turned out to be very different from what was originally intended. On thinking through the idea, I concluded that the American adventure would make little sense to readers in the 1990s unless I could help out with some comparative picture of my British upbringing and background. But, mainly because both my mother and my father died when I was still very young (he, as noted in Chapter 1, when I was barely eighteen), I found myself engaged in a major detective work of reconstruction – almost a book in itself. The idiosyncrasies of my parents began to intrigue me. Out of it all I deduced that my real, English (or, rather, Scottish) family were, at least on my mother's side, infinitely more eccentric (as well as being a great deal unhappier) than that unusual one on which I descended in America.

There was a further problem. It was literary constipation, sheer blockage, that seemed to be my trouble. Until I could fool myself into pretending that I was writing about a totally other, external set of people – like, say, the Macmillans or the Kennedys – there were days and weeks of complete seize-up. Writing about my family, sometimes, too, was depressingly like being dead, writing one's own obituary. On Chapter Two, 'Auriol, My Mother', I got so stuck that I had to be rescued by that patron saint of authors, Drue Heinz, who let me come and stay, alone, in her hide-out on Lake Como. That was bliss, I had a modest villa all to myself, and would spend balmy days working outside beneath a walnut tree, tapping away at my first Apple laptop.

I truly had no recollection at all of my mother, bar a vague aroma of scent and beauty; I had seen so little of her before her untimely death.

She was always away. So the material for these earlier chapters came largely from some thirty scrapbooks that survived her death by drowning in the River Scheldt back in 1930, as well as several steel boxes of her writings. Luckily for me, she threw nothing away. She must have been a kind of squirrel; but perhaps people of her era were. There were albums of faded postcards and photographs of people and faraway places; albums full of signatures of weekend party guests, of invitations, race-cards and even dance-cards. There were boxes full of unpublished short stories, novels, poems, plays and songs. There were books of cuttings of her press articles – which were published – and pay-slips and letters of rejection. And there were two morbid cuttings-books, prepared by unknown hands, of her death. It is largely from this material that I set about the detective work of reconstructing a mysterious family past. (All have been sent off for safe-keeping, with the rest of my archives, to the admirable Gottlieb Center at Boston University.)

Though I had lived with it for years, ever since my father's death in 1944, I had never properly sifted through this material, and in the course of doing so I found what seemed to me an intriguing picture of an era, not only of my own forebears. From this untapped treasure trove I learned a little more about an unusual, and somewhat wayward, clan, which took me wandering still further from that b-and-b letter to America. Yet it was immeasurably worthwhile – at least to me.

Both my paternal and maternal families were Scots. The Hornes were Lowlanders of modest bourgeois extraction; my mother's clan, the Hays, were rather grand, but impoverished, Highlanders, who could trace their ancestry back some six centuries. But there was also an element of decadence: one of my mother's generation, the naughty Lord Erroll, was murdered for his misdemeanour in Kenya. (His demise, in 1940, gave rise to one of the best headlines ever, 'BELTED EARL BUMPED BY BART', and provided substance for a book and much-hyped film, *White Mischief*.) Both families were also singularly unfecund. Out of six Hay siblings, only my mother reproduced; while my father's generation of five bore just two children – myself, and my Cousin Eve.

My father described himself as having been 'educated privately'. That meant that there was not enough money to send him to school, let alone university. Born in 1875, like many an impecunious young Scot of his days

James Allan Horne shipped off to find his fortunes in British India. He must have proved himself an able administrator, and ended the war with a knighthood. After twenty-two years on the subcontinent, he returned home to find a wife.

Auriol Hay was born in 1893. Her parents left each other, and her, early in her childhood. Hers was not a happy life; she grew up even poorer than my father, with no home, and no money. The Great War came, and the holocaust of the Western Front stole away many of her friends, and potential suitors. In 1917 she married a gallant officer on leave from the front, at the British Embassy chapel in Paris, where she had been doing war work. Captain Noel Barran survived the trenches only to be killed in the flu epidemic two years later. Still aged only twenty-six, with no home, no money and no calling, Auriol set to earning a livelihood with her pen – as a foreign correspondent, using her knowledge of German (learned from her uncle by marriage, Graf Münster), at almost exactly the same age that I started off in post-Second World War Bonn. But for a woman to break into such a virtually closed shop as a freelance in the early 1920s would have made earning a livelihood from poetry seem almost child's play by comparison. In the face of repeated rejection by papers, such as was to characterise her whole literary career, she would never take no for an answer. Suddenly she found a home for her journalism in the *Sunday Times*, and a handsome cheque for £3 came in. A first real story, however, arrived when she managed to wangle – through her Münster contacts – an interview with the gruff and surly General Erich Ludendorff, who had hitherto refused to talk to any Allied correspondents. Later, it was Lord Rothermere's *Daily Mail* of 1 December 1922 that printed Auriol Barran's scoop, blazoned across three front-page columns as the lead story, headlined: 'Germany and Russia', 'Secret Agreement', 'War of Revenge', 'A Ten Years Programme'. Here was a first account of the 'Black Reichswehr', General von Seeckt's secret army being raised surreptitiously in Lenin's Russia, against all the edicts of Versailles.

A couple of years later she had met and married my father. There was an eighteen-year age gap between them, but, much more than that, there was a gap of contrasting worlds. He the affluent fifty-year-old bachelor, rooted in his years in India, she the rather bohemian journalist living on a shoestring. How different their friends must have been, for a start: his the world of the Oriental Club and City; hers the international beau monde, German princelings and Grub Street. They were totally different personalities. The omens were not good. Early in 1925, either on a trip to India or Burma, Auriol became pregnant. Was it a mistake, a moment of unheeding passion in the heat, in some rajah's palace? Did she really wish to have children? One was, evidently, to prove enough! I was born on 9 November that year.

Towards the end of the giddy 1920s, Auriol's friends came to note in her a mounting listlessness, the growth of a certain jaded feeling. The Hornes, effectively, separated. Auriol moved to a house in St John's Wood, the resort traditionally of mistresses and the divorced. I seem to have moved in with my father. It looked as if, very soon, she would have to face earning her living again. In September 1930, she was travelling with a Hungarian actress friend, Sári Petráss, from Le Touquet to Holland. After lunch the two set off, late and in a great hurry, evidently a fairly rash thing to do, given the state of the roads in 1930. The following day, 8 September, the British evening press headlined:

KNIGHT'S WIFE DROWNED
AS CAR DIVES INTO RIVER

It seems that the unfortunate driver, pressed on by an impatient Auriol, had – in darkness and mist, and blinded by the lights of Antwerp ahead – driven the car into the River Scheldt, instead of on to the ferry. The logical explanation today would be that he had momentarily dozed off. He managed to escape, the two women, trapped in the back, drowned. The day after the accident, kept from me during my childhood, terrible photographs, published all over the papers, showed the car – registration number 7857 XV – dangling like a large fish from a crane, with Antwerp cathedral in the background. Allan, in Scotland at the time, hastened to the scene of the accident and brought the body home. I was not quite five. Most children who lose a parent even so early retain some recollections. I had little or none – a memory of a scent, of a beautiful, luxuriant, female, all-embracing environment, but an absentee mum. And that is about all.

So that was Auriol, my mother. I retell her story in *A Bundle from Britain*, but if I dwell here on her, unknown, rediscovered, it is perhaps because her image came to beset me as I began the book. It seemed a life so talented yet so fundamentally sad and unfulfilled – but so determined. I suppose that whatever genes I may have inherited as a writer came from her. Auriol may not have been the world's most successful writer, but, my goodness, how she tried! If today I struggle on writing into my eighties it is not least because of the model of determination, of perseverance right to the end, that she left behind.

As I wrote the last words of the book, I felt none of the accustomed fatigue, but instead pure satisfaction, indeed unmitigated delight. I liked to feel I had achieved what I had set out to do: to write a thank-you letter to the USA, expressing my supreme debt of gratitude to, and affection for, America and Americans. I was delighted by the reviews. In *The Times* in the summer of 1993, the distinguished academic and former Provost of King's College, Cambridge, Noel Annan, wrote: 'Many people have love affairs with other countries, but, if you pick America as your mistress, do so while you are a virgin. Alistair Horne had the luck to go there young ... I found this book more than a good read. I found it moving ...' The then US Ambassador in London, Ray Seitz, generally regarded as America's most outstanding envoy in many years, paid the book a heart-warming tribute in the *Spectator*. He followed this up by throwing a party at the American Residence (by chance on my birthday), to which some sixty Bundles came. While the spouses dined off sumptuous Embassy fare, we one-time 'refugees' were given what we might have found in the States as of 1940: a hot dog, a hamburger and a Hershey bar! It was a salutary reminder of life then, but it was a joyous evening.

As might have been hoped, reactions in 'my other country' were even more gratifying. The most exciting of all came in September 1994 in the often surly *New York Times* (which picked *A Bundle* as 'Editor's Choice') from Francine du Plessix Gray, who had her own transatlantic story.* It was quite the nicest review I'd ever had on any book. We had never met, but became good friends thereafter. She described *A Bundle* as 'A paean of gratitude ... this ebullient, generous memoir is far more than a hymn of praise to an America whose idealism and benevolence he finds undiminished to this day ... [It is] the chronicle of a brilliant writer's

---

* Later published as *Them: A Memoir of Parents*, Penguin, 2005.

loyalty and gratitude, and of his lifelong commitment to the art of friend-ship . . . life's greatest treasure.'

Just as pleasing were the quantities of letters I received, out of the blue, from unknown readers who had shared my experiences, or my love of America. One correspondent, however, did write to say that she had found my account of quitting wartime Britain 'smug and offensive'. You can't win them all.

17

THE LONELY LEADER

Two stages in a memorable day: at last a Spitfire!
Duxford Airfield and Senate House, Cambridge.

In defeat, unbeatable; in victory, unbearable.

Winston Churchill on Bernard Montgomery

After finishing *A Bundle*, I was back to contemplating the novel. Then there came a call from a very old friend, from Cambridge days. David Montgomery – Viscount Montgomery of Alamein, son of the great Monty. At Cambridge David had been one of the few of us to study a meaningful subject which wasn't what the feisty Field Marshal would have designated 'useless, quite useless': engineering. Nevertheless, he was an effervescent, dauntless companion, by dusk a daring member of the Night Climbers of Cambridge, whose goal was to place chamber-pots upon the highest pinnacles of King's College Chapel. We both shared an unhappy childhood; he never complained, but his was worse. His father too was an elderly bachelor, marrying late to produce one son; his mother, a wonderful woman called Betty, who brought light, the arts and colour into the life of that dedicated, Jack-Russell-like soldier, died – wretchedly – of an insect bite when David was eight. With his father always away at the wars, David was housed by a series of schoolmasters. Monty must have been a hellish and often embarrassing father, as well as a difficult figure always to defend, but David stuck up for him with unremitting loyalty, prepared to discuss his faults only among close friends.

What prompted David's call in 1992 was that the fiftieth anniversary of D-Day was only two years away. Would I write an account of Monty's last year of the war? He would help in providing all necessary documents, and we would reconnoitre each of Monty's twenty-eight Tactical Head-quarters in that final year, from Portsmouth to Lüneburg Heath, where the final surrender of Nazi Germany was signed. It sounded an exciting project. For him it was something of a filial pilgrimage, for me a voyage of discovery, as new book-subjects always are.

So we set off, on 18 June, close to the date of the historic Normandy landings of forty-eight years previously. The day before I had received, in some astonishment, news that President Mitterrand had conferred upon me the Légion d'Honneur. It seemed a nice omen. Fair, indeed, stood the wind for France! We started off at Southwicke House, aka HMS *Dryad*, now the Royal Navy Navigation School, where the final plans for D-Day had been discussed, with all workers locked in (in Turkish fashion) until the invasion, in order to maintain total secrecy. We then moved on to Broomfield House, the first of Monty's TAC HQs. It was easy to visualise there all the bustle of a hundred men, drivers and support troops, mobile generators, signals and so on.

There followed a luxury crossing of the Channel on a brand-new 27,000-ton ferry, roughly the same size as the British battleships that would have been bombarding the German positions in Normandy. We saw the thin grey ribbon of coast, which those seasick troops would first have caught sight of with apprehension on 6 June, visible half an hour out. No participant that day would ever forget the sight of the vast armada, the largest in history, that simply covered the sea. The figures are mind-boggling. A statistic often forgotten in the US is the fact that British and Canadians were marginally in the majority on D-Day, 83,000 as against 73,000 Americans for the first wave on the beaches. The responsibility for getting them all there rested very largely on the slender shoulders of that one small general. If it was said of Admiral Jellicoe in 1914 that he was the only man who could 'lose the war in an afternoon', it was little less true of Montgomery thirty years later.

So the burden carried by Monty was immeasurable. After the retreat to Dunkirk (when he had been commanding Britain's top division, the 3rd), and the humiliating string of defeats in the Middle East, nobody knew better the inherent frailty of the British Army. But Monty had managed better than anyone to fill it with fight, with what he called 'binge'. And the troops trusted him. Tirelessly before the invasion he would pursue his quest of raising binge, visiting a division a day, seven a week. In those key months of preparation, more controversial – and it rankled especially with the American commanders – was the arrogant manner in which Monty delivered his presentation, on 7 April, of a map of 'Phase Lines'. These laid down that the Seine would be crossed by D+90: in fact he was to beat this target by nine days. To Monty, geographical lines were unimportant; what counted was the destruction of enemy forces within that area. But what would hang like a perennial millstone round his neck was his boastful assumption that Caen, the critical hub on the east of the British/Canadian sector, would be taken on D-Day itself. American critics particularly would never allow him to forget this.

Montgomery's TAC HQ system, which was at variance with the ways of General 'Ike' Eisenhower, the Supreme Allied Commander, and other senior US commanders, had the great advantage of putting him supremely in touch with the forward fighting formations under him. On the other hand, it also suffered the very serious disadvantage that it left him out of touch with senior staffs at SHAEF (Supreme Headquarters), then still back in England; and, with the speed of the advance, that disadvantage would increase. Thus, with every setback, the murmurings and backstabbing of Montgomery's many enemies – British as well as Americans – at SHAEF rose unchecked, and Montgomery was never there to make any effort to explain, and re-explain, his strategy to Ike.

For a few days David and I experienced blinding rain and winds, of the kind that so nearly called off D-Day in 1944, and were to cause appalling damage to back-up supplies two weeks later. So in howling wind and wild seas we visited the beautifully tended US cemetery at Colleville-sur-Mer, which overlooks Omaha Beach, where so many Americans died. We made a recce to the scene of one of the first abortive British attempts to seize Caen from the flank, the small township of Villers-Bocage. The word *bocage* came to have a sinister connotation in Normandy. Notably in the American sector, it denoted medieval sunken lanes, densely fringed by trees, in which a column of tanks could become inextricably stuck, easy prey to the deadly Panzerfaust bazookas of teenage German troops prowling in the undergrowth.

That afternoon after our walk at Villers-Bocage I had a spookily unnerving experience. As we drove around David had been urging me to stop at a British cemetery, just to show me how superbly well tended they were. Most of the US dead had been collected and concentrated at Colleville-sur-Mer, but the British lay in numerous small cemeteries, marshalled by the Commonwealth War Graves Commission. But each time we passed one and David suddenly cried, 'Stop!', it was either on the wrong side of the road or else there was a car behind us. Finally, at random, we stopped at one, at Saint-Charles-de-Percy. The name meant nothing to me. Yet the moment we entered I knew what I would find. Strangely, not having thought of her all these years, that morning Jo had been constantly in my mind, as I recalled that her husband, Mick, had been killed with the 2nd Battalion, Irish Guards, in Normandy in August 1944. From the entrance of the cemetery something guided me, uncannily and unerringly, straight to the grave of Lieutenant M. McConchy, aged twenty-four, buried in the same grave as his tank driver. That said everything about his means of death, a tank 'brewed up', the crew immolated, according to one fellow officer 'there was only a handful of ashes left, hence they were buried together'. *Quis separabit*, the motto of the Irish Guards; in death they were not. It was uncanny. Out of all the thousands of graves, scores of cemeteries in Normandy, how had I been led, so directly, to this one? I felt shaken for the rest of the day, indeed for days afterwards.

Employing his unerring skill as a map-reader, David would track down the site of each TAC HQ using the diary Monty's staff officer Paul Odgers had kept. David always planned our accommodation, where his skill was sometimes mixed. On one occasion we found ourselves staying in a strange *logement* (described, imaginatively, as being in the 'English Manorial Style') where the carpet was on the wall instead of covering the floor; at another (Brussels) in a Novotel completely surrounded by noisome motorways. Like his austere father, David would stipulate rigorously no drink at lunch, so we would picnic somewhere on site – often in pouring rain as it was that sort of summer, which lent a realistic tint of hardship to the undertaking. But each night we would abandon austerity, to celebrate the results of the day's recce, in a liquid manner of which Monty would heartily have disapproved.

By the end of June we had reached Belgium, and David and I broke off the first half of our recce, but not before making a detour to Antwerp, for both personal and military reasons. Without difficulty I found the spot where my mother's car had gone into the Scheldt sixty-two years before. It was painfully easy to reconstruct what had happened: Preedy, the poor chauffeur, very tired, dozing off, bombing down the long, straight boring road from Ghent at night, comes up to the river floodbank at right angles to the river, sees cathedral in the distance, drives straight on, instead of taking the turn-off to the ferry at right angles. All too easy to see, a tragedy that would have been avoided had the new Kennedy Tunnel been in existence in 1930. I mourned, speculated how my life would have been changed if the tunnel had existed. What would she have been like as a mother? How would we have got on? Would I still have become a writer, like her? The Bundles adventure to America in 1940, which fundamentally altered my life, would probably never have happened.

David and I discussed the tragic early demises of our respective mothers. Certainly his childhood would have been different if the much loved Betty hadn't died. Mindful of the precept I had formed while writing about Supermac – namely, that it was the defection of his wife Dorothy to Boothby which had provided the grit in the oyster to drive the rather lank MP of the 1930s upwards to Number 10, I asked him whether he thought Betty Montgomery's tragic death just before the Second World War could have had that kind of influence on Monty's career. No, absolutely not; his father would always have been the single-minded soldier, dedicated to winning a war. I was left wondering, but David should know.

We resumed our recce in September, starting at the Flemish village of Zonhoven, south of Brussels. There we were treated to a rather stodgy reception in David's honour. It was warm-hearted but very formal. Promised a 'frugal light lunch', we found our plates laden by ample Flamands who might have stepped out of a Breughel painting. David made a charming speech, which was followed by recollections offered up by ancient inhabitants: a mother allegedly complaining to Monty, 'Your soldiers have treated my daughter badly,' received the response: 'Madame, you have one daughter. I have 450,000 soldiers to look after. Would you please look after your daughter!' Monty was at Zonhoven when the Germans launched the Ardennes offensive, also known as the Battle of the Bulge. It was the bloodiest battle that American arms experienced in the Second World War. British losses totalled 1,400, while the Germans lost some 85,000 men; but it also expended Hitler's last Panzer reserves, opening the way into Germany.

We moved on into Holland, making an important detour to explore tragic Arnhem. Then we were briskly into Germany, picnicking – typically – in blinding rain, at roughly the spot where Monty and Churchill were memorably photographed on the banks of the Rhine before Monty's armies crossed at Wesel.

At Ostenwalde in the Teutoburgerwald just east of Osnabrück where the TAC HQ had been set up in a very rustic, typical Westphalian farmyard of half-timbered buildings, with a seventeenth-century mansion, we were invited in by a friendly countess, Gräfin Perponcher, who as a young girl witnessed Monty and his caravanserai taking over the Schloss in the last days of the war. We picked up a local story of how the conquering British Field Marshal had been 'defeated' by the frogs in the Schloss lake. His sleep disturbed by their croaking, Monty had organised all the school children in the area to collect the frogs humanely in baskets and move them several miles to another lake. But within a few days they had all hopped back again.

After travelling a total of some 3,000 miles in the course of our two trips, we finally reached our Holy Grail, Lüneburg Heath, where on that historic day of 4 May 1945 – five days after Hitler had blown his brains out in the Berlin bunker – Monty received the surrender of the German forces. Before moving in, we picnicked on sandy fields at the edge of the heath. Breaching David's austere principles, I insisted we celebrate with a half-bottle of *rouge* that had been bouncing around in the boot of the car since Normandy. It was perhaps rash, because – despite all our documentation and meticulous map references – we could not then locate the famous obelisk (of which David had a photograph) built to mark the surrender site. Expecting to find the monument with the utmost ease, we arrived amid a noisy *Schutzfest*, bands playing and a fairground. We asked several Germans, who all insisted, 'A plaque is in the woods, but it is within a forbidden Bundeswehr Tank Range.' Finally we found a young, very overweight Panzer trooper, stubble-chinned, who – with his even more overweight girlfriend – took us to the trig point. There was the concrete base of a monument, but nothing more. It was all too plain (and perhaps understandable) what had happened to the obelisk: the Bundeswehr tanks had used it for target practice.

We left with a sense of extreme frustration, fatigue and disillusionment – no bag of gold at the end of the rainbow! It was a bit like a treasure hunt, where one arrives at the last clue to find somebody else has got there first. There was some incongruity and humour in the drunken jollities of the fair – present-day Germans totally oblivious to the extraordinary epoch-making event that had taken place nearly fifty years before. Our trip ended with a detour to visit my friend Axel von dem Bussche, in Bonn. I knew that he and David would be kindred spirits, but it was to be the last time I would see my old friend. Clearly in increasing pain from his numerous war wounds, he died three months later.

So ended our recce. I think it helped me to understand this strange, unclubbable, antisocial, lonely, aggressive little fighter, who was so totally dedicated to defeating Germans. We – or even the Americans – could not have won the war in the west without him. But, as his own son would admit, with his boastfulness and refusal to admit that things had occasionally not 'gone according to plan', he had been his own worst enemy. In their memoirs, the old generals on both sides of the Atlantic hardly erred in generosity – or accuracy. That may remain for another generation of military historians. A few years later in Hanoi David and I went to meet Vietnam's General Vo Nguyen Giap – a tiny walnut of a man, then aged eighty-seven. He was the last of the great warlords, having won first, at Dien Bien Phu, one of history's most decisive battles, thereby ending nearly a century of French rule. He then went on to defeat the combined might of America and the Republic of Vietnam after fifteen long years of further fighting. Sitting under a bust of Ho Chi Minh, opposite the huge mausoleum of his late leader and close friend, he smiled approvingly when I suggested to him that he and David's father shared the reputation of being perhaps the only generals of the twentieth century never to have lost a battle.

Possibly the last word should go to Winston Churchill, the man who appointed Monty in the first place, who often found himself infuriated by his arrogant intractability, yet recognised his surpassing qualities of generalship. When, after the war, members of his entourage were passing snide comments on Monty, Churchill bit back: 'I know why you all hate him. You are jealous: he is better than you are. Ask yourselves these questions. What is a general for? Answer: to win battles. Did he win them without much slaughter? Yes. So what are you grumbling about?'

All this, and more, I had to mull over, frame and organise over the next year of writing. Superbly helped by that master editor, Peter James, once again it was nevertheless a hard slog, not least to get it out in time for the 1994 fiftieth-anniversary celebrations. During those long months of composition, I had plenty to distract me. In April 1993 there was a muted and dignified ceremony to remember Axel at the small Saxon town of Thale where he was born, and I was invited to give the address – in German. It was a tremendous honour; at the same time I had felt in those last years I owed Axel something of an apology. After years of badgering, in 1985 I had finally persuaded him to try to set down the remarkable story of his life. Knowing of the terrible nightmares of the past that afflicted him, and how difficult Axel found it to write, or even think, of those days, the publisher George Weidenfeld (who was immensely keen to publish Axel's story) and I cobbled together a programme that would render it as easy as possible for Axel. He, with Camilla, would come for a year to St Antony's, as an 'Alistair Horne Fellow', where he would narrate his memoirs to Miriam Gross (then literary editor of the *Sunday Telegraph*, and a German-speaker). There had followed, in George's study, one of the most moving exchanges I can recall: with Axel, the German, declaring that Germany would not be forgiven for the Final Solution for a thousand years; and Weidenfeld, the Zionist Jew, riposting, 'No, forgiveness should begin at once.' It all looked set fair for the memoirs. Camilla loved her year at Oxford, everybody loved Axel. But he simply could not get down to writing. I always felt, thereafter, that in our friendship there was a tinge of resentment at the position into which I had pushed him, but I still think it was worth the risk.

I sat down to writing, honing, polishing and rewriting in my rusty German a 1,200-word address. I practised again and again in front of the mirror, cutting out all portmanteau words that might cause me to stumble. Thale, Axel's home-town of 16,000 inhabitants, nestles beneath the Harz Mountains, in one of the most ravishingly pretty, unspoilt corners of Germany. The next-door town of Quedlinburg has the deserved reputation of being the most beautiful in all Germany, a gem of half-timbered Renaissance buildings which is possibly what Dresden might have resembled in miniature, before the terrible fire-raid of 1945. Lying just inside what used to be Communist East Germany, both towns retained a kind of enchanting shabby innocence happily still preserved from the depredations of modern European society. Inside Thale's modest town hall, hosted by the Bürgermeister, the actual ceremony struck exactly the right note. Speeches were interwoven with singing by the local high-school choir (I had never heard Auld Lang Syne sung in German before). There were no national anthems, there were no flags, no fanfares, no uniforms, no martial music. Pride and sorrow were very properly inter-mixed. As I rose to deliver my carefully prepared homily I was startled to see in the front row Queen Beatrix of the Netherlands. I had expected Richard von Weizsäcker, then still President of Germany, to be there, as he had been Axel's closest friend, but not Queen Beatrix (though I knew her husband Claus had also been close to Axel). I was terrified. But afterwards she came up and in perfect English congratulated me: 'I didn't know the Brits did German!' I think I mumbled, 'Ma'am, they don't – it was all done with mirrors!' Which was roughly true. I just hoped I had got it right. I ended with words, from an old German lament, 'Ich hatt' einen Kameraden / Einen bessern findst du nit' (I had a comrade / You won't find a better one).

Three years later Sheelin and I went to Burma to meet a hero, or rather heroine, of a different ilk. Michael Aris had become a close associate of mine in the St Antony's context, and was on the selection committee for my Fellowship there. He was, by definition, a gentle academic with a passion for Tibetan studies, in which he had helped to establish a specialist centre at Oxford; he later converted to Buddhism. In 1972, he married a beautiful Burmese woman, Aung San Suu Kyi, whom he had met while both were studying in Oxford. They had two young sons, Alexander and Kim, and for a while lived the quiet life of academics in north Oxford. Suu Kyi, however, born in 1945, just as the Japanese were being driven out of Burma, was the daughter of General Aung San, the resistance hero who, fighting against both the Japanese and British, had led Burma into independence after 1945. Aung San was regarded as the only man who could salvage a war-ravaged, backward country; but he and his entire cabinet were assassinated by political rivals in 1947. The country was then ruined by twenty-six years of its own brand of inward-looking socialism.

In 1988 Suu Kyi returned to Burma, at first to tend her ailing mother but later to lead the pro-democracy movement there. In the 1990 general election, the first permitted by the incumbent military regime, she was elected Prime Minister in a surprise landslide, as leader of the National

League for Democracy party, which won 59 per cent of the vote and 394 of 492 seats. But the ruling SLORC (State Law and Order Restoration Council) immediately quashed the results, and set about smashing her party. Suu Kyi, who had already been detained under house arrest before the elections, then remained under house arrest in Burma for almost fourteen out of the ensuing twenty years. Her life, and Michael's and the lives of their young sons in Oxford, were changed radically. In 1991, now a respected world figure, though with no previous political experience, she was awarded the Nobel Peace Prize, one of its youngest recipients. Michael and the two teenage boys remained in Oxford, cut off from their mother, sequestered in Rangoon.

It so happened that, in spring 1997, we had been invited with a group of friends to travel up the Irrawaddy from Rangoon to Mandalay. The invitation was irresistible. I told Michael Aris of our trip and asked if he would like us to take any letters out to Suu Kyi. He arrived with a large suitcase, filled, engagingly, with cosmetics unavailable in austerity Burma. It was not easy. Arriving in Rangoon, after some circuitous telephoning, we took a highly nervous taxi to 54 University Avenue. At the top of the street we were stopped by a police block. The taxi disappeared at top speed. We were quite disagreeably harassed, both by armed soldiers and plain-clothes 'guards', liberally photographed, and made to sign a registration book. Suu Kyi's 'compound' as she called it, consisted of a once elegant, but now badly decayed stucco house overlooking a lake on whose banks some of the worst atrocities occurred in the massacres of 1988; and across which some lunatic American swam, uninvited, in 2009 – thereby adding another eighteen months' house arrest to her already endless sentences. The compound was surrounded by the bravely challenging red flags of her party, but right up against her house was a SLORC security post. It became evident later that our (very outspoken) conversation had been bugged.

Inside we were greeted by a slender, very feminine woman of extraordinarily delicate beauty, with all the natural proudly erect elegance of a Burmese. Wearing a pretty purple jacket with a fresh orchid in her hair, and an embroidered silk longyi, she looked younger than her 52 years. Her eyes moistened as we brought her news of Michael, and home, and handed over his suitcase. On seeing show the photographs of her boys she exclaimed: 'Heavens, Kim's hair is down to his shoulders!'

With an engaging sense of humour, she laughed gaily when I said I intended to photograph the guards, *en revanche*: 'What a jolly good idea!' There was something about her which was still unmistakably Oxford; her perfect, musical English spiced with such expressions as 'rather miffed'. But one sensed a steely seriousness and deep commitment underneath. SLORC, with its parochial orientations, had been swift to latch on to the Oxford connection, attacking her 'foreignness' and claiming that she knew nothing of Burmese politics.

'The trouble is that I know too much,' she explained 'I could not, as my father's daughter, have remained indifferent to all that was going on.'

'Are things getting better?' I asked.

'No, it was worse over the past year, with more arrests of our people in the middle of the night.' Some of them received seven-year sentences. 'But they have miscalculated, our Party wouldn't collapse.'

Though warmly appreciative of what we had brought her, from outside, she ticked me off for coming to Burma at all: claiming that most of the income from tourism and foreign investments only found its way into the pockets of SLORC.

I riposted by observing how, as a writer, I had written about Iron Curtain Soviet Russia and Pinochet's Chile – and where were they now? 'If you open the windows, it can only let air and light in eventually.' We disagreed, politely. In 1997, she was pessimistic about the prospects of the generals ever packing up, and leaving one day – like Pinochet.

The house was austere, with absolutely no concessions whatever to femininity. Sheelin asked about her everyday life: 'It's taken up with politics – three meetings this morning, now your visit this afternoon, then another meeting this evening. I have books and videos, but I don't have time to watch them.'

As we left, Suu Kyi presented Sheelin with a silver 'Fighting Peacock' brooch, the symbol of Aung San's rebellious students in the 1930s. Her parting words were: 'I hope to see you soon back again in a democratic country; it won't be long!'

We left with lumps in our throats; hers was the true anatomy of courage, and of self-sacrifice of the early Christian saint. Having given up all family life for her beliefs, would she win, this frail little lady against all the panoply of evil might of the Rangoon Generals? Outside in the street, I fulfilled my promise to her and – rashly – took a photograph of the thugs manning the checkpoint. The taxi-driver almost had a seizure, setting off even before the door was closed. Meanwhile, a devastating dossier of human rights abuses by the Rangoon regime over the past thirteen years has since been compiled.

Shortly after we returned to England, Michael Aris was diagnosed with terminal prostate cancer. Despite appeals from all over the world, including Pope John Paul II, the SLORC would not allow him to return to see his wife one last time. Instead they urged Aung San Suu Kyi to leave the country to visit him; making it perfectly plain that, once out they would not allow her to return. Michael died on his fifty-third birthday in 1999. Since 1989, when Suu Kyi was first placed under house arrest, he had seen her only five times, the last of which was for Christmas in 1995. The year after he died, she was back under house arrest, as she has remained, on and off, for the past ten years.

Like many others (though not everybody agreed), I could wish she had come out when Michael was dying. All emotion aside, with her youth, beauty and blazing honesty, abroad she would have made an even more powerful beacon of protest for human rights than Solzhenitzyn ever was. Could she not have been a new Mandela? But, no; she insisted, 'I cannot leave my people.' Possibly that very refusal to compromise may have told against her. As the years went by, and she stayed at 54 University Avenue as prisoner of the Generals, increasingly forgotten by the outside world, it seemed tragically as if she were losing the game. The calling of elections in 2010 looked like a cunning ploy by the Junta (now calling itself the Union Solidarity and Development Party). It succeeded in fracturing, for the first time, 'The Lady's' NDF party. Were the elections a sign of strength, or of weakness? On her release following the elections, Suu Kyi herself displayed great moderation, expressing willingness to negotiate with the Government. It is hard to believe that the West's sanctions and feeble bleats of protest over the years have had any effect, but if this odious team really is at last contemplating change, then perhaps it should recall de Tocqueville's historic sentence: 'The most dangerous moment for a bad government is when it begins to reform.' Meanwhile 'The Lady' was free at last. Or is she? Can she be truly free within a country still in shackles?

The following month, on 8 May – the anniversary of VE Day – I was due to receive a doctorate at Cambridge University's Senate House. On various occasions over the years my mentor at St Antony's, Raymond Carr, had urged me to take a doctorate. When I protested that I didn't have time to work up an erudite paper, Raymond riposted, 'my dear fellow, you don't have to. With your published oeuvre all you need to do is to proffer four or five titles, A Savage War for instance, and then the Doctorate Committee at Cambridge will judge whether you qualify.' And so, to my considerable surprise, it happened. As the day of my investiture approached, I discovered by chance the existence at Duxford airfield (in whose development I had been closely involved as a trustee of the Imperial War Museum), a few miles south of Cambridge, of ML-407, the only genuine two-seater Spitfire. It had flown 172 sorties in 1944–5, before being converted for the Irish Air Force, and was currently owned by an attractive Australian widow, Carolyn Grace. With wonderful antipodean alacrity and generosity, Carolyn responded to my pleading. A flight was all fixed for 9.30 a.m. on Saturday, 8 May, just two hours before I would be filing up to the Senate House to receive my doctorate.

On what was to be one of the most exciting mornings of my life, I woke at 5.30, my stomach full of those proverbial butterflies. It was a peerlessly beautiful spring day. Cambridge had never looked more ravishing. After a hearty breakfast of two fried eggs, bacon and sausages, I drove out to Duxford, 7 miles away. There, parked alongside the old control tower, was ML-407, more than matching the beauty of the day, with those voluptuously curved wings that still make the Supermarine Spitfire the best-known aircraft in the world to every small boy – the plane that I, aged seventeen, had so longed to fly.

Carolyn Grace helped me into my flying overalls. They were very tight. Even tighter was the cockpit; I wondered how any larger-than-average pilot ever managed to bale out alive. There was a remarkable economy of very basic instruments – air-speed indicator, altimeter, artificial horizon, compass, rev counter and that crucial oil-pressure gauge. No nonsense like radar. From the front, pilot Peter Kynsey, an immensely experienced flyer, asked politely if I could retract my undercarriage – my feet were resting on his pedals. Suddenly, with a puff of blue smoke, a roar like a lion and a burst of that enormous power of 1,710 horses, the 3 tons of tiny plane set off bumping across the grass. Over the clamour of the Rolls-Royce Merlin engine, Peter was chatty and informative on the intercom. 'Spitfires land much better on grass,' he explained comfortingly. 'Their brakes aren't as good as other planes. I was a bit worried when they insisted on mowing yesterday – you don't want grass cuttings in the carb.'

'No,' I replied, a little nervously, 'that might be inconvenient.'

After an incredibly short take-off (about 300 yards; in a wartime scramble, a Spit could make it, with full boost, in 200), smooth and painless, we were up and away, banking steeply over the M11 motorway as it snaked towards Cambridge. Running at a gentle 1,500 revs, at just under 2,000 feet we were already registering 240 knots. Peter amazed me by saying that this half-century-old veteran could still manage 425 mph, almost as fast as a modern commercial jet. A few minutes later, there was Cambridge in all its glories just below us, the narrow silver ribbon of the Cam. As we flew over the Tudor pinnacles of King's College Chapel, I thought fleetingly of D. H. Lawrence's irreverent remark that the chapel reminded him of an upturned sow. 'Shall we do a victory roll?' said Peter. Before I could answer, the 'upturned sow' of King's was standing above my head. It was an exhilarating notion to do a victory roll right over the place where in two hours' time I would be receiving my Litt D. Then, momentarily, I began to regret those two fried eggs. We went into a tight bank, to look more closely at my old college, Jesus – so tight that I could feel the g-force pressing hard on my cheeks, and I recalled how the extraordinary small turning circle, almost containable within a football field, had saved many a Spit pilot during the war. Classic, too, was its capacity to survive a steep dive: the wings of any Messerschmitt 109 foolhardy enough to try to follow it tended to break off.

Peter, heroically, let me take over on the way back. 'Watch out on the stick,' he warned. 'It's as light as a feather.' Sure enough, I barely touched it and up she zoomed, almost standing on her tail. It was incredibly sensitive – every inch of her winsome skin seems to be tingling with life. I wished I could hurl us into a loop. Darting under the clouds, I lived, briefly and happily, the sweet life of a Spitfire pilot. It all ended too soon. We made a perfect three-point landing on the grass at 70 knots. Half an hour later I was back in Cambridge, in gown and sub-fusc, collecting my doctorate from the Vice-Chancellor as he uttered the age-old formula in Latin.

After the ceremony, blessed Jesus College, in whose courts all those years previously I had been so undistinguished a student, gave a celebratory lunch for all the Hornes. It was indeed a memorable day, made most memorable, of course, by the unbeatable thrill of getting my hands on the joystick of a Spitfire. In a way I felt I had come full circle from that awful day in 1943: no longer wrestling with a chocolate machine in Liverpool, as a failed AC2, now I was a Spitfire pilot, if only for twenty minutes. Following up on that day, Dr Jana Howlett, the zestful College Praelector, kindly put me forward to become an honorary fellow of Jesus. After my rather dismal record as an undergraduate, that was an honour indeed. By comparison with the austere Jesus of the 1940s, the modern Jesus is a bright, cheery place, especially now that it takes in women. I have returned frequently to enjoy College hospitality when working on a book at the University Library (a rather more user-friendly establishment than the Bodleian in Oxford, I found).

Even more astonishing than doctorate and honorary fellowship was the invitation which arrived that autumn from 10 Downing Street of appointment as a Commander of the Order of the British Empire, or CBE. Nominally, I suppose, I was offered it for those ten years beavering away under frostbite conditions at Birch Grove on the Macmillan biography. When the time came for the Queen to hang the decoration and its ribbon round my neck at Buckingham Palace a few months later, I was taken aback when she recollected that I had written the book (Macmillan was generally believed to have been one of her favourites among the nine prime ministers that have passed in and out of the Palace over the previous fifty years of her reign).

I found the investiture ceremony unashamedly exhilarating. And the awards didn't stop there. The following year, equally surprising, came from France (from President Mitterrand, no less) the sonorous award of Chevalier of the Légion d'Honneur, founded by Napoleon in the year (1805) that he was planning to invade Britain. The honour was bestowed on me by the French Ambassador in London, and I have ever since proudly sported my *ficelle* on every Gallic occasion.

David and I were thrilled by the review of *The Lonely Leader*. Even in the US, where Monty remained something of a hate figure, the *New York Times* called it 'as balanced a biography ... as we are ever likely to get ... an admirably fair-minded and therefore persuasive book'.

In June 1994, flatteringly, I was drafted out of mothballs by *The Times* to cover the events marking the fiftieth anniversary of D-Day. It was a moving experience. We sailed from Southampton to Caen, with some 500 veterans and their wives aboard the *Canberra*, which only a dozen years before had been employed taking another landing contingent to the Falklands. The one surviving Lancaster flew over and, with deadly accuracy, showered the ship with a million red poppies. A young trumpeter, his blowing alas wasted by wind and emotion, sounded the Last Post. Ashore I accompanied a group of the 6th Airborne to Pegasus Bridge on the Orne, the crucial landings that had prefaced the invasion. As we came close, there were emotional cries from the veterans who had never returned till that day, of 'My God, there's the quarry I landed in!'

It was also that summer of 1994 that an unexpected enemy struck me, with fearful force. One afternoon taking our Jack Russell, Bumble, for a walk, I found I just could not get up to the top of the gentle hill in the field at the back of Turville. It wasn't the familiar breathlessness of the asthma I had suffered intermittently most of my life, but resembled an icy fist clutching at something somewhere inside my chest. My heart was pounding out of all recognition. There wasn't the acute pain supposedly associated with angina, but this was quite clearly something new, and I didn't like it one little bit.

My friendly NHS doctor gave me a tiny red-and-white puffer and said, alarmingly, 'it's nitroglycerine. Don't put it near a flame. Spray it once or twice under your tongue, when necessary. If it works, come and tell me at once. If it doesn't, come and tell me anyway.' The magic potion, properly called Nitrolingual, the size of a tube of Gold Spot, has a horribly clinical taste, like the inside of a hospital operating theatre, but also an instantaneous, miraculous effect. For a while it worked wonders. But one night in the small hours the dreaded symptoms returned. I slipped out of bed and took two puffs of nitroglycerine. Fifteen minutes later the pounding was back again. It reminded me, horribly, of *Jurassic Park*, the heavy footfalls that preceded the onslaught of the unseen, terrifying monster,

Tyrannosaurus Rex. In no time at all I found myself in Wycombe General emergency ward.

There followed several long days of discomfort, intermixed with extreme boredom. The funny thing with hearts, if there can be anything funny, is that you are either extremely ill or extremely dead – or else extremely bored as all the fuss and bother of recovery goes on. Within an hour or two of being lodged safely in a public ward, I began to feel desperately bored. Small things, like other patients' endlessly chattering visitors, irritated me beyond bearing.

The minor fittings of the ward seemed to have been designed by a socialist think tank. One would have to be a very fit contortionist to turn the light on and off; old-fashioned, compressed-air earphones had square ends that cut painfully into one's ears after ten minutes' listening; neither television nor radio worked very well, and I was too beset with attached wires from cardiac monitors to be able to read comfortably. In a cluster nearby the nurses gossiped relentlessly, largely about plans for when they were 'off'. Between 3 p.m. and 8 p.m., five hours solid, the neighbouring beds had family visitors. There appeared to be nothing resembling a matron or anybody in charge, and the nursing staff did absolutely nothing to reduce the length of the visits or the level of the noise. None of this did anything to allay the ghastly inhibition of using bottle or pan, banned from leaving bed, behind badly fitting curtains.

In a kind of resentful despair, I started writing a diary, no doubt somewhat plaintive in tone. I sent the results in article form to the *Daily Mail*. They published it with glee, under the skilful heading 'An Affair of the Heart', doubtless hoping for the romantic, or lubricious, tabloid readers of the journal would flock to read it. The editors at Northcliffe House were delighted and asked for more. I obliged with two more features, the burden being gratitude to the doctors for my survival and criticism of the appalling bureaucracy of the NHS which rendered the British hospital system so comfortlessly unpleasant and costly for us all. The proceeds of these articles helped pay for a welcome R&R in the sun. I ended up having an angioplasty, then another: a not very agreeable procedure.

Eventually I went home, certified okay. I felt better than ever before, or, in the immortal words of Mae West, feeling like a new man. I scampered up to the top of the hill with Bumble. With a high sense of priorities, John Julius Norwich, not a *Mail* reader and mishearing me on the telephone when I said I had had a 'ticker problem', exclaimed, 'Oh, I thought for a moment you said a pecker problem! Thank God it's not serious.' For all my grumbles about the NHS, I felt intensely grateful – to medicine, to Dr W and Dr S, to my wife who (as is always the case) went through more distress than I did, and to God. With the hymn, I sing: "Tis good, Lord, to be here'. A generation ago, one might might well not have been. Most contritely, and on my knees – and thinking of the old Italian proverb of the blackbird, in summer, who declares, so rashly: 'Lord, now the winter is over I fear Thee no more!' I determined to regard my recovery with a humble and most grateful heart.

18

WHEN THE GOING WAS GOOD

Knocking down the Berlin Wall; in Russia in 1990,
with David Montgomery and General Dmitri Volkogonov.

[Pliny the Younger] never read a book so bad, but he drew some profit from it.

Laurence Sterne, *Tristram Shandy*

No author's life is entirely 'scribble, scribble, scribble' at dusty tomes. I sit with my back to a wall full of books, a hundred and many more, I can't count, that I've reviewed over half a century. Their authors gaze down my neck: some, I fear, reproachfully; most, I hope, with a grateful smile I've learned from many of them. But reviewing has never been my favourite pastime, and I could never boast the skill of a Cyril Connolly. Let's face it – for some us, much of the time – book-reviewing is a drudge. 'Critics are like eunuchs in a harem; they know how it's done, they've seen it done every day, but they're unable to do it themselves,' said Brendan Behan. Another aspect of my literary vagabondage – travel – on the other hand, is a joy and a liberation. While Sheelin takes a sketch-pad to record the places we've been to, I use travel-writing. It is always a special pleasure to combine travel with writing a book, as I had just done in *The Lonely Leader* and as I would shortly do again for an account of Napoleon's battles. But on the whole of course this was about journalism. Leafing through bulging cuttings books, I revisit with delight far-off places and times. You name it, I've been there and written about it.

There were of course the bad or wasted times. Most frustrating of all, probably, was an abortive trip to the Caucasus in autumn 1979. It left a particularly angry taste, because it was designed to be a treat for my twenty-two-year-old daughter Za, after she had got a good degree in Russian from London's School of Slavonic and East European Studies. In the event we spent three abortive days in Moscow, trekking back and forth to the airport for a plane to Tbilisi which never materialised. The excuse: there was snow on the runway (a full inch at Sheremetyevo, and planes were taking off busily); there was bad weather; there was fog in Georgia. We managed to ring my hero, Fitzroy Maclean, who was waiting for us down in the Caucasus. He said he was picnicking in shirtsleeves. So we spent three gloomy nights in the Hotel National in Moscow, waiting. It was impossible to get tickets to the Bolshoi or anything else. Because it was a weekend, it was equally impossible to book a decent restaurant. So we had to satisfy ourselves with a visit to the Lenin Museum. There Za gave tongue to our pent-up frustrations by baiting the slab-faced Intourist guide with pointed questions, in Russian, about the paintings from which Trotsky had infamously been airbrushed out.

'Whose cap is that on the chair?', pointing to the outcast's famous pointed Red Army cap.

'Oh, it's some soldier's . . .'

'Okay, then where is Trotsky?'

'Who he? Never heard of him.'

No father ever felt prouder. Za never let the bone go. A large group of tourists and Russians gathered round. Finally the battered guide called for a superior, who muttered feebly: 'You see, this is Lenin Museum. As Trotsky was always anti-Lenin, how could you expect him to be in it?' I felt it was time to leave, before the KGB arrived. But a point had been made, a mild revenge for all our frustrations.

It was not till we returned to London that I learned from the Foreign Office what would have been the real reason behind our getting stranded in Moscow. It was the time of the US–Iran hostages debacle. Every Soviet airfield in the Caucasus was, apparently, standing by for airborne reinforcements just in case, as might have been half-anticipated, the Americans contemplated following up with a full-scale invasion of Iran. One could hardly have expected the whole truth, but could not Intourist have come up with slightly less fantastical excuses? I recalled that great traveller Peter Fleming, remarking ages ago: 'Every people have their own way of lying. Latins and Arabs lie to please, but only the Russians lie without any discernible motive, and often to their own detriment. It's a way of life.'

The next year, 1980, brought me better travel luck. I received a letter from Conor Cruise O'Brien, then – briefly – editor-in-chief of the *Observer*. He invited me to take part in a series, 'Famous Authors Choose the Holiday of their Dreams'. Aware of the *Observer*'s prevailing state of penury, I assumed that their idea of a freebie hol would probably stretch no further afield than Brighton, and foolishly did nothing about it. Then I ran into Conor at the bar of the Garrick and teasingly said, 'supposing I want to go to China?' He stunned me by replying, 'We'd send you.' I rushed home, replied to the invitation accordingly, only to be told that I was too late – Penelope Mortimer had just booked it. After some reflection, I came back with 'What about China Minor?' – that is Hong Kong, Taiwan and Macao, the offshore islands. So that spring I set off. My old skiing/sailing partner from New York, Van Galbraith (who became US Ambassador to France the following year) joined me on the first leg of the trip, to Taiwan. Through his contacts, we fixed up an interview with President Chiang Ching-kuo, son of Chiang Kai-shek, who lost China to Mao in 1948 and holed up on the island of Taiwan. Very formally, we had had to submit questions well in advance. It was not promising. In the meantime, Russia had invaded Afghanistan and looked increasingly menacing; America had received a bloody nose in Iran; under Carter's flaccid grip the world seemed to be coming apart. So the night before the interview, Van and I agreed we would breach protocol and slip in a fresh question: 'Mr President, what would your reaction be if the USSR now attacked the People's Republic of China?' Perhaps he would welcome them as liberators from the enemy, Mao? In the event the effect was dramatic, like a detonator exploding a landmine. A small man, the President leaped to his feet, seeming to me as if he were actually standing up on top of his desk. 'The Chinese mainland is our sacred territory,' he declared with passion, 'the people there are our brothers. We object to the Communist regime, we cannot compromise with it, but any invader of the mainland would be our enemy. We would not take advantage nor stand by.' It was an heroic notion, the thought of seventeen million Taiwanese rushing to the aid of a couple of billion mainlanders, and it said, to me, a lot about the sense of identity of the Chinese across the globe. It was something of a scoop for the *Observer*.

My next commitment in Taipei was an invitation to give a lecture at the Staff College of the Armed Forces of the Republic of China as Taiwan still designated itself. Most of the audience – a lot of old waxworks as Prince Charles might have designated them – looked as if they had been senior officers in the lost war against Mao. From the menu I had supplied them, they chose as the subject 'The Fall of France, 1940,' based on my book, *To Lose a Battle*. I could hardly have been more astonished: of what possible relevance could that be to Taiwan in 1980? As I entered the lecture-hall, I realised from the profusion of excellent maps – the best I had ever seen – plastered on the walls that the campaign had long been a special subject at the College. My lecture was translated laboriously paragraph by paragraph as I spoke, lasting all afternoon, the audience smiling with glazed politeness over a subject with which they were familiar to excess. As I thanked the general hosting me, I apologised deferentially for having bored the audience with a subject they knew better than I did. With an engaging smile, he gave me a putting-down response: 'Never mind: in Taiwan we love old movies!' It was a taste of the special quality of Chinese humour. I reflected that maybe the older the civilization the more supercilious becomes its mirth towards lesser ones.

Early one morning the Taiwan military flew me off on a visit to its off-shore island of Kinmen – or Quemoy as the West once knew it. Just five miles off the mainland, it had remained an outpost of Taiwan after the debacle of 1948, protected by the mantle of the US Seventh Fleet. Twenty-two years previously, it had come close to providing a casus belli for nuclear war between China and the US, when in August 1958 Mao's forces unleashed on it a devastating artillery bombardment. It went on for several weeks, and was assumed to be the softening-up prior to a full-scale invasion, which would have been met head-on by John Foster Dulles. Harold Macmillan in his diary expressed fears of being 'on the brink of World War Three'. Then, inexplicably, and just as abruptly as it had begun, the shelling petered out. Or, at least – by a peculiarly Chinese gentlemen's agreement – the Communists dropped a few token shells on odd days, the Taiwanese responded with the occasional missile stuffed with pamphlets on even days. The world breathed again, and Quemoy was put on the back-burner. Thoughtfully, I was invited on an even day. It was a real Ian Fleming outing. The ancient DC-4 skipped 50 feet above the waves all the 200 miles from Taipei. There was no sign of an airfield, but suddenly the palm trees moved aside, and we landed on a narrow airstrip, immediately to be towed into a vast cavern that opened in the hillside. In fact, the whole of Quemoy is one great cavern stuffed with weaponry, underground arms factories, bunkers and hospitals. Above, it is a charming, idyllic pastoral Chinese scene, replete with lakes, bamboo groves and pagodas – all artificial – such as one might have found agelessly portrayed in the National Palace Museum. The mainland is so close that, through binoculars, you can actually see Mao's troops in their positions.

My host is Colonel Han, head of 'Psy-Warfare', with bushy eyebrows like Chou-en-Lai. His job seems chiefly despatching propaganda balloons, which, wafted by the prevailing winds, reach out across the lost homeland as far as Sinkiang Province. Apart from literary exhortations against Maoism, they apparently contain condoms – the unhappy mainlanders currently being subject to the one-child policy launched the previous year, and yet prophylactics being at a premium. In a vast wall-map Colonel Han shows me with pride that his balloons have even landed as far away as Paris. One can imagine the surprised delight on the face of some lucky Parisian showered with *capotes anglaises*, courtesy Quemoy.

My sojourn in Taiwan ended with a banquet. To my distress I was confronted with a pile of two dozen of my (pirated) books, to sign for 'honlable fliends'. It was a terrible quandary: as a member of the Committee of Management of the (British) Society of Authors, which had formally protested about the pirate publishing of books in Taiwan, from which no proceeds accrued to the author, should I refuse, walk out and thereby forfeit possibly the Chinese dinner of a lifetime, or should I kowtow? I leave the reader to judge my shameful decision.

Finally, in 1984, I got to visit 'China Major', on an eventful tour along the Silk Route, conducted by the unflappable Gail Joplin. It was the first of many such trips that Sheelin and I would make together. We headed to Urumqi in Xinjiang province on the farthest frontier with the Soviet Union, once turbulent Turkestan. But at an unscheduled stop in a non-place called Aksu, close the border of then Soviet Kyrgyzstan, on the northern edge of the terrifying Taklamakan Desert, the ancient Russian 'Antonov' turbo-prop put down to refuel. While we waited in the spartan airport lounge, our accompanying lecturer, Peter Hopkirk, back to the window, treated us to a chilling account of the Taklamakan (the name meaning, literally, 'Go in and you never come out'). Such were the sand-storms, the 'Karaburan', he said, that whole caravans had been known to be buried without trace inside of twenty-four hours. As he spoke, I noticed over his shoulder the poplars fringing the airport dipping low as a wind hit them; within minutes they had disappeared from sight. 'Peter,' I called

out: 'look behind you!' 'My God, it's a Karaburan!' Soon the plane too
had disappeared in the howling sand-storm.

There was no question of flying on, so we hunkered down for the night
at Aksu. Being so close to the sensitive frontier, Aksu was a prohibited
zone. Probably few westerners had been there since the intrepid Francis
Younghusband stopped there in 1887. 'There were large bazaars and
several inns – some for travellers, others for merchants wishing to make
a prolonged stay to sell goods' he wrote. But not for us; lodged in a
transport workers' 'guest house', discovering conditions that travelling
Chinese expected. We slept in our mackintoshes that night, hoping to be
prophylactically sealed off from the bedbugs. It gave one a small insight
into what life for millions of Chinese must be like.

Kashgar, however, an anchor of the Silk Route, and once scene of
the Great Game, was immediately wonderful. Old gentlemen with fur-
trimmed hats, knee-length quilted jackets with wide sleeves, forked white
beards and marvellous weather-beaten faces smiled benevolently from
behind their silk carpets in the bazaar. The zany canopies threw eccentrically shaped shadows across a scene of amazing colour, and a million
delicious smells wafted out from the spice stores and kerbside kitchens.
It is the Middle East of a past century, but these are the Uighur and
Mongol descendants of Genghis Khan and Tamburlane, distrusted and
persecuted by the Han Chinese; they regard us as men from Mars. We
spend the next ten days ambling back along the Silk Route, via Turfan,
the extraordinary Buddhist Thousand Caves of Dunhuang, which had
been lost for centuries until re-discovered by the 'Foreign Devils', Sir
Aurel Stein and Sven Hedin.

Up till 1984, few Brits have visited Kashgar and 'Turkestan' within
recent memory. One of the last, Peter Fleming, wrote it up in his classic,
News from Tartary, while his Swiss lesbian travelling companion, Ella
'Kini' Maillart (they must have been a strangely assorted couple) gave an
entirely different – but equally engaging – account in her *Forbidden
Journey*. Returning from our trip to 'Tartary', I recalled that it was the
fiftieth anniversary of Peter's great journey, which took him and Kini
some seven months of considerable adventure and hardship, compared
to our three weeks. Peter Fleming certainly found rougher places than
Aksu. So I wrote a piece, humbly in his memory, for *Time & Tide*, which

helped focus in my mind's eye an exciting, exotic trip, that was, alas, as always, far too short.

The fall of the Berlin Wall on 9 November 1989, my sixty-fourth birthday, was one of the most exciting and most significant events of my life, well, of all our lives. Recalling my time in Germany in the 1950s, never in a million years – short of nuclear war – could I have dreamt that I would live to see the Iron Curtain rolled back. It, the division of Germany, seemed, literally, to be set in concrete. I remembered how ruthlessly the June 1953 Berlin revolt had been crushed. The fall of the wall, without a drop of blood being shed, was a real triumph of the human spirit, of *vox populi*, and perhaps of the media too. That 1 January 1990, with grateful humility I thanked the gods that, for the first time in my life, here was a New Year's Day one could greet without a sense of fear, either from the shadow of Hitler or the heirs of Stalinism. The world was at peace with itself, for the first time in my life. For how long? Within a year we were at war in the Arab world. It didn't surprise me.

The fall of the wall dwarfed all literary enterprises, even thoughts, but for me at least it opened some new windows. In the spring of 1990, *Harper's* sent me to West Germany's Coburg, on the edge of what had been the Iron Curtain, to do a piece on Prince Albert's childhood home of Rosenau, where he had lived prior to marrying queen Victoria. A modest country house in the midst of woods, it had just been done up, brilliantly, though perhaps a trifle exuberantly in its choice of colours. I know of no royal house where I could more happily live; no wonder poor Albert disliked cold and draughty Windsor, whose drains were eventually to kill him. In 1990 Coburg claimed to be the most prosperous town in Germany. But by night you could see the lights of Gotha, the other half of Albert's princely domain, twinkling some 15 miles away – now its very poor relation. For the previous five decades Gotha had been just on the wrong side of the Interzonal Frontier, its inhabitants gazing with envy at the lights of fatly rich Coburg. Sheelin and I drove over the wire the day it came down. The contrast was staggering. Albert's family palace in Gotha was in a state of dilapidation, the lawns unmown, weeds growing out of the roof. We moved on to Goethe's Weimar, again superficially shabby and unloved, but with the bones beneath five decades of Communist neglect of a grand and romantic cultural inheritance. The house of the German Enlightenment and, later, the Bauhaus Movement, it had also been the seat of Germany's first unhappy experiment with democratic rule. From Weimar, we drove to Berlin. Somewhere along the line we managed to collect a ticket from two aggressive Vopos, for driving without seat belts. It was a pleasure to be able to pay them an on-the-spot fine in Ostmarks which in a few days' time would be totally worthless. Once in Berlin, where there was still a heady atmosphere of fiesta, we rushed to the wall to chip off our own trophies. I wondered whether the revellers could have any concept of what those seven-odd decades of Weimar inflation, Hitler and Stalinism, had been like for the now liberated East Germans.

In the autumn of the following year I finally made it to the Caucasus, with Sheelin and a congenial group of friends. It was an exciting trip to a Soviet Union then in the process of dismantlement, part of a world-shaking series of events of which the fall of the wall was the most dramatic. But for me, professionally and historically, the most thrilling moment came right at the beginning, in Moscow. Through the good offices of historian Hugh Thomas I was put in touch with a Colonel-General Dmitri Volkogonov, the head of the Institute of Military History in the Red Army. Only a few years younger than myself, Volkogonov was a doctor of philosophy and a doctor of history, as well as being director of the arm of the Soviet military concerned with psychological warfare. As the four-star general in charge of political commissars, he was by definition regarded as one of the truest of the true in the world of Soviet Communism. But by the middle of Leonid Brezhnev's rule he began to feel serious doubts about the Soviet regime. These at first related only to Stalin, under whose purges both of Volkogonov's parents had died. He spent nearly twenty years compiling a revisionist biography of Stalin,* in which, though he forthrightly described the dictator's crimes, he showed that he was an admirer of Lenin, holding that Stalinism was a perversion of true Leninism. That his book would be controversial was obvious to others, but it became apparent that, in effect, Volkogonov was attacking not just Stalin but the whole Communist regime. Once the book was published, consequences were not slow in coming. Shortly after my visit,

---

* *Stalin: Triumph and Tragedy*, Grove Weidenfeld, 1991.

he was fired from his job as director of the Institute by Mikhail Gorbachev. But history will surely recognise him as one of the leaders of the movement to expose the crimes of the Soviet regime and exorcise its malignant influence from Russia. He opposed the use of force in ethnic disputes and was to criticise Boris Yeltsin for his decision to invade Chechnya.

General Volkogonov invited me to address his Institute when I was in Moscow. Like the Taiwanese, he invited me to submit a menu. As it was shortly after publication of the second volume of Macmillan, I included a proposal to speak about the Cuban Missiles Crisis of 1962. It was accepted. Rather like the exam student who leaps upon the one question he feels he can answer, I was delighted. I hoped it would give me an opportunity to learn what Moscow's input in that episode, so hideously dangerous to all humanity, might really have been. It was an extraordinary experience. The host, a short rather unmilitary figure, covered with decorations (though he had never fought a battle), greeted us warmly in his office before the talk. His Stalin biography had just been published. Almost apologetically he said, 'We don't always write the books we want to, but things are changing. We now have the benefit of newly opened documents.' He went on to explain that his Institute's criterion was 'to publish what we should not be ashamed of in twenty-five years' time', adding something most of us already felt: 'Maybe you are witnessing very historic days in Russia. We are on the brink of a very important period in our history. The river of time is irreversible!' I replied that, in the West, we believed that 'History needs to be rewritten at regular intervals, at least every twenty-five years.'

We then filed into a large auditorium, past imposing paintings of the Defence of Moscow of 1941, the Kursk Offensive of 1943 and the Civil War of 1918–21. Facing me were over 200 senior officers in uniform, and some civilians, who gave me a warm welcome. My lecture was read out in Russian while I remained seated – for all I knew, it might have been a chapter out of *Lady Chatterley*. It was a strange experience, sitting there scrutinising the tough, hard-bitten faces of men who had been training to kill us over the previous five decades, and I wondered what was on their minds. I was a little disappointed by the questions. Coming so soon after *glasnost* they were somewhat hesitant, and the British Ambassador, Sir Rodric Braithwaite, seated next to me, whispered that the interpreter was not up to it. I wish there could have been more time. They asked general questions: what were Stalin's miscalculations in 1939? What had been the goals of US and British strategy in the Cold War? There was some cynical laughter in response to a follow-up question: Had these been achieved? Perhaps the most interesting contribution was a criticism of the significance of the executed Colonel Penkovsky in the Cuban Missiles Crisis; one officer (identified by Braithwaite as KGB) said he had known him well; and, yes, he knew all about the specifics of Soviet rocketry.

But the most remarkable thing about the event was that it could have happened at all. It may even have been something of a special landmark in British–Russian relations. After it was over, we were presented with archival photographs, and Sheelin, the artist, disarmingly with a handsome book of Soviet paintings. The host and several of his senior officers then came over to the British Embassy for lunch, where they were greeted by the Defence Attaché, a brigadier, and his team, all in full uniform. It was, Sir Rodric confided to me, possibly the first time that there had been a full-dress get-together since 1945. With me was my old friend David Montgomery (whom one of the Russian generals, perhaps over-excited by the vodka, confused with his late father). There were indeed many libations and toasts, reminiscent of those few good wartime interludes between Zhukov and the teetotaller Monty. I was left with the feeling that we had been privy to quite an historic occasion.

From Moscow we flew, via Kiev, to Tbilisi, capital of Georgia. In the squares statues of local boy, Stalin, were being wrenched off their plinths. One of Lenin was trussed up in what looked like an immense French letter, presumably for sale to some western collector. Our hotel looked as if a camel train had passed through it. A rat ambled through our bedroom; fortunately poor Sheelin, infected with 'flu by the Ambassador, thought it was only a mouse. In a restaurant one evening, dashing Georgian males tried to steal all the women in our party, plying them with champagne and flowers. Our terrified guide warned us: 'these Georgian men get very excited by foreign women, and won't take no for an answer. But if you men go after theirs, there will be a *bloody mess!*' So we creep out, in pairs, through the back door. We took off to Tsinandali, where in a famous tragedy in 1854 written up by Lesley Blanch in *The Sabres of Paradise*, two

Georgian princesses from the Tzarina's entourage, a French governess and the children, were hijacked by the legendary Chechen independence-fighter, Shamyl. The hostages were kept in his mountain harem for many months until the Tsarist Government agreed to exchange them for his son. A lovely Italianate villa, with Gothic windows and Turkish lattice-work porches, Tsinandali percolated wistfulness.

Back in Russia, near Pyatigorsk, we passed, among Cossack horsemen, a vast, concrete statue (already beginning to disintegrate) which marks the high-water mark of the German invasion – 400 hundred miles east of Rostov, and only a few miles short of the Grozny oilfields, and the Caspian Sea beyond. Years later when Ukraine was invited to join NATO, I reflected on that statue and how tactless the West could be to even contemplate what the prospect of coal-scuttle helmets again so close to Stalingrad would signify to the Russians. How offensively dumb can you be? In Pyatigorsk our charmless hotel sports rows of dread fruit machines in the foyer. An augury of NATO and Western civilization perhaps.

I embarked on many of these foreign trips not just to write the incidental travel article but with a more coherent goal in mind. At the end of 1990, just as the First Gulf War was about to hot up, the irrepressible Julian Amery, who had been a great ally when I was writing about his father-in-law, Harold Macmillan, and was close to the Sultan of Oman, Qaboos Bin Said Al-Said, invited me to join in a freebie to Muscat to celebrate Sultan Qaboos's fiftieth birthday, and the twentieth anniversary of his accession to the throne. We were a group of mixed Americans and Brits, spooks and MPs prevalent. One was an old friend, Anthony Cavendish, of SIME days, Alan Clark and Jonathan Aitken – a figure who always struck me as about to be engulfed in scandal, as, indeed, he soon would be (in 1999 he went to prison for perjury). A small man with deeply penetrating eyes, Sultan Qaboos came across as one of the last of the world's benevolent despots. A confirmed bachelor, he was hands-on everywhere, all the time. Apart from being the cleanest country in the world (and not just in the Middle East), Oman has to be the best run of all Arab states (a longer visit there twenty years later confirmed my view). Oil rich, it remains deeply attached to Britain, whose forces saved it from its greedy neighbours on at least two occasions in recent years.

But what lent topical interest to our 1990 visit was an unscheduled appearance at a lunch by US General Norman Schwarzkopf, then commanding the huge Allied build-up in Saudi Arabia for the first Gulf War. At first sight we irreverent Brits giggled privately at the massive ambling figure in a uniform far too tight for his bulk, but this soon ceased after 'Stormin'' Norman got up to speak. With outspoken clarity, he exposed to us, in extraordinary detail, how the land campaign to drive Saddam out of Kuwait, 'Desert Storm', was going to unfold two months later – his 'left-hook strategy' which in fact crushed the Iraq forces in just four days. Two years later when I interviewed him on publication of his autobiography, *It Doesn't Take a Hero*, I questioned him about his apparent indiscretion that day. He replied, 'Frankly our strategy was so watertight, and Saddam such an incompetent military leader, it would have made no difference how much he knew of our plan.' What, then, had been his principal worry? He and his British opposite number, General Peter de la Billière, both came up with the same instant response: the media. 'In 'nam [where Schwarzkopf had been a courageous battalion commander], he said, 'we had eighty journalists, and it took thirty-six hours to get copy on screen in the US. In Iraq we had two thousand and eighty, and reports were on screen immediately. So, in case we had heavy casualties, I banned all TV screens from any of my command bunkers.' I asked him what might have happened, in June 1944, if there had been CNN on Omaha Beach. He replied, memorably: 'There would have been no D+1.'

In spring 1992 I was invited back to Israel to participate in a major international conference on biography, down in the Negev, and to give lectures in both Tel Aviv and Jerusalem. It was my first visit since 1969, two years after the Six Day War, when I had had that explosive exchange with General Ezer Weizman. I was curious to see how things had moved on. Sheelin came with me, her first visit to Israel, as a confirmed Judaeophile.

After I had lectured at Tel Aviv University on the Algerian War (*A Savage War* having been translated into Hebrew along with my other books), we drove ourselves off to Sidi Boquer near Beersheba in the Negev. Making the Negev desert bloom was one of the great achievements of David Ben-Gurion, the founding father of Israel. Next to where he retired, the simple dwelling still called Ben Gurion's Hut, is the university named after him, a thriving campus with over 17,000 students. It was there we chewed over the art of biography for the next three days. The participants were central casting: a very Indian Indian, straight out of E. M. Forster, who knew everything; an excitable Italian who never stopped talking; a morose Spaniard with Franco-style moustache, and an earnest Californian who bored us all to death with psychobabble about the importance of the mother-figure in biography. *Cherchez la mère!* And there was my old host from Moscow, General Dmitri Volkogonov.

Following my two meetings with the sturdy little general, events incongruously linked Volkogonov's destiny with St Antony's College, Oxford, where his books had found a prestigious translator in the shape of Dr Harry Shukman. Appointed Defence Adviser to Boris Yeltsin in 1991, after being sacked from his post with the Soviet Army where I had found him, he had then been stricken with cancer, which eventually was to kill him in 1995. Harry arranged for Volkogonov to receive treatment at Oxford's Radcliff Hospital. He was there when, trapped in Moscow's 'White House' in October 1993, Yeltsin was besieged by anti-government insurgents. Volkogonov, from his Oxford hospital bed, was called upon to give advice to Yeltsin. The means of transmission was the St Antony's fax machine – never a reliable device at the best of times – with Harry doubling back and forth as messenger boy. As a result of the general's directives, the siege was lifted, the rebels crushed, and the Yeltsin cabinet liberated.

Here was the most frustrating thing about the whole visit to Sidi Boquer: I was sequestered with one of the most interesting men in the world, and we could not communicate – no common language and no competent interpreter! I was made nervous on being introduced to the conference by an Orthodox Jew who exposed me as having been a British officer in Palestine in 1947 – on 'the wrong side'. But there was friendly laughter. Altogether, the atmosphere at Sidi Boquer was warm and welcoming, but under the surface I sensed tensions there and elsewhere that I had not found back in 1969. Even here in the remote desert helicopters were out at night, roaming restlessly. Everywhere there were signs of Israel on the alert, determined not to be caught out again as at Yom Kippur in 1973.

The University sits on the edge of a vertiginous canyon, recalling *Seven Pillars of Wisdom*, close to Lawrence's 'Wilderness of Zin'; even closer, some twenty miles away, is Dimona, the home of Israel's secret, secret nuclear weapon. One evening, as dark came down, we were taken out ibex-spotting. Related to the wild goat, ibex are huge, relatively rare animals, with great curling horns. Except for the birds and frogs, storks and white eagles, there was total silence and emptiness around us. Then pebbles began mysteriously falling, dislodged by the invisible ibex high above us. Suddenly we spotted more than fifty, scampering at phenomenal speed, from one perilously tiny ledge to another, as quickly as skiers, down to water. Somehow the ibex, with their precarious footholds, evoked the very essence of Israel in the world, clinging on in the face of impossible odds, never seeming to slip or fall, where only one slip would result in calamity.

After a few days' rest and superb snorkelling in Egypt's Taba, at a hotel later blown up by Arab terrorists on the Gulf of Aqaba, we drove back into Israel, heading south to Jerusalem via the West Bank. Fortunately, it was one of those rare good years, of relative tranquillity. We were able to travel everywhere, in a hired car with Israeli number plates, without apprehension. Travelling first to Masada, we passed pathetic Bedouin encampments, looking more impoverished and tattier than I recalled from the past – perhaps because their beautiful traditional camel tents are now replaced with dirty plastic. Masada is, as one might expect, a haunting place. Sheelin found it more moving than any other place in Israel, more than Galilee, Bethlehem or even Jerusalem. One can vividly imagine the terror within that last Jewish stronghold as those organisation-men, the Romans, slowly and methodically pushed their ramp up to the impregnable escarpment, and finally the mass suicide of all the inhabitants, leaping off the cliffs. Masada has left such an indelible imprint in the whole Jewish psyche that one thinks of it constantly, especially in the context of nearby Dimona, which houses what to me seems like the modern-day Masada weapon – to be used only at the last extremity, when a new Holocaust is impending.

Travelling through the Occupied Territories of Judaea and Samaria was a disturbing experience. The Arab communities, with their goats and their donkeys, dust and minarets, seemed little changed as I remembered them in 1946–7 – only the population had increased tenfold. It was still the world of the Old Testament, redolent with history and charm, but alongside was the bustling, successful world of the New Testament in Israel, as modern and Western-orientated a world as anything in Europe or North America. But everywhere you looked in the West Bank, there were the fresh pink and white concrete blocks of new Israeli settlements, and overlooking them, like bossy governesses, on every strategic hilltop an Israeli army fort or outpost. The whole West Bank was gridded like a military map; there was not even the pretence of a Palestinian state – just a mosaic of fragments separated by Israeli strategic roads or girdles of settlements. How can a viable nation be created out of this?

And that, as I write, was nearly two decades ago. Now the settlement population in the West Bank alone totals some half-million Israelis – equal to the overall population of Israel when founded in 1948. How, one wonders, recalling the historic nightmare created by the Sudetenland and by the Polish Corridor of pre-1939 days, could one ever create a viable Arab Palestinian state out of this interlocking, interwoven mess? Perhaps this is what the dyed-in-the-wool Zionists (and they form the majority of the new settlers) are hoping for, an Eretz Israel that reaches from the Mediterranean to the Jordan, in which the indigenous Arab population is once more reduced to its biblical role of 'hewers of wood and drawers of water'. Having seen, later, what Housing Minister Ariel Sharon's ruthless construction plans had done around East Jerusalem, and around Tiberias up on the ravishing Sea of Galilee in the north, we both left Israel in deep gloom, which nothing that has happened since has done anything to dispel.

Arriving in Jerusalem, from the north, we were confronted by the huge, eyeless unfinished buildings of Sharon's ring strangling the Old City. We lunched with President Chaim Herzog, the man who came to my rescue when I was assaulted by General Weizman. He recalled the episode well. A gentle man with a military moustache, looking like a British Army major (which he once was, in the Second World War), he was born the son of a Chief Rabbi of Ireland, and charmed Sheelin's Irish blood with anecdotes of old Dublin. We talked about the recent Gulf War: the West, he observed 'always gets it wrong; they were wrong on the Iraq–Iran War, wrong about Kuwait, wrong to halt. They should have gone on for two

days more, with air power, no need to go to Baghdad . . . Saddam is still a
very evil and dangerous man.' During the war, Herzog had had a narrow
escape from one of Saddam's Scuds; in hospital, with bronchial trouble,
in Tel Aviv: 'I was nearly blown out of my bed by a Scud.' He had to
broadcast to the nation from his bed; 'but nobody knew it!' He could
only speak for a few minutes at a time, because of the bronchitis, and had
to refuse a gas mask (there was widespread fear in Israel that the Scuds
would contain nerve gas). For the same reason, Herzog thought the Israeli
Army would have struck at Saddam if many more Scuds came.

 I left Israel frankly disturbed. The mood had changed radically since
the heady atmosphere after the Six Day War. No longer one of tri-
umphalism; gone was the cocky self-assurance, 'we can beat any combination of Arabs'. That, in itself, was no bad thing; but replacing it was
a lack of confidence, in leaders, in security, in the ability to find a reliable
lasting peace and in Israel's image in the world. More shocking was the
attitude to the Arab population one found growing in diverse places.

 Towards the end of 1992 an enticing invitation arrived from New York,
from Professor Arthur Schlesinger Jr. Dear Arthur! To me he was always
the antithesis of what Belloc's 'remote and ineffectual don' signified:
eminent academic, great historian, superb speaker, always able to lighten
his talk with wit and humour – something rare among American academics. But apart from that I don't think I ever met anyone more capable
of enjoying all that life had to offer than diminutive Arthur. In his early
days at Harvard, when I first came across him, he seemed to have a slightly
underdeveloped sense of humour. In the late 1950s, he had a somewhat
fierce encounter with my former room mate Bill Buckley. Arthur and Bill
were politically at opposite poles. Arthur had written a scathing review
of one of Bill's books, ending on a highly sarcastic note: 'but I envy his
rhetoric!' Bill, then a relatively unknown figure, but with an already
irrepressible sense of mischief, grabbed at this last remark by Arthur and
printed it, totally without context, as a puff on the jacket of his next book:
'". . . I envy his rhetoric." Arthur Schlesinger, Jr.' Arthur, quite rightly, was
furious and sued for 'invasion of privacy'. It was a drawn-out and ill-
humoured affair. Eventually, as Arthur himself once so generously
observed, 'There comes a time with age when all contemporaries become
friends' – and so it was with Arthur and WFB.

Arthur's career had changed radically with the election of John F. Kennedy. From being just an esteemed Harvard historian, overnight he became the scribe at the court of Camelot. He knew everyone, from Kurt Vonnegut and Norman Mailer to Philip and Katherine Graham, from Leonard Bernstein, Walter Lippmann and George McGovern to Carlos Fuentes, Peter Hall, Lauren Bacall, Marlene Dietrich and Jackie Onassis. He loathed and despised Richard Nixon and in turn was on Nixon's 'hate-list', only to find him, in post-Watergate life, to be a next-door neighbour in New York.

Arthur had become a good friend of mine in the late 1970s when I was writing the Macmillan biography. With his intimate knowledge of the Kennedy era, he was immeasurably helpful. From then on he and the deliciously towering Alexandra and Sheelin and I remained the closest of friends. I was always struck with Arthur's generosity, not only with his time, but with his material and his friends. He was one of those rare things: a liberal who laughed. Apart from that invaluable commodity of laughter, one of the many things that impressed me about Arthur, as an historian, was his incredible range of interest in the raw stuff of history – people. He couldn't walk down Fifth Avenue without wondering what it, and the people on it, would have looked like a century before. I remember one evening Arthur ringing me up and asking me if I was doing anything, before saying, 'I have been asked to a party given by Hugh Hefner at the Bunny Club. Why don't you come along?' It was a particularly terrible evening. A pretty face plus a wagging white tail is not always a recipe for success – not much between tail and ears – but it gave a hint of Arthur's eclecticism, his endless range of interests. (The next day, I had an appointment signing books at Scribner's on Fifth Avenue. There was a long queue out on the pavement, and my hopes rose. But no, they were queuing for Hugh Hefner's autograph, not mine. I was at a small table, back of shop.)

I think this interest in everything, and everybody, plus his capacity for laughter, was what made Arthur truly, as he has been called, 'a historian of hope'. We shared many convivial holidays together – Morocco, Florida, the south of France. Wherever we were, by mid-morning in some remarkable way Arthur had managed to read all the worthwhile journals and knew exactly what was happening in the world anywhere. The humour with which he spiced his observations was utterly enviable. My wife used to infuriate me by saying, 'Why can't you be more like Arthur?'

Arthur's invitation was to take part in a conference in Morocco in January 1993, marking the fiftieth anniversary of the wartime Casablanca Conference, the top-level meeting headed by Roosevelt and Churchill, at which was decided not just the future strategy of the Second World War but – to some extent – the shape of the world after the war. I was invited to give, at an essentially US-organised conference, a British historian's viewpoint. At the same time Arthur asked, could I suggest a distinguished Frenchman to put a French view, given that de Gaulle had played an important (if involuntary) role?* With alacrity, I proposed the name of Maurice Druon, an old friend from the Franco-British Council (on which we sat together for many years), who held the imposing title of Secrétaire Perpetuelle of the French Academy, a writer whom I greatly admired and who I was sure would put up a powerful case for de Gaulle. Maurice accepted, and I looked forward to a week of listening to his exquisite French and indeed sonorous English. *Hélas!* as he arrived from Paris the next plane, from Washington, DC, brought in Pamela Harriman, an old friend of Maurice's, and the two disappeared discreetly for much of the conference.

It was a good conference. Arthur and former ambassador Bill vanden Heuvel, who held the ring as a superb chairman, had put together a remarkable convocation. Present were children and grandchildren of major participants in 1943: Roosevelts, Churchills and a de Gaulle son-in-law; and also the son of Harry Hopkins, the egregious confidant to FDR. But what got the conference off the ground, and made it unlike other international get-togethers, which tend to skirt the thresholds of tedium, was the audience we all had with King Hassan in Fez. Ushered through countless, spookily empty courtyards, we were presented formally to the King – a middle-aged Arab monarch who had seen everything (including two all but successful assassination attempts) and had every-

---

* FDR, who hated de Gaulle, tried to arrange a shotgun marriage there between the two rival French generals, de Gaulle and Giraud, dubbing them privately the 'bride' and 'groom'. The Conference also established the questionable policy of 'unconditional surrender' of the Axis Powers, decided on the invasion of Sicily and Italy, and agreed that there would be no cross-Channel invasion in 1943.

thing – and now seemed, frankly, bored. Then Pamela Harriman took over. Aged seventy-two she looked wonderful. Certainly King Hassan thought so. Suddenly everything changed. It was the most extraordinary performance. I had known and admired Pamela in Washington in the 1980s when I was working on the Macmillan book and she was married to Averell Harriman. He was then in his nineties, almost totally deaf – and demanding. We all knew of the unkind reputation she had for studying beautiful ceilings of the great and rich, but as far as gossipy Georgetown knew (and it always knew everything) she never put a foot wrong. She came across as a totally one-man woman; that is, one at a time. Personally, I could never quite get the sex-symbol aspect of Pamela – she didn't bowl me over. I may be quite wrong, but I always sensed with her that power mattered more than the delights of the boudoir. And throughout her varied career her use of power was prodigious. Without her networking Bill Clinton might well not have made it into the White House in 1992 (perhaps alas), and it was pay-back time: she was about to be given the much coveted job of US Ambassador to Paris.

Now, in the royal palace of Fez, we watched her turn her charm on the jaded monarch. As she gave him her total attention for little more than five minutes, it was like watching a powerful laser-beam at work. King Hassan II wriggled, melted and succumbed. It was remarkable, and just as remarkable was the effect it had on the rest of our visit to Morocco. From then on, for the remainder of the week all twenty or thirty of us became VIPs. The red carpets were everywhere; we were treated to luxurious banquets; exotic fantasias with charging white Arab steeds were laid on, and – in Marrakech – we were received around a lake by several score musicians deafeningly blowing trumpets, pounding drums and crashing cymbals. It was like a scene out of *One Thousand and One Nights* – and all thanks to Pamela. I can't remember much of what we discussed at the conference.

19
LA BELLE FRANCE, ENCORE

Willie Rushton's cartoon (in fact, his last) for the *Literary Review* critique of
How Far From Austerlitz.

Paris was built like Nebuchadnezzar's statue, of gold and mud.

Voltaire

The fall of the Berlin Wall provided me not just with new opportunities for journalism but with a new book. Back in the 1970s, the resourceful George Weidenfeld had invited me to write a heavily illustrated book on Napoleon. Though the library catalogues list over 600,000 titles on Bonaparte, what historian can resist having another go? Out of it (in 1979) came *Napoleon: Master of Europe, 1805–1807*, taking the Emperor of the French at the high tide of his ambition, as he stood aboard that raft at Tilsit on the River Niemen – the one-time little Corsican émigré, the diminutive *petit-caporal*, dictating his terms to the conquered rulers of continental Europe. It was the headiest of moments, replete with triumph, but fraught with consequence for the world. The book was my only literary infidelity to the House of Macmillan in forty-five years. Like an iceberg, more research went into it than was visible. George produced a lavish and exquisite coffee-table book. I was delighted; but it did not become a bestseller. For me as a military historian, there had been a big disadvantage in preparing the book: I had been unable to visit the sites of Napoleon's great battles of 1805–7. Austerlitz, the greatest, Jena/Auerstadt, Friedland and Eylau all lay in Eastern Europe, then under Soviet dom-ination. My old guru, Maurice Oldfield, then head of MI6, urged me not to consider making a trip to Czechoslovakia to visit Austerlitz. It was very soon after the Soviets' brutal crushing of Dubček's Prague Spring, and the Eastern Bloc Security services were on high alert. With my intelligence background – modest as it had been – he cautioned: 'They might easily grab you. Remember what happened to that poor Jim Prideaux John le Carré wrote about? We might not be able to get you back.'

Then, following publication of *The Lonely Leader*, a senior Macmillan editor, William Armstrong, came to me with the proposal that I write a new full-scale history of Napoleon, fleshing out my 1979 book and taking the story right to the end – to Waterloo, 1815. It would be an account of the world's greatest military genius, who in 1807 had stood at the summit but lost everything (and ruined Europe) because of his inability to know when, or how, to stop. Encouraged by the critical reception of *Master of Europe* in 1979, I liked the idea at once; I could visit the battlefield of Austerlitz (now Slavkov, to give its Czech name) without being troubled by the KGB.

Starting off from Vienna, I was accompanied by David Mynett, a good friend, skilled professional artist, superb lecturer and considerable Napoleonic buff in his own right – an unbeatable choice of travelling companion. We headed north to the city of Brno, some two and a half hours' drive, 70 miles away. It was late November in 1995, almost exactly the time of year Napoleon had arrived to fight his greatest battle. As we approached Brno, an unpromising industrial city amid the rolling Moravian hills, to encourage David I read to him from the 1805 diaries of that dashing cavalryman, Joachim Murat. The streets, wrote Murat, were filled with 'extremely pretty women, got up in the most tasteful and tempting way'; after their 1,000-mile march from Paris the French spent the evening feeding and wassailing sumptuously. No such luck in 1995. There was not a female of any kind to greet us in Brno, and we had the greatest difficulty finding anywhere to eat at all.

The following morning shortly after dawn we moved the few miles to the Turan (now Žuran) Hill where Napoleon had set up his HQ that morning of 2 December 1805. The brilliance of his famous *coup d'oeil* was that, over the previous days, he had carefully studied both the peculiarities of the land where the superior Austrian and Russian forces* would bring him to battle and the weather patterns. Now we had the good fortune to find the weather perform exactly as it had 190 years before, and as Napoleon had then expected it would. There was snow on the ground, and a hard frost, just as there had been that morning in 1805 – good hard going for Prince Bagration's elite cavalry. At 8 a.m. the Pratzen Heights to the

---

* Napoleon had 73,100 men, 139 cannon, against the Russian Army commanded by Tsar Alexander I himself, and General Kutuzov, plus the Austrian Army together totalling 85,700 men, 278 cannon. The whole battle is immortally described in Tolstoy's *War and Peace*.

east were beginning to emerge from the thick fog in the valley of the Goldbach. There Marshal Soult's shock-troops would have been waiting, hidden, for their charge up the slopes of the Heights which would decide this important battle. Then, exactly as it had in Napoleon's day, at 10 a.m. the sun came out: 'Le beau soleil d'Austerlitz'. Napoleon would have observed General Kutuzov's forces, as he had anticipated, moving off the Pratzen so as to strike the French on their right flank. He gave the order to Soult's invisible force to attack, rolling up the surprised enemy, finally to obliterate them as they fled into the frozen Satschen ponds at the southern end of the battlefield.

As he sketched away in the bitter cold, David, the artist, could hardly contain his excitement. He was depicting exactly what Napoleon would have seen. To add a touch of reality, he allowed himself the poetic licence of putting in a cannon beneath the hazy sun. I was to use his sketch, executed in little more than half an hour, for the book jacket. It was perfect. But what, to me, was thrilling beyond belief was to be able to see every feature of this particularly compact battlefield, astoundingly little changed in the intervening two centuries. The farming villages of 1805 were all there, grown but little; roads were all but unchanged; no woods had grown up to obscure the contours. All at once the amazing genius at work in choosing this site for battle against a superior foe, who was moving in for the kill, became plain – as did every detail of Napoleon's plan. On no battlefield that I have ever visited was the course of it laid out before my eyes with such extraordinary clarity; not even at Verdun, or Sedan, or Villers-Bocage, or on the Golan Heights. One could not fail to see in most minute detail how it had all evolved and developed. No military historian could ever have had a more satisfying experience.

That one day at Austerlitz cost the Allied side 16,000 dead and wounded, 11,000 captured, 185 cannon and 45 flags seized; Napoleon lost but 1,288 dead and 6,993 wounded. After the successive triumphs of 1806–7, the map of Europe was indeed rolled up as he stepped on to the raft floating on the Niemen. Yet the stellar success on the Pratzen was to carry within it the seeds of his defeat, just as the breakthrough at Sedan in 1940 had presaged Hitler's end – with *folie de grandeur* leading both to eventual doom in Russia. In 1805 Napoleon also missed one vital trick, which would eventually destroy him and lay the foundations of the century of

Pax Britannica. Almost without his noticing it, on 21 October, a month before he arrived at Austerlitz, his dream of world conquest had been destroyed far behind his back by Horatio Nelson at Trafalgar. 'Those distant, storm-beaten ships, upon which the Grand Army never looked, stood between it and the dominion of the world,' in the immortal words of US Admiral Mahan. (On the other hand, one might ask, how could the Grand Army have set eyes on the Royal Navy ships, any more than the Kaiser's or Hitler's land-locked armies were to do a century later?)

From Austerlitz/Slavkov we moved on to study, and sketch, the bloody battlefields of Aspern-Essling and Wagram, both fought in 1809. Wagram, though Napoleon emerged victor after losing a quarter of his effectives, was the first battle to reveal flaws in the master's touch, and hints of the end-game. David filled a sketchbook with a dozen superbly evocative works, I filled a notebook. Frozen, at Vienna airport we restored ourselves liberally with Hungarian *barrack pálinka*, apricot brandy, before tottering on to the plane.

Back home, having written the book (it was published in 1996), I decided on the title *How Far from Austerlitz? Napoleon 1805–1815*, drawn from a somewhat bizarre children's lullaby by Rudyard Kipling which begins

> 'How far is St Helena from the field of Austerlitz?'
> You couldn't hear me if I told – so loud the cannons roar.

I thought it a good title; so did the reviewers on the whole, and they also approved of the book. One dissenting voice was the prestigious *History Today*, which accused me of making 'specious' parallels between Napoleon and Hitler. Certainly some of the triter parallels are specious, but others deserve to be made. On a purely military level, both led their nations to destruction on the endless steppes of Russia. In a curious coincidence, each started their invasion within the same twenty-four hour span in June; for a variety of reasons, for both it was already too late in the season. What in fact destroyed the Grande Armée and the Wehrmacht equally wasn't 'General Winter', but 'General Summer': the heat killed off Napoleon's cavalry, his most potent weapon; the dust wore out Hitler's invincible Panzers – small facts which many historians overlook. By way of fundamental contrast between the two 'Masters of Europe', Hitler after twelve years in power bequeathed to Germany nothing but a mountain of skulls and rubble. In terms of civil, non-military accomplishments alone, Napoleon, on the other hand, had he never fought a single battle would still have to be rated one of history's great leaders for the system of administration and the civil reforms he left behind him in France. One modern historian, Martin van Creveld, rates him as 'the most competent human being who ever lived'. I can't go that far; he killed too many men (it used to be said that the French were a race of tall men before Bonaparte), and it was his style of warfare that led to the mass butcheries of the twentieth century. But one of the aspects of this extraordinary human being that always astounded me was his capacity to think laterally. On campaign in faraway Egypt he would be contemplating the art collections of Paris; fighting one of his grimmest battles in East Prussia he would be fussing about the working of the fountains in the capital. From every one of his battle TAC HQs would fly horsemen by the hundreds with non-military orders for the hard-pressed civilians in Paris.

Eight years later I had an invitation, from Orion Press, to return to his non-martial components, in one of a series titled 'The Age of Napoleon'. In it I was able to concentrate on his contributions to the world of the arts, to Paris city planning, furniture design, dress and decor, and decorum. It was illuminating and fun. If nothing else it succeeded in being, at less than 200 pages, one of the shortest books ever written on the great man. It went into many languages, including Slovak and Korean. Imagine my surprise when an uninterpretable volume landed on my doorstep: it turned out to be from Albania, one of the few countries of the world where the Emperor never set foot and one which, you might have thought, had the least interest in his achievements.

In personal and professional terms, however, what was most important about *How Far from Austerlitz?* was that it led me on the road back to Paris (bringing, incidentally, great contentment to my wife). Research took me to the magnificently revamped Musée de l'Armée, inside Napoleon's Invalides. There I found some amusement at the restructuring of the Empire galleries: sumptuous during *la Gloire*, they ran in a straight line from Rivoli through Austerlitz, years of triumph. Come 1815 and you reached a corner; on turning it, you were abruptly in the battles of the Restoration, the terrible, historic defeat of Waterloo somehow seemed to have disappeared. I asked a sleepy young attendant, 'Mais où est Water-loo?'

'Waterloo? Connais pas.' And then, after consulting a colleague, 'Il n'y a pas de Salle Waterloo.' One wonders whatever brought the poor man to St Helena.

Thanks largely to geography, we Brits in our history have been spared the terrible defeats suffered by our proud neighbours, but would we try to gloss them over as France does? I recall de Gaulle's pain in having to confer with Macmillan in a room in Admiralty House hung with paintings of Trafalgar and other French naval defeats; or of President Chirac's state visit to Windsor in 2004 when, for the benefit of Gallic pride, the Waterloo Room had to be redubbed 'the Music Room' for the evening.

When Vichy's Admiral Darlan was assassinated by a young French zealot in Algiers in December 1942, Winston Churchill observed to the House of Commons – in exasperation moderated with great sympathy – that 'the good Lord in his infinite wisdom did not choose to make French-men in the image of the English.' Had I been an MP in the House that day, I would have cried 'Hear, hear!' At regular intervals the startling fact comes home to me too that the French don't even think like us. And I thank the good Lord for his inventiveness and generosity in putting so different a nation just across the Channel from us. I recall the happy years I spent on the Franco-British Council, wrestling with the Sisyphean task of improving the Entente Cordiale – that ethereal, intangible umbilical cord, like the Special Relationship with America. We were all good friends, got on wonderfully well with each other, lunched lavishly together alter-nately in our respective capitals and parted *d'accord* with all our mutual resolves. Yet, a week or two later, when the French minutes arrived in London, they would bear absolutely no relation to what we Brits thought had been agreed.

Every two years we would host a monumental beanfeast, alternating between our countries, to which the heads of government and the great and the good would be invited. We would agree on inviting seventy-five a side. So the Brits would go home and instantly send out seventy-five invitations to a first eleven; some twenty would refuse, so we would dutifully invite a second eleven of another twenty, until our list was full. But what did *nos chers collègues* do? Absolutely nothing for two months;

then, under pressure, they would send out 100 cards and get 105 accept-
ances – the extra five representing mistresses whom French invités wanted
to include. Hair-tearing in London. But Paris would insist 'It will be all
right on the day.' Sure enough, there would be a score of drop-outs on
the day, and each team would field exactly the magical seventy-five. But
the difference was, whereas the Brits' team would consist of the biggest
beasts available, all too often the French would be second-raters, *petits
fonctionnaires* instead of ministers and chefs de cabinet, with little to offer.
But we loved, or affected to love, each other.

So, *vive la différence!* That is why, in effect, I write about French rather
than British history. It is, quite simply, rather more exciting. We have the
Repeal of the Corn Laws; they have 1789, Napoleon, the Siege of Paris
(heroic balloonists, eating rats and all that) and the Belle Epoque. French
history seems to move in a series of great surges; they go to the brink of
the abyss and sometimes pull back at the last minute (as happened in
Paris's near-revolution of 1968). Or else they go over the brink, and then
recuperate with the most astonishing revitalization – as they showed
with the flowering of the Impressionists, which followed the catastrophic
defeats of 1870 and the Commune.

As André Maurois, a great Anglophile, explained in a passage that
I have quoted more times than I can count:

> France's history, a lasting miracle, seems more dramatic than that of other
> countries. Like Greece in another age, it has the special privilege of deeply
> moving the people of the earth to the point where they take part in France's
> quarrels. The story of Joan of Arc, that of the kings of France, that of the
> French Revolution, that of the Marne, that of the Resistance, form a part
> of the heritage of all mankind. If England has preserved in the modern
> world Rome's imperial and judicial tradition, Paris has played, both in
> letters and in the arts, the role of Athens ... For five centuries, 'everything
> which was French was universal, and everything which was universal was
> French.'*

Maurois ended his account of his country's history by pointing to an
unarguable fact: 'Being a Frenchman was and will remain a dangerous

---

* André Maurois, *A History of France*, 1949; he is quoting Etienne Gilson.

business; it is all the more honourable.' *D'accord!* And, whatever the Little Englanders may say, France today remains the most civilised country the world has to offer.

Thus, as the old century came to its gory close, I went back to writing about Old France – or Old Paris to be exact. In the exotic history of this extraordinary city, the handmaidens of beauty – sex, violence and mayhem – are never far removed, which undoubtedly helps to make its story so fascinating. Over the years of researching various books there, I had kept what Churchill in the Second World War called his 'discard box', where he would file material that he would later use in his majestic histories. Particularly as a result of my weekend rambles when I explored the *Fall of Paris* sites of 1870–1, I realised that I had come to know Paris far more intimately than London or New York. It is, of course, a wonderfully compact city; a foreign correspondent friend once claimed that he had walked from Montmartre to Montparnasse in 45 minutes. That was in the traffic-free '50s; and of course it was downhill much of the way. I challenged him, but have never tried it. In the course of my researches for what came to be entitled *Seven Ages of Paris* – in that it told the story of the city in seven eras, from that of its twelfth-century founder Philippe Auguste to Charles de Gaulle in the twentieth – a funny thing (actually, it could have been rather unfunny) happened to me on the way to *l'Opéra*. I had spent the morning studying the surrounding artefacts of Prefect Haussmann on the Rue de l'Opéra and was quietly taking a break in the Café de la Paix. Perhaps it was a curious choice, but I've always wondered if the old cliché was true that, sitting there, you would see the whole world pass by, and it was raining and I was hungry.

Seated under the glass-enclosed terrace, I had just paid my bill (the receipt reminds me that it was 14.14 on 7 April 2001) when boum! – something smashed into the plate-glass window 6 feet from me, on a level with my head and with considerable impact. The window, a large slab about 4 feet by 7, shattered from top to bottom, but fortunately it must have been made of reinforced safety glass because – like the windscreen of a car – only a few fragments splintered inwards. In the centre of the spiders' web of cracks was a crater, about 1½ inches across, almost certainly the mark of a bullet of some sort, too powerful to have been an airgun – possibly a light rifle with a silencer? It seemed unlikely to have come from the crowded street, but across the road, on the top floor of a building across the boulevard, there was an open window, lined up with the hole in the window, and with my head. Had it been ordinary glass, or no glass at all, without a shadow of doubt I would have had to travel home at Foreign Office expense. If I had been a man of action like the intrepid Max Hastings, with whom we had been hobnobbing in the Embassy the previous night, I would have whizzed out to see if there was a Jackal figure sliding out of the building, reassembling his lethal crutch. However, as an Italian at the next-door table moved off as quickly as Marshal Graziani in the desert, I decided there was no point awaiting the questioning of some Inspector Clouseau. The management did not seem especially perturbed, almost suggesting this was an everyday event, and there was no instant wail of sirens, such as there used to be in the good old days when the riot cops of the CRS would arrive to beat up a few harmless students.

Brushing off the odd sliver of glass back in the safety of our hotel, I set to wondering what it was all about. What had the unseen assailant got against the Café de la Paix – surely not just an excesssive bill for an indifferent lunch? A protection racket? Had my Italian neighbour been a Mafia target? Or what had someone got against me? If it had been at a time when I was writing about the Algerian War and the OAS, it would not have been unduly surprising, because some rum things did occur. But that was three decades before. Sheelin, unbelieving till I brushed the glass slivers off my collar and out of my turn-ups, flatteringly suggested a jealous husband? But not guilty. The mystery remains.

I couldn't resist closing *Seven Ages of Paris* with an epilogue on Père Lachaise cemetery, named after Louis XIV's father-confessor, who – poor man – died of hypothermia among the splendours of Versailles in that bitter climate-change winter of 1709, the bitterest cold ever recorded in Paris. It's easy to forget that, as well as being the city of light and life, Paris is also a city of the dead. From Héloïse and Abelard to Edith Piaf and Oscar Wilde, anybody who was anybody is buried out there in the marble orchard which graces Paris's east end. You only have to stroll round its ornate and extravagant tombs and vaults to appreciate how much the French bourgeoisie mind about death, and their *placement* there. I remember once in the 1960s lunching *à trois* with Nancy Mitford and

Gaston Palewski, who arrived in a terrible stew over his booking in Père Lachaise. He had just been up there and had been told that he could only be placed on a waiting list and, to his great distress, could not be guaranteed a site 'with a view over Paris'. His indignation was boundless: 'Moi, Président de Gaulle's closest colleague, Président du Conseil Constitutionnel, the highest constitutional authority in France.' Teasing him, Nancy told him to hang on a bit: 'After all, every once in a while don't they dig up the old bones, and then grind them up to make cosmetics for Chanel?' Palewski was not appeased.

Macmillans and Knopf in New York both did a beautiful job in producing the book. I particularly liked the British jacket, with one of the balloons of Paris soaring over the city. Among reviewers, Antonia Fraser picked up on it, selecting it as a 'Book of the Year' in the *New Statesman*. In America, my new friend and a great writer, novelist and biographer, herself half French by birth, Francine du Plessix Gray, could not have been kinder in the *New York Times*: 'How much happier life could be if one could read a book as riveting as Alistair Horne's *Seven Ages of Paris* every week of the year.' That certainly helped it become a steady bestseller in New York.

With publication of *Seven Ages*, I decided – with heavy heart – to part from Macmillans. It was a wrench, but things had changed. Nicky Byam Shaw, my friend and long-term publisher who had stood by me so valiantly throughout the Harold Macmillan saga (and to whom I dedicated *Seven Ages*) was retiring to live in New Hampshire. The crofters had sold out to a big amorphous German group, earning the lucky grandsons some thirty big ones each. I didn't feel at ease with the new management, which seemed directed towards making Jeffrey Archer their flagship author (when I wrote berating them for backing crook books instead of the cook books on which past family fortunes had been founded, they seemed unamused). As a final break with the past, for economy reasons they had purchased characterless offices the wrong side of King's Cross. Mr Dan and Mr Harold would not have been happy there. So, enticed by George Weidenfeld, ever determined in his pursuit of authors, I moved to Orion – located lunchably close to the Garrick Club.

My editor there would be a much respected veteran of the trade, one of the last of the old school of publishers who actually liked books – Ion

Trewin. The proposal was for a full-scale history of France. The year 2004 would be the centenary of the Entente Cordiale, that milestone in Franco-British relations, which predated the sacrificial deaths in Flanders fields of a million Britishers and men of the Commonwealth eleven years later. The date would, as they used to say in Fleet Street, be a good peg on which to hang such a history. I had no shortage of material: the MS of *Seven Ages* having been (as usual) horribly overweight, the sagacious Peter James had rigorously red-pencilled anything which did not strictly relate to Paris. So I had been left with yet another vast discard box of material. I also bore in mind criticism from well-meaning readers who thought that, in the earlier book, I had underplayed such important subjects as the Revolution in provinces during those 2,000 years of French history.

With the 1904 centenary around our necks, we agreed on the title *Friend or Foe: An Anglo-Saxon History of France*. It was, I admit ruefully, one of the least inspired. It made the book sound far too parochial, too much of an anti-Frog rant. Sadly, I lost the services, temporarily, of Peter James. He had done five of my last books, each requiring a lot of work, and said – with engaging honesty – that he had had enough of what he called 'Horneana' for the time being. Ion, too, an outstanding operator, was at a crux. He had semi-retired from Orion and was deeply committed to writing his own biography, on the naughty Alan Clark. (As I wrote to him at the time: good publishers should not be permitted to write good books too – unfair on their authors.) So the editing of *Friend or Foe* was delegated to a young and inexperienced junior. It was not what I had sought in leaving Macmillan. Nor, in switching agents from Michael Sissons to Andrew Wylie at about the same time, did I get what I wanted there, but that is another story. The reviews were nonetheless positive, the *Independent* even declaring with largesse that 'Horne in top form is not to be missed.' In New York, employing the much more majestic title of *La Belle France: A Short History*, Ash Green at Knopf produced a distinctly more handsome book. But it didn't sell as well as I had hoped, certainly not like *Seven Ages*. When I taxed Ash with this, he explained with laconic Yankee style: 'Well, we Americans are funny people. We love Paris but hate the French!' The timing was, of course, unfortunate: 2004 was a time of maximum US–French coolness, those ungrateful Frogs, forgetting about Belleau Wood and Omaha, having told George W. Bush that they were not joining him in Iraq.

Working in, and on France, it was my friends there that made it especially worthwhile. One of the principal joys of working in Paris in the 1980s and 1990s was the presence there of Van and Bootsie Galbraith. Although he was intermittently a banker in London, Van spent much of his life in Paris, a career culminating with his appointment as Ronald Reagan's controversial, and irrepressible, ambassador in 1981.

Van was no ordinary mortal. To begin with, he did not know the meaning of the word fear; trepidation was simply not in his vocabulary. We first met in the 1960s, when he drove me up into the Swiss mountains to Bill Buckley's domain in Rougemont. Unfamiliar with driving on icy, snowbound roads, Van bounced off the snow banks between road and precipice at least six times, without betraying the least sense of alarm. We became fast friends. He headed my very short list of people I would have gone into the jungle with. (Much as I loved him, I would not have ventured in with Bill Buckley. He would have got distracted by some philosophical issue and wandered off lost.) Apart from his courage, demonstrated not least through years of fighting cancer, Van's great assets were his unquenchable optimism and a formidable sense of humour (often Rabelaisian). He could be, and often was, one of the funniest raconteurs you could meet, and quite indestructible on the ski slopes. We skied and sailed together, over many years and in many seas; it was always fun. But there was much more to Van. He had an acute mind, and total political dedication to what he construed the Right Way (invariably spelled with a capital R.). We disagreed powerfully on many issues, notably – in recent years – on the Middle East. But never once did he lose his temper in argument; nor did he ever lose that unquenchable optimism, day by day, that it was 'all going to be alright'. And we were going to come out of the jungle in one piece.

As Reagan's ambassador in Paris (where we saw him often, and where Bootsie with her artistry transformed the Embassy into a place of charm and joy), Van distinguished himself more by force of personality, possibly, than by diplomatic craft. He was Bill Buckley's closest friend from Yale days, and it was unquestionably Bill's influence with Reagan that got him the job. He must have been a constant worry to those correct professionals down in Washington's well-named Foggy Bottom, yet I suspect his bravura personality appealed to the Gipper. Nobody could have changed his style less on becoming an HE. Van told President Mitterrand – in his excellent French, and over the media – exactly what he thought of his having Communist ministers in his Cabinet, and as a result it took ten years for him to receive the statutory Légion d'Honneur. When it did come (from Chirac), as a lifelong Francophile Van wore it with pride and a smile. He died in 2008. I miss him.

Both *Seven Ages* and *La Belle France* brought enjoyable lectures and events in their wake, not least in that most magical of all bookshops that crouches beneath the shadow of Notre Dame, Shakespeare and Company. They led to two more coupled oeuvres on France, the first being *The Age of Napoleon* in 2004. Then, when my thoughts and energy had wandered far away, to the USA and Henry Kissinger, an unexpected call from an unfamiliar quarter asked if I would write the text on a very special production on the French Revolution. Carlton Books had already published a magnificent and lush production on Napoleon (I could wish I had been invited to do it). In a large, coffee-table format, *The French Revolution* combined text with lavish maps, contemporary illustrations and copies of original documents concealed in small envelopes. With knowledge stored over the past, I thought I could provide the necessary text, as well as advising on the illustrative material, without too much sweat. In fact, it turned out to be much more of a labour than I had idly expected, especially since each of the texts for the twenty-seven chapters, though totalling little more than 25,000 words, or a tenth the length of a book like *La Belle France*, had to fit exactly to the page. Vanessa Daubeny was an accomplished but exacting editor. The finished result was superb, and – at £30 – a snip. But how many sixth-formers or university freshmen, at whom the book was essentially angled, could afford £30 in the hostile economic climate of 2009? Yet I felt it was a worthwhile effort, and, once again, I had learned much from the research.

But the real problem, for me, in writing about the French Revolution was what could I say that was the least bit positive? This was one good reason why I may have skimped over it in *Seven Ages*. What an appalling wastage of human spirit! What wanton destruction! What unnecessary misery, and not least for the section of society, the underprivileged, by and for whom it was nominally launched! I cannot see that much good came out of it. Well, it did inspire what is still arguably the world's greatest national anthem. Art? Who but David? One other plus, though that may seem frivolous: 1789 gave birth to the Paris restaurant as we know it; as the Revolution was lopping off the heads of most of the employers, the out-of-work chefs found a niche creating their own restaurants in the capital – and, subsequently, elsewhere.

But did it fulfil that war-cry of Liberté, Egalité or Fraternité? It had improved the lives of the peasants, but wrecked France's agriculture. Égalité? The under-classes of Paris, who thought the Revolution was their affair, ended up little better off than before. Only the bourgeois prospered – as indeed they were to do after those three successive revolutions in the nineteenth century; and French women were almost the last to receive the vote in all Europe. Yet it created the country that I have loved for more than six decades, the country that provided the terrain for my literary vagabondage.

20

KISSINGER

Bill Buckley, Henry Kissinger and AH, in Bill's study, Wallack's Point, Connecticut in 2005. (Note the 'poor paintings' – by Chagall – on the wall.)

There cannot be a crisis next week. My schedule is already full.

Henry Kissinger

Towards the end of my work on that ambitious run of books on France – *Seven Ages of Paris, La Belle France* and *The Age of Napoleon* – I felt I had written enough on France for the time being. What should I do next? The thought of that long-contemplated novel still haunted me. Shortly after the first Gulf War I hatched a plan with Bill Buckley, 'Project Z' we called it, to write a joint thriller about Iraq. It would involve the quest, by evil Saddam Hussein, for a super-weapon that would terrorise Israel. I was to do all the technical stuff and the historical background, he the dialogue and the fictional drama. But it never got off the ground. Collaborating with Bill and his incredible schedule was like being lashed to the tail of a hurricane. So, encouraged by friends and publishers, I set to writing the present book, a kind of autobiography beginning where *A Bundle from Britain* left off. It would be, specifically, the life of a writer – not in any way a family portrait (my children preferred it that way). I had reservations: had I had a sufficiently interesting life? It had certainly been a long one, and along the way I had encountered many people whose lives had been much more interesting. Anyway, I would have a go. It would be timed for publication in 2005, marking the half-century from when I had first started my career as a book-writer. Of course, as usual, things slipped.

When I was already well into the writing, yet one more startling surprise occurred. In 2003 I received another of those stiff envelopes from Number 10. In it was an invitation to accept a knighthood, 'in recognition of services to French History'. I was stunned; I thought I had been given every possible award, far more than I deserved, already. Curiously, the honour came in the Foreign Office list. Some of my clever friends remarked, 'that's for spies, not writers. Now we know!' No comment. Of course I accepted, with delight. I thought of that famous remark by

Harold Macmillan, regarding his own life: 'Things never turn out quite how you expect, dear boy – but never miss an opportunity ...' It goes without saying that you don't choose the gongs you are given, any more than you can choose your parents. Peter Carrington, the most decorated man I know, with gongs ranging from the Order of the Garter down, once remarked that the one he most valued was the Military Cross, 'because I won it'. I suppose if a genie had offered me any choice I would have coveted beyond all others that RAF ribbon of diagonal purple and white stripes, the DFC. But the die was not cast that way. This time the investiture would be held by Prince Charles – the Queen, for almost the first time in her dutiful life, being confined for an operation on her knee. But the proceedings were quite as impressively circumstantial as I recalled from ten years previously.

We were a select band of knights. I shared the honour with an old friend, Michael Pakenham, who had just ceased being a highly successful ambassador to Poland, and Mick Jagger. Mick arrived late, dressed more for a gig than for Buckingham Palace, wearing trainers and what looked like a piece of dead, grey rat around his neck. The immeasurably smart colonel of the Scots Guards who was instructing us looked down from a great height and remarked with pointed courtesy: 'Oh, Sir Michael, how good of you to turn up!' Mick somehow managed to slip out of the investiture, to reappear haranguing the media in the courtyard. I am much honoured by the title, though I use it as little as possible. It sometimes seems archaic in this egalitarian age, if not positively counter-productive when it comes to making, for instance, an NHS appointment.

Then, just after the K, early in 2004 the telephone rang. It was my British publisher, George Weidenfeld, with an extraordinary proposal. Would I write the official life of Dr Henry Kissinger? I could hardly have been more surprised; it was a hugely flattering and tempting suggestion. But I felt I had now reached an age to be deterred by the mass of material that the work would involve (it was rumoured that, whereas Supermac measured his archives in feet, Kissinger's had been assessed by weight and totalled 33 tons). And I was more than halfway through my own memoirs. Although flattered, I declined.

Immediately I regretted the decision. How could anyone turn down an offer to write about one of the most interesting men of our times? So

I flew to New York to see Kissinger. We lunched and I came up with a counter-proposal. Maybe I could write about just one year, one key year, in his life?

'Which year?'

'1973?'

To my relief, his response was immediate: 'I think that's a great idea.'

So a deal was struck. At about the same time, the brilliant Oxford-based – and young – historian Niall Ferguson contracted to do the longer-term project, the whole official life. Niall and I talked over the two projects between ourselves and decided there need be no conflict. I started work.

But why 1973? First and foremost, it was the Big Year: the year of the signing of the pact to end the Vietnam War, the year of détente with the Soviet Union, but also the year when all hopes were undermined by Watergate. It was the year that Kissinger won the Nobel Peace Prize and became Secretary of State (he had been National Security Advisor since 1969), buttressing an increasingly debilitated President, who was under threat of impeachment. That October the world was rocked by the surprise Yom Kippur War in the Middle East; the previous month, in far-off Chile, Allende had been overthrown in a brutal coup by Pinochet. In fact, it was the year everything happened.

From a pile of Kissinger's books on the floor in Turville the owlish countenance gazed up at me for almost five years. That was the time it took me to write the story of one year in the life and activity of one statesman, the 56th US Secretary of State. It says perhaps more about his restless activity and those colossal archives than about my indolence, or indeed about three major illnesses that befell me one after another – none of which I could blame on my subject.

The work did not begin on exactly an auspicious note. For reasons which I won't go into, the project sparked a nuclear explosion between George, my publisher, and Andrew Wylie, my agent. There was a dreadful scene, just before a formal dinner in the French Embassy, where I feared momentarily that George might suffer a seizure. I had to make a choice. In the event, Wylie sacked me. It hadn't been an easy relationship. I had left Michael Sissons of PFD, who had supported me so loyally over the arduous work on Harold Macmillan, because I was unhappy with his representation in America, which I considered was paramount for me.

Wylie, strongly recommended to me by Arthur Schlesinger, came apparently joined at the hip with a highly reputable British literary agent, Gillon Aitken – himself a most likeable man. However, within a few months of my signing up, Wylie and Aitken had split up. I opted, with reservations, to stay with the Wylie faction. America was the keynote. In effect, it turned out to be the reverse of my plaint against Sissons/PFD. From time to time, I made my discontent known to Andrew. Whingeing and criticism were not his thing. So, at his instance, we parted. Though he continued to represent me honourably over the Kissinger book in New York, for the first time in my life I was agentless. An examination by *The Author* journal informed me that I was unique among British authors in the number of literary agents I had had: most normal writers over a normal career have one or two, at most three – and several publishers; I had had five agents, but only a couple of publishers. Something wrong somewhere. They could say I was not very good with agents. True, but in the course of the past half-century, though I have met many poor, under-funded authors, and some struggling publishers, I never met an agent on the bread line.

Operating without an agent for the next five years had some of the beneficial elements of bachelorhood. On the other hand, it was a lonely existence and I know I missed a few openings that a good agent might have brought an author. But I was indebted to Wylie for introducing me to two of the best editors on the US scene: Ash Green of Knopf (who did, superbly, my last books on France) and Michael Korda of Simon and Schuster, who elected to publish my Kissinger book. Michael was one of the legendary publishers of the transatlantic world, and we formed an instant rapport. He himself wrote one of the most engaging biographies of our times, *Charmed Lives*, about his eccentric uncle, Alex, the famous film producer/director, and other members of a most unusual clan, and he went on to write numerous other first-class books. Regrettably, by the time the Kissinger project came along Michael was already semi-retired living up at Millbrook, NY, within miles of where I went to school, tending the horses of his English wife, Margaret, and writing his own excellent books. The publishing process was to prove an unexpectedly rough ride, the roughest; without Michael Korda, and some valuable long-range back-up from London, the coaches would have left the track, catastrophically.

Those 33 tons of material were dispersed between various centres in Washington – notably the Library of Congress and Kissinger's own office on K-Street (I came to think it was named after him). To try to delve through them, I managed to get myself short-term fellowships at the Woodrow Wilson Center and the august Library of Congress, seated on Capitol Hill, just behind the Congress buildings. At the Woodrow Wilson I found myself among old friends, still, from the 1980s – like Sam Wells – and under the inspired aegis of ex-Congressman Lee Hamilton. As twenty-five years previously, I found it a superbly congenial place to work whence you could meet anyone you wanted to (Washington remained a city of wonderfully open doors). Lunches informally at circular tables in the WW had something that reminded me of St Antony's at its best; conversation was informed and uninhibited. Though I was duly grateful for their patronage, at the Library of Congress things were rather different. We worked in internal offices along an interminable corridor without opening to the light of day. It reminded me of the Pentagon at its worst. To find lunch you had to walk miles to a spiritless canteen. Any sense of collegiality was stifled. Perhaps worst of all, for a whole precious month my office was two doors down from one tenanted by that great Czech patriot, former President Václav Havel. But we hardly met; he was guarded by two zealous non-English-speaking security men who spirited him in and out of the building. His English was surprisingly imperfect, and non-interaction with one of the world's most interesting men reminded me of the wasted days in the Negev alongside General Volkogonov. As some philosopher once said, you can waste an hour, but never waste a man. Nevertheless, as we said farewell in 2005, he signed a copy of one of his books for me, picking up a red ballpoint to draw in a disarming red heart.

From my two bases, I was able to interview all the leading actors from Kissinger's year of 1973. It was surprising how many were still around, after thirty years. Perhaps they had all been very young, or maybe working for so tough a taskmaster was beneficial to longevity. Once again, I found no closed doors. Of the many I interviewed, two stand out, both ex-military men. One was Al Haig, Nixon's Chief of Staff in 1973, and the man who as Reagan's Secretary of State had courted outrage when he declared 'I'm in charge' after the 1981 shooting of the President. The other was Brent Scowcroft, Kissinger's deputy (and successor) at National Security. They were very different men. I found Haig's evidence not entirely reliable, nor him very likeable. Scowcroft, an educated former airman, came across as totally trustworthy. It was he, not the ultra-loyal Haig, who suggested to me that Nixon might well have been 'off the wall' with drink that crucial night in October 1973 when the US raised the state of military alert, in response to a Soviet threat of intervention in the Middle East. Kissinger, as newly appointed Secretary of State, was then in the hot seat.

Of course, the most valuable and indeed enjoyable factor in the course of the years of research and writing was the unstinting access to the subject himself that I was granted. Often I came back to that first connecting link through the person of Harold Macmillan, without which I would probably never have met Henry Kissinger. The terms of engagement were similar, but with one important difference: with both Macmillan and Kissinger I was promised full access plus an affidavit of non-interference, neither subject requiring to read my manuscript; but while there was attached to the Macmillan agreement the additional proviso that the biography was not to be published in his lifetime, Kissinger wished to be able to read in print what anyone was to write about him. (He was, nevertheless, always generous enough to assure me of his continuing friendship whatever I should write!) There was another, telling difference in the way we worked: while I always addressed Macmillan formally as 'HM' with Kissinger it was always 'Henry'.

Kissinger would suggest meetings in New York, or in his office in Washington where the indispensable Rosemary Niehuss (a very Wasp blonde whom I dubbed 'Miss Moneypenny') held sway. Most agreeable were my numerous visits to Kent, his and Nancy's idyllic country hide-out in the depths of upstate Connecticut. There peace was so absolute you never heard a plane (otherwise the restless Doctor would almost certainly have wanted to be on it), and there were occasional sightings of black bears in the woods. One hard winter, the bears consumed a neighbour's pony. You don't tangle. I could sometimes imagine that Henry, if cornered, could resemble one of those otherwise cuddly black bears; but I only saw it once, when a paw lashed out after I had committed an indiscretion with a DC columnist. I would be lodged in great comfort,

indeed luxury, in the guest house superbly furnished by the thoughtful
Nancy. From jelly beans to Imodium every possible requirement was
catered for. In the early mornings I would work on boxes of archives
shipped in by Rosemary, or on my own notes and questionnaires, as wild
deer came and grazed insouciantly a yard or two from the house. Mid-
morning, I would amble down to the main house, half a mile through
the woods, for a session. The great man's office lay at the top of the house,
accessible by the most terrifying steep staircase, like some Aztec pyramid
where the riser is twice the depth of the step. Often Henry would be
watching baseball, his favourite sport, on a vast screen. I remarked I had
always found it an incomprehensible sport. 'But it's not a sport!' he
interjected. 'It's a science – its mathematics: that's why it fascinates me.'
One of the men whom he had found most imposing was the great Joe
DiMaggio (married briefly to Marilyn Monroe). Along with Chairman
Mao, DiMaggio was one of the very few who, Kissinger said, 'would fill
the room' he entered.

In contrast to Harold Macmillan, Kissinger eschewed the use of a
tape-recorder; perhaps the harsh memories of Nixon and the notorious
Watergate tapes were too vividly in his mind. So I had to rely on my
handwritten notes, which I transcribed – on tape – later in the day. More
difficult were the mid-morning and afternoon breaks in the ferociously
heated salt-water swimming pool, surrounded by Nancy's very English
herbaceous border. Comparable to Macmillan and his table-talk, some
of Henry's best thoughts would emerge from the pool while he was
exercising in leisurely fashion. Out from the wallowy depths would flow
peerless recollections of Brezhnev in Moscow or San Clemente, of Golda
Meir and of his hero Sadat. That was even more difficult to record: no
notebook would have survived the water. Then we would often lunch –
always delectably, no Scottish Macmillan cold ham here, and à trois with
Nancy. As a young woman, Nancy had had a political indoctrination
on the staff of Governor Rockefeller. She was always included in every
conversation. I came away from every visit to Kent impressed by the depth
of affection that bonded this physically somewhat incongruous couple,
and by his reliance on her. (Sheelin, with her artist's antennae, picked up
on this in her first visit to Kent.) It all made for a happy atmosphere in
which to work.

After our evening work sessions, often the house would be filled for dinner by an intriguing miscellany of 'locals', writers, eminent doctors, academics from nearby Yale, New York gallery directors and Oscar and Annette de la Renta. It was always convivial; Henry loved good conversation, which he tended to dominate in professorial style, and the social life. Sometimes, rather sadly, I would recall in contrast the final, lonely and austere years of Harold Macmillan. After his retirement from government in 1976 with the fall of the Republicans and the advent of Carter, Kissinger led a life that was still crammed with interest and action. Under the George W. Bush administration, he would be invited almost monthly to the White House, or State Department, where the President or Condoleezza Rice would listen attentively to his accrued wisdom, while his professional and social life thrived on a multiplicity of levels. Though I always saw in Macmillan that essentially tragic side, there was nothing tragic in Kissinger's make-up. Had there been he would always have been saved by the restless intellect, the bon vivant bursting to escape, and by Nancy. Questioning him, and listening, was often like playing with a Chinese chess-player; his mind seemed to function on six different levels simultaneously.

Was he open with me during our many long sessions together? His long-time colleague Brent Scowcroft warned me, 'Henry could tell the same story ten different ways to ten different people and never fib!' He could be very opaque regarding questions about his private life. I once asked him what day he and Nancy had become engaged, to which he replied, 'You'll have to ask Nancy!' Did I like him? Yes, once the book was published I could say so. As I progressively became aware of the mountainous problems he faced in 1973 I respected his achievements all the more. I would in any case find it impossible to write a biography of someone whom I fundamentally disliked as a person. For all his image as a cold practitioner of realpolitik, I also came to detect in Henry a highly emotional being, and a soft heart. In office, he was recognised as being a tough taskmaster, yet all but an infinitesimal number of his old staff remained affectionately loyal, many continuing to clock up long years of service. In 2008, after I had been hospitalised with a triple heart-bypass, Henry would ring Sheelin almost daily to offer sympathy and kind advice (he, of course, trumped me by having had a quadruple!).

Did Kissinger ever express to me any lingering regrets? Yes: repeatedly, the failure to achieve a lasting peace in Vietnam. It continues to haunt him. My researches persuaded me, however, that the Watergate disaster was as much to blame for that defeat as any delinquency on the part of Kissinger's unceasing efforts in peace negotiations. I often feel that perhaps the harshest blow fate dealt him was to award him for Vietnam the poisoned chalice of the Nobel Peace Prize, in October 1973, in the middle of the Yom Kippur War. The honour swiftly turned to ashes in his mouth; in April 1975, with the fall of Saigon, he returned the gold medal. If only those honour-bestowing Scandinavians could have hung on for another few months! Surely history would accord Kissinger the Nobel Prize for achieving at least a first semblance of peace in the Middle East.

Henry Kissinger is renownedly sensitive about his position in the history books – sometimes, I would tell him, excessively so. But it is understandable. He remains for many a controversial figure. In the US I found people either hate him or love him – there is no halfway house. At the time of writing, Henry is still going strong, the mind as restlessly busy as ever, as he flies off to Moscow (where he has become close to Vladimir Putin, who trusts him), to China, Japan and Korea, and frequently to his native Germany. I speculate often about what he would like his legacy to be. I think it would be to achieve a major advance towards anti-proliferation of the scourge of nuclear weaponry. Here he continues to pursue the line of his major successes in détente with the Soviets, dating back to 1973. He once warned a troublesome Muscovite ambassador to 'hold his water or I will send him to Siberia. I know Brezhnev better than he does. Ask him if he has ever been kissed on the mouth by Brezhnev, as I have.' Not a memory that everyone would relish, nevertheless it speaks of the unique intimacy Kissinger established with those tricky players in the Kremlin. That is something I believe history will reveal to be of great moment, and a lasting testimony to one of America's most remarkable statesmen.

Just as in 1980–1, when I was working in the US on Macmillan, the Kissinger research gave me wonderful opportunities to catch up with old friends, and particularly to see as much as possible of Bill and Pat Buckley. On one happy occasion, we travelled together down to the family home in the South, which I remembered with affection from wartime visits – Camden, South Carolina. There we participated in debates organised by younger brother Reid Buckley's prestigious school for speakers, a foundation at least as badly needed in America, among businessmen and politicians, as in Britain. The standards were exacting. It was a pleasurable interlude, but I was concerned by my old friend's state of health. He seemed to have little puff, was unable to walk far, struggled for oxygen; it was hard to see someone once so fit struggle for breath. I wondered whether it could possibly be the onset of emphysema, the dread disease which was to kill his sister Jane a short while later. He hotly denied it, swiftly changing the subject. I was left wondering, and worrying.

Later in 2005 there was a halcyon interlude for Bill. It was the fiftieth anniversary of his founding of *National Review*, which had in effect launched the conservative movement in the US. Bill and Pat were honoured at a special event in the White House. All the surviving Buckley clan were there, so were the big guns of the US media and politics. It was a grand occasion. I was invited, as one of seven (and the only alien) to contribute a homily; it was a great honour, but, alarmingly, I was slotted to appear after Henry Kissinger and several of the wittiest and most trenchant speakers in the capital. The President, George W. Bush, appeared and delivered a heartening tribute at the end of the ceremony. He then escorted Bill and Pat back into the White House proper, for a cosy lunch *à quatre*. I questioned Bill about it later.

'Al, I think I may have put my foot in it!'

How, I asked?

'Well, you know, on the way into the small private dining room, there are some shelves – vitrines. The President stopped at one and took out a revolver. "That", he said, in a voice of awe, "was the gun we took off Saddam Hussein when we caught him." "Mr President," said I, "now that's very interesting. Why, I remember President Eisenhower once showing me the pistol with which Hitler shot Eva Braun!" George W. looked a bit discomfited. Do you think I was tactless?'

Oh, Bill – only you could have got away with such a supreme piece of one-upmanship and wandered off with a smile!

A year or so later, in May 2007, I was invited back to the White House on my own account. Staying with the Kissingers at the end of 2006, before we went off to speak at Yale together, I brought Henry a copy of the new edition of *A Savage War of Peace*. It had just been republished by the *New York Review of Books* in their Classic Book series, with a new preface I had written relating the Algerian saga to Iraq. Typically, Henry read it overnight and asked if I had another copy; he would like to send it to President Bush. I thought no more of it. Then, a couple of months later I was granted sudden media fame when a CNN reporter asked the President how he was planning to spend the Martin Luther King holiday. He replied: 'Reading a book – by Alistair Horne ...' As, rather unfairly, book-reading was presumed not to be the favourite indulgence of the forty-third President, the item made news. In the middle of a snowstorm, the US media – corralled by that skilled interviewer Charlie Rose – trooped down to Turville. The book which – through the lethargy of publishers – had previously been selling in the Pentagon on a black-market basis at hundreds of dollars a copy, suddenly took off.

There followed an invitation to a tête-à-tête in the Oval Office in May 2007. Perhaps even more than 10 Downing Street or Buckingham Palace, the atmosphere in this rather modest house whence radiates the greatest power in the world is awe-inspiring. People speak in whispers. In the Oval Office were assembled nine of the President's top aides, including the all-powerful Carl Rove and Steve Hadley, a successor of Kissinger's as National Security Advisor. It was somewhat unnerving. What had I to say that could possibly justify the presence of all these important figures? But George W. was disarmingly courteous, showing me round this room, no larger than an average drawing-room, where so much history had been made, explaining the great desk, a present from Queen Victoria in 1880 (and fashioned from the timbers of HMS *Resolute*), and how it had been modified for FDR's wheelchair and for his Scottie, Fala, to hop in and out from underneath the desk. We then sat down and talked. It all lasted more like an hour than the statutory twenty minutes. On this and a later occasion in London, the much denigrated President seemed remarkably relaxed, with all the time in the world, sharply tuned-in, well read (contrary to the uncharitable view of him) and a most attentive listener. He looked as though he had just come from a week's holiday on a boat – no stress, no strain. It was a very different image to the robotic figure seen on television. There was no hardship in conversing with the most powerful man in the world; I was made to feel totally at ease.

He quizzed me pointedly about de Gaulle's exit from Algeria. 'How did he get out?' I replied: 'Very badly, Mr President. He lost his shirt. He had to give up everything.' The President looked glum, then, accepting the parallels with Iraq, remarked: 'We are not going to lose. We are not going to get out in a hurry.' It was a theme he repeated with emphasis several times: 'We are not going to lose. We are not going to run.' Catching me off-balance, he suddenly popped the question, 'who are your five best British prime ministers?' Momentarily fazed, I couldn't think of more than four. They included Macmillan. I then added, 'I'm afraid I can't add Tony Blair to the list!' He looked disappointed, and replied: 'All I can say is that whatever Blair has said to me on foreign affairs he has always been as good as his word, he has always done exactly what he said he was going to do. I think he is a great man.' I groaned inwardly. He then questioned me intensively about Macmillan, and – surprisingly – about Dorothy and Boothby. I observed how lonely at the top Macmillan had found life as PM, and didn't he find it so too? He laughed, 'No – look at all these guys! I long for peace, to be by myself sometimes. They give me no peace!'

As I took my leave, he expressed his admiration for Henry Kissinger, praising him especially for his great help with Putin – 'though I think maybe he's a bit too kind on the guy!' I left the White House with a positive impression of Bush's personality, somewhat unexpectedly, but puzzled that so thoughtful a man could appear to have been so misinformed, so misled, by his advisers on Iraq. That same evening, at a dinner, I met for the first time Colin Powell, leader in the first Gulf War and more recently Secretary of State. The moment Powell came into the room I was struck by the sense that here I was meeting a man of extraordinary stature and integrity. My plate was more than full that day. But Washington was not a happy town. Bush was deeply unpopular, the dreadful echoes of Abu Ghraib were still ricocheting around, Nevertheless I left it with many regrets. As always, it had been a fruitful and happy place to work.

So ended the three-year research phase of the Kissinger book. To me, research was always the best part of any literary effort. Now began the slog of writing, followed by the worse slog of editing, proofreading and repeat proofreading. This time the process was the toughest ever. In the first place, there was a 3,000-mile gulf between me and the publishers in New York, Simon and Schuster, who were masterminding production. Worse, there was a split in command between them and Michael Korda, buried away on his farm up at Millbrook. With his sure touch, and the experience of having edited both Nixon and Kissinger, he gave me a report on all the chapters as I wrote them. I obeyed Michael's injunctions almost to the letter. They were enormously helpful. But there was also a zealous young woman, nominally in charge as senior editor who came up with her own set of editorial queries. These totalled some thirty per chapter on just the first three, then stopped. Some were helpful, many were not; all involved a great deal of extra work. Meanwhile in London, Ion Trewin at Weidenfeld & Nicolson was producing his own comments. I was poleaxed. Dealing as best I could with her first batch, I waited for her input on the remaining thirteen chapters. They never came through. Then, in the run-up to Christmas, Simon and Schuster – one of America's top publishers – hit the buffers. Fifteen per cent of their staff were sacked, including the senior editor. In the ensuing mayhem, somehow the illustrations for Kissinger got lost. The editorial work had to be cleaned up in London, by the brilliant young Bea Hemming at Weidenfeld.

The whole episode of Simon and Schuster was an unhappy one – about the worst I have ever had in publishing. But for Michael Korda, the project might well have foundered. Apart from him, as commissioning editor, I was never made to feel that the publishers had their heart in it. There was little sympathy for, or interest in, either Kissinger or Nixon. The PR department at Simon and Schuster would send me pages-long question-naires to fill in and ask 'What's new in the book?' It's not easy for the author to see the wood for the trees. What was new, I proposed feebly, was a new look at Nixon, a much underrated President; a first authorised account from Kissinger himself, with much new first-hand material; and the fact that it was by an outsider, a Brit, with perhaps a different lens of objectivity.

Then, on top of the labours of production, in 2006, 2007 and 2008 I was struck down by a series of unexpected major illnesses, starting with pneumonia contracted in a frosty May in Southern Italy and culminating with that heart-bypass, over which my subject was so warmly solicitous.*

Nevertheless, despite all vicissitudes, eventually the book came out, with the title *Kissinger: 1973, The Crucial Year* in New York in June 2009 and, that September, in London as *Kissinger's Year: 1973*. (The latter was, I thought, a slightly snappier title, and the London edition also had a more striking jacket.) I went to the US to promote it, a tour that included an appearance on the *Charlie Rose* show. But was Henry, a man highly sensitive about his image and his place in history, and an academic perfectionist, happy with the result? He and Nancy generously gave not one but two splendid dinners, one in New York, one up at Kent. He was graciously welcoming and full of smiles – though a number of, mostly minor, criticisms came out at a morning tutorial we had at Kent. Then, when I returned home, I received a blast of fury. It was as if he hadn't read the small print, and that someone had alerted him to offending passages in the book. They principally concerned his Vietnam nego-tiations and highly technical details of rocketry talks with the Russians. I suddenly felt what it must have been like to be a member of his staff who had underperformed on an important task. But I also felt he was being unfair, that *he* had got it wrong in this instance, not the poor bloody biographer. I bit back, and fearfully awaited his response. Back came an e-mail with just one word: 'PEACE!'

Whatever it was that had upset him, Henry forgave me. In October 2009, submitting to the allure and enticement of Warden Margaret Mac-Millan, he came over to give a talk at St Antony's. He spoke for an hour and a half, without notes and without pause. I was up on the dais, with the Warden, supposedly as moderator, firing questions, but I was supernumerary, and neither of us could get a word in. From a packed, tough Oxford audience, Kissinger got a standing ovation. There was no demo, no nasty questions about Chile or Cambodia. (I felt he was almost disappointed.) In the annals of the College, indeed of the University at

---

* One day while I was recuperating in hospital, he telephoned, urging me to get up and exercise and recounting how, when he had had his quadro, on his daily walks he had made a target of a red fire-extinguisher twenty yards down the corridor. When, one day, he finally made it to the extinguisher, he embraced and kissed it.

large, the evening was judged to have been an outstanding success. The Doctor palpably enjoyed himself. He spent the night with us at Turville, leaving at 7 a.m. to host a dinner for Chinese grandees in New York. His parting words of comfort words were: 'Alistair, if they don't like the book, it's me they hate, not you!'

Yes, the reviews were frankly disappointing, both at home and in the US, whether for the reason generously proffered by the subject or not. In the harshest review I've had on any book ever, the *Washington Post* began a longish demolition with 'Poor Alistair Horne . . .' That said about everything, though it went on: 'He might have thought more about the idea first. Kissinger's version of events has been told, retold and retold again.' But, then, I had been pretty rude about the *Post* in its handling of Watergate in 1973. Eminent journals can have memories like elephants. Speaking privately, the editor of the prestigious *New York Review of Books* dismissed the book as 'a love story' and declined to review it at all. In the UK press, what was particularly gratifying to me personally was David Owen's support, in the *Daily Telegraph*, for what I had written about Chile; in taking on 'the traditional view of the international Left who hold Kissinger personally responsible for the overthrow of Salvador Allende'. This, coming from a former foreign secretary, and one-time socialist politician seemed to carry particular weight on an issue where I had tried so hard, over many years, to realign accepted views.

It had been quite a slog, but it had also been – in the word Harold Macmillan so often chose – fun. I would not have missed the opportunity for anything. I had learned a lot – always, for me, the main point of writing books. Among other things, I had learned just how difficult it was to have been the first Jewish secretary of state in America. When Kissinger first came to that office, in September 1973, he had – predictably – two major critics: first, the Arab world; secondly, the Russians, with their long, innate history of anti-Semitism. Third came the Israelis, under the sturdy Golda Meir (whom he irreverently nicknamed 'Miss Israel'), always pressing Kissinger to do more for them, simply because he was Jewish. But fourthly, and – at least to me – the most unexpected, as well as the most troublesome to him, there was the indigenous and all-powerful Jewish lobby at home, in Washington and New York. In the book I tried to give full play to all these pressures on a newly appointed US Secretary of State, coming to office at a time of unprecedented challenge in the Middle East, plunged almost at once into the Yom Kippur War. To me it made his achievements there all the more remarkable.

21

LA PENULTIMA

Bertie 'the Biter', wants to have a go at Apple No. 1 as much as the author.

It is one of the bad effects of living in one's own time that one never knows the truth of it till one is dead.

Horace Walpole

Instead of saying, 'let's have one last *copita*, for the road, superstitious Andalusians always talk about *la penultima*. So this chapter is, I promise, *La Penultima* ... The completion of *Kissinger* was also a time of searing loss. In England, I had already lost two of my dearest and oldest friends: in 2002, Miles Norfolk; in 2006, Peter Rawlinson – two people whom I admired as much as I enjoyed their company, both of them leading Roman Catholics with great hearts. Then, within a period of just a year, from 2007 to 2008, there fell four irreplaceable friends in America: Arthur Schlesinger, Van Galbraith, and Bill and Pat Buckley.

First, on the last day of February 2007, it was Arthur – aged ninety. Only a few months previously, in New York, Sheelin and I had taken him out for lunch. Though his essential merriment never left him, he was painfully frail and had difficulty eating, but wouldn't have his favoured Martini because he said he had to work that afternoon. I teased him: 'Arthur, surely at your age you can't work in the afternoon?' He replied, 'I have to, otherwise I can't fit in my eight hours writing a day.' *Eight hours a day!* I wished I could remember when I had last achieved that! He survived long enough for his final book* to be published, the last of some thirty, full of piquant wit and erudition.

Barely two months later, Pat Buckley was taken off to hospital. She was to face one more operation in a series on her legs – those incredibly long, slim adornments once rated 'the best in the business' in New York. Much of the pain and suffering she went through seemed to stem from a cata-strophic ski accident she had suffered in her beloved Rougemont back in 1965. For this I could never quite cease to suffer remorse: had I not urged

---

* *Journals 1952–2000*, Penguin 2007.

her and Bill to join us in the Chalet Bärgsunne five winters previously, she might never have taken up skiing, and the accident would never have happened. Her legs were simply not designed for skiing. So, after years of pain, she went into Stamford Hospital. Unthinkably, amputation was threatened. Septicaemia set in, and a short while later she died.

Bill was shattered; he never quite recovered. For all the nuclear rows they had had in latter years, without Pat. Bill could not survive. A deep moroseness set in. The iron seemed, in the words of Sartre, to have entered his soul. On television, to his friend Charlie Rose, he admitted that his life was complete and that he longed for death. I reproached him, as he had indeed often reproached me in moments of extreme Black Dog, reminding him that, for so devout a Catholic, 'Despair is a mortal sin.' He denied that it was despair; he was just world-weary. But, not just Pat, so much of value in his life had abandoned him, perhaps predominantly his hearing – which meant that he could no longer enjoy the banter of general conversation, or, worse still, experience the delight that music and his own playing of the harpsichord gave him. Then deafness forced him to give up his *Firing Line*, the longest-running show on serious US television. Bit by bit, like the peeling of an onion, life was stripped from him.

To me, however, he remained to the end the wonderful companion he had always been, over some sixty-five years. Physically, emphysema and then diabetes were added to the burden he was already shouldering. Without Pat, he neglected himself. Shortly after her death, he was found in a semi-coma on a train returning from Washington. Rushed to hospital, lovingly tended (though he was an impossible patient) by his one and only son, Christo, he pulled through. Though 3,000 miles apart we would telephone each other two, three times a week. During the arduous slog of the Kissinger book, his unfailing support and encouragement never flagged. Then one day he rang, in a gloom, to announce: 'Al, for the first time in my life I don't have a book to write!' (He'd already published more than fifty.) Almost reflexively, I replied: 'Why don't you write a book about Ronald Reagan? No one knows him better than you. After all, you created him!' He thanked me warmly, than sat down to hammer out what would be his last testament. It was all but complete when the Reaper came.

When you have had a friend all your life, you somehow tend to invest them with immortality, you think they'll be there for ever. Periodically in that last year, Christo would warn me, 'Pup's a very sick man,' but – 3,000 miles away – I would refuse to accept it. The first intimation came when that November we hatched a plan for me to fly out and, on my way to New York, join him in at his temporary writing hide-out in Florida. But he changed his plans at the last minute; I had to bin the tickets. I realised he was not his old self. We had one last happy reunion, at Wallack's Point. Paradise though it always was, gazing out over Long Island Sound, without Pat it was a house without a soul.

Two months later, in January 2008, Bill's closest buddy from Yale days, and a friend of mine for many years too, Van Galbraith, died, after a ten-year battle against creeping cancer. I went to see him in New York in that last month; his outrageous sense of humour was there to the end. For, however long his death had seemed inevitable, it left a gaping hole in our world.

We had barely returned home from saying farewell to Van in New York when the telephone rang in Turville. It was Christo, with the news that his father had been found dead by his desk in his cluttered garage/office in Wallack's Point, at that battle-worn computer apparently writing a column. He died in the saddle, as he would have wished. Happily, my daughter Camilla, Bill's goddaughter and friend from childhood of Christo, happened to be in New York and went to the funeral. Sheelin and I flew over for the memorial service. It was a grand affair, a full Catholic mass in New York's St Patrick's Cathedral, which was packed, bursting at the seams. Only Christo and Henry Kissinger delivered lay eulogies; they were brilliant, and moving, but both nearly broke down. I could not have done it. Said Henry, in his tribute: 'we mourn him for his civility even to adversaries, his conviviality, his commitment and, above all, the way he infused our lives with a very special presence ... all of us give thanks to a benign Providence that enabled us to walk part of our way with this noble, gentle and valiant man who was truly touched by the grace of God.' There was something profoundly touching, and American, about a Jew addressing the convocation at this most holy of Catholic churches in the US.

Across the board in America the outpouring of grief, admiration and affection was no less extraordinary. Ronald Reagan (who had died four years earlier) was quoted as having once remarked, in praise of Bill: 'You didn't just part the Red Sea – you rolled it back, dried it up and left exposed, for all the world to see, the naked desert that is statism ... And then, as if that weren't enough, you gave the world something different, something in its weariness it desperately needed, the sound of laughter and the sight of the rich, green uplands of freedom.' The outpouring came not just from friends and fans, but – perhaps astonishingly, given how, as a controversial polemicist, Bill had never spared his opponents – from far and wide. Tribute was paid to his remarkable industry – 4.5 million words in 5,600 newspaper columns over the years, and all those published books, but even more to his 'graceful, often self-deprecating wit' and his personal kindness (*Time* magazine). In Britain, where he was not a household name, the *Independent* provided an admiring list of his attributes: 'Editor, novelist, wit, polemicist, bon viveur, one-time CIA agent, failed New York mayoral candidate, scourge of liberals and, not least, an accomplished harpsichordist', before adding that another reason for liking him 'surely, was his personal charm, humour and grace. Even at his most excoriating, Buckley was hard to dislike.' It was as if America collectively – and not just America – had suddenly realised that it had lost a truly Renaissance man, a rarity in this age: a hero in our times devoid of heroes.

I too realised, suddenly, what a great man had been my friend for those sixty-five years. Of course I had known it, but there it was facing me in lapidary sentences. But the eulogies didn't make the pain any less. Sixty-five years is a long time; in terms of the American history we learned as boys together at Millbrook School, it would stretch from Appomattox at the close of the Civil War to the Great Depression of 1929. 'Goodnight, sweet prince, and flights of angels sing thee to thy rest,' Camilla wrote in a valedictory note.

To me Bill was indeed ever a prince among friends; he really taught me the meaning of friendship. His was never wanting; he was always there, always with his cheery 'Hi, Al!' I sometimes pondered over what our friendship was based on. Perhaps it was because there were 3,000 miles separating us. But perhaps because we also had an unspoken acceptance of each other's essential loneliness as writers. Strange, for someone so gregarious, but I always felt that the speed of Bill's phenomenal mind induced a certain isolation – to wit, his impatient urge to leave any, even the most fun, dinner party by 10 p.m. I introduced him to skiing; he led me to Bach. I think I may have disappointed him: in not converting to Catholicism, in not following his conservatism all the way and in not having my book on Henry Kissinger (which I dedicated to him) ready for him to read. But he never chided.

It was more than just friendship I owed Bill. In his perpetual striving for excellence, he was, professionally, a lifelong beacon. He wrote over fifty books, I some twenty, but I doubt I would have written any but for Bill's example and constant exhortation. In our youth, we had both venerated Antoine de Saint-Exupéry, for his eloquence and carefree courage. In *Wind, Sand and Stars* Saint-Exupéry wrote:

> Thus is the earth at once a desert and a paradise ... life may scatter us and keep us apart; it may prevent us from thinking very often of one another, but we know that our comrades are somewhere 'out there' ... bit by bit, nevertheless, comes over us that we shall never again hear the laughter of our friend, that this one garden is forever locked against us. And at that moment begins our true mourning ...

Yes – and no. I cannot quite accept that this great spirit is not still 'out there', somewhere. I shall hear his laughter, and the 'Hi, Al!' every remaining day of my life.

Less than a month after Bill's memorial service, I flew back to New York to deliver a eulogy at a service for Van. All those bereavements, the death of Bill in particular, brought with them some warning, some intimation of mortality, that I too might be nearing the buffers.

I suffer from chronic asthma. So do far too many people these days.* As air pollution has worsened it has apparently become one of the most prevalent and apparently incurable diseases. It's a beastly affliction. I've had it since I was nine, on and off; in 1943 I lied about it so as to get into the RAF and, mysteriously, never had it again over the next fairly arduous four years in the forces, in many asthma-inducing circumstances. On

* Asthma affects 7 per cent of the population of the United States, 6 per cent of British people and a total of 300 million worldwide.

demob, it came back with a bang. So is there something psychosomatic about asthma? Doctors really don't seem to understand, or know how to cope with it, much better than they did when I was a child. It's the same old potions: antibiotics and prednisolone, prednisolone and antibiotics.

If you have never had it, try to imagine what it's like to be buried alive, slowly suffocating. I sometimes think of the wretched, innocent civilians of Hué, buried alive in their hundreds by the vengeful Viet Minh during the Tet Offensive of 1968, or the victims of Iran's Revolutionary Guard, dying slowly in shallow earth pits, unable to breathe. The chairman of the British Asthma Council shocked guests at a recent gala by telling them to breathe through a straw to experience what an asthma attack feels like. That was what hit me one Friday in March 2010 in Marrakech where we were on holiday. It struck in the middle of the night. I got out of bed and sat up in a chair, struggling for air. No improvement. It was the worst attack I could remember. At one moment I thought I might not make it to the dawn; would the overworked ticker simply give up? After a quite eventful life, is this how one goes – not with a bang but a whimper, I wondered? I just wanted to tell Sheelin, who was still sleeping, how much I loved her, and how wonderful she was, and what a nuisance I had been. Just in case . . . But I couldn't raise the puff to get out a word. When I heard the muezzin that dawn, I gave thanks to the Almighty whom both our religions share.

The hotel (a hide-out so magical that I reveal its identity only to my most discerning friends) called a doctor at 7 a.m. He came at once and stayed for an hour. Dr M, fiftyish, trained in Paris and Lille, had an encyclopaedic knowledge of chest problems. Diagnosing asthma cum severe bronchial infection, he started, to my surprise, by warning me that we had come in the worst week for asthma, with maximum pollen count from the olive trees. Yet Marrakech is where Churchill famously went in 1943 to recover from pneumonia under its pure blue skies. He would not have fared well now. With a population grown to over a million, its skies are often clouded with pollution. Asthma is a major concern, now endemic in Marrakech, and is exacerbated by those olive trees in the spring.

Dr M's English was rudimentary, his French excellent, his earthy sense of humour a delight – always good for a patient. He then prescribed and provided a compendium of six sets of pills, one appropriately called Exomuc, then asked me to lower my pants and gave me a painful shot of cortisone in the bum. One thing he did not have with him was alcohol for swabbing the skin round the injection. In the bathroom he discovered an exotic phial of Sheelin's best scent and sprayed that on the assaulted area with the words, 'Better not tell the manufacturer what part of your anatomy it was used on!' As he left he gave himself two bursts of Gardenia behind the ears: 'It may make my wife suspicious, but it will impress my colleagues in the clinic no end.' By Sunday we had become good friends. In true Arab fashion, he kissed me on both cheeks and called me 'my friend'.

There are always complications. Thanks to my sleeping in an armchair, my ankles had swollen with oedema. Under Dr M's ministrations, I began to feel a little better, though able to walk only a few paces before puffing. But it was a slow up-and-down process, good days followed by bad ones – not the best way to spend time in Marrakech, and certainly not for my long-suffering consort. On the Tuesday I was carted off to a *pneumologue* for X-rays and so on. The *pneumologue* was on the second floor in a pretty unpromising suburb, a *banlieu* which the tourist never sees, a red hell of hot dusty charmless streets with no green anywhere. In rural slums around it we passed an intermix of the most desperately poor encampments – the worst I have seen anywhere in the world – juxtaposed with opulent villas under construction. At the *pneumologue*'s it took six hefty Moroccans to hoist the shaky wheelchair up two flights of concrete stairs, as though I were some medieval despot in a palanquin. Following the session I decided to risk it and walk down.

We had to postpone our flight home by three days. When I got back to Turville I was immediately and – for once – gratefully popped into the local hospital for three days of welcome oxygenation. In consequence, sickness in Marrakech delayed the present memoirs yet again. The asthma had gone, temporarily, but when will the dark enemy come back? Coupled with thoughts about the victims of Tet, I ruminate on Orwell's *Nineteen Eighty-Four*, and its terrifying apocalypse of Room 101, orchestrated by the fearsome O'Brien: 'I told you that you knew the answer already. Everyone knows it. The thing that is in Room 101 is the worst thing in the world.' If that which confronted Winston Graham in Room 101, the 'worst thing in the world' for him, was rats, mine is being buried alive. That's how it will be, I expect.

But, for the time being, God has been merciful. Since that dread brush with eternity in Marrakech, I have been permitted to return to my desk: to complete these memoirs, write articles on asthma, Barbados, Aung San Suu Kyi, the new Savoy Hotel, book reviews on Dien Bien Phu, update introductions for some of my own books, and start work on a study of battles of the twentieth century. I haven't been exactly idle, but finishing this literary vagabondage gives me time to construe whether over a half-century at it could possibly constitute a success. But then, for a writer, what is success? I find myself rereading a book that has languished on my shelves these many years, Cyril Connolly's *Enemies of Promise*. Then a highly regarded and feared critic, Connolly is now largely a forgotten figure, but in his book he wrote meaningfully of the 'weeds' that can smother an author, likening them to those in George Crabbe's 'Blighted Rye' in his poem 'The Village'. Of all the noxious weeds, Connolly set success, 'the Slimy Mallows', as 'the most insidious' that confront an author: 'a kind of moving staircase from which an artist, once on, has great difficulty in getting off'. In support, he quotes Trollope – 'success is a poison that should only be taken late in life, then only in small doses' – and Somerset Maugham – 'success improves the character of a man, it does not always improve the character of an author.'

For Connolly himself, a constant worry was 'how to live another ten years', meaning, how 'to write a book that will hold good for ten years'. On that score I suppose I could plead success in that *The Price of Glory* has been consistently in print for almost fifty years, with several others well over Connolly's ten-year mark. Yet I have never written the novel I set out to write all those years ago, while still in the army. I regret this. That is failure. And any conceits of a long literary life were somewhat watered down with a New Year's present of 2011, in the shape of my Public Lending Right return from Ireland: the handsome sum of €13.68. I have certainly never made a fortune from the pen. I suppose if I had taken the option of going to Harvard, back in 1947, and thence on to the Business School, instead of to our Cambridge, I might look back on a rather more prosperous career. But I doubt it would have been a happier one, or offering as much fulfilment.

In one of his more acidic moments, Dr Johnson declared: 'No man but a blockhead ever wrote, except for money.' Thence, I must be a kind of 'blockhead', but one of a large company: I am certainly poorer than when I started on my literary vagabondage. The profit-and-loss account doesn't look brilliant.

Why does one write? Of course it's a kind of compulsion. My wife observes consolingly, 'Well, you couldn't really do anything else!' True. In my Walter Mitty life, I would been delighted – alternatively – to have been a *good* landscape painter or to have run an art gallery, preferably with someone else's money. But, no, I wouldn't have chosen differently; I've had a wonderfully rewarding and interesting life, in terms of people, places and events – and performing on my own terms. My fellow historian, Arthur Schlesinger, had perhaps the most unquenchable intellectual curiosity of any writer I've ever known. I'd like to think that some fraction of that enquiring, inquisitive mentality is what has sustained me. There is always something, somebody, new over the next hill. My new book, for instance, brings me to study twentieth-century naval battles in the Pacific: *terra incognita* up to now. But the exploration enthrals me.

There's no denying that writing can be a tough and lonesome pursuit. That's what drives many a writer to the bottle, or the pursuit of illicit, and often illusory, loves. Like actors, we authors are a vain, insecure lot, lusting after praise and reassurance. Our profession is, however, nowhere near as harsh as the stage, where even the most successful actor has constantly to wait for the telephone to ring: a life 'fraught with disappointments', wrote Somerset Maugham, who knew the theatre well:

> Long stretches of idleness must be endured. The prizes are few and can be held but for a short time. The rewards are inadequate. The actor is at the mercy of fortune and the inconstant favour of the public. He is forgotten as soon as he ceases to please.

The well-meaning lady who would ask me 'What do you *actually* do?' would also assume that the writing of a book is also the end of story. But of course it's not; it's more like the one-tenth of an iceberg you see above the water. The invisible nine-tenths below the surface constitutes the drudge of editing, rereading one's increasingly leaden sentences again and again, checking proofs, providing and selecting illustrations and maps;

then the labour of helping promote and sell the finished product. Of the residual, visible 10 per cent, perhaps half is occupied in researching a book, which an Oxford don once dubbed 'a state of resentful coma', but which, to me, is where all the fun is to be found. The actual 5 per cent that represents the writing can often be a terrible sweat, an unnatural act to one born with a slothful temperament, or with a tendency to distraction when even the act of tidying the desk can come as a welcome diversion.

I have been blessed with much good fortune; never had a book turned down by a publisher, and – on the whole – treated with exceptional kindness by the critics. Mostly I've been lucky with my editors; one may complain of the lapses, the desuetude, of publishers and literary agents, but that may be largely ritualistic – my present editor groans: 'authors *always* complain about their publishers'. If I were to presume to offer advice to a new young writer, to learn from the crass mistakes I have made, I would say select your literary agent as carefully as you would a marriage partner, perhaps with even greater care than your publisher; and, having made the choice, don't row with them. They always win in the end. And perhaps another caution, learned the hard way: don't be too grand for the 'box'. Vulgarian, debasing, and lowest-common-denominatorish as TV may be, that's where the money, and the publicity – if not the future – lie. For unless you embrace TV, it's hard to make a living wage.

We historians are motivated by an urge to understand, to learn. But do we think we can 'do good' by influencing politicians and leaders with the lessons we have learned? It's always rewarding to be heeded. Or do we write merely to entertain, or for our own satisfaction? Writing in the comfortable nineteenth century, Samuel Butler, the satirical novelist and author of *The Way of All Flesh*, reckoned that an author should write only for readers 'of between twenty and thirty, as nobody read or changed their opinions after that'. A qualification that would not embrace many movers-and-shakers today. I wrote *The Price of Glory* with impassioned anti-war sentiment. It came out in the only year since VJ-Day when Britain did not lose a serviceman in war, America had not yet become deeply embroiled in Vietnam, and five years before Israel and the Arabs savaged each other in the Six Day War. I can't claim to have had any influence on the Vietnam War; though my books published in Israel did have an influence, apparently, on their military assessments. On the other hand as the Cuban Missiles Crisis broke in October 1962, President Kennedy was reading Barbara Tuchman's great, admonitory book on 1914, *The Guns of August*. Might it have persuaded him to step back from the awful brink of nuclear war? President George W. Bush read, in early 2007, my book on the Algerian War, *A Savage War of Peace*. Had he read it *before* going into Iraq in 2003, might it have caused him to pause and reflect? I would like to think so. On the other hand, such was the bellicose commitment of his advisers, that lethal alliance of born-again Evangelicals and committed Zionists, as with those hell-bent trains that had 'left the station' in 1914, it seems improbable.

Thinking back on places, people and things of which I've written over the past half-century is an invigorating trip down memory lane. How lucky, how spoilt we were! By way of comparison the state of the world today is hardly encouraging. Going back to Square One, the British armed forces, which employed me for four highly formative years, now – after the depredations of successive Labour and Tory administrations – seems reduced to its feeblest state since I was demobbed in 1947. Egypt, where I spent two exciting and instructive years is, as I write, currently tearing itself apart, and threatening the precarious balance in the Middle East as a whole. My whole writing life has been bracketed by the dark clouds emanating from that hate-torn fragment of the globe which now menaces all of us. In 1946 the killers of the Jewish Irgun and Stern brought terrorism out of Pandora's box. On 9/11 Al Quaeda gave it an extra spin towards perfection – the human bomb. Where will it end now?

On unhappy Palestine, still in bondage since 1967, the historian may be entitled to note the parallel of some sombre dates: between 1870 and 1914, the period when France's Alsace-Lorraine was under the boot of Prussia until the war which would restore it (at a cost, incidentally of some sixteen million lives), was of exactly the same duration as that from the Israeli occupation of the West Bank, which followed the Six Day War, to the present day. How much longer will the Arab world go on shouting into the wind, without extremists demonstrating their impatience with another atrocity directed against the West? Equally, one might ask, plaintively, why should one's grandchildren, and their grandchildren, continue to be plagued by what is basically parochial, internecine savagery between two sets of Old Testament tribes, and which bears so little relevance to Western ethos?

It's perhaps somewhat more cheering to come back nearer home, to Germany and France, whose conflicts equally bedevilled the first twenty years of my life, but are now in a state of residual peace. Germany, where I cut my teeth as a writer and whose future direction so preoccupied the minds of us journalists back in the 1950s, has turned out to be one of the world's most respected democracies, its economy a constant triumph. And France is, gloriously, forever France, like a beautiful and capricious woman, impossible but eternally exquisite.

As for my adoptive country, the US of A, and my own England, one may weep at where the occasional fits of arrogance and imbecility take us, and – we writers especially – at the constant devaluation of the language which accompanies that chimaera called 'progress'. Yet life goes on, the things we value survive. Few countries offer a better quality of life than Britain, or a more congenial environment for the writer – for all the menaces of global warming – which now freezes us to death every winter. And which, if we believe the experts, can destroy this country, and civilisation as a whole, at one lash of its all-powerful paws.

So at what point should a writer put up his hands, switch off the computer, and call it a day? I remember that doyenne of English novelists, Rumer Godden, at a publisher's party celebrating her ninetieth birthday, declaring with force: 'You don't give up writing, it gives you up.' Recently the great tenor, Placido Domingo, at 69, put it more succinctly: 'If I rest, I rust.' Amen to both. Like Placido, I'm incapable of resting. At the risk of sounding pompous, presumptuous or fulsome, I suppose I go on writing not least to repay gratefully some of the pleasure and enlightenment that writing has given me for over half-a-century.

ACKNOWLEDGEMENTS

My distinguished colleague at St Antony's, Timothy Garton Ash, observes, 'History is History, but Memoirs are the art of the fallible.' Quite so. I like to think I am blessed with a better than average memory – I can recall all the names in my class at prep school – but I am constantly made aware of gaps, fallibility, in the hard disk. So this memoir is drawn from a multiplicity of recorded sources: fragmentary diaries (alas, I failed to keep one consistently), boxes full of random notes, and copious correspondence and cuttings (my long-suffering wife complains that I am a squirrel, storing everything).

The problem facing every autobiographer is to know how much to include. As it was, my exigent editors – quite rightly – cut one-third of the original manuscript, while advisedly I pruned some references to intelligence activities.

I have been reminded of Rumer Godden's rather mystical remark: 'everyone is a house with four rooms. ... Most of us tend to live in one room most of the time but unless we go into every room every day, even if only to keep it aired, we are not a complete person'. Being a record of a writer's life, this book then is written essentially from within the 'Writing Room'. I must apologise to many friends and acquaintances who helped the writer on his way, yet fail to appear; on the other hand, some may feel pleased to be left out.

Most especially I am beholden to my children, Camilla, Zaza and Vanessa – and to Renira – for their kindly understanding of why they, and my grand-children, play a much lesser role in these pages than they played in the real whole House, and less than they deserve. Their infrequence in no way reflects the deep, unalterable love I feel for them all.

In the publishing world, among many, I owe gratitude to my literary agents, Andrew Wylie of New York and Michael Sissons of PFD in London; and in Orion to the commissioning editor, Ion Trewin (since retired), and Alan Samson. Above all, in the toilsome work at the pit face,

I have had the remarkable good fortune to have had two of the best editors in the business: Peter James and Bea Hemming. Peter is now so sought after that he chooses you, not the other way round. I have had the great privilege for him to 'do' six of my books. He never misses a trick. Bea is simply one of the brightest of young editors, as charming as she is bright. Whatever either tells me to do, I stand to attention. I am beholden, too, to the sharp-eyed proof-reader, Dr Anthony Hippisley. In the very few cases where I may have rejected their advice, the fault is entirely mine for whatever mishaps may have ensued.

And I cannot forget Janet Robjohn, whose ebullient and optimistic good humour sustained me through much of the writing of both this book, *Kissinger*, and others. Above-and-beyond-the-call of secretarial services, she also took off our hands (at great risk and frequent wounds to herself) Bertie, 'the Biter', and gave him a happy home.

Most of all I owe an everlasting debt of gratitude to the sternest critic of any, my wife Sheelin. She has lived with this memoir for many years, often questioning whether I should be working on it at all, but always offering sensible advice – accompanied by liberal resort to the red pencil. She protests that, without its demands, she might have painted many more pictures; but I doubt I could have written it, or other books, without that smile which still, and always, pervades even the Writing Room. She has my eternal gratitude and love.

Finally, I feel (in the phraseology of the immortal King James Bible) that 'it behoves me' to express thankfulness to the Good Lord for permitting me to experience, and to survive, perhaps the most interesting, and exciting times in all history: from the destruction of Hitler to the bloodless Fall of Communism, the Landing on the Moon, the advent of my Apple laptop, to the revolutions in the Middle East, and the crash of the House of Murdoch, still being played out as I write. I would not have missed a second of these thrilling years – except maybe some of those many frustrating hours related in Chapter One, trying to 'do something' in the Second World War. Fortune has been very kind to me, and I am indeed grateful for the blessings she has given me.

INDEX